XML Specification Guide

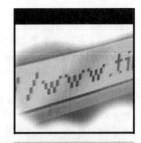

XML Specification Guide

Ian S. Graham
Liam Quin

Wiley Computer Publishing

John Wiley & Sons, Inc.
NEW YORK · CHICHESTER · WEINHEIM · BRISBANE · SINGAPORE · TORONTO

Publisher: Robert Ipsen
Editor: Cary Sullivan
Managing Editor: Brian Snapp
Electronic Products, Associate Editor: Mike Sosa
Text Design & Composition: NK Graphics

This publication is designed to provide accurate and authoritative information in regard to the subject matter covered. It is sold with the understanding that the publisher is not engaged in professional services. If professional advice or other expert assistance is required, the services of a competent professional person should be sought.

Library of Congress Cataloging-in-Publication Data:

Graham, Ian, 1955–
    XML specification guide / Ian Graham, Liam Quin.
        p.   cm.
    "Wiley computer publishing."
    Includes index.
    ISBN 0-471-32753-0 (pbk. : alk. paper)
    1. XML (Document markup language)   I. Quin, Liam.   II. Title.
QA76.76.H94G7335   1999
005.7'2—dc21   98-49441
                                                              CIP

Printed in the United States of America.

10   9   8   7   6   5   4   3   2   1

*To the memory of my father, Eric Stanley
Graham, 31 December 1921 to 23 July 1998.
Loved, admired, and sadly missed.*
—Ian S. Graham

*This book is dedicated to my mothers,
who never met.*
—Liam R. E. Quin

Contents

Preface

XML and the "New" Web

The Web began, like many revolutionary things, with relatively little fanfare and far from the public eye. The idea that started it was pretty simple: "Let's see if we can build a simple distributed hypertext system so that researchers can write documents together, even though they are not at the same physical locations." From this simple idea sprang the three founding ideas of the Web: the hypertext markup language (*HTML*, for writing the documents to be displayed and edited), the hypertext transfer protocol (*HTTP*, for getting the documents from one place to another), and uniform resource locators (*URL*, for actually referencing documents and other resources in a way that could be written into the HTML documents).

Well, we all know what happened. The "little" idea became the model for a new generation of software development, and a whole new industry of content providers, webmasters, e-commerce, Intranets, portals, and so on. Some people became rich and/or famous, while most (like us) did not. But behind the scenes, many who were watching this process understood that times really were changing, and that this new Web model was going to profoundly change the way application software of all types was designed, built, and distributed. And some of these people started to look for ways to improve these new technologies, and help push along that process.

The problem was that although HTML, HTTP, and URLs were useful and exciting technologies, they were insufficient for designing large-scale Web applications. This was not really surprising—it was in fact their simplicity that allowed for the initial rapid growth of the Web, and of Web-compatible software. However, for truly large-scale distributed applications development, something more was needed.

As a result, HTTP, URLs and HTML quickly evolved to incorporate new features, and to make the technologies more robust. However, it soon became apparent that one of the weakest links was HTML. Or, perhaps to put it better, it soon became apparent that HTML was inappropriate for many of the data markup requirements of these next-generation Web applications.

The reason was that the business of distributed applications was distributed information processing—and that meant that the Web needed a universal format for encoding and distributing data that could be understood equally well by any machine on the Internet. Although HTML appeared to fill this model of a universal and widely understood format, it was insufficient in that it enforced a specific view on the data it contained. Quite simply, elements such as **H1**, **P**, **DIV**, and **TABLE** were fine for describing content for display by a browser, but they were woefully inappropriate for describing a purchase requisition, an automotive part, access control restrictions, or the structure and timing of a multimedia presentation.

After much effort at constructing extensions to HTML, or at designing special, application-specific mini-languages, it quickly became evident that the Web needed a new language—one that had the "Web-flexibility" of HTML—that is, the ability to be intelligently processed far from the machine that "created" the data—combined with the syntactic flexibility of a language like the Standard Generalized Markup Language (*SGML*). Indeed, SGML was first considered for this purpose, as it is a powerful and complex international standard expressly designed for "defining" different, special-purpose markup languages—HTML itself is defined using SGML. But, SGML was seen by the Web community as far too complex for easy Web application development, and was also burdened with a number of features that make it very inflexible in a distributed environment like the Web. What was needed was a language that spanned the worlds of HTML and SGML—a language that had the rich ability to define new languages, like SGML, but also the Web-portability of HTML.

The obvious choice was to develop a "stripped-down" SGML—and after approximately eighteen months work by over one hundred well-respected industry experts, the result of this process was the eXtensible Markup Language, or XML. XML was designed, like HTML, as an SGML application—that is, the rules for constructing XML documents were defined such that XML text could be processed correctly by SGML software. XML was also designed to support "arbitrary" markup, so that the language could be used to mark up data from widely different applications, but using a single, universal format. XML also inherited a mechanism from SGML that allowed for specification of the allowed structures of such documents, so that the syntax for classes of documents could be defined and enforced.

At the same time, XML was designed to be much simpler than SGML, and in particular was designed for use in a distributed environment like the Web, where data—marked up in XML—may be far from the machine from whence it came.

The designers of XML also felt it important that the specification for XML be small, so that it would be easy for a developer to assemble simple XML processing software, without too much fuss—certainly one of the lessons of the Web was that simplicity breeds applications! As a result, the XML specification is only 30 pages long, and is written in a style that software developers love—concise and to the point. On the other hand, the official SGML specification runs to several hundred pages, and is exceedingly hard to understand and implement. Even the HTML specification runs to some 360 pages!

The result has been an explosion of XML development, with XML emerging as the core data-distribution language for application development on the Internet. Indeed, although it can in principle be used like HTML as a simple document distribution mechanism, its future lies in more exotic areas, such as collaborative authoring of large documents, electronic commerce transactions, encapsulation of EDI data, synchronized delivery of multimedia, encoding of mathematical expressions for distribution and sharing in applications such as Mathematica and Maple, and much more. HTML will probably never disappear, but under the surface XML will have an ever-growing role in actually moving large quantities of information from one place to the other, and in keeping the applications behind the Web interface happily talking to each other.

Who Is This Book For?

This book is designed for developers—that is, people who are or will be designing XML applications, or writing software that will process XML. The intent of this book is to provide such people with a sound introduction to the language, and also to provide a useful reference to the gritty details, so that developers will know exactly what the XML specification says and what it means. Indeed, this book comes complete with the full specification for XML, in an annotated form. Our experience is that the XML specification is very carefully and concisely written, but that this conciseness can—at times—lead to confusion for software designers. We have thus added many annotations that, we hope, clarify some of the more complicated parts, and that also provide some background as to the intentions of the specification as written. Indeed, the specification is in many places quite vague as to how specific features should be implemented or used, and we provide some guidance as to useful ideas to try—or particularly bad ideas to avoid!

Finally, the conclusion of the book covers some technical details (such as coded character sets and encodings, language identifications, etc.) that are defined in specifications separate from that for XML. Some of these external specifications are themselves quite complex, and we felt a simple yet technical introduction to these areas would be helpful to XML implementors.

So—if you think this is the book for you, please look to the next section for a more detailed description of the book content and organization.

Organization of This Book

This book is organized into three main parts. Part 1 is a "bootstrap" tutorial of XML. It is designed for those familiar with the concepts behind markup (for example, knowing HTML, or a language such as troff or LaTeX) and who want a fuller, albeit informal introduction to the structure, syntax, and rules of XML. This part of the book consists of ten chapters, each of which examines—using example documents and/or markup "snippets"—particular aspects of the XML language. These sections are designed to be clear (we hope!), progressive (each successive example introduces new features on top of previous ones), and concise (we tried to keep this part of the book short and to the point).

Part 2—the core component of this book—is an annotated version of the XML 1.0 specification, published by the World Wide Web Consortium. This technical specification is the *normative* definition of the XML language, and defines both the structure of the language and the terminology needed to understand the definition. For such a specification, this document is actually a marvel of clarity and conciseness. However, its very conciseness can make it difficult to understand for non-experts, and we have added annotations that provide extra clarification, background material, and occasional illustrative examples. Part 2 consists of six chapters and six appendixes, corresponding directly to the chapters and appendices of the official specification.

Part 3 of the book concludes with seven technical appendices covering issues not appropriate elsewhere in the book, and that provide additional views on the official specification, or technical information relevant to understanding the XML specification, but not discussed in detail therein. Appendix A is an "annotated" version of the formal grammar specification for XML. This appendix was created by extracting the grammar rules from the XML specification (in Part 2), re-ordering them to make them easier to follow, and adding notes explaining the rules and their relationships. This is useful as a grammar "quick reference," particularly when combined with the production rule index given on the inner back cover of the book.

Appendix B gives a technical introduction to character set issues, and in particular to the Unicode/ISO/IEC 10646-1 character set that serves as the "document character set" of XML.

An important related issue is that of language, since language choice can affect important aspects of document processing, such as the appropriate choice of quotation marks. XML supports a special attribute (**xml:lang**) for indicating the language relevant to a block of markup. The value assigned to this attribute must be a language identifier, as defined in Internet RFC 1766. Appendix C covers RFC 1766 in some detail, and explains how such language identifiers are written.

Appendix D looks at the main features of XML that are different from HTML. This is a useful quick-reference section for people who are familiar with HTML, and who want a quick highlight of the important differences between HTML and XML.

Appendices E and F introduce the ideas of XML namespaces and XML schemas. These two new features of XML (not yet fully specified, but defined in several discussion drafts) will allow proper merging of markup tags and tag rules (as specified by a DTD, for example) from different DTDs, which will permit easier integration of disparate XML markup. Appendix F discussed schemas—a proposed mechanism for using the XML language itself to specify the types of syntactic and grammatical constraints that currently must be defined using a DTD. Schemas and namespaces in fact go hand-in-hand, and will permit much more flexible integration of XML-based applications than is currently possible.

Finally, Appendix G covers some "good practice" guidelines for writing markup declarations in a DTD. It is hard enough getting the DTD correct, without worrying about errors in your markup, and the guidelines in this short appendix will help you prepare DTDs that are both easier to read and easier to debug!

Notation

In this book, we try rather carefully to use notation that distinguishes special meanings of parts of the text without making the text look jumbled or difficult to read. In general, XML markup examples are shown in a fixed-width Courier font. Where an example is long (covering more than one line), it is generally placed in its own block of text, separate from the preceding and following descriptive text. Inside such examples, we often use boldface to highlight parts of the markup that are particularly relevant to the surrounding discussion. On the other hand, we italicize code text that is a "variable" corresponding to a value that would be set by an XML author. An example of this use is:

> The structure for a parsed general entity reference is:
>
> ```
> &ent-name;
> ```
>
> where *ent-name* is the name chosen for the entity. . . .

Note, however, that inside a *document type declaration* (the special part of an XML document that defines the grammatical rules that must be followed within a document), we italicize the *names* of element-types or entity names. An example, corresponding to the element type **item** and the entity **resto,** is:

```
<!ENTITY resto "Liam's Chowder House and Grill" >
<!ELEMENT item (desc, price, graphic?) >
<!ATTLIST item
          type (appetizer|entrée|dessert|drink) "entrée"
>
```

Within regular text, we use boldface for the name of a particular element, attribute, or entity (as also illustrated just above), and italic text to indicate particular filenames or URL references. For example, given the markup

```
<stuff href="foo.html"> here's &frieze; stuff </stuff>
```

we might write: "The value of the **href** attribute on the element **stuff** is a URL pointing to a useless resource (the file *foo.html*), whereas the entity **frieze** corresponds to . . . "

Last, we have tried, in these examples, to use markup layout that is both attractive and useful. Of course, the latter is of particular importance for authors, and we have chosen layouts that lead to more accurate markup, and fewer errors. For example, in longer declarations, we always break to a new line at places corresponding to breaks in the meaning of the markup components. Thus, an unparsed entity declaration (this will make more sense upon reading Chapter 6 of Part 1) is written as:

```
<!ENTITY ent-name
    SYSTEM "/path/to/resource.ext"
```

```
     NDATA my.Notation
>
```

Note how placing the enclosing angle brackets at the beginning of the lines makes it easy to see where this element begins and ends, while the placement of the different logical parts of the declaration (SYSTEM and NDATA) on separate lines makes it easy to spot errors in these parts. We similarly italicize names of entities and elements, when they are used within the declarations, to help make them easier to spot.

The Supporting Web Site

This book is its own Web application, in that much supporting material related to the book is available over the Web, at the book's supporting Web site. This site contains technical tables relevant to XML developers, as well as annotated versions of the XML grammar specification, and some useful interactive tools for exploring this specification. This Web site appears in several different locations—some of which are included as references in this book. However, you can access the entire Web site via the publisher's Web server, by accessing the link:

www.wiley.com/compbooks/graham-quin

Acknowledgments

I first want to acknowledge the friendship and support of my co-workers at Groveware, Inc., and at the University of Toronto. A book is a lot of work, and has left me—at times—a little more tired and grumpy than I should be. Their support and patience during this process was greatly appreciated.

More specifically, I would like to thank those who reviewed parts of this book, and who provided useful feedback and criticism. In particular I would like to thank Martin Dürst, who reviewed Appendix B, and helped to make the discussion far clearer than would otherwise have been possible. Any errors are, of course, my own.

Last, I would like to thank my wife, Ann Dean, who has once again tolerated the many "missing" weekends and sleepless nights that arose as I was madly trying to correct "one last example" or understand "one more convoluted aspect of Unicode." Of course, these battles are never over, but

the thought that she will be alongside during and after the battles makes
the whole effort worthwhile.

—Ian S. Graham, Toronto

I would like to thank my partner, Clyde Rogers, for his patience and support.

—Liam R. E. Quin

XML Specification Guide

PART

One

XML Overview and Bootstrap

Part 1 of this book is intended as an "XML bootstrap"—a phrase made famous by the many XML presentations and workshops presented under that title. A bootstrap is a quick and accelerated introduction to a topic, and is designed to quickly bring you up to speed on a given topic. The intent of this bootstrap is to quickly familiarize you with the basic ideas of XML, and with how the language is applied. We also try to introduce, with explanations, the essential terminology of XML. However, in no case do we formally define the rules or grammar of XML. This is left to Part 2, where the actual XML specification—which contains all the formal details—is presented, with annotations. The goal of Part 1 is to give you a quick and gentle (but not too gentle!) introduction to XML, while Part 2 (and some of the more technical appendices in Part 3) gives a more technical background, when you are ready to study the details.

Introduction to XML

As mentioned in the preface, an XML document is a sequence of characters that encode the *text* of a document (for example, the words in a dictionary or novel, or the text of a database entry) plus the *logical structure* of the document and *meta-information* related to that structure. The formalism of

XML simply specifies how this is done. Or, perhaps it is not so simple—considering the number of books on the topic, and their sizes!

Indeed, XML is both simple and complex. It is simple in principle—the ideas behind how it works are pretty straightforward, and can be outlined using a few simple examples. It is more complex by application, however, as the rules of XML are precisely defined, and understanding the details of this processing can be nontrivial. In a sense, it is a bit like carpentry—the tools and tricks look easy, but the reality is slightly different!

Structurally, an XML document consists of a sequence of characters that can represent what is called *markup* (the part that encodes structural information) or *character data* (the actual text being "marked up"). The XML specification explicitly defines which characters can appear in an XML document, based on the specifications of the *Unicode / ISO/IEC 10646* character set standards.[1] XML lets the document text contain just about any printable character from this character set, but forbids most non-printable control characters (things like "form feed"). XML places much tighter restrictions on the characters that can be used in *markup*. This is done to make it easy for an XML processor to *parse* the markup, and divide the document into its component parts.

Indeed, the XML specification doesn't care much about the text content—it is mostly concerned with the rules for placing logical and structural information within the content. Thus, the XML specification defines how markup components (e.g., tags) are represented within the document, and what specific characters can be used to compose those markup components. In XML, the rules for constructing valid markup are expressed as *production rules* using the notation of an *extended Backus-Naur Form* (*EBNF*). Essentially, these rules state how a particular XML expression (such as a start-tag), can be written, or *produced*, using other expressions defined elsewhere in the BNF. The lowest-level components expressed in an EBNF, such as the definitions for a *letter* or *white space*, are given in terms of the *Unicode* characters that are allowed as letter or white space characters.

In the XML specification, each production rule is numbered. In Part 1 of this book, we sometimes refer to production rules by this numbered index, placed inside square brackets. For example, the rule for white space is defined by production rule [3] (one or more space, tab, carriage return, or line feed characters). The complete EBNF for XML is given throughout Part 2 of this book (as part of the annotated specification), and also in concise

---

[1.] These two specifications (which are equivalent, for all practical purposes) define characters for most of the world's languages, and define what is, in essence, the first truly "international" character set. In this book, we generally refer to this unified standard as UCS. See Part 3, Appendix B for details about character sets in general, and Unicode and ISO/IEC 10646 in particular.

(annotated) form in Part 3, Appendix A. You can look to either place to find the referenced rule. Note also that there is an index of the productions given on the inside back cover of this book, which you can use to quickly look up the productions and their meanings.

One of the things we don't discuss in Part 1 of this book is how the piece of software processing a document extracts the characters from a data file. On a computer, a document is stored in a binary format, and the process by which characters are stored in this format is known as a *character encoding*. When an XML processor reads an XML document, it must read in a sequence of bytes and convert this stream of encoded data into an in-memory representation of the original characters. In Part 1, in effect we are looking at text after this process is complete, and assume that we can directly look at the text without worrying about the original encoding. However, if you are curious about character encoding issues (they are complex, and interesting) you can look to Part 3, Appendix B.

Part 1 is written so as to introduce the ideas of XML using a set of increasingly complex examples. In doing so, we introduce the various components of XML markup, and show how they work and interact with one another. We also try to point out places where the interpretation of markup is tricky, or counter-intuitive to those who don't have a background in SGML. And, last, we introduce the vocabulary of XML—there are many precisely defined terms, and it is important to understand these terms and their meanings when reading XML documentation or working with XML software. Terms with explicit and important meanings in the context of XML, when they are introduced, are noted in italics. These terms are defined or explained further in the Glossary at the end of this book.

CHAPTER

1

A Basic XML Document

Terms Covered: prolog, XML declaration, encoding declaration, start-tag, end-tag, empty-element tag, comments, entity, well-formed documents, valid documents

Figure 1.1 shows an example of a simple XML document. This document corresponds to a restaurant menu, and has a structure that defines items on the menu, complete with descriptions of the items, prices, and references to pictures of the items.

Formally, an XML document consists of *markup* and *character data*. Markup is simply the text that conveys information about the logical structure of the document, with the character data being the text that is "marked up." In XML, markup is denoted by text surrounded by left and right angle brackets (< and >; strictly speaking, the less than and greater than symbols)—and character data is everything else. In Figure 1.1, the markup is shown in boldface, while the character data content is not.

Structurally, an XML document has two basic parts: a single *prolog*, and a single *document element*. The prolog provides general information about the document, but does not represent the actual structure of the document. In Figure 1.1, the prolog consists of the markup `<?xml version="1.0" ?>`. There can be other things in the prolog (namely, a document type declaration, comments and/or processing instructions), which we discuss in later chapters.

The other main part is the actual character data and markup corresponding to the "document." This is contained within the *document element*, which we discuss later in this chapter.

```
<?xml version="1.0" encoding="UTF-8" ?>

<menu date="12nov1998">

  <rname>Liam's Chowder House and Grill</rname>
  <item type="appetizer">
    <desc>Warmed leek salad, coated with a balsamic vinegar and
          goat cheese dressing</desc>
    <price units="usd">6.95</price>
    <graphic gtype="gif"
             src="http://www.goodfood.com/menu/leek-salad.gif"
/>
  </item>
  <!-- Following Item is tasty! -->
  <item type="appetizer" >
    <desc>Prosciutto ham with melon</desc>
    <price units="usd">7.95</price>
    <graphic gtype="jpeg"
             src="http://www.goodfood.com/menu/ham-melon.jpeg" />
  </item>
</menu>
```

Figure 1.1 A simple XML document illustrating XML declaration, start-tags, end-tags, empty-element tags, and attribute declarations. The parsed tree structure corresponding to this document is illustrated in Figure 1.2.

1.1 The XML Declaration

The first line in Figure 1.1, `<?xml version="1.0" encoding="UTF-8" ?>`, is an *XML declaration*. An XML declaration simply states that the data that follows is an XML document, and optionally indicates the version of the XML specification that the document complies with. If present, an XML declaration must be the first thing to appear in a document, before any other markup or text. The declaration in Figure 1.1 says that the following data is an XML document complying with Version 1.0 of the XML specification. The encoding declaration `encoding="UTF-8"` says that the data file containing this text (i.e., the data that an XML processor is reading) is encoded using the UTF-8 encoding of the Unicode/ISO 10646 character set.

In addition to the version number and encoding, an XML declaration can also declare a document to be standalone or non-standalone (`standalone="yes"` or `standalone="no"`). A standalone document is essen-

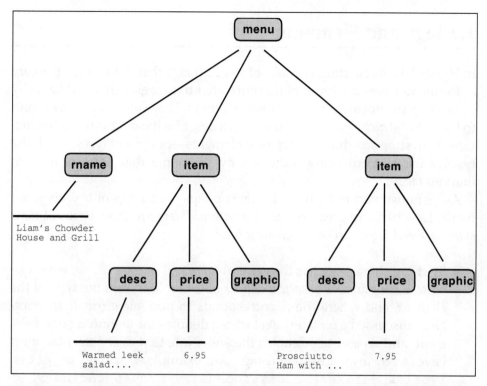

Figure 1.2 An illustration of the parse tree created upon analyzing the structure implied by the markup in Figure 1.1. Note how the tree structure has a single root node—the *document element.*

tially one that can be read in and processed independent of any other *external entities* (i.e., external files or resources). We discuss this in a bit more detail in the next chapter.

Note that, formally, an XML declaration is optional. However, you really should include it, as it provides a useful way of indicating the type of the data, and also a way of informing software about character encoding used to create the binary representation of the document, as discussed in Part 3, Appendix B. It will also mean that your XML documents will still work when (and if) XML 2.0, or some other future version of XML, is published.

Finally, note the use of double quotes to surround the values in the declaration. XML lets you use either single or double quotes, so that the declaration can equally be written as:

```
<?xml version="1.0" encoding='UTF-8' ?>
```

XML uses quotations marks to delimit many different types of strings, and allows either single or double quotes in all cases.

1.2 Tags and Elements

In Figure 1.1, the markup consists of markup *tags* that define the structure of the menu (there are types of markup other than tags, discussed later) by organizing the document into a tree of *elements*. These elements correspond to the *logical structure* of the document. To describe the details of such structure, XML supports different types of elements—or *element types*—with the type of the element being indicated by the name that appears in each markup tag.

As demonstrated in Figure 1.1, markup tags are strings of text enclosed by the less-than and greater-than characters. There are three types of tags: *start-tags*, *end-tags*, and *empty-element tags*:

- **Start-tag.** A start-tag has the general form `<gi-name ...>`, where *gi-name* is the name or *generic identifier* (*GI*) that identifies the type of the element, and where the ... corresponds to possible *attribute specifications* (discussed a bit later). A start-tag denotes the beginning of an element, and an end-tag denotes the end. Note that every start-tag *must* have a corresponding end-tag. An example start-tag is: `<item type="appetizer" class="nondairy nonvegetarian">`.

- **End-tag.** An end-tag has the general form `</gi-name>`, where *gi-name* is the name identifying the type of element that tag is ending. Note that, unlike a start-tag, an end-tag cannot contain attribute specifications. An example end-tag (corresponding to the preceding start-tag example) is: `</item>`.

- **Empty-element tag.** An empty-element tag has the general form `<gi-name ... />`, where *gi-name* is the name identifying the type of the element. Like a start-tag, an empty-element tag can contain *attribute specifications*, denoted here by the three dots. However, unlike a start-tag, an empty-element tag stands alone—there is no corresponding end-tag: An empty-element tag denotes an element which is *empty* and which cannot contain any other markup or text. An example empty-element tag might be `<linebreak/>`, to indicate a forced line break in some text.

1.2.1 Element Nesting and Parse Trees

In a real document, elements are nested so as to define structure for the character data making up the document. This means that element start- and stop-tags must nest, and cannot overlap. Thus, the following markup

```
<elem1> asdf <elem2> adsf  </elem2> asdf </elem1>
```

is correct (**elem2** is nested within **elem1**), while the markup

```
<elem1> asdf <elem2> adsf  </elem1> asdf </elem2> <!-- ERROR! -->
```

is forbidden, since the two elements overlap, and do not nest.

Figure 1.2 illustrates how the elements from the document in Figure 1.1 can be represented as an ordered tree defining the document structure. Note also that the document has a single top-level element, called the *document element* (here the element named **menu**) which contains all other elements in the document. This is a requirement of XML—every XML document must have exactly one element, called the *root* or *document element*, that contains the entire document tree.

1.2.2 Attribute Specifications

Start-tags and empty-element tags can also contain *attribute specifications*, which specify attributes for the element and assign values to those attributes. Attributes are simply named quantities that define properties about a specific instance of an element. For example, in the empty-element tag

```
<graphic gtype="jpeg"
         src="http://www.goodfood.com/menu/ham-melon.jpeg" />
```

the attribute **gtype** is assigned a value indicating (in this example) the type of the graphic being referenced by the element, while the attribute **src** is assigned a URL indicating where the file can be found. One can think of attributes as a way of assigning properties to a particular instance of an element. Alternatively, one can think of an element type as corresponding to a *class* of elements, and a particular instance of an element of a given type (along with any attribute declarations) as corresponding to an *instance* of that class of elements. Thus, in Figure 1.1, all the different elements named **graphic** are different instances of an element of type **graphic**.

XML has many rules about how attributes can be used. In particular, an attribute can be specified *only once* in a given element. Thus it would be illegal to have an element specified `<graphic gtype="gif" gtype="jpeg"/>`. Furthermore, attribute values must be placed within quotation marks, either double (as in the preceding example) or single quotes (e.g., `gtype='jpeg'`). In addition, an attribute value can never contain a literal less-than (<) character, nor can it contain the quotation character that is used to surround the value (if it did, then software parsing the markup would not be able to locate the end of the value string). Finally, the ampersand character can only appear as the leading character of a *character* or *entity reference*. Such entities are discussed in later chapters. We will also discuss, in Part 1, Chapter 3, Section 3.3.4, how to use such references to include "escaped" versions of the <, &, and quotation characters that are otherwise forbidden in entity values.

Note that you must use the ASCII single or double quote characters to surround attribute values—you cannot use "smart" quotes, or the grave or apostrophe characters.

1.2.3 Element and Attribute Names

XML strictly defines the allowed characters that can be used in an element or attribute name. Formally, these strings must be *names*, where a *name* is a string consisting of a single *letter*, underscore, or colon followed by any number of *name characters*. Because XML is designed to work in a multilingual environment, the definitions of *letter* and *name character* are quite detailed (see production rules [4] and [5] in Part 2 of the book), and provide support for characters from non-Latin based languages such as Arabic, Hebrew, Chinese, and Japanese. For more details on these issues, you are referred to the detailed XML specification (Part 2) or to Part 3, Appendix B.

Case-Sensitive Element and Attribute Names

Attribute and element names are *case-sensitive*. Thus, the start-tags `<elem>` and `<Elem>` correspond to different element types, and the attributes `Type` and `type` are distinct: the start-tag `<Elem Type="type1" type="input">` is perfectly valid, since the two attributes have different (albeit confusingly similar!) names.

1.3 Comments

XML comments can provide commentary on the markup or character data content of the document, but they are not themselves considered part of the character data. Comments are marked by the start string <!-- and stop string -->, and can contain any characters other than the string -- (two minus signs) or the string --> that ends the comment. Production rule [15] gives the specific rule for producing a comment.

> **NOTE** Notation for Production Rule References
>
> **Throughout this book, references to the productions rules of the XML grammar are given using the notation [*nn*], where *nn* is the reference number for the production rule. These rules are defined within the XML specification (Part 2 of this book), and are also summarized in Part 3, Appendix A. There is also a production rule index inside the back cover of this book.**

Comments can appear anywhere inside an element, or within character data that lies inside an element, or they can appear before the document element or after it. Thus, the following document is correct:

```
<?xml version="1.0" ?>
<!-- Here is a comment before the document -->
<body>
  <title> This is the title of the document </title>
  <para> Here is an exciting paragraph. Isn't this fun.
      <!-- boy oh boy oh boy..... -->  Maybe you should try
      preparing dozens of XML example documents..</para>
</body>
<!--* document is ended:  this comment is outside the
    * document element -->
```

and has comments inside, in front of, and after the document element. However, comments cannot appear inside markup tags—you cannot place a comment inside a start-, end-, or empty-element tag.

1.4 A Document Entity

XML refers to physical units that make up a document, such as files on disk or resources accessible via URLs, as *entities*. This name originates with SGML, and is used to help distinguish the concept of the *physical containers* of data that make up a document from the perspective of a document as a *logical* collection of markup elements defining the logical structure. Thus, the data content of Figure 1.1 is an entity, which an XML processor might read from disk.

We use the word "entity" instead of "file" because XML uses several different types of entities (not all are files, for example), each of which can only be used in specific ways. Thus it is important to distinguish between a "file" and an "entity," although in many cases the difference will seem small.

XML supports a mechanism, called an *entity reference*, for including one entity within another—this is a bit like the "include" feature of many programming languages, albeit with some special—and distinct—features. We will discuss these features, and entities, in more detail, in Chapters 3, 4, and 5 of Part 1.

1.5 Well-Formed XML Documents

The XML document listed in Figure 1.1 is *well-formed*. Indeed, the XML specification states that "A data object is an XML document if it is well formed, as defined in the specification." The XML specification gives eleven well-formedness constraints (applied on top of the formal grammar for XML, as expressed by the production rules of the EBNF) that must be satisfied for a document to be XML. An example well-formedness constraint is:

> The Name [5] in an element's end-tag must match the element type in the start-tag.

which expresses, more formally, the element nesting rules described previously.

The purpose of well-formedness constraints is to ensure that an XML document can be accurately parsed—that is, that a document can be read by an XML processor and unambiguously parsed to produce an element tree and properly defined attributes and values associated with each node of that tree. If a document is not well-formed, then this process cannot be done reliably. If an *XML processor* (the software that processes XML data, perhaps on behalf of another application) detects that a document is not well-formed, then it must stop processing the data, and must return a fatal error to the application. The XML specification is very explicit about this—if a document is not well-formed, then an XML processor must not attempt to continue processing it.

1.6 Markup Design Goals

Lastly, we will look at the rationale for the markup design of Figure 1.1. Structurally, the markup models a menu by using a top-level **menu** element that in turn contains an **rname** element, containing the name of the restaurant, followed by multiple **item** elements corresponding to items in a menu. Each **item** element contains three other elements: a **desc** element containing a text description of the item, a **price** element containing the cost, and a **graphic** element that indicates the location of an image of the item.

Attributes are used to set properties for the specific elements. For example, the **date** attribute corresponds to the date of the menu, while the **units** attribute indicates the currency units used by the content of the price element (U.S. dollars). The **graphic** element takes two attributes: The **type** attribute defines the format of the referenced graphic resource, while **src** is assigned a URL at which the resource can be accessed.

Note that there is nothing in the XML markup in Figure 1.1 to indicate specific rules for where these elements can be placed, how these elements can be nested, which attributes are supported by specific elements, or what types of values are allowed for a given attribute. Such rules can be specified via a *document type declaration*, discussed in the next chapter.

Similarly, there is no built-in meaning for the names of the elements, nor for the attributes and attribute values—these semantics must be defined separately, and are to a large degree outside the scope of XML. Recall that XML can mark up the structure of a document, and encode meta-information, such as the schema by which a document can be constructed, but it cannot assign meaning to that markup, or to the metadata. This is left to the application designer, who will need to design software that understands the ramifications of the XML document structure, so that the data can be accurately processed.

1.7 Valid XML Documents

An XML document is said to be *valid* if, in addition to the well-formedness constraints, the document satisfies an additional twenty-three validity constraints. Whereas well-formedness constraints ensure that a document is syntactically correct, validity constraints ensure that a document satisfies a well-defined schema: These extra constraints ensure that a schema for the document is present, that the schema is complete (there are no missing parts that, if included, could change the schema), and that the document element is consistent with those rules.

To understand validity constraints, we must first understand how a document type declaration can define a schema for a document. This is the topic of the next chapter.

CHAPTER

2

Declaring Markup: The Document Type Declaration

Concepts Covered: Document type declaration, element type declarations, content models, attribute list declarations, string attribute types, enumerated list attribute types, internal entities, general entities, entity references, standalone documents

The previous chapter examined the structure of element-level markup—that is, the markup that organizes the text of a document to give it structure and meaning. However, provided the basic markup rules were followed, there was no specified syntax for the nesting or placement of these elements, or even their names. Consequently, documents such as the one listed in Figure 1.1 are essentially free-form, and can have entirely arbitrary elements, attributes, and hierarchical structures.

Often, however, there are specific rules that an author (or XML application designer) may wish to impose on the structure of a document—for example, that only certain named elements can be used, and that these elements must be "nested" in certain ways (e.g., a **menu** element must contain a **desc** and a **price**). Indeed, this is an important aspect of markup, since intelligent processing of marked-up data requires that there be some defined structure, and some common way for defining structural rules, and verifying that those rules are obeyed.

In order to impose such requirements, XML needs a mechanism for defining syntax rules for a document or class of documents. Indeed, XML supports such a mechanism via a markup component called the *document type declaration*. This chapter introduces this concept, while the next several go into the details of how it works. Indeed, most of the hard parts of XML are associated with understanding how the document type declaration (and its contents) work and affect the processing of the document element and its content.

2.1 The Document Type Declaration

Figure 2.1 is a reworked version of Figure 1.1, including a single new component—a *document type declaration*. A document type declaration defines syntax rules for the elements and attributes of a document, and also defines entity and notation declarations. This chapter looks only at declarations governing document syntax—entity and notation declarations are looked at in later chapters.

2.1.1 The Document Type Declaration Internal Subset

As mentioned in Chapter 1, a document type declaration is part of the document prolog, and must appear in front of the first element of the document. It must also appear after the XML declaration. A document type declaration begins with the string:

```
<!DOCTYPE string [
```

and ends with

```
]>
```

where `string` (a *Name* [5]) is the internal identifier for the declaration, and essentially names the document element type to which the declaration applies. Consequently, the name specified in the declaration must match the name of the root element of the document. Note, in Figure 2.1, how these two names match (**menu**).

The content of the document type declaration (the markup declarations between the strings `<!DOCTYPE string [` and `]>`) is called the *internal document type declaration subset*, or internal DTD subset, or often just the internal subset. It is called "internal" because it is actually a part of—or internal to—the document entity being processed. Not surprisingly, there is also a thing called the "external subset," which we will discuss in Chapter 5 of Part 1.[1]

[1.] A document type declaration can actually begin with `<!DOCTYPE string external-identifier [` , where *external-identifier* references another entity (e.g., file) containing markup declarations like those inside the internal subset. Indeed, if the entire document type declaration is in this external entity, the declaration can take the form `<!DOCTYPE string external-identifier >`, omitting the square brackets. We will discuss this "external" part of the docu-

A document type declaration contains *markup declarations*—declarations that define the allowed grammar for the use of elements and attributes, and that define reusable component parts for the XML document (i.e., entities). There are four types of markup declarations: element type declarations, attribute-list declarations, entity declarations, and notation declarations. This example looks only at element type, attribute-list, and some simple entity declarations. Entity declarations are also discussed in more detail in Chapters 3, 4, and 6 of Part 1, while notation declarations are discussed in Chapter 6.

2.1.2 Internal General Entity Declaration

The first line in the document type declaration

```
<!ENTITY resto "Liam's Chowder House and Grill" >
```

declares an entity named **resto** to be equivalent to the string inside the double quotes (you could equally well use single quotes). This particular entity is an *internal entity*, because the actual content of the entity is given in the declaration. By contrast, *external entities* (discussed in Part 1, Chapter 4) are those whose content is external to the document, for example in a file. The value for an internal entity is given by the quoted string present in the declaration. Note that this value cannot contain the quotation character used to delimit the value (here the double quote "), or the characters & and % when they are not part of a *character* or *entity reference* (the % is used to reference *parameter entities*).

This type of entity is also called a *parsed entity*, as it contains parsable XML markup and character data. By definition, all parsed entities must contain good (i.e., well-formed) XML—and all internal entities are parsed entities.

This form of entity declaration (i.e., beginning with <!ENTITY resto . . .) defines what is called a *general entity*. General entities are used, or *referenced*, using the notation &resto; where resto is the entity name. Such references can appear in a variety of places. This particular entity is used in

ment type declaration (the collection of all the external parts of the document type declaration is called the *external subset*) in Part 1, Chapter 5.

[2.] There is a second type of entity declaration (beginning with <!ENTITY % ent-name...—note that the space after the % character is required) which defines a *parameter entity*. Parameter entities are referenced using the notation %ent-name;—note how the percent character references this special type of entity. Parameter entities can only be used (referenced) inside a document type declaration. We discuss them in more detail in Part 1, Chapters 3 through 5.

```
<?xml version="1.0" encoding="UTF-8" ?>
<!DOCTYPE menu [
<!--* menu has any number of items, each item containing
    * a description, price, and optional graphic.
    * -->
<!ENTITY  resto "Liam's Chowder House and Grill" >
<!ELEMENT menu (rname,(item,extend?)*) >
<!ATTLIST menu
         date  CDATA   #REQUIRED
         ref   CDATA   #IMPLIED
         rest  CDATA   #FIXED    "&resto;"
>                                               <!-- ENTITY USED
HERE -->
<!ELEMENT item (desc, price, graphic?) >
<!ATTLIST item
         type (appetizer|entrée|dessert|drink) "entrée"
>
<!ELEMENT desc (#PCDATA | emph)* >
<!ELEMENT price (#PCDATA)* >
<!ATTLIST price
         units CDATA   #REQUIRED
>
<!ELEMENT graphic EMPTY >
<!ATTLIST graphic
         gtype CDATA #REQUIRED
         src   CDATA #REQUIRED
>
]>
<menu date="12nov1998">
  <rname>&resto;</rname>                        <!-- ENTITY USED HERE
                                                    -->
  <item type="appetizer" >
    <desc>Warmed leek salad, coated with a balsamic vinegar and
          goat cheese dressing</desc>
    <price units="usd">6.95</price>
    <graphic gtype="gif"
             src="http://www.goodfood.com/menu/leek-salad.gif"
                                                    />
  </item>
  <!--* Following Item is tasty! * -->
  <item type="appetizer" >
    <desc>Prosciutto ham with melon</desc>
    <price units="usd">7.95</price>
    <graphic gtype="jpeg"
             src="http://www.goodfood.com/menu/ham-melon.jpeg"
                                                    />
  </item>
</menu>
```

Figure 2.1 The example document shown in Figure 1.1, but equipped with a document type declaration (shown in boldface). The *names* of the elements and entities being declared are shown in italics.

two places: within the **rname** element of the document, and within the attribute-list declaration for the **body** element.

Note that an entity name must be a *name*, as defined by production rule [5].

2.1.3 General Entity References and Replacement Text

As mentioned above, internal general entities can be referenced within a document by means of a general entity reference. Such entity references take the form

```
&ent-name;
```

where `ent-name` is the name of the entity in question. The actual content of an internal entity (that is, the text present in the definition of the entity) is called the *literal entity value*: Thus the literal value for the entity **resto** is the string:

```
Liam's Chowder House and Grill
```

When entity references `&resto;` are expanded (i.e., when an XML processor parses the document), they will be replaced by this text.

Formally, the text that replaces an entity reference is called the *replacement text*. In the preceding case, the replacement text and the literal entity value were the same—but this is not always so. The literal entity value and the replacement text may be different because entities can themselves contain entity references—for example, the `resto` entity might have been defined by:

```
<!ENTITY  resto "Liam's Chowder House &stuff; and Grill" >
```

where the literal entity value contains the entity reference `&stuff;`. It is now less clear what to use as replacement text for `&resto;`—should it be replaced by the value inside the double quotes, or by the value inside double quotes *after* replacing `&stuff;` by the contents of that reference?

We will actually not answer that question here—we need to introduce some other concepts (namely: character references, parameter entities, and external/internal entities) before we can properly explain the rules for constructing replacement text. We will do so in the next few chapters.

Valid Locations for Internal General Entity References

Internal general entities can be referenced from three places in a document:

- from inside element markup (e.g., inside the **rname** element, at line 21 in Figure 2.1)
- from inside an attribute value (as in the declaration for the attribute **rest** at line 10 in Figure 2.1)
- from inside another internal entity declaration (as in the example in the previous section)

General entity references cannot appear anywhere else. In particular, they cannot appear within the document type declaration, other than inside an attribute value or internal entity value. A second type of entity, called a *parameter entity*, is designed specifically for use in the DTD, and is introduced in the next chapter.

2.1.4 Element Type Declarations

Element type declarations define the name for an element type, and the *content model* for that element type—that is, what other element types are allowed inside an element of the declared type, and the rules by which those *child* elements can be present. Element type declarations take the form

```
<!ELEMENT elem-name
        content-rule
>
```

where `elem-name` is the name of the element, and `content-rule` defines the content model supported by elements of the named type. As an example, the rule

```
<!ELEMENT menu
        (rname,(item)*)
>
```

says that elements of type **menu** must contain one element of type **rname**, followed by zero or more elements of type **item**. We introduce the rules for specifying content models in the next three subsections.

EMPTY Content Models

The notation for content models is in general complex, but there are two simple forms. The declaration

```
<!ELEMENT elem-name EMPTY>
```

means that the element of the indicated type is *empty*—it can only be present as an empty-element tag. An example is the declaration for the graphic element in Figure 2.1:

```
<!ELEMENT graphic EMPTY >
```

ANY Content Model

In contrast, the declaration

```
<!ELEMENT elem-name ANY>
```

means that elements of the indicated type can contain anything—any mixture of character data (text) and elements. In the absence of a document type declaration, an XML parser will generally assume that any non-empty element has a content model of ANY.

Element-only Content Models

Element types that can contain only other elements as children (that is, they can contain other elements, but cannot contain character data) are said to have *element content*. In this case, XML provides several ways of specifying the elements that are allowed within an element of the indicated type. The grammar for expressing these rules is detailed in production rules [47] through [50] (Part 2 of this book, Chapter 3, Sections 3.2.1 and 3.2.2). This section briefly reviews the notation for these rules, and gives some simple examples (it's really not very complicated), but you are referred to the official specification for further details.

The content model uses special characters to denote element grouping, ordering, choice, or allowed repeat sequence. Using the symbol **a** to refer to "elements of type a" and **b** to refer to "elements of type b," we can illustrate the grammar with the following simple examples:

- **Fixed order is indicated by a comma.** Thus the expression **a,b** indicates **a** followed by **b**.
- **Choice is indicated by a vertical bar.** Thus, the expression **a | b** indicates a choice of either **a** or **b**, but not both.

- **A repeat rule is indicated by the characters *, ?, + or by no character.** The characters *, ?, or + (or no character) following an expression indicate the allowed repeat sequence for the expression. The symbol * corresponds to "zero or more," ? to "zero or one," and + to "one or more." The absence of a symbol corresponds to "one and only one." For example, the expression **a,b*** indicates a single **a** followed by zero or more **b**'s, while the expression **a?** | **b+** indicates either zero or one **a**, or one or more **b**'s.

- **Round brackets group expressions for treatment as a unit.** Thus the expression (a,b)* means zero or more occurrences of the sequence **a** followed by **b** (e.g. "**a b**" or "**a b a b**", or "**a b a b a b**", and so on).

It is now simple to understand the content rules given in Figure 2.1. For example, the content model for the menu element (Figure 2.1, line 7):

```
(rname , ( item , extend?)*)
```

means that a **menu** element can contain a single **rname** element, followed by zero or more occurrences of an **item** element, each of which may be followed by an optional **extend** element. Note that the document in Figure 2.1 (which does not have any **extend** elements) is consistent with this content model, since such elements are optional.

Mixed Content Models

Element types that allow both elements and character data as content are said to have *mixed content*. The declarations for such elements are much less complex than those for elements that can only contain other elements. Indeed, there are only two forms:

```
<!ELEMENT elem-name (#PCDATA)* >
```

This form says that elements of the indicated type can only contain character data (the notation #PCDATA corresponds to a character data sequence containing zero or more characters), and cannot contain child elements. Note that, in this special case, the * following the (#PCDATA) is optional.

```
<!ELEMENT elem-name
     (#PCDATA | elem1 | elem2 ... )*
>
```

This form indicates that elements of the indicated type can contain any amount of parsed character data intermingled with any number of any of the elements listed in the content model. Thus, this content model can restrict the types of elements allowed within an element, but cannot specify the number or order of them.

Although these declarations are pretty simple, it is still easy to make mistakes. One common mistake is to repeat the same element type name in a mixed content declaration, for example:

```
<!ELEMENT elem-name
      (#PCDATA | elem1 | elem1 | elem2... )*
>
```

where the repeated items are in boldface. This is an error, and violates one of the XML *validity* constraints.

NOTE   **Only One Element Type Declaration per Element Type**

XML expressly forbids having more than one element type declaration for a given type of element. Thus markup of the form:

```
<!ELEMENT book ( pref? , chapt* , app*) >
<!ELEMENT book ( pref? , chapt* , app* , glos) > <!-- ERROR! -->
```

is invalid. This means that you cannot use subsequent declarations to override previous ones. The only way to allow alternative markup models is via *conditional sections* and *parameter entities*, discussed in Part 1, Chapter 5, Section 5.4.

Constraints on Character Data Inside Elements

The only constraints on character data (PCDATA) content of elements are those arising from the XML grammar (production [14])—such content cannot contain the character < (it would be interpreted as the start of a tag), the character & (unless the start of an entity reference), or the special string]] > (the end of a *CDATA section*, as discussed in Part 1, Chapter 9, Section 9.1.1).

Beyond these limitations, there is no way within XML to constrain the actual text content within an element that has #PCDATA in its content model. Thus, you cannot, for example, restrict an element to contain only digits, or uppercase letters A-Z, and so on. If such constraints are desired, they must be applied externally by the application creating XML data. You might use attributes to indicate constraints (e.g., <invoice content= "digits"> ... </invoice>), but the actual *application* of these constraints is outside the scope of XML.

This issue is recognized as a significant weakness of XML, and efforts are underway to make it easier to describe the allowed content of elements.

See Part 3, Appendix F, where we discuss current proposals for using XML markup itself, as opposed to DTDs, to define schemas for XML documents.

2.1.5 Attribute-List Declarations

An attribute list declaration defines the set of attributes that are associated with a given element, and can set several restrictions on the allowed attribute values. An attribute list declaration has the general form

```
<!ATTLIST elem-name attribute-definitions >
```

where `elem-name` is the name of the element type for which the attributes are being declared, and `attribute-definitions` is a sequence of attribute definitions defining the name, type, and default value (if any) of each attribute associated with the indicated element type.

The general form for a single attribute definition is

```
att-name type default-declaration
```

where `att-name` is the name for the attribute, `type` is a keyword or expression defining the type of the attribute, and `default-declaration` defines the default value. The possible values for the default-declaration, and their meanings, are:

- `#REQUIRED` The attribute *must* be specified in all elements of the declared type—there is no default value.

- `#IMPLIED` The attribute can optionally be specified in elements of the declared type—there is no default value.

- `"attr-value"` The attribute can optionally be specified in elements of the declared type—the default value (if no value is specified for a given element) is given by the value inside the double (or single) quotes.

- `#FIXED "attr-value"` The attribute value cannot be assigned a different value in an element instance. Instead, *every* element of this type has the fixed value given within the double (or single) quotes.

There are ten different ways to specify the `type` (essentially the *type* of the attribute). In this example we look at the specification of two attribute types: strings and enumerated lists. The other type specifications will be discussed in Chapters 6 through 8 of Part 1.

Enumerated-List Attribute Types

Enumerated lists are lists of predefined values, where an attribute value can take only one of the listed values. In this case, *type* is just a list of possible values as given by expressions of the form

```
( value1 | value2 | value3 )
```

where *value1*, *value2*, and *value3* are the allowed attribute values (production rule [59], Part 2, Chapter 3, Section 3.3.1). Note the brackets that group the collection of choices. Each value must be a *name token*—a special type of string defined by production rule [7] (Part 2, Chapter 2, Section 2.3).

An example of such an attribute specification is found in Figure 2.1, in the lines

```
<!ATTLIST item
        type (appetizer|entrée|dessert|drink) "entrée"
>
```

Note how the default declaration sets a default value of entrée, and allows this value to be overridden by any element in a document—as is in fact done by the **item** elements in Figure 2.1. Enumerated type attribute definitions can also use the #FIXED, #IMPLIED, or #REQUIRED default declarations, as described previously.

String-Type Attribute Types

String attribute types are indicated by the *type* keyword CDATA. Such attributes take, as values, any string of valid XML characters, with three restrictions: The strings cannot contain left angle brackets (<), ampersand characters (&) unless they start entity references, or the quotation character used to surround the string. If you really need them, these characters can be included using character or entity references, as described in the next chapter.

String types are generally used for attribute values that cannot be defined ahead of time, such as URLs, time/date strings, or values defined at user input. Three examples of string-type definitions are found in Figure 2.1:

```
<!ATTLIST menu
        date  CDATA    #REQUIRED
        ref   CDATA    #IMPLIED
```

```
        rest   CDATA    #FIXED    "&resto;"
>
```

Note that the content of the third attribute (**rest**) is fixed, and is defined using an entity. When an XML processor parses an XML document, it must appropriately expand such entities, replacing them by their proper replacement text. This process is rather complex, and is discussed in more detail in the next chapter.

> **NOTE** Restrictions on Characters in String-Type Attribute Values
>
> An attribute value string cannot contain the characters <, & (unless it is the start of an *entity reference*), or the quotation character used to delimit the string. Note also that if there is a general entity reference inside the literal string of an attribute value, it must refer to an *internal entity*, as discussed in Chapter 3.

Combining Attribute-List Declarations

It is legal to have more than one attribute-list declaration for the same element type—software that parses the markup declarations will appropriately merge the attribute definitions in the two declarations. It will do this for each individual attribute in two ways:

- by *incorporating* a new attribute definition if the named attribute was not defined in a previous declaration
- by *ignoring* a subsequent attribute definition if the named attribute was defined in a previous declaration

For example, given the following two declarations:

```
<!ATTLIST menu
        date   CDATA     #REQUIRED
        ref    CDATA     #IMPLIED
        rest   CDATA     #FIXED      "&resto;"
>
<!ATTLIST menu
        date   CDATA     "October 12 1998"
        locat  CDATA     "21 Groverton Blvd, Toronto Ont"
        rest   ( open | closed | redirect) "redirect"
>
```

then the preceding rules state that the italicized definitions will be used, leading to the following "merged" declaration understood by the processor:

```
<!ATTLIST menu
        date   CDATA    #REQUIRED
        ref    CDATA    #IMPLIED
        locat  CDATA    "21 Groverton Blvd, Toronto Ont"
        rest   CDATA    #FIXED    "&resto;"
>
```

2.2 A *Valid* XML Document

The document listed in Figure 2.1 is both *well-formed* and *valid*. It is well-formed in that the markup is correctly constructed upon expanding all entity references, replacing them by the corresponding replacement text. Of course, Figure 2.1 contains only one declared entity (an internal general entity)—the *well-formedness* constraints are more complex when external entities are involved.

The document is also valid, in that it contains a document type declaration, and in that the document is consistent with the syntax specified by the document type declaration. A second validity constraint is that the document type declaration declare any entities required in the document, and this is indeed the case. Needless to say, proof of validity is more complex when external entities are involved, as discussed later.

2.3 XML Models for Document Processing

As mentioned in Chapter 1, there are two "modes" for an XML document, well-formed and valid. A well-formed document is one that obeys the rules for writing XML markup, but where the actual syntax for the document may not be defined (as in Figure 1.1, where there is no document type declaration), or if present may be incomplete. The XML specification defines a set of well-formedness constraints that must be satisfied for a document to be called well-formed. A well-formed document is essentially a lowest common denominator XML document—anything less, and the document is not XML.

On the other hand, a valid document is one where a grammar for the document is specified (by the document type declaration), and the document is consistent with that grammar. The XML specification defines a set of validity constraints that must be satisfied (along with the well-formedness ones) by a document that is valid. The validity constraints essentially state what extra steps need to be taken to verify that the document type declaration is properly constructed, and that the element content is consistent with the grammar defined in the DTD.

Because the requirements of these two models are so different, software processing the document (an *XML processor*) must understand the difference between these two modes. For these reasons, XML defines two classes of XML processor—a *validating* processor, and a *non-validating* processor. A validating processor can only process valid XML documents, and rigorously checks that the document is valid as defined by the document type declaration. A validating processor must read and check everything in the document type declaration, and must verify that all validity and well-formedness constraints are satisfied.

A non-validating processor is not required to check the document for validity. Thus, while a non-validating processor may read the element type declarations, it does not have to (and probably does not) check that the document is consistent with the content models stated in these declarations. However, a non-validating processor must read markup declarations of the internal subset and extract any internal general entities that are needed inside the markup (for example, the entity **resto** in Figure 2.1) as well as any default attribute values set by attribute-list declarations (for example, the value for the attribute **rest**). Actually, a non-validating processor must stop reading the internal subset if it encounters external parameter entity references it cannot process, since those external entities might change the document type declaration—we will talk a bit more about this in later chapters.

These two models arose from experience with the World Wide Web, in which HTML documents were found to be quite usable despite the absence of a document type declaration. Thus, XML decided on a two-pronged approach, one in which full validity was preserved (as might be required of a document editor), and one in which correctness was sufficient (as in a document viewer, such as a Web browser).

2.4 A *Standalone* XML Document

The document listed in Figure 2.1 is also a *standalone* document. A standalone document is one that can be unambiguously processed independently of any markup declarations that are external to the document (i.e., that are in external entities). Since this example document references no external entities, it can safely be called standalone. (Documents that do reference external entities may or may not be standalone documents, depending on the content of those entities.[3])

Being standalone is very useful in a distributed environment such as the Internet, as software retrieving a standalone XML document can safely begin processing it before downloading any declared external entities. This can mean a significant performance boost for the application. On the other hand, if a document is not standalone, then the software must first download all the external entities before beginning processing, since these entities will affect, in an unknown way, how the document should be parsed. For example, the content of an external entity might affect the default value for an attribute, or change the definition of an entity.

A document can become non-standalone when markup declarations (that is, document type declaration content) are moved to an external entity. There are several ways in which this can be done, and we will look at some of them in the next example. Conversely, one can always pre-insert all external entities to create a standalone version of any given document.

The *XML declaration* supports a standalone declaration for explicitly indicating whether or not a document is standalone. The possible forms are `standalone="yes"` and `standalone="no"`, with the obvious meaning associated with the wording. Either single or double quotes can delimit the yes or no values. An example XML declaration is then:

```
<?xml version='1.0' standalone="yes" ?>
```

If a document contains no external entities, then it is standalone by default, and this declaration is unnecessary (although it certainly cannot hurt!). This declaration is most useful for documents that reference external entities, but where the document author knows ahead of time that the external entities will not affect the processing of the document type declaration, and that the document is standalone.

[3.] A document can be standalone if no attribute value defaults or general entities are defined in the external DTD subset (the part of the DTD that is in entities outside the document entity) or if such things are defined in the external subset, but are not actually used in the document.

Internal Entities and Character References

Concepts Covered: Internal, general, and parameter entities (declarations and references), character references, entity replacement text

The previous chapter introduced the idea of a *character reference*—a way of indirectly referencing characters that might otherwise be forbidden. An example is a less-than character as text inside an element—it would be interpreted as the start of a markup tag if it was not "escaped" in some way. Indeed, before we talk more about entities it is important to introduce character references, as they are often used to escape text inside an entity value.

Chapter 2 also introduced the concept of an internal general entity—in essence, a way of defining named, reusable strings of text. Such entities can be referenced (i.e., used) in only certain contexts—namely, within the content of an element, within the value of an attribute, or inside another internal entity definition. They cannot be used inside the document type declaration. There is a second type of entity, called a *parameter entity*, designed for use in this context, which we introduce in this chapter.

Finally, Chapter 2 discussed how the defined values for internal entities could themselves contain entity references. The handling of such cases is one of the more complicated things you will have to deal with when constructing XML documents, and this chapter spends some time outlining the issues involved.

3.1 Character References

XML provides a special type of markup, called a *character reference*, for indirectly referencing each valid XML character by its code position (i.e., its location) in the Unicode ISO/IEC 10646 character set. The position can be given as either a decimal or a hexadecimal number. As an example, the character "õ" (letter "o" with a tilde on top) is at position 245 (decimal) or F5 (hexadecimal) in the Unicode character set, and can be referenced using one of the following three references:

EQUIVALENT REFERENCES	CHARACTER
õ õ õ	õ

The prefix &# in front of the number indicates a decimal character reference, while the prefix &#x indicates a hexadecimal reference —note that this expression must use lowercase letter "x." Of course, the actual character õ can be directly included in the text file, provided it is defined in the character set being used to encode the text.

Character references are used for two purposes: to encode characters that might be difficult to enter as proper Unicode characters, or to "escape" characters that would otherwise be interpreted as markup in some way. As an example of the first case, when entering text using a typical North American keyboard, one might use a character reference to include Cyrillic or Chinese characters. Indeed, this mechanism is your only option if the document is to be stored using a character encoding (such as ISO 88591-1) that does not support explicit Cyrillic or Japanese script!

Character references are also useful for escaping characters that would otherwise be interpreted as markup, the start of an entity or character reference, or the closing quotation of a string (e.g., in an entity or attribute definition). For example, the text "<a>" (a mathematical notation for the average of the variable a) in the following

```
<para> The average of a, <a> is given by ...
```

must be escaped when present as character data content, as it otherwise looks just like a markup tag. Thus, the text could be written as:

```
<para> The average of a, &#x3C;a&#x3E; is given by ...
```

where the character references for the two escaped characters are shown in boldface.[1] Similarly, if you are using single quotation marks to surround an attribute or internal entity value, then the possible value `Mr. 'Big'` would need to be encoded to escape the quotation symbols, as illustrated in the following markup snippets:

```
<!ATTLIST elem
        size CDATA 'Mr. &#x27Big&#x27;'
>
<!ENTITY silly 'Mr. &#x27Big&#x27;'>
.....
<!-- and finally as an explicit attribute .... -->
<elem size='Mr. &#x27Big&#x27;'> ... </elem>
```

3.1.1 Valid Locations for Character References

Character references can be used in three places: as part of PCDATA content (that is, as part of the text content of an element), as part of the text of an internal entity definition, or as part of the text of an attribute definition (either in an attribute-list declaration, or in a specific instance of an element). They cannot, however, be used within markup declarations (other than at the two places just noted) or inside markup tags (other than inside attribute values).

To use references appropriately, particularly within attribute and entity declarations, you also need to know when, during processing by an XML processor, such references are replaced by the corresponding characters. We will discuss this issue later in this chapter (Section 3.3), and also in Chapter 10.

3.2 Internal Parameter Entities

For use inside the document type declaration, XML supports a second type of internal entity, called an internal *parameter entity*.[2] Such entities can *only*

---

[1] Special entity references can also be used to escape these characters, as discussed in Sections 3.3.3 through 3.3.5. Indeed, a document author should use the entity references for the < and > characters, as opposed to the character references described here. However, software automatically processing text might use character references as described here.

[2] Like general entities, parameter entities can be internal (as discussed here) or external. The processing and handling of external parameter entities is discussed in Part 1, chapters 4 and 5.

be referenced within the document type declaration, and generally contain text that is used in this context—namely, markup declarations. Indeed, these entities are generally used to *parameterize* a subset of the grammar for a given class of documents.

The notation used to declare and reference internal parameter entities is only slightly different from that used for general entities, as illustrated in the following example declarations:

Internal general entity   <!ENTITY *ent-name "literal value"* >

Internal parameter entity   <!ENTITY % *ent-name "literal value"* >

Parameter entity declarations use a percent character in front of the entity name (you must have white space between the percent character and the name). The two types are also referenced differently—parameter-entity references again use the percent character before the name, as opposed to the ampersand:

General-entity reference   &*ent-name*;

Parameter-entity reference   %*ent-name*;

Like general entities, parameter entities must be declared before they are used. XML is designed to allow single pass construction of the document type declaration, and this is only possible if all entities are defined prior to their use.

3.2.1 Scope for Parameter-Entity References

As mentioned above, parameter-entity references are only valid inside the document type declaration. Indeed, it is only in the document type declaration that the % character is interpreted in a special way (denoting the start of a reference) . Thus, in the following markup:

```
<para>
Here is a nice %string; of text
</para>
```

the string %string; is treated as ordinary text.

A parameter-entity reference can also be used within the definition of another parameter entity, or the definition of an internal general entity. Indeed, Table 3.1 defines those places where parameter and internal general entities can be referenced. A bit later in this chapter, while discussing

Table 3.1   List of locations where parameter and internal general-entity references are valid. The locations that differ between the two entity types are italicized.

ENTITY REFERENCE TYPE	WHERE VALID/USEFUL
Parameter entity	internal parameter or general entity declaration, *document type declaration*
Internal general entity	internal parameter or general entity declaration, *element content, attribute value*

an example document, we will investigate further how these entities are actually used in these contexts.

NOTE Only References to Internal General Entities in Attribute Values

Only general-entity references are allowed in an attribute value. Furthermore, such references must point to an *internal entity*.

3.2.2 Names for Parameter and General Entities

Parameter and general entity names do not conflict. This is actually implied by the fact that they are *addressed* using different notations. As a result, it is acceptable (albeit confusing!) to declare parameter and general entities having the same name, as in:

```
<!ENTITY   blobbie "This is a test general entity" >
<!ENTITY % blobbie "This is a test parameter entity" >
```

with the respective references being &blobbie; and %blobbie;.

3.2.3 Literal Entity Values and Replacement Text

The definitions of an internal parameter or general entity (the *literal entity value*) can consist of text (except for the characters &, %, and the quotation character enclosing the value), character references, parameter-entity references (starting with a %), or general-entity references (starting with an &). However, the *replacement text* (the text put in place of a reference to an internal entity) for these entities will consist of the same text with the character references and parameter entities expanded, but with the general entity references left as-is. To see what this means in practice, we have constructed the following example XML document.

3.3 Internal Entity Example

Figure 3.1 is a reworked version of the document Figure 2.1 designed to illustrate the use of internal parameter and general entities, as well as character references. To do this we have done two things: modified the entity named **resto** to use a disallowed character (the quotation characters that surround the value), and created a new parameter entity named **menu-attrs**, which contains the attribute-list declaration for the **menu** element type.

3.3.1 Replacement Text for Internal Entities

When an entity reference is used, it is replaced by its *replacement text*. The replacement text for all internal entities is determined by scanning (i.e., reading and processing) the literal entity value, and processing it as follows:

1. Parameter-entity references are replaced by the replacement text of the corresponding parameter entity.
2. Character references are replaced by the corresponding character.
3. General-entity references are left as-is. General-entity references are only replaced when the entity is used within the content of an element, or in the context of an attribute value.

The reasoning behind these rules is simple. In order to process the document, an XML processor must first expand and process the document type declaration in order to extract any relevant grammatical rules, default attribute values, and so on, that are relevant to the document. Since parameter entities are designed to contain markup declarations, they must be immediately expanded so that the grammar can be analyzed. Any general-entity references that lie within the expanded DTD simply define properties (such as attribute values) relevant to this grammar, and can be expanded when required (i.e., when an attribute value is set, or when element content is processed).

As examples, let's first look at the internal general entity named **resto**. In this case, the literal text contains two character references, which reference

```
<?xml version="1.0" encoding="UTF-8" ?>
<!DOCTYPE menu [
<!--* menu has any number of items, each item containing
    * a description, price, and optional graphic.
    * -->
<!ENTITY   resto "Liam's Chowder &#x22;House&#x22; and Grill" >
<!ENTITY % menu-attrs "<!ATTLIST menu
     date CDATA #REQUIRED
     ref  CDATA #IMPLIED
     rest CDATA #FIXED &#x22;&resto;&#x22;
     >"
>
<!ELEMENT menu (rname,(item,extend?)*) >
%menu-attrs;

<!ELEMENT item (desc, price, graphic?) >
<!ATTLIST item
        type (appetizer|entrée|dessert|drink) "entrée"
>
<!ELEMENT desc (#PCDATA | emph)* >
<!ELEMENT price (#PCDATA)* >
<!ATTLIST price
        units CDATA   #REQUIRED
>
<!ELEMENT graphic EMPTY >
<!ATTLIST graphic
        gtype CDATA #REQUIRED
        src   CDATA #REQUIRED
>
]>
<menu date="12nov1998">
  <rname>&resto;</rname>                       <!-- ENTITY USED
                                                       HERE -->
  <item type="appetizer" >
    <desc>Warmed leek salad, coated with a balsamic vinegar and
          goat cheese dressing</desc>
    <price units="usd">6.95</price>
    <graphic gtype="gif"
          src="http://www.goodfood.com/menu/leek-salad.gif"
                                                        />
                                                (continues)
```

Figure 3.1 The example document shown in Figure 2.1, but modified to use internal parameter and general entities, and also character references. The changes relative to Figure 2.1 are shown in boldface. Once again, the names of elements and entities being declared are shown in italics.

```
(continued)
  </item>
  <!--* Following Item is tasty! * -->
  <item type="appetizer" >
    <desc>Prosciutto ham with melon</desc>
    <price units="usd">7.95</price>
    <graphic gtype="jpeg"
              src="http://www.goodfood.com/menu/ham-melon.jpeg"
                                                               />
  </item>
</menu>
```

the quotation character used to surround the string. Thus the replacement text will be the same string but with these references replaced by the designated characters, as shown in Table 3.2.

The internal parameter entity **menu-attrs** has literal text containing character references and general-entity references—here, the character references were used to "escape" the double quotation characters around the third attribute value specification. To create the literal text, the character references are replaced by the corresponding characters, while the general-entity reference is untouched, following from rule 3. Again, the "before" and "after" versions are shown in Table 3.2.

When the parameter **menu-attrs** is referenced, it is replaced by the replacement text given in the table. Then, when the processor begins processing this markup declaration (after having replaced all the parameter entities) and encounters this attribute list, it will detect the general reference `&resto;` in the attribute value for **rest**, and will replace this reference by the appropriate replacement text. Note that the quotation characters in the replacement text for `&resto;` do not prematurely end the quoted value, since they are included indirectly via the entity reference. Finally, the reference `&rest;` in the body of the document (within the **rname** element) is similarly replaced by the listed replacement text.

In the preceding example, note that we could also have written the literal entity value for the parameter entity **menu-attrs** as:

```
<!ENTITY % menu-attrs "&#x3C;!ATTLIST menu
     date CDATA #REQUIRED
     ref  CDATA #IMPLIED
     rest CDATA #FIXED &#x22;&resto;&#x22;
     &#x3E;"
  >
```

Table 3.2 Literal entity values and the corresponding replacement text for the general entities defined in Figure 3.1.

ENTITY: *RESTO*	
Literal Value	Liam's Chowder **"**House**"** and Grill
Replacement Text	Liam's Chowder "House" and Grill

ENTITY: *MENU-ATTRS*	
Literal Value	<!ATTLIST *menu*
	date CDATA #REQUIRED
	ref CDATA #IMPLIED
	rest CDATA #FIXED **"&resto;"**
	>
Replacement Text	<!ATTLIST *menu*
	date CDATA #REQUIRED
	ref CDATA #IMPLIED
	rest CDATA #FIXED "&resto;"
	>

where the changes relative to the declaration in Figure 3.1 are shown in boldface. Note that this will lead to the same replacement text as that shown in Table 3.2, since the two extra character references will be replaced by the characters < and >.

NOTE Space Characters Added Around Parameter Entity Replacement Text

When a parameter-entity reference is replaced, the replacement text is padded with a leading and trailing space character. Space is never added before or after the replacement text of general-entity references.

NOTE Limits on Parameter Entity Values

The internal parameter entity used in Figure 3.1 contained an entire markup declaration. Indeed, when a parameter entity (internal or external) is used within the document type declaration *internal subset* (the part inside the DOCTYPE), this is the only thing the entity can contain. This is required to ensure that the markup will be seen as well-formed by a non-validating XML parser, which can choose not to process references to external parameter entities, but which must still be able to verify that the markup declarations are well formed. This issue is discussed again in Chapter 5 of Part 1, when we discuss the *external DTD subset.*

3.3.2 Nested Parameter-Entity References

Parameter entity definitions can contain parameter-entity references, which can lead to some odd structures. For instance, in the following example:

```
<!ENTITY part0
     "<!ELEMENT grumpy ANY>"
>
<!ENTITY part1
     "%part0;<!ELEMENT sneezy ANY>"
>
<!ENTITY part2
     "%part1;<!ELEMENT dopey EMPTY> "
>
%part2;
```

the replacement text used in place of %part2; is evaluated as follows:

1. The replacement text of **part1** is evaluated by replacing %part0; by its replacement text. Thus this replacement text for **part1** becomes:

```
<!ELEMENT grumpy ANY> <!ELEMENT sneezy ANY>
```

Note how a space character has been added in front of and after the replacement text for **part0** (the space before is hard to see).

2. Then, the evaluation of the replacement text for **part2** replaces the reference to %part1; by this text, so that the replacement for %part2; is:

```
<!ELEMENT grumpy ANY> <!ELEMENT sneezy ANY> <!ELEMENT dopey
EMPTY>
```

Note again the space character added in front of and after the replacement text for **part1** (again, the space in front of the text is hard to see).

The official specification gives some more complex examples of this process, and the oddities that can result from it! Please see Part 2, Chapter 4, Section 4.5, and Part 2, Appendix D for some "graduate" examples of entity reference replacement text processing.

NOTE Infinite Entity Recursion Is Forbidden

You can reference other entities from within an entity declaration, but you cannot allow infinite recursion of entity inclusion—for example, **entity-1** includes **entity-2**, which includes **entity-1**, which includes . . . and so on. Be careful when including an entity within an entity, that you have not indirectly introduced an infinitely recursive structure!

3.3.3 Escaping Characters in Markup Content

Within character data content or markup elements, entity references are expanded *before* the markup and character data are processed. This lets you use general-entity references (particularly external ones) to "include" large blocks of markup and character data, stored for example in another file. An example might be to use the entity reference &chap1; to include an entire first chapter of a book (that is, all the text content plus any relevant markup) into an overall "book" document, as in:

```
<book>
&chap1;
&chap2;
...
</book>
```

However, because parsing is done *after* the references are replaced, you need to be careful when you want to escape markup that lies inside an entity. As a simple example, consider the following character data content of an element in a document, written so as to "escape" the text for two markup tags and an ampersand character:

```
<para> The tags &#60;a&#62; &#38; &#60;b&#62;  are ...
</para>
```

This is well-formed, since the character references "escape" the substring "<a> & <b>" so that <a> and <b> are not seen as markup elements when the document is parsed by an XML processor, and the ampersand is not seen as the start of an entity reference.

Suppose that now we naively move this markup into a declared entity, and use this entity instead. The following attempt will fail:

```
<!ENTITY nomarkup "&#60;a&#62; &#38; &#60;b&#62; ">
<para> The tag &nomarkup; are ... </para>
```

because the *replacement* text for the **nomarkup** entity is the string `<a> &`
`<b>`, so that the markup content, upon replacing the entity, becomes:

```
<para> The tags <a> & <b> are ... </para>  <!-- ERROR! -->
```

The processor will now interpret the strings `<a>` and `<b>` as markup, and
the bare ampersand as the start of a character or entity reference, which is
incorrect and leads to ill-formed XML.

To properly escape the markup, you in effect need to "doubly" escape
these characters. A correct entity declaration would be:

```
<!ENTITY nomarkup
        "&#38;#60;a&#38;#62; &#38;#38; &#38;#60;b&#38;#62; "
  >
```

for which the replacement text is the string `&#60;a&#62; &#38;`
`&#60;b&#62;`. The markup will then be expanded into

```
<para> The tags &#60;a&#62; &#38; &#60;b&#62; are ... </para>
```

which is what we wanted.

This procedure is cumbersome, to say the least! In Section 3.3.5 we will
see how you can use the special pre-defined entity references `&lt;` (<)
and `&gt;` (>) to more easily escape text sequences containing markup.

3.3.4 Escaping Characters in Attribute Values

Attribute values cannot contain the less-than character, as mentioned earlier, so that this character must be escaped if it is to be included in an
attribute value specification. For example, the following declarations and
attribute-value assignments are well-formed:

```
<!ATTLIST menu  tasty CDATA "&#60;yum!" >
...
<menu tasty="&#60;yum!" >
```

and safely "escape" the attribute value `<yum!`.

However, just as was the case inside markup, this mechanism cannot be
used if the character is escaped inside an entity that is in turn referenced
inside the attribute value. For example, in the following:

```
<!ENTITY  misused "&#60;yum!" >
.....
```

```
<menu  tasty="&misused;>
... </menu> <!-- DANGER — bare "<" appears here! -->
```

the replacement text for the entity **misused** is the string `<yum!`, so that when the reference is replaced in the explicit markup, the resulting effective markup is:

```
<menu tasty="<yum!" >
... </menu>
```

However, the XML processor must now *rescan* this text so that it can convert the data and markup into a parse tree. Unfortunately, this re-scanning encounters the bare less-than symbol, which is disallowed.

Consequently, if you wish to escape a less-than symbol (or, similarly, an ampersand) you must doubly escape the character, using the sequence in `&#38;&#60;`. For example, consider the entity:

```
<!ENTITY  misused "&#38;#60;yum!" >
.....
<menu  tasty="&misused;>
... </menu> <!-- less than is properly escaped here -->
```

In this case, the replacement text for misused is the string `&#60;yum!`, so that the "effective" markup is:

```
<menu tasty="&#60;yum!" > ...
</menu>
```

The text can now be safely rescanned, as there is no illegal less-than character inside the attribute value. Furthermore, when the text is rescanned the character reference `&#60;` is converted back into the less-than character, and the attribute is assigned the correct value `<yum!`.

Again, this procedure is awkward. We discuss in the next section how to use special pre-defined entity references to far more easily escape special characters such as `<`, `>`, and `&`.

3.3.5 Predefined General Entities

The procedures described in Sections 3.3.3 and 3.3.4 are rather awkward, and prone to errors by authors and software alike. For convenience and to help avoid these errors, XML *predefines* the following five entities, corresponding to the ASCII characters that most commonly need to be "escaped":

```
<!ENTITY lt      "&#38;#60;">
<!ENTITY gt      "&#62;">
<!ENTITY amp     "&#38;#38;">
<!ENTITY apos    "&#39;">
<!ENTITY quot    "&#34;">
```

It is much easier to use these predefined entities to escape markup or entity references. For example, the entity defined earlier in Section 3.3.3:

```
<!ENTITY nomarkup
        "&#38;#60;a&#38;#62; &#38;#38; &#38;#60;b&#38;#62; "
>
```

can be rewritten, using these entity references, as:

```
<!ENTITY nomarkup
        "&lt;a&gt; &amp; &lt;b&gt;; "
>
```

This is, needless to say, much easier to write without making a mistake, and much easier to read!

Although these are predefined (you don't need to declare them in a well-formed document) they will need to be declared in any document destined to be used with older SGML software, since such software may not support these predefined entities.

Parameter and General Entities

Concepts Covered: External parsed entities (declarations, general, parameter, references), text declaration

The example documents in the previous chapters were self-contained—that is, all the data relevant to the document was found in the document entity, which in turn contained internal entities that defined "chunks" of data for reuse within the document. However, not everything needs to be inside the document—XML supports mechanisms for declaring and including *external* entities, which are typically files or resources accessed via a URL. These mechanisms are similar to the "include" features of many programming languages. However, the XML mechanisms are significantly more complex, as we shall see in this and the following two chapters.

XML supports two types of external entities: *general* and *parameter*. General entities can themselves come in two flavors: *parsed* and *unparsed*. A parsed general entity contains data that may represent markup or character data—for example, a collection of elements and text. Such entities are declared so that they can be used within the document—in a manner similar to the internal entities discussed in the previous chapter.

An unparsed entity contains data that is, as far as the XML processor is concerned, not XML. Typical examples might be RTF or PostScript files, binary data such as images or programs—or the data might even be an XML document. XML documents can never use entity references to included unparsed entities, but can use a special type of attribute to relate an element to specific unparsed entities. This chapter only looks at parsed general entities—unparsed entities are discussed in Chapter 6 of Part 1.

Note that an XML processor only knows the nature of a given external entity (parsed, unparsed, general, or parameter) from the way in which the entity is *declared* in the document type declaration.

External parameter entities are *only* used within a document type declaration, and must always be parsed entities. We talk briefly about this type of entity in this example, and provide more detail in Chapter 5.

4.1 External Parsed General Entity Declarations

Within an XML document, the existence of external parsed general entities is indicated using a general entity declaration. Such declarations can take one of two possible forms:

```
<!ENTITY ent-name
      SYSTEM "uri-reference"
>
<!ENTITY ent-name
      PUBLIC "public-id"
      "uri-reference"
>
```

where `ent-name` is the name of the entity being declared, `uri-reference` is a system identifier, consisting of a URI (such as a URL) indicating a location for the entity, and `public-id` is a *public identifier* for the resource. Public identifiers are a legacy from SGML, and provide an indirect way of referencing external resources—an XML processor may use the value of the public identifier to try to generate an alternative URL for locating the entity (this is sometimes accomplished by looking up the public identifier in a catalog file). However, note that an XML entity declaration must always specify a valid system identifier, in addition to the public one.

Figure 4.1 contains a "reworked" version of the document listed in Figure 2.1, wherein the document has been decomposed into a single document entity and two external entities. In the document entity (the entity that serves as the root for the document), the declaration

```
<!ENTITY items
      SYSTEM "http://www.groveware.com/examp/items.xml"
>
```

```
(A) Document Entity-Root document for the Entity Tree
<?xml version="1.0" encoding="UTF-8" ?>
<!DOCTYPE menu [
<!-- menu has any number of items, each item containing
     a description, price, and optional graphic. -->
<!ENTITY  resto "Liam's Chowder &#x22;House&#x22; and Grill" >
<!ENTITY % menu.cont
          "<!ELEMENT menu ( rname,(item,extend?)* ) >"
>
<!ENTITY % item-grammar
          SYSTEM "http://www.groveware.com/examp/grammar.xml"
>
<!ENTITY    items
          SYSTEM "http://www.groveware.com/examp/items.xml"
>
%menu.cont;
<!ATTLIST menu
          date CDATA #REQUIRED
          ref  CDATA #IMPLIED
          rest CDATA #FIXED    "&resto;"
>
%item-grammar;
]>
<menu date="12nov1998">
  <rname>&resto;</rname>
  &items;
</menu>


(B) Parameter Entity: item-grammar
http://www.groveware.com/examp/grammar.xml
<?xml version='1.0' encoding='ISO-8859-1' ?>
<!ELEMENT item (desc, price, graphic?) >
<!ATTLIST item
          type (appetizer|entrée|dessert|drink) "entrée"
>
<!ELEMENT desc (#PCDATA | emph)* >
<!ELEMENT price (#PCDATA)* >
<!ATTLIST price
          units CDATA  #REQUIRED
>
```

(continues)

Figure 4.1   Effectively the "same" document as that shown in Figure 2.1, but broken up into external general and parameter entities. The relationship between these entities is illustrated in Figure 4.2.

```
(continued)
<!ELEMENT graphic EMPTY >
<!ATTLIST graphic
          gtype CDATA #REQUIRED
          src   CDATA #REQUIRED
>


(C) General Entity: items
http://www.groveware.com/examp/items.xml

<?xml version='1.0' encoding='UCS-2' ?>
<item type="appetizer" >
    <desc>Warmed leek salad, coated with a balsamic vinegar and
          goat cheese dressing</desc>
    <price units="usd">6.95</price>
    <graphic gtype="gif"
             src="http://www.goodfood.com/menu/leek-salad.gif" />
  </item>
  <!-- Following Item is tasty! -->
  <item type="appetizer" >
    <desc>Prosciutto ham with melon</desc>
    <price units="usd">7.95</price>
    <graphic gtype="jpeg"
             src="http://www.goodfood.com/menu/ham-melon.jpeg" />
</item>
```

defines the external parsed general entity named **items**, located at the given URL.

External general entities are referenced just like internal ones—that is, by the notation *&entity-name;* , where *entity-name* is the name of the entity. And, just like internal ones, they must be declared before they are referenced. Looking to the bottom of Part A of Figure 4.1, you will see how the reference to **items** is of the expected form, and that this entity is declared in the DTD, prior to its use.

4.2 External Parameter Entity Declarations

External parameter entities are declared almost identically to external general entities-the only difference is the presence of the percent character preceding the entity name. For example, Figure 4.1 declares two parameter entities, via the markup:

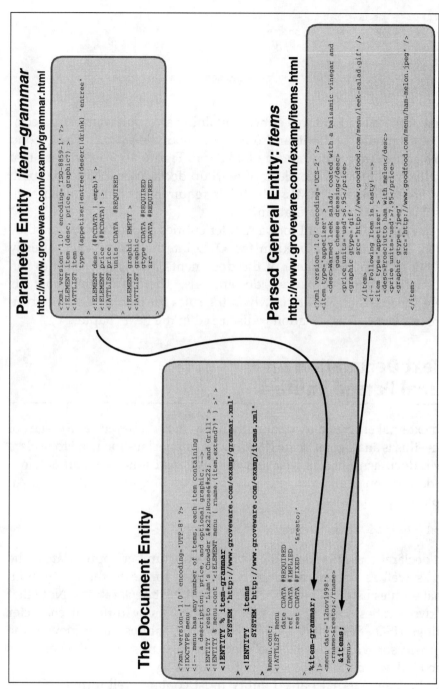

Parameter Entity *item-grammar*
http://www.groveware.com/examp/grammar.html

```
<?xml version='1.0' encoding='ISO-8859-1' ?>
<!ELEMENT item (desc, price, graphic?) >
<!ATTLIST item
          type (appetizer|entree|desert|drink) 'entree'
>
<!ELEMENT desc (#PCDATA | emph)* >
<!ELEMENT price (#PCDATA)* >
<!ATTLIST price
          units CDATA #REQUIRED
>
<!ELEMENT graphic EMPTY >
<!ATTLIST graphic
          gtype CDATA #REQUIRED
          src   CDATA #REQUIRED
>
```

Parsed General Entity: *items*
http://www.groveware.com/examp/items.html

```
<?xml version='1.0' encoding='UCS-2' ?>
<item type="appetizer" >
    <desc>Warmed leek salad, coated with a balsamic vinegar and
          goat cheese dressing</desc>
    <price units='usd'>6.95</price>
    <graphic gtype='gif'
             src="http://www.goodfood.com/menu/leek-salad.gif" />
</item>
<!-- Following item is tasty! -->
<item type="appetizer" >
    <desc>Prosciutto ham with melon</desc>
    <price units='usd'>7.95</price>
    <graphic gtype='jpeg'
             src="http://www.goodfood.com/menu/ham-melon.jpeg" />
</item>
```

The Document Entity

```
<?xml version="1.0" encoding="UTF-8" ?>
<!DOCTYPE menu [
<!-- menu has any number of items, each item containing
     a description, price, and optional graphic. -->
<!ENTITY resto "Liam's Chowder &#x22;House&#x22; and Grill" >
<!ENTITY % menu.cont "<!ELEMENT menu ( rname,(item,extend?)* ) >" >
<!ENTITY % item-grammar
         SYSTEM "http://www.groveware.com/examp/grammar.xml"
>
<!ENTITY items
         SYSTEM "http://www.groveware.com/examp/items.xml"
>
%menu.cont;
<!ATTLIST menu
          date CDATA #REQUIRED
          ref  CDATA #IMPLIED
          rest CDATA #FIXED "&resto;"
>
%item-grammar;
]>
<menu date="12nov1998">
  <rname>&resto;</rname>
  &items;
</menu>
```

Figure 4.2 Diagram illustrating the relationship between the document entity and the related external general and parameter entities listed in Figure 4.1.

```
<!ENTITY % menu.cont
    "<!ELEMENT menu ( rname,(item,extend?)* ) >"
>
<!ENTITY % item-grammar
    SYSTEM "http://www.groveware.com/examp/grammar.xml"
>
```

The first of these is an internal entity containing a complete markup declaration, and should be familiar from the previous example. The second declares an external entity, and by looking to Figure 4.1 you will see that this entity contains a whole block of markup declarations. Note that both entities are well-formed XML, which is a requirement of parameter entities, as it was of parsed general entities.

The use and valid content for parameter entities depends on where they are used. When they are used in the DTD internal subset (i.e., directly inside the DOCTYPE element of the document entity), such entities can only contain complete markup declarations. There are other contexts (namely, the external subset), in which the rules for parameter entity content are less strict. This situation is discussed in the next chapter.

4.3 Text Declaration for External Parsed Entities

Parsed external entities may optionally have a *text declaration* at the start of the file—this is analogous to the XML document declaration used to declare an XML document, except that text declarations cannot contain a standalone declaration (i.e., standalone="yes" or standalone="no"). An example is:

```
<?xml version='1.0' encoding='ISO-8859-1' ?>
```

Text declarations can specify the XML version number appropriate to the entity, as well as the character encoding used to create the entity. Both external entities listed in Figure 4.1 begin with text declarations. Note that these two entities state that they are encoded using different character encodings (ISO-8859-1 and UCS-2). When the entities are retrieved, the XML processor will transform the character content so that all characters are encoded, within the processor, in the same way.

Note that an external parsed entity must contain well-formed XML—that is, it must be well-formed independent of any knowledge of the intended use of the entity. Thus, a parsed entity cannot contain partial elements (e.g., start-tags without the corresponding end-tags), or partial

Table 4.1   Examples of some ill-formed and well-formed external parsed entities, with explanations.

EXTERNAL PARSED GENERAL ENTITY (ILL-FORMED)

```
< ?xml version='1.0' encoding='ISO-8859-1' ?>
```

```
<linkTo href="path/to/file.xml">linked text
```

> The preceding general entity is ill-formed, as it is missing an end-tag.

EXTERNAL PARSED GENERAL ENTITY (ILL-FORMED)

```
<!ATTLIST menu   stuff "menu-stuff" >
```

> The preceding entity is ill-formed, as the start-tag is in error (the ! cannot be used as the start of an element name), and there is no end-tag. Note that this was declared as a general entity, which means that it will be well-formed only if it matches the well-formedness constraints that apply to the content of elements.

EXTERNAL PARAMETER ENTITY (WELL-FORMED)

```
< ?xml version='1.0' encoding= "UCS-2" ?>
```

```
<!ATTLIST menu   stuff "menu-stuff" >
```

> The preceding entity is well-formed parameter-entity content, but would be ill-formed if it were declared as a general entity.

EXTERNAL PARSED GENERAL ENTITY (WELL-FORMED)

This quick brown fox jumped over the lazy

Dog. This pen is mightier than the sword.

Actions speak louder than words.

Good men are hard to find.

Good examples are even harder.

> The preceding entity is well-formed character data content, without any tags. Of course, an entity may itself be well-formed, but may lead to an invalid document. For example, if the preceding entity were included inside an element that had *element content* (that is, is declared to only allow elements inside it) then the document would not be valid.

markup (for example, the first few characters of a start-tag, but not the ">" character that ends it). Table 4.1 gives some examples of badly formed entities, with explanations of why these particular entities are not well-formed. Also shown are some entities that are well-formed.

4.4 Replacement Text for External Entity References

When an external entity reference is used, it is replaced by the content of the entity. The rules for generating replacement text for an external entity are very similar to those used for internal entities. The rules are:

1. (External) parameter-entity references are replaced by the replacement text of the corresponding entity. This rule is only relevant for external parameter entities, as parameter-entity references are not recognized within the content of external general entities.

2. Character references are replaced by the corresponding characters.

3. General-entity references are only replaced when the entity is used within the content of an element, or in the context of an attribute value.

Thus, except for the small change to the first rule, external parsed entities are parsed in essentially the same way as internal entities.

In practice, the processing model is somewhat different. Upon encountering an external entity reference, an XML processor simply deletes the characters making up the entity reference, and then goes off and reads the data content of that entity, continuing recursively through all contained entity references. When this process is completed, the processor takes up in the original document entity at the point just after the original entity reference.

For example, given the following external entity (references within this entity are shown in boldface):

```
&#60;item type="appetizer" >
    <desc>Prosciutto ham with melon</desc>
    <price units="usd">7.95</price>
    <graphic gtype="jpeg"
            src="&urlref;" />
&#60;/item>
```

then the replacement text for this entity, upon applying rules 2 and 3 above, will be:

```
<item type="appetizer" >
    <desc>Prosciutto ham with melon</desc>
    <price units="usd">7.95</price>
```

```
    <graphic gtype="jpeg"
            src="&urlref;" />
</item>
```

4.5 Multiple Declarations of the Same Entity

A DTD can contain multiple declarations for the same named entity. For example, the following is perfectly legal markup:

```
<!ENTITY address "123 Markham Avenue, Toronto, Ontario" >
<!ENTITY address "321 Bloor Street West, Toronto. ">
<!ENTITY address SYSTEM "dir1/stuff.xml" >
```

However, once an entity is declared, an XML processor must *ignore* any subsequent declarations for the same named entity. Thus, an XML processor would ignore the second and third declaration listed here, and would use the first defined value.

This is true for all types of entities, including external and internal. This ensures that a non-validating XML processor can establish the identity of an external entity via a declaration in the part of the DTD that it reads, and not worry that a subsequent declaration—perhaps in an external entity it does not read—can change the already-set value.[1] This rule lets you create an external DTD that can be shared by many users, and lets those users override specific (perhaps generic) entity values within each specific instance of a document.

4.6 Allowed Locations for Character and Entity References

It can be confusing to figure out where entity references can and cannot be used. As mentioned in the previous chapters, it is illegal to use general-entity references inside the document type declaration or inside a markup declaration (except inside attribute or entity values)—this is instead the realm allocated for parameter-entity references. Similarly, parameter entities have no meaning inside the document element.

At the same time it is useful to know how entity references are handled when they are valid. We have discussed these rules in previous examples, but it seems useful to summarize them together in one place. This is done

---

[1] Recall that a non-validating XML processor is one that does not validate markup, but that may read the content of the document type declaration to obtain values for internal entities, and default values for attributes.

in Table 4.2. These rules are more formally stated in Section 4.4 of the official specification (see Part 2 of this book).

4.6.1 Forbidden Characters in Entity and Attribute Values, and Inside Elements

It is also useful to recall which characters are explicitly forbidden in attribute values, internal entity values, or as text content within a non-empty markup element. These rules were also discussed in the previous chapters, but can be usefully summarized as shown in Table 4.3. These characters can be present, of course, as character or entity references. However, for internal entity values you must be careful that the resulting replacement text is well-formed wherever the entity is referenced.

> **NOTE** Parameter-Entity References Not Recognized In Attribute Values
>
> **Parameter-entity references are not recognized in the context of an attribute value. Thus, in the attribute-list declaration:**
>
> ```
> <!ATTLIST writing
>         todo CDATA "I've got %things; to do"
> >
> ```
>
> **the string** `%things;` **is *not recognized* as a parameter-entity reference, so that the actual value for the entity todo is the string:** `I've got %things; to do`.

Table 4.2 Entity and character references allowed in internal entity declarations, in attribute specifications, and in the text content of non-empty elements. Please see Table 4.3 for a list of characters disallowed in similar contexts.

CONTEXT FOR THE REFERENCE	TYPES OF REFERENCES ALLOWED IN GIVEN CONTEXT
Internal parameter entity	■ *parameter-entity reference* (included in the *literal entity value* containing the reference; any expanded quotes resulting from the inserted replacement text do not end the literal string)
	■ *general-entity reference* (valid, but the reference is not replaced in the replacement text—it is only replaced when the internal parameter entity is used. Note that you *cannot* use a general-entity

Table 4.2 *(Continued)*

CONTEXT FOR THE REFERENCE	TYPES OF REFERENCES ALLOWED IN GIVEN CONTEXT
	reference within an internal parameter entity that is referenced from directly within the document type declaration. Thus, the only place you can really use an internal general entity is within a parameter entity that is used within another internal general entity definition. This is not terribly useful, so that you might as well avoid using general-entity references in this context.)
	■ *character reference* (replaced, in the replacement text, by the indicated character)
Internal general entity	■ *parameter-entity reference* (included in the *literal entity value* containing the reference; any expanded quotes resulting from the inserted replacement text do not end the literal string)
	■ *general-entity reference* (valid, but the reference is not replaced in the replacement text—it is only replaced when the internal general entity is used)
	■ *character reference* (replaced, in the replacement text, by the indicated character)
Attribute value specification	■ *internal general-entity reference* (included in literal value; any expanded quotes resulting from the replacement text do not terminate the literal string)
	■ *character reference* (replaced by the indicated character)
Inside the document type declaration (but not in any of the preceding three contexts)	■ *parameter-entity reference* (replaced by the replacement text)
Inside non-empty element	■ *general entity reference* (external entities need be included only if validating)
	■ *character reference* (replaced by the indicated character)

Table 4.3 Characters explicitly disallowed within internal entity declarations, attribute specifications, or in the text content of non-empty elements. Such characters must be *escaped* in these contexts.

CONTEXT	DISALLOWED CHARACTERS
Value for an internal parameter or general entity	& (except when the start of an entity reference)
	% (except when the start of an entity reference)
	quotation character (' or ") used to surround the entity value
Attribute value specification (in declaration or in an element)	< & (except when the start of an entity reference)
	quotation character (' or ") used to surround the entity value
Inside non-empty elements	<
	& (except when the start of an entity reference)
	the string]] > (end of CDATA section)

External and Internal Document Type Declaration Subsets

Concepts Covered: external subset, internal subset, conditional sections

As mentioned in the last chapter, the markup declarations (plus any comments) appearing inside the document type declaration (i.e., between the brackets [and] that delimit the content of a DOCTYPE element) are referred to as the *document type declaration internal subset*, also known as the *DTD internal subset*, or sometimes just the *internal subset*. The internal subset consists of those markup declarations that occur directly within the document entity—and nothing else. Because these declarations are present within the document they describe, there are some restrictions placed on the way in which parameter entities can be used. These restrictions are described in the next section.

A document type declaration also supports what is known as a *document type declaration external subset*, also known as the *DTD external subset*, or sometimes just the *external subset*. The external subset is entirely external to the document entity, and consists of external entities that are related to the document in two different ways:

- by an explicit external subset declaration in to the document type declaration (i.e., in the DOCTYPE element)

- as external parameter entities referenced by parameter entity declarations and referenced, either directly or indirectly, from the internal subset or from the explicit external subset just mentioned

Because the markup declarations in the external subset are present in an entity separate from the document they describe, the restrictions placed on parameter-entity usage are less severe than those placed on parameter entities used within the internal subset. These restrictions, and their ramifications, are discussed in this chapter.

5.1 Document Type Declaration Internal Subset

As mentioned, markup declarations that appear inside the document type declaration (i.e., inside the DOCTYPE element) are referred to as the *document type declaration internal subset*. Within this internal subset, parameter-entity references can be used to include additional markup declarations—these can be references to either external entities or internal ones. However, within the internal DTD subset, parameter-entity references can only appear in two places:

- where markup declarations can occur (i.e., the entity can contain an entire markup declaration, to be included in the internal subset)
- inside the value for an internal entity declaration

Parameter-entity references cannot occur within attribute value specifications (they are not recognized there), nor within markup declarations—that is, they cannot contain "parts" of a markup declaration.

For example, in Figure 4.1 the declaration for the **menu** element was completely contained within the internal parameter entity named **menu.cont**, so that this declaration is invoked, in the internal subset, via the markup

```
<!ENTITY  % menu.cont
   "<!ELEMENT menu ( rname,(item,extend?)* ) >"
>
%menu.cont;
```

However, markup of the form:

```
<!ENTITY  % menu.cont
     "( rname,(item,extend?)"
>
<!ELEMENT menu (%menu.cont;*) > <!-- Illegal reference! -->
```

is illegal inside the internal subset, since the entity is not referenced from a location where markup declarations can occur.

5.1.1 Processing by Non-Validating XML Parsers

This special rule (no parameter entities inside markup declarations) is present to ensure reasonable processing of well-formed XML by a non-validating parser. A non-validating parser will take an XML document and convert it into a tree of data and associated attributes, but is not required to check the structure of the document against the grammar defined in the DTD. Furthermore, the XML specification says that non-validating parsers can entirely *ignore* external entity references (parameter or general). This rule is in place to allow documents to be handled independent of any related entities. As a result of this decision, the rules for writing markup declarations inside the internal subset must ensure that the markup is well formed, even if some parameter entities are not replaced. Of course, the markup

```
<!ELEMENT menu (%menu.cont;*) >
```

is not well formed when the entity reference is not replaced, so that this type of inclusion is forbidden inside the internal subset.

Note that parsing the internal subset for internal general entity and default attribute values must cease as soon as the processor encounters an external parameter-entity reference that it does not retrieve, since this external entity may contain declarations that override declarations in the internal subset occurring *after* the un-expanded reference.

5.2 External Subset (1): External Parameter Entities

The situation is different inside an external parameter-entity referenced from the internal subset. Since such entities are external to the document, they are considered to be part of the external DTD subset. This means that the rules for using parameter entities are significantly less stringent, as illustrated in the following.

Consider Figure 5.1—a reorganization of the documents in Figure 4.1 such that the declarations are placed in an external parameter entity. Figure 5.2 shows an illustration of these different components and how they are related, and indicated which parts of the document type declaration are in the internal and external subsets.

There are two ways that Figure 5.1 differs from Figure 4.1. First, the declaration for the menu element is now found in an external entity

```
(A) Document Entity

<?xml version="1.0" encoding="UTF-8" ?>
<!DOCTYPE menu [
<!-- * menu has any number of items, each item containing
     * a description, price, and optional graphic.
     * -->
<!ENTITY   resto "Liam's Chowder &#x22;House&#x22; and Grill" >
<!ENTITY   % menu.cont
           SYSTEM "http://www.groveware.com/examp/menu.xxx"
>
<!ENTITY   % item-grammar
           SYSTEM "http://www.groveware.com/examp/grammar.xml"
>
<!ENTITY   items
           SYSTEM "http://www.groveware.com/examp/items.xml"
>
%menu.cont;
%item-grammar;
]>
<menu date="12nov1998">
  <rname>&resto;</rname>
  &items;
</menu>

(B) External Parameter Entity: item-grammar
http://www.groveware.com/examp/grammar.xml

<?xml version='1.0' encoding='ISO-8859-1' ?>
<!ELEMENT item (desc, price, graphic?) >
<!ENTITY % grap2
       SYSTEM "http://www.mysite.org/datafile"
>
<!ATTLIST item
           type (appetizer|entrée|dessert|drink) "entrée"
>
<!ELEMENT desc (#PCDATA | emph)* >
<!ELEMENT price (#PCDATA)* >
```

(continues)

Figure 5.1 A reorganization of the documents listed in Figure 4.1, so that the declaration for the menu element is found in an external entity (the file *menu.xxx*—note that the filename suffix, here *.xxx*, is not significant). The differences between this figure and Figure 4.1 are shown in boldface. Note the more flexible use of parameter entities from within external parameter entities, compared with the forms allowed within the internal subset.

(continued)

```
<!ATTLIST price
          units CDATA  #REQUIRED
>
%grap2;

(C) External General Entity: items
http://www.groveware.com/examp/items.xml

<?xml version='1.0' encoding='UCS-2' ?>
<item type="appetizer" >
    <desc>Warmed leek salad, coated with a balsamic vinegar and
          goat cheese dressing</desc>
    <price units="usd">6.95</price>
    <graphic gtype="gif"
             src="http://www.goodfood.com/menu/leek-salad.gif" />
  </item>
  <!-- Following Item is tasty! -->
  <item type="appetizer" >
    <desc>Prosciutto ham with melon</desc>
    <price units="usd">7.95</price>
    <graphic gtype="jpeg"
             src="http://www.goodfood.com/menu/ham-melon.jpeg" />
</item>

(D) External Parameter Entity: menu.cont
http://www.groveware.com/examp/menu.xxx

<?xml version='1.0' encoding='UCS-2' ?>
<!ENTITY % menu.model "(desc, price, graphic?)" >
<!ELEMENT menu ( %menu.model;* ) >



(E) External Parameter Entity: grap2
http://www.mysite.org/datafile

<!ELEMENT graphic EMPTY >
<!ATTLIST graphic
          gtype CDATA #REQUIRED
          src   CDATA #REQUIRED
>
```

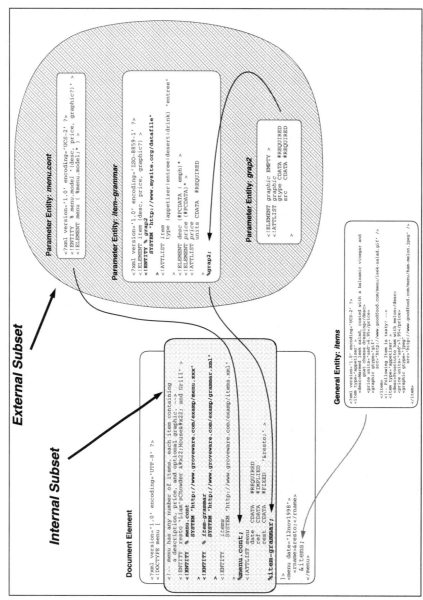

Figure 5.2   Diagram illustrating the relationship between the document entity and the external general and parameter entities declared and listed in Figure 5.1. This figure also notes the entities that make up the *external DTD subset*, and the markup within the document entity that makes up the *internal DTD subset*.

menu.cont (the file *menu.xxx*, part D). Note how the entity **menu.cont** uses an internal parameter entity to contain just the *content model* for **menu** elements, and then references this entity from within an element declaration. Second, the external entity **item-grammar** (part B) has been modified to itself reference an external entity (**grap2**) which contains the declarations for **graphic** elements.

This use of parameter entities as containers for sub-parts of a declaration is perfectly valid within the external subset, provided the sub-part are themselves well-formed data that correspond to a "complete" grammatical XML expression, or token (recall that the XML processor will add space characters in front of and after every inserted parameter entity). For example, if a parameter entity contains part of a content model, it must define an entire grouping of content model rules, and not a partial one (i.e., it must have matching round brackets, and cannot begin or end with the sequence ("|") or connector (",") symbols). Similarly, the parameter entity cannot contain just part of a literal string used in a declaration. Table 5.1 illustrates some common errors in this regard.

5.3 External Subset (2): Explicit External Subset

A document type declaration can also specify, at the beginning of the document type declaration, the location of a special entity containing an external DTD subset. As with external entities, this can be referenced using a system identifier or system and public identifiers. An example is:

```
<!DOCTYPE name SYSTEM "url/of/file/doc.dtd"
[
    <!-- Internal DTD subset -->
]>
```

which identifies the resource *path/to/file/doc.dtd* as an external DTD subset. Note that the preceding declaration could also be of the form (differences in boldface):

```
<!DOCTYPE name PUBLIC "public-id"
                "url/or/file/doc.dtd "
[
    <!-- Internal DTD subset -->
]>
```

where `public-id` is a public identifier for the external subset. Public identifiers, and their use, were discussed in the previous chapter, in section 4.1.

Table 5.1 Three examples of internal parameter-entity declarations, showing correct and incorrect (with explanation) use of parameter-entity references. Note that the "valid" uses described here are only valid within the external DTD subset (i.e., inside an external parameter entity).

VALID	INVALID
	Incomplete expression: unmatched round brackets
<!ENTITY % *cont* "(a | b)" >	<!ENTITY % *cont* "(a | b" >
<!ELEMENT zippy ((%*cont*;)*,w);	<!ELEMENT zippy ((%*cont*;))*,w);
	Incomplete token in entity value
<!ENTITY %*tg* '#FIXED' >	<!ENTITY %*tg1* "'#FIX" >
	<!ENTITY %*tg2* "#ED'" >
<!ATTLIST blob	<!ATTLIST blob
CDATA %*tg*; "Tgif!" >	CDATA %*tg1*;%*tg2*; "Tgif!" >
	Entity contains only partial literal value: unmatched value delimiter (" character)
<!ENTITY *val* "'Value for Zip!'">	<!ENTITY *val* 'for Zip!'" >
<!ATTLIST zip CDATA %*val*; >	<!ATTLIST zip CDATA "Value %*pval*; >

The preceding markup implies both an external and internal subset. However, the internal subset can be left off, in which case the document type declaration takes the simple form:

```
<!DOCTYPE name SYSTEM "url/of/file/doc.dtd " >
```

Like the internal subset, the external subset must (upon processing of any entities defined and used within it) consist of a series of complete markup declarations. However, because it is an external entity, this entity does not have any of the restrictions on parameter-entity usage imposed within the internal subset. The ramifications of this are shown in Figure 5.3, which is a reworked version of Figure 5.1, with all markup declarations moved to the external subset. Note how the external subset (*doc.dtd*, Part B in Figure 5.3) can use parameter entities to represent sub-parts within markup declarations.

```
(A) Document Entity

<?xml version="1.0" encoding="UTF-8" ?>
<!DOCTYPE menu SYSTEM "path/to/file/doc.dtd" >
<menu date="12nov1998">
  <rname>&resto;</rname>
  &items;
</menu>

(B) Explicit External Subset:
path/to/file/doc.dtd
<?xml version='1.0' encoding='UCS-2' ?>
<!ENTITY  resto "Liam's Chowder &#x22;House&#x22; and Grill" >
<!ENTITY items
         SYSTEM "http://www.groveware.com/examp/items.xml"
>
<!ENTITY % menu.model "(desc, price, graphic?)" >
<!ELEMENT menu ( %menu.model;* ) >
<!ATTLIST menu
         date  CDATA    #REQUIRED
         ref   CDATA    #IMPLIED
         rest  CDATA    #FIXED    "&resto;"
>
<!ELEMENT item (desc, price, graphic?) >
<!ATTLIST item
         type (appetizer|entrée|dessert|drink) "entrée"
>
<!ELEMENT desc (#PCDATA | emph)* >
<!ELEMENT price (#PCDATA)* >
<!ATTLIST price
         units CDATA  #REQUIRED
>
<!ELEMENT graphic EMPTY >
<!ATTLIST graphic
         gtype CDATA #REQUIRED
         src   CDATA #REQUIRED
>
```

(continues)

Figure 5.3   An example document type declaration that has all markup declarations within an explicit external subset. Note how the external subset defines all general entities referenced from within the document entity.

(continued)

(C) External General Entity: *items*
`http://www.groveware.com/examp/items.xml`

```
<?xml version='1.0' encoding='UCS-2' ?>
<item type="appetizer" >
    <desc>Warmed leek salad, coated with a balsamic vinegar and
          goat cheese dressing</desc>
    <price units="usd">6.95</price>
    <graphic gtype="gif"
          src="http://www.goodfood.com/menu/leek-salad.gif" />
</item>
<!-- Following Item is tasty! -->
<item type="appetizer" >
    <desc>Prosciutto ham with melon</desc>
    <price units="usd">7.95</price>
    <graphic gtype="jpeg"
          src="http://www.goodfood.com/menu/ham-melon.jpeg" />
</item>
```

Note also in Figure 5.3 how the external subset defines all the general entities that are referenced from within the document entity, and that by implication the **resto** entity, which was previously an internal general entity, is now an external one.

5.3.1 Processing Order: Internal and External Subsets

Given all these different parts of the document type declaration, it is important to know the order in which the declarations will be evaluated. In general, the procedure is as follows, and is very specific:

1. **The internal subset is processed first**. If the XML processor is not validating the document, it may choose not to retrieve any external entities. In this case, processing of the internal DTD subset *must stop* when the processor encounters a reference to a non-retrieved external

parameter entity, since this could contain declarations that affect the interpretation of the document.

2. If external parameter entities are being included into the internal subset, then each parameter-entity reference is replaced by the replacement text of the referenced entity, and the processor treats the expanded markup as if it were part of the internal subset. Once processing of the external entity is finished, processing continues at the markup declaration that followed the parameter-entity reference in the internal subset. This continues until the entire internal subset is processed.

3. If the document type declaration itself references an explicit external subset (by a SYSTEM or PUBLIC identifier on the DOCTYPE element), then this entity is processed last, after the internal subset.

The purpose of this model is to allow document authors to create and use general entities as they wish, without needing to worry that the entities they define will be somehow overridden by an entity with the same name that is defined in the external subset. Recall the following rules:

1. If two or more entity declarations declare the same named entity, then the first one encountered is used, and subsequent ones are ignored.

2. If two or more attribute declarations for a given element type declare default properties for an attribute of the same name, then the properties resulting from the first such declaration are used, and properties from subsequent specifications for this named attribute are ignored.

3. If there is more than one element declaration for the same element type, then the document is not valid, and processing of the document type declaration must stop. If the document is being processed by a validating processor, then it must report a fatal error to the application, and must stop processing the document completely. If a non-validating processor is being used, it may continue to process the element content.

Thus the two document entities shown in Figure 5.4 use declaration in the internal subset to *override* entity declarations found in the explicit internal subset shown in Figure 5.3.

As a result, you can use an explicit external subset to define an overall grammar for a document, as well as a default set of entities, and can then use declarations in the internal subset to override specific entity declarations and attribute value specifications. Note, however, that you cannot use

```
(A) First Example Document
<?xml version="1.0" encoding="UTF-8" ?>
<!DOCTYPE menu SYSTEM "path/to/file/doc.dtd" [
<!ENTITY resto "Ian's Happy Clam Shack and Pub" >
]>
<menu date="12nov1998">
  <rname>&resto;</rname>
  &items;
</menu>


(B) Second Example Document
<?xml version="1.0" encoding="UTF-8" ?>
<!DOCTYPE menu SYSTEM "path/to/file/doc.dtd" [
<!ENTITY resto "Justin's Chicken-Only Takeout Joint" >
<!ENTITY items
        SYSTEM "my/items/food.xml"
>
<!ENTITY more-items
        SYSTEM "path/to/more/food.xml"
>
]>
<menu date="12nov1998">
  <rname>&resto;</rname>
  &items;
  &more-items;
</menu>
```

Figure 5.4 An illustration of how declarations in the internal subset can override entity declarations in the external subset. The new declarations, relative to part (A) of Figure 5.3, are shown in boldface. The external subset being referenced (*path/to/file/doc.dtd*) is shown in Figure 5.3 (B).

these declarations to change the content model, since the XML specification explicitly forbids two element declarations for the same element type, as discussed earlier in Chapter 2, at the end of section 2.1.4.

If you need to change content models, XML provides conditional sections and parameter entities, as described in the next section.

5.4 Conditional Sections

The external subset supports an additional and important feature known as *conditional sections*—this form of markup is not allowed in the internal subset. A conditional section allows portions of an entity to be conditionally included or ignored in the grammar. These two options are indicated by the following syntax:

```
<![ INCLUDE [
   <!-- Markup declarations to include as part of the DTD -->
]]>
<![ IGNORE  [
   <!-- Markup declarations to ignore as part of the DTD -->
]]>
```

with the obvious associated meaning (the white space between the keywords INCLUDE or IGNORE and the preceding (<![) and following ([) text is optional). Each section can in turn contain markup declarations, parameter-entity references, or additional conditional sections.

Of course, these declarations are pretty useless as they stand. However, a judicious use of parameter entities makes these expressions very useful for toggling in and out different blocks of the declaration. An example is shown in Figure 5.5—simply by changing the values of the **debug** and **production** entities, we can choose to include or exclude those markup declarations required by debugging tools.

```
<!ENTITY  % debug      'INCLUDE' >
<!ENTITY  % production 'IGNORE'  >

<![%debug;[
   <!ELEMENT event-handler (
      reference , tracing* )*
   >
   <!-- other declarations to use when debug mode is enabled
   --> ]]>

<![%production;[
   <!ELEMENT event-handler
      (reference)*
   >
   <!-- other declarations to use when production mode is
        enabled, and debugging is disabled -->
]]>
```

Figure 5.5 An illustration of the use of parameter entities and conditional sections to conditionally include or exclude different groups of attribute-list declarations.

Conditional sections can be nested, with the expected behavior. That is:

- Everything within a section marked IGNORE is ignored—an XML processor will not include sections marked INCLUDE if they are inside a section marked IGNORE.

- Within a section marked INCLUDE, an XML processor will ignore any sections that are marked IGNORE.

Of course, you must be careful to escape (e.g., using character references) any strings of the form]]> that appear inside a marked section, as they will otherwise be interpreted as the end of the conditional section.

CHAPTER

6

Unparsed Entities and Tokenized Attribute Types

Concepts Covered: unparsed entities, notation declarations, entity tokenized attribute types

In Chapters 4 and 5 we discussed external parsed entities—entities (typically files) that contain well-formed XML data. We also described how in order to use such entities we needed to declare them in an XML document using an entity declaration, and reference them in a document using an entity reference.

We also mentioned *unparsed* general entities—that is, entities (files, or whatever) that do not contain XML.[1] Such entities can correspond to non-XML text, such as RTF, WordPerfect, or PostScript files, or they can correspond to binary data such as image files or executable programs. XML for the most part does not care about the nature of such resources. However, XML does care insofar as it has a mechanism for declaring the existence of such objects, and a mechanism for referencing them, from within markup, using a special attribute type. These two issues are the subjects of this example.

In general, an XML processor does not handle unparsed entities itself. Rather, it passes information about unparsed entities (their locations, how they are referenced from within the XML document) to the overall application.

[1.] Unparsed entities must be general entities, since all parameter entities must contain well-formed XML.

In a DTD, an *unparsed* entity is declared via one of two possible declarations:

```
<!ENTITY entity-name
     SYSTEM "uri-to-resource"
     NDATA tname
>
<!ENTITY entity-name
     PUBLIC "public-id"  "uri-to-resource"
     NDATA tname
>
```

Except for the extra text in boldface, these are identical to parsed general entity declarations, discussed in Chapter 4, where *entity-name* is the name of the entity, and the SYSTEM and PUBLIC identifiers are as described in that chapter. The special token NDATA says that the entity is unparsed, while the final string, *tname*, is a *name token* [7] that identifies the format, or *notation*, of the unparsed entity. For example, the declaration

```
<!ENTITY logo-graphic
     SYSTEM "images/files/logo.gif"
     NDATA gif
>
```

declares an unparsed entity named **logo-graphic** that corresponds to the file *logo.gif*, of the *notation* **gif**.

Several unparsed entities can share the same notation. Thus, a DTD might easily contain the following declarations:

```
<!ENTITY gra-mort
     SYSTEM "images/morticia.gif"
     NDATA gif
>
<!ENTITY gra-fest
     SYSTEM "images/u-fester.gif"
     NDATA gif
>
<!ENTITY gra-thin
     SYSTEM "images/thing.gif"
     NDATA gif
>
```

which declares three unparsed entities, all of notation **gif**. Of course, the entities themselves must have different names—and must have names distinct from those used for any parsed general entities.

6.1 Notations and Notation Declarations

In a valid XML document, every *notation* type that is used *must* be declared in the DTD via a *notation declaration*. Such declarations are very similar to entity declarations, and take either of the forms

```
<!NOTATION notation-name
    SYSTEM "uri-to-resource"
>
<!NOTATION notation-name
    PUBLIC "public-id"  "uri-to-resource"
>
```

where `notation-name` is a *name* [7] that identifies the notation. Notations are a way of defining auxiliary resources that can be used to interpret or appropriately process unparsed entities of the defined notation. For example, the declaration

```
<!NOTATION gif SYSTEM "apps/gifview.exe" >
```

might indicate that the notation **gif** is associated with some application program (*gifview.exe*), which can be used to interpret any unparsed entity of notation type **gif**.

This particular interpretation or use of notations is inherited from the SGML world, where documents generally resided on a single machine, and where it made sense to reference "support" applications in this way. It makes less sense on the Web, when one generally does not want to let a remote document start up arbitrary local programs! Another possible interpretation would be to use a notation to reference an applet that could in turn be downloaded and run—in a secure environment—to handle objects of the declared notation.

An alternative is to use a notion to specify a *list* of allowed types of unparsed data, as in the following:

```
<!NOTATION notation.Image
    SYSTEM "image/png:image/jpeg:image/gif:text/postscript"
>
<!ENTITY picture.Liam
    SYSTEM "http://www.site.org/imagelib/files/"
    NDATA notation.Image
>
```

Here, the notation **notation.Image** indicates that the document author prefers image files of the indicated types, where the types are given as a sequence of MIME content types, perhaps listed in decreasing order of preference. Then, if the application were to decide to retrieve the unparsed entity **picture.Liam** from the indicated remote site, it could use *content negotiation* (a feature of the HTTP protocol implied by the URL given here) with the remote HTTP server to negotiate the retrieval of the image in the best available format.

In general, the XML specification is very (and safely) vague on how notations should be handled, and simply says (see Part 2, Chapter 2, Section 4.2):

> **Notation declarations provide [a name and external identifier for the notation] which may allow an XML processor or its client application to locate a helper application capable of processing data in the given notation.**

This formally allows all of the preceding interpretations. Note also that the actual implementation of any of these choices is outside the scope of the XML processor, but is instead the responsibility of the application making use of the XML processor—all the processor does is note existence of a notation, and pass on the related information to the application.

As illustrated in the preceding text, one role of a notation is to identify, by name, the format of one or more unparsed entities, and to perhaps suggest a way to process or view the entity. However, XML supports two other uses for notations:

- to define the format of an element using a special type of attribute
- as a reference to an application, such that an XML document can send instructions to the application

These two tasks draw on two additional features of XML—*notation attributes* (attributes which can only take, as values, names of defined notations), and *processing instructions* (which define a set of instructions to be sent to a defined notation). These features will be discussed in Chapter 7.

6.2 ENTITY Tokenized Attribute Types

Of course, declaring unparsed entities is useless without a way of referencing them from an XML document. XML forbids the use of entity references to reference unparsed entities—it makes no sense to "include" non-XML data into an XML document. Instead, unparsed entities must be referenced using a special type of tokenized element *attribute*. These types *must* be declared in an attribute-list declaration (or else the XML processor does not

know the special role of these attributes), using the attribute type keyword
ENTITY or ENTITIES. An example is:

```
<!ATTLIST foot-pic
        sfoot ENTITY #FIXED "my-foot"
>
```

These are tokenized types, since the type declaration keyword implies the
type of token that can appear as an allowed attribute value (a name token)
and also implies that the allowed values must be names that are defined as
unparsed entities in the document type declaration.

The value ENTITY defines attributes that can only take, as their values, a
single unparsed entity name, while ENTITIES means that the attribute can
have a value consisting of one or more space-separated unparsed entity
names. Note that these entities must be declared before they are used, just
as with parsed entities.

As an example, consider the following block of declarations (the notation declaration for the type GIF is omitted):

```
<!ENTITY  my-foot
      SYSTEM "images/foot.gif"
      NDATA GIF
>
<!ENTITY  lfoot
      SYSTEM "images/my-left-foot.gif"
      NDATA GIF
>
<!ENTITY  rfoot
      SYSTEM "images/my-right-foot.gif"
      NDATA GIF
>
<!ENTITY  bfoot
      SYSTEM "images/my-baby-foot.gif"
      NDATA GIF
>
<!ENTITY  elbow
      SYSTEM "images/my-elbow.gif"
      NDATA GIF
>
<!ELEMENT foot-pic ANY >
<!ATTLIST foot-pic
      sfoot    ENTITY   #FIXED "my-foot"
      mix-foot ENTITIES "lfoot rfoot bfoot"
>
....
<foot-pic mix-foot="rfoot elbow hamster" />
```

Note how the value assigned to an ENTITIES is a *space-separated* list of name tokens, and that these name tokens must correspond to unparsed entities defined in the DTD. If the entities named in an attribute-list declaration or within an attribute-value assignment are not declared, then the document is not valid XML, although it is still well-formed.

Figure 6.1 shows a rewritten version of the example document from Figure 5.1, modified to illustrate the use of unparsed entities, notations, and entity tokenized attribute-list types. For simplicity, this document places all the XML markup into a single file (the document entity), with the only logical changes being:

- the use of unparsed entities to reference two "generic" images (note that we have left off the filename extension) previously referenced, as explicit image types, by **src** attributes
- the use of a notation declaration to declare a list of preferred image file formats, using the extended MIME notation supported for content negotiation by HTTP 1.1
- a change in the DTD so that **graphic** elements use entity names to reference the desired graphics
- changes to the markup to use entity names to reference the image files

Superficially, this is not that different from the previous version. However, this form may lead to a more robust document, since the entity declarations can in principle be maintained separate from the document body (for example, in an external entity), allowing for easier link maintenance, while the notation mechanism lets the document pass to the application information relevant to retrieval and/or processing of the external unparsed data.

```
<?xml version="1.0" encoding="UTF-8" ?>
<!DOCTYPE menu [
<!--* menu has any number of items, each item containing
    * a description, price, and optional graphic.
    * -->
<!ENTITY  resto "Liam's Chowder &#x22;House&#x22; and Grill" >
<!ENTITY l-salad
    SYSTEM "http://www.goodfood.com/menu/leek-salad"
    NDATA imgTypes
>
<!ENTITY h-melon
    SYSTEM "http://www.goodfood.com/menu/ham-melon"
    NDATA imgTypes
>
<!NOTATION imgTypes
    SYSTEM "ImageData: image/gif:image/jpeg:image/png;
q=1" >

<!ELEMENT menu ( rname,(item,extend?)* ) >
<!ATTLIST menu
        date  CDATA    #REQUIRED
        ref   CDATA    #IMPLIED
        rest  CDATA    #FIXED   "&resto;" >
<!ELEMENT item (desc, price, graphic?) >
<!ATTLIST item
        type (appetizer|entree|dessert|drink) "entree"
>
<!ELEMENT desc (#PCDATA | emph)* >
<!ELEMENT price (#PCDATA)* >
<!ATTLIST price
        units CDATA  #REQUIRED >
<!ELEMENT graphic EMPTY >
<!ATTLIST graphic
        src   ENTITY #REQUIRED
>  <!-- * Now the src attributes of graphic elements must
        * reference, by name, the unparsed entities defined
        * above. -->
]>
<menu date="12nov1998">
  <rname>&resto;</rname>
```

(continues)

Figure 6.1 A rewrite of the document in Figure 5.1, such that all markup is located in the document entity. In this example, external parsed entity declarations, notation declarations, and entity-type attribute-value specifications (in boldface) are used to reference the external image files.

```
(continued)
<item type="appetizer" >
    <desc>Warmed leek salad, coated with a balsamic vinegar and
        goat cheese dressing</desc>
    <price units="usd">6.95</price>
    <graphic src="l-salad" />      <!-- references a defined
                                                entity -->
  </item>
  <!-- Following Item is tasty! -->
  <item type="appetizer" >
    <desc>Prosciutto ham with melon</desc>
    <price units="usd">7.95</price>
    <graphic src="h-melon" />      <!-- references a defined
                                                entity -->
  </item>
</menu>
```

CHAPTER

7

Notation Attribute Types and Processing Instructions

Concepts Covered: processing instructions, notation attribute types

As illustrated in the preceding chapter, notations can identify, by name, the format of one or more unparsed entities. However, there are two additional features of XML that make use of notations—*processing instructions*, and *notation attributes*. Processing instructions are designed for sending instructions from the XML document to an external application, while notation attributes provide a way of defining a notation useful for interpreting or processing the *content* of a markup element that corresponds to a defined notation. These two features are discussed in the following sections.

It must be noted, for Web-based applications, that processing instructions and notation attributes are among the less-useful features of XML. You are best advised to avoid using these features unless they are specifically required for compatibility with existing SGML-based data.

7.1 Processing Instructions

A *processing instruction*, or *PI*, provides a way for an XML document to send a message to an external application. This allows an XML document to contain information relevant to the processing of the document but that may not be relevant to the document itself. For example, the processing instruction might recommend a memory stack allocation to a secondary program that will process the XML data, or it might contain an instruction to printing software, indicating the printer to which the formatted output of the application should be sent. Indeed, the XML specification does not say what processing instructions should be used for; it only states that an XML processor must forward information from the processing instruction to the application on behalf of which the processor is analyzing the XML markup.

Processing instructions have the general form

```
<?target-name string-of-chars ?>
```

where `target-name` *may* be the name of a notation, and `string-of-chars` is a character string that is the instruction to be sent to the notation. Note the use of the word "may"—there is no requirement that `target-name` be the name of a notation, although this is one common implementation. Target-name can be any *name* [5], provided it does not begin with the string "XML" in any case variation (i.e., `XML`, `Xml`, `xml`, etc., are forbidden). Names beginning with these letters are reserved for future use. The value `string-of-chars` can be any string of valid XML characters, provided the string does not contain the sequence ?> (which ends the PI). Thus, an example PI is:

```
<?psprinter psprint -g1000 paper="8.5x11" ?>
```

which might indicate sending the instruction `psprint -g1000 paper="8.5x11"` (get ready to print at resolution of 1000 dpi, onto 8.5 by 11 inch paper) to the external application notated by the name `psprinter`.

Obviously, if a processing instruction uses a notation to indicate the target of the PI, then this notation must be declared. For example, the markup

```
<!NOTATION psprinter
        SYSTEM   "/root/progs/psex"
>
```

binds the name `psprinter` to the application at the indicated location. An XML application that invokes the processing instruction might then launch the program */root/progs/psex* and use the string `psprint -g1000 paper="8.5x11"` as a command line argument.

Note, of course, that the security risks described in the previous chapter (section 6.1) apply here also, so that this type of use for notations is not recommended for Internet-distributed documents.

WARNING: Security Hazards of Processing Instructions

No Internet application should allow local invocation of arbitrary processing instructions via arbitrary notations. For example, if the notation referenced the

program /bin/rm, **or the command** del, **with the processing instruction containing the instruction** -rf /* **or** C:* , . . . **well, the ramifications of that are too horrifying to contemplate!**

7.1.1 Placement of Processing Instructions

Processing instructions can appear almost anywhere in an XML document—in the prolog, within the document type declaration, after the prolog and before the document element, within the document (or other) markup element, and even after the end-tag of the document element. Inside the prolog, a PI could be used to provide overall instructions to an external application, for example providing configuration parameters to a printer driver (as in the above example). Within the markup content, a PI could provide more specific instructions. For example, the instruction

```
<?psprinter pagebreak ?>
```

might instruct the printer to break to the next page at that point in the document.

Of course, many processing instructions can be mimicked by appropriate element markup, or by adding attributes that define appropriate properties (making sure, of course, that the application understands the new attributes!). For example, the markup element <pagebreak/> could indicate a location at which a page break must occur, while an element such as

```
<ifPrinting resolution="1000" paper-size="8.5x11">
```

could communicate the desired printing parameters.

7.2 Notation Attributes

Notation attributes are an enumerated type of attribute that can only take, as allowed values, one of a defined list of notations. Like entity-type attributes, notation attribute must be declared in an attribute list declaration. The intent is to indicate that the *content* of an element must be processed in some way, with the notation attribute indicating the tool (or type of tool) needed to do that processing. As an example, consider the following declaration, which declares elements of type **frog** to use a notation attribute, with the two possible values. Following this is an example of a **frog** element, and the element content.

```
<!ATTLIST frogs
      pproc NOTATION (base64gif|base64jpeg)  "base64gif"
>
.
.
.
<frogs pproc="base64gif"
>R0lGODlhawCzAPcAAAAAAAEBAQICAgMDAwQEBAUFBQYGBgcHBwg1CAkJCQoKCgs
LCwwMDA0N
DQ4ODg8PDxAQEBERERISEhMTExQUFBUVFRYWFhcXFxgYGBkZGRoaGhsbGxwcHB0d
HR4eHh8f
HyAgICEhISIiIiMjIyQkJCUlJSYmJicnJygoKCkpKSoqKisrKywsLC0tLS4uLi8v
LzAwMDEx
MTIyMjMzM0Q0NDU1NTY2Njc3Nzg4ODk5OTo6Ojs7Ozw8PD09PT4+Pj8/P0BAQEFB
QUJCQkND
Q0REREVFRUZGRkdHR0hISElJSUpKSktLS0xMTE1NTU5OTk9PT1BQUFFRUVJSUlNT
U1RUVFV
 .  .  .
</frogs>
```

The implication of this notation type is that **frog** elements contain base 64-encoded data, with the two notations corresponding to base 64-encoded GIF or JPEG images. I know this, of course, because I made up the example and chose notation names that were meaningful. In practice, the corresponding notation declarations (not shown in this example) would need to reference software that can appropriately process the content of this element, or alternatively would need to contain information that could be passed back to the application such that it understood the special handling required by the content of that element.

Note that this example overloads two concepts (image file type and encoding type) onto the same notation attribute. A better choice might be to use two attributes: a notation-type attribute to indicate the image type, and an enumerated list type to indicate the encoding mechanism. For example:

```
<!ATTLIST frogs
      imgtype NOTATION (gif|jpeg|pict)  "gif"
      encoding NOTATION (uuencode|base64)  "base64"
>
.
.
.
<frogs imgtype="base64gif" encoding="base64"
```

```
>R01GODlhawCzAPcAAAAAAAEBAQICAgMDAwQEBAUFBQYGBgcHBwgICAkJCQoKCgs
LCwwMDA0N
. . . . .
```

This separates the two concepts more cleanly, but will require additional intelligence by the application processing the data.

CHAPTER 8

ID and Name Token Attribute Types

Concepts Covered: ID, IDREF, **and** IDREFS **attribute types,**
NMTOKEN **and** NMTOKENS **attribute types**

There are five additional attribute types that have not yet been discussed, and that serve special purposes in XML. These are all *tokenized types*, as their values must be string tokens that satisfy syntactic rules specified by the corresponding type declaration. In this sense they are similar to the ENTITY type attributes discussed in Chapter 6, which could only take, as values, names associated with declared entities.

Tokenized attribute types are most useful within valid XML documents—the XML processor can check the attribute values, and determine if they are "correct" (i.e., valid) or not. This is analogous to the case with enumerated attribute types, for which the XML processor can validate any assigned attribute value against the allowed list of values, and detect errors if there is no match.

8.1 ID and IDREF Attribute Types

ID, IDREF, and IDREFS attribute types are designed for *labeling* and *referencing* elements in XML documents. For those familiar with HTML, attributes of type ID are analogous to the HTML **NAME** attributes, used to identify specific anchor (**A**) elements by name, while the IDREF attribute is analogous to the use, in HTML, of identifiers within **HREF** attributes to reference named anchors. However, the XML mechanism is much more flexible, as any element can have an ID-type attribute, while XML validity constraints can ensure, in a valid document, that addressed locations are unique, and that all references to addressed location are valid (i.e., every reference refers to a defined location).

The ID type declares an attribute to be an element *identifier*. A declaration for such an attribute must take one of the two forms illustrated in the following two examples:

```
<!ATTLIST item
     ref  ID #IMPLIED
>
<!ATTLIST pez-mints
     ref  ID #REQUIRED
>
```

Both these examples declare the attribute **ref** to be of type ID. Aside from #IMPLIED and #REQUIRED, no other default value declarations are allowed. Also, an element type can have *at most* one attribute of type ID. Thus the declaration

```
<!ATTLIST item
     ref ID #IMPLIED
     refy ID #IMPLIED
>    <!-- Invalid declaration-can't have two ID type attrs -->
```

is invalid, since there are two attributes of this type.

Within the document content, the element item we just declared would typically take the form:

```
<item ref="loca-32" >  ... </item>
```

where the *value* assigned to this attribute must be a *name* [5]. Within a given document (that is, within the document entity *including* all included external entities) ID-type attribute values must be unique—that is, no two attributes of type ID can have the same value. This is independent of the actual name used for an attribute of type ID. For example, given the declarations

```
<!ATTLIST item
     ref ID #IMPLIED
>
<!ATTLIST sub-item
     partid  ID #IMPLIED
>
```

the following markup is invalid, since the two attributes of type ID are assigned the same value:

```
<item ref="loca-32">
   <sub-item  partid="loca-32">
    stuff about the item
   </sub-item>
</item>  <!-- error - two identical ID attribute values! -->
```

8.1.1 Using IDs: IDREF and IDREFS Attributes

Attributes of type IDREF and IDREFS are used to *reference* elements labeled by ID attributes. IDREF attributes are declared using attribute-list declarations of the form:

```
<!ATTLIST  itemize
    ref-to   IDREF   #IMPLIED
    refb-to  IDREF   #REQUIRED
    topref   IDREF   #FIXED "rx-23b"
    cref     IDREF          "fxjk-22b"
>
```

Note that a single element can have multiple attributes of type IDREF, and that these attributes can have fixed or default values, if you wish. A specific element could then be written as

```
<itemize ref-to="x32-bkjq" refb-to="aq3fdllds">
```

which essentially creates cross-references to the elements with indicated values for an attribute of type ID.

This only works, of course, if the referenced locations are defined. Indeed, in a valid XML document, *every* location referenced by an attribute of type IDREF or IDREFS must be defined by an attribute of type ID somewhere in the document. In other words, if an IDREF or IDREFS attribute references a name, then this name must also appear as the value of an attribute of type ID, somewhere in the document.

IDREFS is equivalent to IDREF except that the value can take one or more space-separated name values, which thus can reference more than one location. Declarations for attributes of type IDREFS are equivalent to the one given previously for the element **itemize**, except that forms such as

```
<!ATTLIST  itemizers
    topref  IDREFS  #FIXED "ref1 ref2"
```

```
       cref    IDREFS        "Oogie boogie woogie"
  >
```

are possible. Note how this lets an element reference multiple locations within the document. Indeed an explicit **itemizer** element of the form

```
<itemizer cref="t-23  x-23  indexpg"> ... </itemizer>
```

uses the **cref** attribute to reference three other elements present (and named via attributes of type ID) somewhere in the document.

There are many possible uses for ID and IDREF(S) attribute types. For example, they can be used to link one section of a document to a related section, such as a footnote or glossary entry. Logically, you can think of these attribute types as adding one-to-one, one-to-many (using IDREFS), or many-to-one (many elements using IDREF to reference the same ID) relationships that are not (or cannot) be expressed using the element-based tree structure of the underlying document.

8.1.2 IDs and Non-Validating XML Processors

ID and IDREF attributes will function as expected if an application is using a validating processor, since the processor will require that ID-type attribute values be unique, and that IDREF values exist somewhere in the document. However, this cannot be guaranteed for a non-validating processor, for the following two reasons:

■ Some attribute-list declarations may not be processed, due to external parameter entities that were not included into the document. These missing declarations may define ID type attributes (including default values) that are thus not recognized by the XML processor.

■ Some ID values may be defined in general entities that are referenced in the document, but that were not included.

Thus it is impossible for a non-validating XML processor to maintain the integrity of ID-based unique names, or ensure valid cross-references using IDREF or IDREFs attributes.

On the other hand, although it is not stated in the XML specifications, you should never design a non-validating XML processor that makes things worse! Thus, if a non-validating processor knows that there are attributes of type ID, and that some values have been assigned to them, then it should not let a document editor choose new values for attributes of type ID that conflict with these already defined values.

The ID-based linking mechanisms provide only a limited way of creating "pointers" to parts of or locations within a document. Much work is currently underway to develop "Xpointer" extensions to XML, that will allow much richer mechanisms for declaring and referencing pointers within XML documents. For up-to-date information on Xpointers, please see the Xpointer section at www.w3.org/XML/.

8.2 NMTOKEN and NMTOKENS Attribute Types

The NMTOKEN and NMTOKENS attribute types allow specification of attributes that can only take name tokens [7] as allowed values. Attributes of type NMTOKEN can take only one such value, while attributes of type NMTOKENS can take one or more white space–separated values. Some examples of declarations are:

```
<!ATTLIST  items
    attr1 NMTOKEN "sneezy"
    attr2 NMTOKEN #REQUIRED
    attr3 NMTOKEN #IMPLIED
    attr4 NMTOKEN #FIXED "grumpy"
    attr5 NMTOKENS "bashful clumsy dopey sleepy"
>
```

Other than restricting the type of strings allowed in the attribute value, NMTOKEN does not have much practical advantage over CDATA. NMTOKENS, however, provides a useful way of listing values that can be separated into individual tokens by an XML processor (since the processor understands how name tokens are constructed, and how to separate one token from the next).

The NMTOKEN type is also used with a special predefined attribute, named **xml:lang,** for identifying the human language of the text content of a given element. This special attribute is described in the next chapter.

CDATA Marked Sections and Language Identification

Concepts Covered: language identification, CDATA marked sections

The previous eight chapters covered most of the structural issues associated with XML, including the nasty details of how document type declarations work. This chapter and the next cover some of the smaller details that did not easily fit in these preceding discussions.

This chapter covers two issues—a mechanism for escaping marked-up text, allowing markup to be included within elements without being processed, and a means for identifying the human language relevant to the character data content of an element. Both issues are of course relevant (and important) to creators of XML content, so that we chose to present these points together in this chapter.

9.1 Escaping Marked-Up Text

Sometimes you may wish to place XML (or other markup) inside an XML element, and treat this content as a blob—that is, as character data, ignoring the markup. One practical situation where this is necessary is the containment of HTML markup within an XML document. If not "escaped" in some way, the XML parser will attempt to parse the HTML tags—and will fail, since the HTML markup rules are not consistent with the syntax of

XML (e.g., empty elements do not end with the characters />, some end-tags are optional, etc.).

One way to do this is to place the data in a separate file, and reference it as an external unparsed (non-XML) entity. However, often one wishes to treat the "blob" as some sort of character data (e.g., for text indexing), or to be able to serialize the XML and non-XML data as a single entity, for example to send the data as an e-mail attachment or as an HTTP message.

A second alternative is to pre-process the non-XML text, and "escape" every instance of the characters & and < using character references. This will work, but requires special markup to indicate sections that have been so encoded, and application software that can handle the encoding/decoding required to maintain the correct state of the data. For example, the HTML document:

```
<html>
  <head>
    <title>  L'angst &agrave; la Poubelle --
            Une Histoire    </title>
  </head>
  <body> ....
  </body>
</HTML>
```

could be escaped and placed within an XML element as follows:

```
<web format="html">
&lt;html&gt;
  &lt;head&gt;
    &lt;title>  L'angst &amp;agrave; la Poubelle --
            Une Histoire  &lt;/title&gt;
  &lt;/head&gt;
  &lt;body&gt;   ....
  &lt;/body&gt;
&lt;/HTML&gt;
</web>
```

where the "escaped" HTML is marked in italics. The application handling these data would need to understand that the attribute specification `for-mat="html"` means that the content of the element is encoded HTML, and that it must be processed accordingly.

9.1.1 CDATA Sections

On the other hand, XML provides a special markup structure, known as a *CDATA section*, that can be used to contain and escape blocks of text containing characters which would otherwise be recognized as markup. Such sections begin with the special string < ! [CDATA [and end with the string]] >. These two strings are, amazingly enough, called *CDATA section delimiters*. A CDATA section can contain any sequence of characters, except for the string]] >. Thus the following markup (section delimiters in bold-face)

```
<![CDATA[
<html>
   </head>
     <title>  L'angst &agrave; la Poubelle --
              Une Histoire    </title>
   </head>
   <body> ....
   </body>
</HTML>
]]>
```

is a CDATA section containing the HTML document given previously. Note that neither the < nor the & characters are escaped—indeed, they must not be escaped, as the XML parser will never unescape data contained within a CDATA section.

CDATA sections, however, cannot contain binary data, such as image files or executable programs. Recall, as discussed in the introduction to Part 1, that XML documents can only contain those Unicode characters specifically permitted by the XML specification. When an XML processor reads XML text data, it assumes that the document text is encoded in some way, decodes the byte stream into an internal representation of the actual characters (usually as 16-bit unsigned integers), and then checks to ensure that the characters are valid according to the XML specification. A binary file, however, will contain bytes (a) that should not be decoded into characters in the first place, and (b) that, when decoded, correspond to invalid characters. Such data will be immediately rejected by any XML processor.

As a result, the only way to include binary data within an XML document is by encoding the data in some way, such as *base64* or *uuencode*, and then including the resulting data within the document. Such data are guaranteed to contain only valid ASCII characters, and the resulting encoded data can be included in an XML document, within a CDATA section or within regular markup—provided the string]] >, if it occurs in the text, is escaped in some way. Note that such strings cannot occur with base64 encoded data, as these characters are not used in the base64 encoding algorithm.

9.2 Language Identification

The character data inside an XML document can represent characters from most of the world's languages—and indeed, many characters "belong to" more than one language. How these characters should be processed, however, can depend on the language. For example, different languages can have different rules for alphabetical ordering (e.g., the alphabetical ordering for the characters e, è, é, ê, ë, È, É, Ê, and Ë), or for case folding (i.e., conversion of a letter from one case to another. For example, in France, the letter " é" is capitalized as "E", whereas in Quebec, the letter is capitalized as " É"). For applications processing XML content, it is thus important to know the language applicable to a given block of markup.

XML defines a special attribute, named **xml:lang**, for identifying the language of element content, and of attribute values associated with an element. The value assigned to this attribute must be a name token, and must take the form specified in RFC 1766—the Internet specification for language identifiers. The details of RFC 1766 are given in Part 3, Appendix C. Briefly, a language identifier takes the general form

```
lang-subcode
```

where the string `lang` identifies the language, and `subcode` identifies some variant of that language. The `lang` string is most often a two-letter code (from ISO 639) identifying a language, for example "en" for English, while the subcode is usually a two-letter code (from ISO 3166) identifying a national variant (for example, "US" for the United States). Some examples of language identifiers are: `en-US` (US English), or `fr-QC` (Quebec French).

NOTE Case-Insensitive xml:lang Attribute Values

Note that, unlike all other attribute values, the values for language identifiers are *case-insensitive*, so that the identifiers `EN-US`, `eN-uS`, et cetera, all identify the U.S. variant of the English language. This is required for compatibility with the rules specified in RFC 1766.

In our menu document example, we could use **xml:lang** to denote menu item descriptions written in different languages. An example is shown in Figure 9.1.

Note that in a valid XML document the **xml:lang** attribute must be declared to be of type NMTOKEN.

```
<!DOCTYPE [
<!-- * lots of missing declarations ... this is, after all
     * only a snippet!
     * -->
<!ELEMENT item
    (desc*, price*, graphic?)
>
<!ELEMENT desc
    (#PCDATA | emph)*
>
<!ATTLIST desc
         xml:lang NMTOKEN "en-US"
>
]>
<menu date="12nov1998">
  <rname>&resto;</rname>
  <item type="appetizer" >
<desc xml:lang="en-US">Warmed leek salad, coated
         with a balsamic vinegar and goat cheese
         dressing</desc>
    <price units="usd">6.95</price>
<desc xml:lang="fr">Une salade chaude de chevre et poireau,
vernissez d'une sauce balsamique</desc>
    <price units="ff">35.00</price>
    <graphic gtype="gif"
          src="http://www.goodfood.com/menu/leek-salad.gif" />
<!-- more missing content -->
</menu>
```

Figure 9.1   A markup extract illustrating the use of xml:lang to indicate the human language relevant to the content of an element—the places where the attribute is used are shown in boldface. Note how an attribute-list specification is used to set a default value (here U.S.–style English).

CHAPTER

10

White Space Handling and String Normalization

Concepts Covered: white space handling, the xml:space attribute; string normalization

In most of the preceding chapters, we have been very lazy about our use of white space—XML defines white space to be any sequence of one or more space (SP), tab (TAB), carriage return (CR), or line feed (LF) characters. Indeed, within markup declarations or inside markup tags one can be pretty loose with white space, and use it to help structure the markup for easy reading by people, as opposed to software. This is because white space, in these contexts, is not really important—it simply serves to separate one part from another (e.g., in a start tag, the name of an element from the name of an attribute), so that it doesn't really matter how much space there is.

Of course this is not always the case. Sometimes (such as in a poem) white space is an important part of the text, and it is thus important to be able to indicate in the markup when this is the case. XML has a way of doing so, discussed in the first section of this chapter.

Similarly, white space may have specific importance within the markup—for example, within the literal strings that define system identifiers or attribute values. In these cases too we need specific rules for stating when white space is significant and, when it is, how it should be handled. This aspect of white space handling comes under the general category of string normalization, and is discussed in the second half of the chapter.

10.1 White Space Handling in Markup Elements

White space may or may not be significant inside markup. Within markup elements that take character data content, white space is usually only important insofar as it signifies separation between words or symbols. Extra space is often used to structure the text so that it is easy to read in a text editor (e.g., so that lines are not too long), or to align markup element start- and end-tags for easier readability, but this does not really affect the processing, display, or interpretation of the text. An example is the markup from Figure 1.1, repeated in the following:

```
<menu date="12nov1998">
  <rname>Liam's Chowder House and Grill</rname>
  <item type="appetizer" >
    <desc>Warmed leek salad, coated with a balsamic
          vinegar and goat cheese dressing</desc>
    <price units="usd">6.95</price>
    <graphic gtype="gif"
          src="http://www.goodfood.com/menu/leek-salad.gif" />
  </item>
  <!-- Following Item is tasty! -->
  <item type="appetizer" >
    <desc>Prosciutto ham with melon</desc>
    <price units="usd">7.95</price>
    <graphic gtype="jpeg"
          src="http://www.goodfood.com/menu/ham-melon.jpeg" />
  </item>
</menu>
```

Note how the line breaks were introduced to make the text fit in fewer than 70 columns, while space characters were used to indent the text, so that the element nesting is obvious. A second example—one in which white space is important—might come from a piece of poetry, somewhat lazily encoded as follows:

```
<stanza>
Oh what a tangled Web we'll weave,
      ... If our 'ML's to succeed
Far beyond our parser's sigh
  Let us validate at first try
</stanza>
```

where the white space is used to mark the end of lines in the poem, and also to add indents to appropriate lines.

As far as the XML processor is concerned, white space is just another part of the data, of equal importance with all other characters, so that the processor *must*, in handling this data, preserve all these characters, and forward them on to the application (e.g., an XML editor, database, etc.) that will manipulate or store the data.

However, the *application* (e.g., the editor that is employing the XML processor to handle the XML data) may choose to eliminate extraneous white space, should it deem it unnecessary. Certainly in terms of the element structure, extra white space is probably irrelevant. However, it may be important for other reasons, such as to preserve an easily hand-editable document, or to preserve space characters and line breaks in poetry, as illustrated in the example just given.

XML supports a special attribute, called **xml:space**, that indicates, to the application handling the data, that white space should be preserved within the associated element. This is an enumerated-list type attribute and can take two possible values: `preserve`, to indicate that white space must be preserved, or `default`, to indicate that the application can use whatever default white space handling mechanism it traditionally uses. Of course this attribute must be declared in a valid document, and a typical declaration would be:

```
<!ATTLIST elem  xml:space ( default | preserve ) "preserve" >
```

The effect of this attribute will cascade through all elements lying within the element to which this attribute was applied, unless specifically overridden by another **xml:space** attribute.

10.1.1 Handling of End-of-Line Characters

End-of-line character sequences are handled somewhat differently—the XML specification requires that all end-of-line character sequences be normalized to a single, standard form. Current computers use various character sequences to denote the end of a line. The common end-of-line sequences are: the two-character sequence CR LF (carriage return–line feed; used on all Microsoft operating systems), a single CR (carriage return; Macintoshes), or a single LF (line feed; UNIX and variants). XML requires that all such sequences be converted to the single character LF before the data is sent on to an XML application. This is in fact trivial to do—the XML processor can normalize the data as it reads it, even before the XML processing begins.

10.1.2 White Space in Elements with Element Content

Elements that take element content can only contain other elements, and cannot contain character data. In this case, XML allows white space to be placed between the tags, but also notes this as a special case. In particular, if there is white space inside an element that takes element content, then a validating XML processor *must* make special note of this fact to the application handling the document (see Part 2, Chapter 2, Section 2.10). Furthermore, having white space here means that the document can never be *standalone*.

It is thus safest to omit all white space *between* tags, and, if necessary, introduce space or line breaks *inside* the tags. One convenient place to introduce space or line breaks is just before the > character (or the sequence /> for empty-element tags) that ends a tag. For example, the following markup is syntactically correct XML

```
<element
  ><child
  /><child2
  /><child3
  /></element
>
```

and typographically reproduces the element nesting levels without adding white space between the elements.

10.2 Normalization of Attribute Values and PUBLIC Identifiers

The last finicky detail we will cover is the way in which attribute values and system identifiers are *normalized* prior to being used. In the case of a PUBLIC identifier (a string given as the location identifier for an external entity, a notation, or the external DTD subset), the value must be normalized before the XML processor attempts to locate the resource. In the case of an attribute value, the value must be normalized before it is checked for validity (for example, to see if it is defined in the list of allowed values) and before it is passed on to the application.

10.2.1 Normalization of PUBLIC Identifiers

A public identifier is normalized in the following way:

1. All strings of white space characters are normalized to a single space character.

2. All white space at the beginning and end of the identifier is removed.

For example, if an entity declaration was of the form

```
<!ENTITY arthur-dent PUBLIC
      "   -//Groveware//    standard docman content// EN "
      "  http://www.utoronto.ca/ian/books/    stuff.html  " >
```

then the PUBLIC identifier is normalized to the string

```
"-//Groveware// standard docman content// EN"
```

before the processor attempts to retrieve the resource. Note that this is still an invalid URL—URLs cannot *contain* space characters!

Note that a SYSTEM identifier (such as the URL given in the preceding example) is not normalized—the string given is used, as-is, as a reference to the indicated resource. Normalization is not done because the sequences of white space in the URL may have meaning—for example, they may refer to a file that, indeed, has two consecutive space characters in the filename.

10.2.2 Normalization of Attribute Values

Attribute values are normalized in the following way:

1. Character references are replaced by the corresponding character.

2. Entity references are replaced by their replacement text; if the replacement text contains an entity reference, the process is continued until all entities have been recursively replaced.

3. The white space characters SP, TAB, CR, and LF are each replaced by an SP character. However, the character sequence CRLF is treated as a special group and, if present, is replaced by a single SP.

4. This completes the normalization if the attribute is of type CDATA. If it is not of type CDATA, then the final stage of normalization is to:

   a) eliminate all leading and trailing space (SP) characters

   b) replace sequences of multiple space (SP) characters within the string by a single SP (i.e., collapse all strings of space characters to a single space character)

Note how this normalization process (steps 1 and 2) is essentially just an extra step beyond the generation of replacement text, as described in Chapter 3, Section 3.2.3.

For example, consider the following attribute declaration list, and the subsequent instances of elements specifying values for those attributes:

```
<!ATTLIST  spunky
        href CDATA #IMPLIED
        loc  ID    #IMPLIED
        type ( happy | sad | depressed ) "happy"
>
<!ATTLIST refer
        xref IDREF #IMPLIED
>
......
<spunky href="  http://bighead.com/yippee.html"
        loc=" x23 "
        type="
                depressed       "
>
<refer xref="x23">
```

Consider first the **href** attribute. Here the normalized value will be the string (excluding the quotation marks):

```
"  http://bighead.com/yippee.html"
```

including the (two) leading space characters, since this is a CDATA attribute and the normalization rules do not remove these characters. As a result, this URL reference will be incorrect.

On the other hand, the normalized value for **loc** is the string "x23", since this is not of type CDATA, and the fourth normalization rule removes the leading and trailing space. Consequently, the **xref** attribute of the **refer** element will reference this location. For the same reason, the normalized value for the **type** attribute is `"depressed"` (the leading space and line breaks are normalized away) so that this attribute will be valid if the XML processor checks this against the allowed list of values.

10.2.3 Normalization by Validating and Non-Validating Parsers

Validation is straightforward for a validating parser, since it unambiguously knows the type of each attribute, and can invoke the correct normalization algorithm. Things are much tougher for a non-validating processor, which will possibly not know the types of all the attributes it needs to normalize. The XML specifications state that such a processor must use the best information it has to normalize attribute values. If it encounters an attribute for which it does not know the type, then it must assume the attribute to be of type CDATA.

PART Two

Extensible Markup Language (XML) 1.0 Specification

W3C Recommendation 10-February-1998

Part 2 of this book contains the actual XML Specification itself. We have included the entire text together with our annotations and comments. We have kept the specification unchanged, except for some words inserted in [square brackets], but we have added references to the glossary where terms such as ⌜parameter entity⌝ appear, and we have added references to production numbers where production names appear, such as Name[5] to indicate a reference to production [5], Name.

Within the specification, **boldface** is used when a term is defined.

Cross references in the specification text itself are always to chapters within the specification, of course; references within our annotations may be to other parts of this book, so we have made that explicit.

THIS VERSION:

www.w3.org/TR/1998/REC-xml-19980210
www.w3.org/TR/1998/REC-xml-19980210.xml
www.w3.org/TR/1998/REC-xml-19980210.html
www.w3.org/TR/1998/REC-xml-19980210.pdf
www.w3.org/TR/1998/REC-xml-19980210.ps

LATEST VERSION:

www.w3.org/TR/REC-xml

PREVIOUS VERSION:

www.w3.org/TR/PR-xml-971208

EDITORS:

Tim Bray (Textuality and Netscape) <*tbray@textuality.com*>
Jean Paoli (Microsoft) <*jeanpa@microsoft.com*>
C. M. Sperberg-McQueen (University of Illinois at Chicago) <*cmsmcq@uic.edu*>

Abstract

The Extensible Markup Language (XML) is a subset of ⌜SGML⌝ that is completely
described in this document. Its goal is to enable generic SGML to be served,
received, and processed on the Web in the way that is now possible with HTML.
XML has been designed for ease of implementation and for interoperability
with both SGML and HTML.

Status of this document

This document has been reviewed by W3C Members and other interested
parties and has been endorsed by the Director as a W3C Recommendation. It is
a stable document and may be used as reference material or cited as a
⌜normative reference⌝ from another document. W3C's role in making the
Recommendation is to draw attention to the specification and to promote its
widespread deployment. This enhances the functionality and interoperability of
the Web.

This document specifies a syntax created by subsetting an existing, widely used
international text processing standard (Standard Generalized Markup
Language, ISO 8879:1986(E) as amended and corrected) for use on the World
Wide Web. It is a product of the W3C XML Activity, details of which can be
found at *www.w3.org/XML*. A list of current W3C Recommendations and other
technical documents can be found at *www.w3.org/TR*.

This specification uses the term ⌐URI⌐, which is defined by [Berners-Lee et al.], a work in progress expected to update [IETF RFC1738] and [IETF RFC1808].

The list of known errors in this specification is available at
www.w3.org/XML/xml-19980210-errata.

At the time of writing (late in 1998) there were no significant errata at that URL.

Please report errors in this document to *xml-editor@w3.org*.

In a few places in this book we have commented on errors, and of course we have already sent these to the xml-editor address given here, so you should only send errors that we have not pointed out!

CHAPTER 1

Introduction

Extensible Markup Language, abbreviated XML, . . .

⌜Markup⌝ is the name given to annotations that explain text.

```
Jack and Jill   <───────────────── title
When Jack and Jill climbed the hill,  <─────── paragraph
they were tired. Jack had lost his shoes and
was barefoot, and Jill had already lost the
Golden Orb of the Realm.
```

The labels *title* and *paragraph* are markup.
In XML, the markup might look like this:

```
<Title>Jack and Jill</Title>
<Paragraph>When Jack and Jill climbed the hill,
they were tired. Jack had lost his shoes and
was barefoot, and Jill had already lost the
Golden Orb of the Realm.</Paragraph>
```

The markup here is included in the text, using a computer language. In fact, XML lets you extend the language by adding your own kinds of markup. For example, we might say that we want to relate the title and the text of the story, and also to label the Important Artifact that Jill lost, like this:

```
<Story>
<Title>Jack and Jill</Title>
<Paragraph>When Jack and Jill climbed the hill,
they were tired. Jack had lost his shoes and
was barefoot, and Jill had already lost the
<artifact>Golden Orb of the Realm</artifact>.</Paragraph>
</Story>
```

XML is an extensible markup language because you can use it to define your own ways of marking up texts or other structures.

. . . describes a class of data objects called ⌈XML documents⌉. . .

The term "data objects" is used here to avoid saying "document"; XML can represent things that are not normally thought of as documents: Almost anything with nested structure, such as a tax form, a spreadsheet, a database table, or even a C++ or Java object's internal data, can be represented as XML documents.

. . . and partially describes the behavior of computer programs which process them.

Partially because XML marks up data rather than procedures. In other words, XML markup says *what* something is, such as a title or paragraph or a spreadsheet formula; it does not say how to interpret that data, nor does it limit the data to a single use or interpretation. XML can provide suggestions on what to do with the data, both formally and in human-readable comments, but does not try to give a complete description.

XML is an ⌈application profile⌉ or restricted form of ⌈SGML⌉. . .

This means that you can make use of existing SGML tools to *read* XML files, but to *process* XML you need to use XML-specific tools, or to run a program or script to transform the output of other tools into XML. XML files can also be created "by hand" in a plain ⌈ASCII⌉ or Unicode text editor.

. . . of ⌈SGML⌉, the ⌈Standard Generalized Markup Language⌉, ⌈ISO 8879⌉.

The ⌈Standard Generalized Markup Language⌉ was published as an international standard in 1986, over a decade ago. It is known by its ISO standard number, ⌈ISO 8879⌉, or by its initials, ⌈SGML⌉.

By construction, XML documents are ⌐conforming SGML documents⌐.

This sentence is saying that you don't need to go and read the ⌐SGML⌐ standard: Any document that conforms to the XML specification will necessarily also conform to the SGML specification, because XML was designed that way. It was a design goal of XML that all XML documents also be SGML documents, but it was another goal that XML users (and developers) not have to read the SGML specification in order to work with XML.

XML documents are made up of ⌐storage units⌐ called ⌐entities⌐ which contain either ⌐parsed⌐ or ⌐unparsed data⌐.

A ⌐storage unit⌐ will usually be a file; the file could, for example, be downloaded using ⌐HTTP⌐ or ⌐FTP⌐, or it could be generated on demand by a program. The terms ⌐storage unit⌐ and ⌐entity⌐ are used to remind the reader that the contents might be downloaded over a network, or for some other reason might be something other than a static disk file.

In this case, one might simply say that an XML document is made up of one or more files. You can include one file within another (much as you can using the #include facility in the C and C++ programming languages) and you can also refer to another external file (as you do when you incorporate an image in ⌐HTML⌐). Included files must be in the correct XML format (i.e. they are ⌐external parsed entities⌐). External files can be in any format, whether XML or not, since the XML parser doesn't look at their contents; they are said to contain ⌐unparsed data⌐.

Suppose you have a definition of how you represent a spreadsheet formula in XML, and you need to use this in several documents. You could put this definition in a file called *formulas.xdd* and include it like this:

```
<!ENTITY % Formulas
    SYSTEM "formulas.xdd"
>
%Formulas;
```

Note that there are several different kinds of ⌐entity⌐ in XML; the kind of entity being described here is an ⌐external parameter entity⌐, and *not* an ⌐internal entity⌐ or a ⌐general entity⌐.

See Part 1 of this book for introductory material about ⌐external entities⌐ and Part 2, Chapter 4, *Physical Structures,* for the gory details.

⌐Parsed data⌐ is made up of ⌐characters⌐, some of which form ⌐character data⌐ and some of which form ⌐markup⌐.

An XML file is a stream of ⌜characters⌝; it contains both ⌜markup⌝ and text (⌜character data⌝), with the text sitting between pieces of markup.

The term ⌜character⌝ is used in the Unicode sense (described below and also in Appendix B, in Part 3 of this book); a ⌜character⌝ in XML does not refer to a byte, but to the result of reading one or more bytes to make the internal representation of a character.

Not all byte values (and not all sequences of byte values) represent legal characters, so that it is not possible to include arbitrary binary data in an XML document without encoding it, for example with MIME ⌜Base64⌝.

⌜Markup⌝ encodes a description of the document's ⌜storage layout⌝ and ⌜logical structure⌝.

The ⌜storage layout⌝ of a document is the way it is divided into separate entities (or files, if you prefer to call them that). The ⌜logical structure⌝ is the way the document is divided into chapters, paragraphs, tables, rows, columns, database tables, or whatever. See the illustration in Chapter 1 of Part 1 of this book.

In fact, the markup does more than encode a description of these structures: It actually describes them directly.

XML provides a mechanism to impose constraints on the ⌜storage layout⌝ and ⌜logical structure⌝.

There are two sorts of constraints here: constraints on the ⌜storage layout⌝ of the document, and constraints on the ⌜logical structure⌝ of the document.

The constraints on the ⌜storage layout⌝ are limited to saying what file formats are allowed.

The possible constraints on the logical structure of a document are numerous and sophisticated: You can specify (for example) that a footnote can't contain chapters, or that an image must have an associated textual description. If you use the optional XML ⌜schema⌝ facility (still a draft at the time of writing), you can also say that a birthday must be a date, or that a shoe size must be numeric.

A software module called an ⌜XML processor⌝ is used to read ⌜XML documents⌝ and provide access to their ⌜content⌝ and ⌜structure⌝.

The XML processor is a convenient abstraction; it is not necessary to have a separate module (or class) to read or process XML, although it may be a good idea to do so for other reasons.

The part of the program that reads XML is often informally referred to as an ⌜XML parser⌝.

It is assumed that an ⌜XML processor⌝ is doing its work on behalf of another module, called the ⌜application⌝. This specification describes the required behavior of an XML processor in terms of how it must read XML data and the information it must provide to the ⌜application⌝.

If you use a separate module in the software you write, you may also find it convenient to use, as an interface between the application and the parser, one that has already been defined: either the ⌜SAX⌝ or the ⌜Document Object Model⌝ (⌜DOM⌝) interface.

There are a number of ⌜XML parsers⌝ available, both commercial and free, that save you from having to write your own.

Whether you write your own XML reading module or use someone else's, you will have to arrange that all of the necessary information in the input gets communicated correctly to the rest of the program, and also to perform the required error checking for ⌜well-formedness⌝ and ⌜validity⌝.

1.1 Origin and Goals

XML was developed by an ⌜XML Working Group⌝ (originally known as the ⌜SGML Editorial Review Board⌝) formed under the auspices of the ⌜World Wide Web Consortium⌝ (⌜W3C⌝) in 1996. It was chaired by Jon Bosak of Sun Microsystems with the active participation of an ⌜XML Special Interest Group⌝ (previously known as the ⌜SGML Working Group⌝) also organized by the W3C. The membership of the XML Working Group is given in an appendix [of this specification]. Dan Connolly served as the Working Group's contact with the W3C.

The XML Working Group had approximately eleven members or so at any given time. The Special Interest Group was open only to W3C members and invited experts, and for the first year had approximately 100 members, consisting of industry experts and academic researchers in related fields. The process was that the Working Group would pose a series of questions to the Special Interest Group, who would then discuss the issues; the Working Group would then make an informed decision. It is worth noting that a number of people in both the Working Group and the Special Interest Group were also members of the ISO Working Group responsible for the publication and continued development of SGML itself, so that there was a lot of cooperation. Liam Quin, one of the authors of this book, was in this group from its inception.

The design goals for XML are:

These goals were stated at the very outset of the work on XML, were agreed upon by all parties, and have remained more or less intact. They are very helpful in understanding why XML ended up the way it did, and should also be read carefully before proposing any changes or extensions to XML.

1. XML shall be straightforwardly usable over the ⌈Internet⌉.

SGML predates the ⌈World Wide Web⌉ and ⌈HTTP⌉, and as a consequence left unspecified some things that made it difficult to use over the Web; different implementations did not work together well. It was clear from the start that XML would not succeed unless it was as easy to use as ⌈HTML⌉ in many applications.

2. XML shall support a wide variety of applications.

This requirement effectively ruled out the idea of a fixed set of tags or properties (such as is found in HTML, for example). All of the markup must be defined to be useful for specific applications, and hence must not be part of the base XML specification.

3. XML shall be compatible with SGML.

Every ⌈valid⌉, ⌈conforming XML document⌉ is also a valid, ⌈conforming SGML document⌉. This is important because SGML is an international standard: It will still be possible to read an SGML document ten, twenty, or even 100 years from now.

4. It shall be easy to write programs which process XML documents.

The people involved with designing XML hoped that programmers would use XML as the file format of choice, so that you'd be able to take the output of one program and use it with another, or edit configuration files with an XML editor, or do entirely unexpected things such as loading all the part numbers and quantities from an invoice directly into a spreadsheet or database.

In order for XML to become ubiquitous in this way, it had to be easy for programmers to implement, both so that they would want to do so and so that budgets for the work would be approved.

5. The number of optional features in XML is to be kept to the absolute minimum, ideally zero.

Every optional feature is one more thing that programmers might decide they don't have time to implement; this means that interoperable documents can only really safely use features that are not optional. Worse, optional features make the specification much harder to understand.

6. XML documents should be human-legible and reasonably clear.

Over a decade of experience with SGML has shown the value of marked-up documents that a human can look at and understand directly without needing special tools.

7. The XML design should be prepared quickly.

At the time this was written, HTML was being developed rapidly, and it seemed as if it would soon become entirely unmanageable because of its large and growing set of elements and functionality.

Furthermore, a number of companies with large amounts of data marked up in ⌜SGML⌝ were looking for a way to distribute this over the ⌜World Wide Web⌝, but felt unable to use ⌜HTML⌝ because of the loss of information involved in moving to a less application-specific markup.

The XML design was largely frozen after six months, and published as a W3C recommendation approximately 18 months after the work was started; this is very fast for any sort of widely used and international standard.

8. The design of XML shall be formal and concise.

The ⌜SGML⌝ standard (ISO 8879:1986) is approximately 200 pages of dense prose; SGML is defined in English (augmented with a formal grammar) rather than in a formal notation, and the entire standard must be read before any of it can be implemented. Implementing SGML is difficult, partly because of the way in which the many optional features interact and partly because the standard is written in a style unfamiliar to most programmers.

The desire that XML be widely implemented (reflected in goals 2 and 4) meant that the XML design had to be short, and also that it had to be written in a way that would be comfortable to most programmers. ⌐Extended Backus-Naur Form¬ (⌐EBNF¬) was used, augmented with ⌐regular expressions¬ for more compactness.

The entire XML grammar is given in Part 3, Appendix A of this book.

9. XML documents shall be easy to create.

This is pretty straightforward; clearly if no one can make the documents, there won't be much demand for software to process them. In practice, this meant that consideration had to be given to documents created by humans as well as those documents automatically generated by software.

10. Terseness in XML markup is of minimal importance.

People have frequently suggested ways of changing the XML specification in order to make XML documents shorter, usually at the expense of robustness in the face of errors. None of these ways have been much more effective at reducing file sizes than using standard compression utilities, so that clarity and robustness were (and are) considered far more important than saving space in uncompressed XML files.

> **This specification, together with associated standards (⌐Unicode¬ and ⌐ISO/IEC 10646¬ for characters, Internet ⌐RFC 1766¬ for language identification tags, ⌐ISO 639¬ for language name codes, and ⌐ISO 3166¬ for country name codes), provides all the information necessary to understand XML Version 1.0 and construct computer programs to process it.**

This statement is claiming that it is not necessary to read any standards other than those listed here in order to work with XML. You don't need to read the ⌐SGML¬ or ⌐HyTime¬ standards, for example.

The standards mentioned here are all listed in the Glossary; any Internet Request For Comments may be downloaded free of charge from ftp. internic.net, whereas the ISO standards must in general be paid for.

> **This version of the XML specification may be distributed freely, as long as all text and legal notices remain intact.**

Where appropriate, we integrated published corrigenda into the specification text, and have indicated where we have done so. We have also silently corrected a very few minor typographical errors. With this exception, the text is intact, as are the legal notices. Where we have inserted text into the standard to clarify, we have done so using [square] brackets.

1.2 Terminology

The terminology used to describe XML documents is defined in the body of this specification.

In other words, the XML specification (unlike this book) does not have a separate glossary, but simply defines terms wherever they are first needed.

The terms defined in the following list are used in building those definitions and in describing the actions of an XML processor:

Like most standards and specifications, the XML specification uses terms like *shall* and *must* very precisely. Wherever we thought the use of one of these words in the main specification itself was not clear, we marked it with a reference to the glossary, or pointed it out explicitly in our annotations.

may: ⌐Conforming documents⌐ and ⌐XML processors⌐ are permitted to but need not behave as described.

For example, "A processor may report an error in this case." That is, the processor is *permitted* to report an error, but it is not *required* to do so.

must: ⌐Conforming documents⌐ and ⌐XML processors⌐ are required to behave as described; otherwise they are in error.

For example, "Processing instructions must be passed through to the application." If you were to write an XML processor that did not pass processing instructions through to the application, but instead swallowed them up silently, you would not have written a correct XML processor.

error: A violation of the rules of this specification; results are undefined. Conforming software ⌐may⌐ detect and report an error and may recover from it.

There are two classes of error that may be found in an XML document: a *fatal error* (see below) and an *error*. An error is something that a good, well-written ⌜parser⌝ will report whenever possible, but not all errors can be detected reliably. For example, an XML document transmitted or stored in the ISO 8859-8 character encoding might be incorrectly labeled as being in the ISO 8859-1 character set; although this is in error, it would be very difficult or impossible to detect automatically.

> **fatal error: An ⌜error⌝ which a conforming ⌜XML processor⌝ ⌜must⌝ detect and report to the ⌜application⌝.**

Note the use of the word ⌜must⌝. here.

> **After encountering a ⌜fatal error⌝, the processor ⌜may⌝ continue processing the data to search for further errors and may report such errors to the application.**

Note the use of the word ⌜may⌝; an XML parser is entirely at liberty to stop reading input altogether if it encounters a fatal error. Any part of the input that has already been passed back to the ⌜application⌝ is not affected: There is no requirement that the portion of the document before the fatal error was found be recanted or deleted or ignored in any way.

> **In order to support correction of errors, the processor may make unprocessed data from the document (with intermingled character data and markup) available to the application.**

The character data and markup are intermingled because the parser has not separated out the markup from the data.

> **Once a fatal error is detected, however, the processor must not continue normal processing (i.e., it must not continue to pass character data and information about the document's logical structure to the application in the normal way).**

In the discussions of the XML Working Group and Special Interest Group, this policy was called the ⌜Draconian⌝ error handling policy. Once a ⌜fatal error⌝ is encountered, the document must be rejected. This policy was chosen largely to encourage people to transmit correct documents.

Hence, after a ⌜fatal error⌝ is detected, all useful processing must halt.

> **at user option: Conforming software may or must (depending on the modal verb in the sentence) behave as described; if it does, it must provide users [with] a means to enable or disable the behavior described.**

The *modal verb* here is either ⌜may⌝ or ⌜must⌝; if something is done ⌜at user option⌝, the user is asked, or perhaps the software can be configured, whether or not to do it each time. In applications of XML for which there is no human user, the most appropriate decision may have to be specified by the designer of the software, but even there it is best to provide configuration options in case the circumstances of use change in the future.

> **validity constraint: A rule which applies to all ⌜valid⌝ ⌜XML documents⌝.**

XML documents fall into two classes: ⌜well formed⌝ and ⌜valid⌝. A validity constraint applies only to documents that claim to be valid.

> **Violations of validity constraints are ⌜errors⌝; they must, ⌜at user option⌝, be reported by ⌜validating XML processors⌝.**

The phrase ⌜at user option⌝ here means that people using XML in an interactive system must be able to configure the XML software they are using so that it does (or does not) report validity errors. This clause makes less sense in environments in which there is no human user, although if a human user instigated an operation which fails because of a validity error that was detected, the user should be able to see the exact error.

Since users can turn error reporting on or off, the ⌜XML processor⌝ detecting and generating the errors must send them back to the ⌜application⌝ to handle, rather than dealing with them directly. For example, a parser library written in C++ should not put error messages on *stderr* or *cerr*, but instead should provide them to the application calling the parser, perhaps through a C++ exception or using a callback.

> **well-formedness constraint: A rule which applies to all well-formed XML documents. Violations of well-formedness constraints are ⌜fatal errors⌝.**

There are a number of places in the grammar for XML where there are well-formedness constraints; *every* XML document must meet these. If an ⌜XML document⌝ fails to meet one of these well-formedness constraints, the document isn't even XML. Any XML processor that detects a violation of one of these well-formedness constraints must report the error back to the application, and must stop supplying parsed XML to the ⌜application⌝; automatic silent error correction is *not* permitted. (See ⌜fatal error⌝, described above.)

It may seem somewhat draconian to prohibit error correction. In fact, this is because of lessons learned with HTML: Error correction and recovery encourage authors to make documents that are not correct, because they don't need to fix all the errors.

match . . .

The verb to match has three separate meanings in XML: for matching strings, for matching rules in the XML grammar itself, and for matching ⌜content models⌝ in ⌜element type declarations⌝. The three kinds of matching are described in the following paragraphs.

(Of strings or names) Two strings or names being compared must be identical. . . .

This might at first appear to be an error in the specification: If you know that you have two identical strings, you don't need to compare them. What is meant is that the following sentences describe how an ⌜XML processor⌝ determines whether two strings or names are in fact identical.

. . . Characters with multiple possible representations in ISO/IEC 10646 (e.g. characters with both ⌜precomposed⌝ and ⌜base + diacritic⌝ forms) ⌜match⌝ only if they have the same representation in both strings. . . .

There are two ways of representing an "ô" in Unicode: either as a letter "o" followed by a ⌜combining⌝ circumflex, or as a single byte, the precomposed "o circumflex" character. If one string uses the first form and the other uses the second, the two strings will presumably look identical on a user's screen, but will *not* match one another according to these rules. See Appendix B in Part 3 of this book.

. . . At user option, processors may normalize such characters to some canonical form. . . .

Normalize here means that the XML processor could turn the precomposed "ô" (say) into the two-character sequence described in the previous annotation, so that the two strings in that example would then ⌜match⌝. It is ⌜at user option⌝ because it's not always acceptable to rewrite users' data in that way. For example, if you opened a document in an editor and changed a single word, you might not expect every accented character (such as ô) in the whole document to be changed from one representation to another when you saved the file!

. . . No ⌜case folding⌝ is performed . . .

This means that names (and other strings) are ⌜case sensitive⌝: earwig and EARWIG are different.

Accents are often omitted on ⌜uppercase⌝ words in France, so that rôle and ROLE might be expected to be the same in a case-insensitive environment; in Quebec, however, the accents are retained, so that rôle and RÔLE would be the same word, and ROLE would be another, possibly quite different word. In order to avoid this sort of problem, and to make sure that the same document would be interpreted everywhere, the XML specification says that role and rôle and ROLE and RÔLE and Role (and all other combinations!) are all distinct.

This also means you can't use uppercase in a ⌜start-tag⌝ and lowercase in the corresponding ⌜end-tag⌝.

. . . [matching] (Of strings and rules in the grammar) . . .

That is, matching of strings in the grammar and matching of rules in the grammar, as opposed to strings in XML documents or rules in XML document type definitions; such other strings were dealt with above.

. . . A string matches a ⌜grammatical production⌝ if it belongs to the language generated by that production . .

This is a formal definition of how ⌜BNF⌝ and ⌜EBNF⌝ work. See Part 1 of this book, and also Appendix A in Part 3 for a more detailed explanation.

. . .[matching] (Of ⌜content⌝ and ⌜content models⌝). . .

In this context, "matching" means that the content of an element in a document matches the content model given in the DTD; this applies only to validity of the document, and not to its well-formedness.

. . . An element ⌜matches⌝ its declaration when it conforms in the fashion described in the constraint "Element Valid". . . .

This is also referred to as matching a ⌜content model⌝; see the notes under *Element Valid* near the start of Part 2, Chapter 3, "Logical Structures," for more details.

> **for compatibility:** A feature of XML included solely to ensure that XML remains compatible with SGML.

A cynical reader might infer that there were SGML features that the XML working group had wished that they could change. Although this is correct in some ways, SGML was in fact changed for XML; see the next item, ⌜for interoperability⌝.

A better reading of this definition is that XML is designed so that every XML document is also an SGML document; in some cases this has been specified explicitly as *for compatibility*, and in others it follows because the XML definition is compatible with the SGML definition (⌜ISO 8879⌝).

> **for interoperability:** A non-binding recommendation included to increase the chances that XML documents can be processed by the existing installed base of ⌜SGML⌝ processors which predate the ⌜WebSGML Adaptations Annex⌝ to ⌜ISO 8879⌝.

> The document referred to, the ⌜WebSGML Adaptations Annex⌝ to ⌜ISO 8879⌝ (⌜SGML⌝), was produced by the ISO working group responsible for SGML, chiefly in order to facilitate the XML process. This is not a ⌜normative reference⌝: a developer is not required to read that document in order to write conformant XML software.

There are a large number of existing installations using both commercial and freely available SGML software, so the interoperability of XML documents with SGML software gave XML a running start in terms of available software and users.

Documents

A data object is an XML document if it is ⌜well-formed⌝, as defined in this specification. . . .

The XML specification obviously can't say anything about files or other kinds of data objects that are not, and do not claim to be, XML. Something that is not ⌜well-formed⌝ is not an XML document. Well-formedness, then, is the most important essential nature of an XML document. All XML documents must be well-formed.

. . . A ⌜well-formed⌝ ⌜XML document⌝ may in addition be ⌜valid⌝ if it meets certain further constraints.

There are two kinds of XML document: ones that are well-formed and ⌜valid⌝, and ones that are well-formed but not valid. Validity, then, is something extra on top of well-formedness.

The reason for the separation is that in many environments it is possible to do useful work with well-formed documents without any need to check to see whether or not they are valid.

Each XML document has both a logical and a physical structure. . . .

The ⌜physical structure⌝ is how the ⌜XML document⌝ is stored, whether it is made up of one file or many smaller ones, and exactly how they are referenced. The ⌜logical structure⌝ can be thought of as a data structure a program might build in memory after reading the ⌜physical structure⌝ of the document.

Part 1 of this book has some examples and illustrations of physical and logical structures.

> **. . . Physically, the document is composed of units called ⌜entities⌝. . . .**

XML uses the term ⌜entity⌝ for many things, but in this context the specification is referring to ⌜external entities⌝ and the ⌜document entity⌝, which may informally be called file entities.

> **. . . An entity may refer to other [external] entities to cause their inclusion in the document. . . .**

For a C or C++ programmer, this is a little like the `#include` construct, except a little more formal. You first declare a name, such as `MyDefs`, for the file you want to include, and associate that name with a URL. A partial URL such as `mydefs.xmd` will work fine (there is no significance to the `.xmd` suffix as far as XML is concerned, so you can use anything you like).

Here is an example of how to include a file using an external entity:

```
<!ENTITY % MyDefs
    SYSTEM "mydefs.xdtd"
>
```

Having made the association between the name, the URL, and the fact that this is an ⌜external entity⌝, you can include the file in your document like this:

```
%MyDefs;
```

You can include it any number of times, and the `mydefs.xmd` file might itself define and/or include other entities.

The entity in this example is an ⌜external parameter entity⌝, and can only be used within the ⌜document type declaration⌝ (⌜DTD⌝) part of the document; it presumably contains definitions. You can include XML text files using ⌜external general entities⌝ as shown in more detail in Chapter 4 of the XML specification.

. . . A document begins in a "root" or ⌜document entity⌝. . . .

The document must also *end* in the same entity in which it started, in order to be ⌜well-formed⌝.

. . . Logically, the document is composed of declarations, elements, comments, character references, and processing instructions, all of which are indicated in the document by explicit markup. . . .

The ⌜markup⌝ is explicit because it is right there in the document, clearly visible.

Note that it is possible in SGML (the more powerful parent of XML) to have markup that is inferred by the SGML processor (e.g., with the SGML OMITTAG feature that is not found in XML), even though there is nothing in the document stream to indicate its presence. For example, end-tags for HTML paragraphs are often left out; an HTML parser must infer their presence at the right place automatically. This sort of processing is difficult both to specify and to implement, and also often baffles users who create documents containing hard-to-find errors. For all these reasons, and also to minimize the size an XML parser needs to be, XML only supports explicit markup that is right there in the document.

. . . The logical and physical structures must nest properly, as described in Section 4.3.2, *Well-Formed Parsed Entities*.

There are examples of logical nesting in Part 1 of this book. Chapter 4 of the XML specification, "Physical Structures," describes nesting of physical structures in detail.

2.1 ⌜Well-Formed⌝ XML Documents

This section describes the conditions a document must meet in order to be a ⌜well-formed⌝ ⌜XML document⌝. Since all XML documents must be well-formed, there is no such thing as an XML document that is not well-formed: Such a thing is simply not an XML document at all, but a pile of characters with pretensions to glory.

A textual object is a well-formed XML document if:

Here, textual is as opposed to binary: Every XML document has at its core a document entity (see above) that is in essence a text file, some of whose text is actually markup.

1. Taken as a whole, it matches the production labeled document[1].

We have used the notation document[1] in this book to refer to the production rule numbered [1]; in this case, document[1] says that a document must contain a prolog[22], a single XML element[39], followed by Misc[27] (optional comments and white space).

1. It meets all the ⌜well-formedness constraints⌝ given in this specification.

The well-formedness constraints are abbreviated WFC, and are described in prose rather than in the ⌜EBNF⌝ for the language. These WFCs are not optional: Every XML document must meet them.

2. Each of the ⌜parsed entities⌝ which is referenced directly or indirectly within the document is ⌜well-formed⌝.

You must not include a file which contains errors. Note, however, that a ⌜non-validating processor⌝ (see Section 5.1, "Validating and Non-Validating Processors") is not required to process ⌜external entities⌝, and is not of course required to detect well-formedness ⌜errors⌝ in external parsed entities that it does not read.

Document

```
[1] Document ::= prolog[22] element[39] Misc[27]*
```

This first production says that document is defined as a prolog[22] followed by an element[39] (exactly one element, in fact) followed by zero or more things that match Misc[27]. A prolog is defined to be a sequence of completely optional items, so that in fact a minimal ⌜XML document⌝ consists of just a single element[39]. An element] is defined to be either an ⌜empty-element tag⌝ or a ⌜start-tag⌝, content[43], and an ⌜end-tag⌝. The Misc[27] at the end allows for ⌜white space⌝ (among other things) after the end of the document; the specification is not clear on whether such space is ⌜ignorable white space⌝, but it would appear not.

Matching the document production implies that:

1. It contains one or more elements.

Although production [1] (document) requires exactly one element[39], that element can itself contain other elements, since element is defined as allowing content[43], which in turn can contain elements as well as text and other items.

2. There is exactly one element, called the root, or ⌈document element⌉, no part of which appears in the content of any other element. . . .

This root element is the one that is mentioned in the document production.

. . . For all other elements, if the ⌈start-tag⌉ is in the content of another element, the ⌈end-tag⌉ is in the content of the same element. More simply stated, the elements, defined by start- and end-tags, nest properly within each other.

For example, `<B><I>Bold Italic</B></I>` is illegal, because the start-tag `<I>` is in the content of the B element, but the end-tag `</I>` is not. This example must be written as `<B><I>Bold Italic</I></B>` instead.

As a consequence of this, for each non-root element C in the document, there is one other element P in the document such that C is in the content of P, but is not in the content of any other element that is in the content of P. P is referred to as the ⌈parent⌉ of C, and C as a ⌈child⌉ of P.

In the following fragment, P is the parent and C the child:

```
<P>starting text<C>content of C</C>trailing text</P>
```

Next, consider the following fragment:

```
<P>
    <Clear>
        <C><Mud>glug glug glug</Mud></C>
    </Clear>
</P>
```

Here, P is the parent of Clear, and Clear is the parent of C. P is not the parent of C because, although C is contained in P, it is also contained in

Clear, and Clear in turn is contained in (i.e., in the content of) P. The rule says that the child must not be in the content of any other element that is inside its parent. Mud, in turn, is a child of C but not of Clear or of P. Mud is in the content of C, Clear, and P. If this all seems very complicated, the glossary entry for ⌜child⌝ may help, and hold on to the simple idea that ⌜parent⌝ and ⌜child⌝ are immediate relations, just as one's grandfather is not normally one's parent in real life, and one's granddaughter not one's own child.

2.2 Characters

The term ⌜character⌝ is a very deceptive one. Computer representation of characters is a very complex area, especially where internationalization is an issue. See Appendix B in Part 3 of this book for an introduction to the way characters are viewed in the international standards community and hence in XML.

The most important concepts are given in the following discussion.

The Unicode consortium (www.unicode.org/) has defined a single 16-bit character set that is intended to cover most or all of the writing systems currently in use in the world.

The International Organization for Standards, ⌜ISO⌝, in conjunction with the International Electrochemical Commission (⌜IEC⌝), has published a compatible standard called ⌜ISO/IEC 10646⌝ which specifies a 32-bit character set, believed to be large enough to represent all of the world's writing systems, both past and present.

Almost all XML documents should therefore be able to use one of the ⌜character encodings⌝ of Unicode or ISO/IEC 10646, such as ⌜UTF-8⌝ or ⌜UTF-16⌝. In fact, UTF-8 is backwards-compatible with ⌜ISO 8859-1⌝, the 8-bit ⌜coded character set⌝ known as ⌜Latin 1⌝, which is already used by HTML.

> **A ⌜parsed entity⌝ contains text, a sequence of characters, which may represent ⌜markup⌝ or ⌜character data⌝. . . .**

A ⌜parsed entity⌝ is what we normally think of as an XML file, so it's no surprise that it has text in it. Here, though, ⌜text⌝ is given the formal meaning of *a sequence of characters*, including markup characters. This is not at all the same as the informal definition.

In the following example of text, the markup has been highlighted:

```
<Note>Jack's <Artifact type="HeadGear"> Crown</Artifact>
has been lost!</Note>
```

... A ⌈character⌉ is an atomic unit of text as specified by ⌈ISO/IEC 10646⌉. ...

The word "atomic" here means that a composite character must be treated as a whole: XML has no interest in anything beneath the level of a character. Note that although some ⌈encodings⌉ (such as UTF-8) may use multiple ⌈octets⌉ (bytes) to represent a single ⌈character⌉, this is not what is being referred to here.

Note also that this is a ⌈normative reference⌉ to ISO/IEC 10646. This standard is not freely available, but must be purchased from one's national standards body. It is therefore not possible to be sure you have written fully conformant XML software without some expenditure.

... Legal ⌈characters⌉ are tab, carriage return, line feed, and the legal ⌈graphic characters⌉ of ⌈Unicode⌉ and ISO/IEC 10646. . . ..

See Appendix C to the XML specification for a list of graphic characters. Note that this rule means that non-graphic control characters other than the white-space ones explicitly listed here are not allowed to appear in XML documents. You can't put Backspace in an XML document, for example, either as its ASCII code (Control-H) or as a ⌈character reference⌉ (&#8;).

This in turn means that you cannot expect to include binary data such as an image directly in an XML file.

You can use an ⌈external unparsed general entity⌉ with an associated ⌈notation⌉, a link using the World Wide Web Consortium's XLink proposal (see www.w3.org/XML/), or you could perhaps use ⌈MIME⌉ ⌈base64⌉ encoding for inline image data, but you can't include the image directly.

This is no surprise for people who have worked with Internet Mail messages in MIME format, or with HTML, or even with including graphic icons and images in C, C++, or Java programs.

... The use of "⌈compatibility characters⌉", as defined in section 6.8 of [the ⌈Unicode⌉ specification], is discouraged.

See Appendix B in Part 3 of this book for information on the ⌈compatibility characters⌉. As their name suggests, they are provided for users of legacy systems, and should not be used in new software or documents.

Character Range

```
[2] Char ::= #x9 | #xA | #xD | [#x20-#xD7FF]
            | [#xE000-#xFFFD] | [#x10000-#x10FFFF]
____/* any Unicode
____ * character, excluding
____ * the surrogate blocks,
____ * FFFE, and FFFF.
____ */]
```

The character FFFE is used for byte order detection: If a Unicode document starts with the two octets (bytes) FE and then FF, in that order, it is assumed that the document has been stored with every pair of octets in reverse order, so that in an 8-bit encoding, *happy boys* would appear as *ahpp yobsy*, and in a 16-bit Unicode file (more to the point) the sequence #x002E (the Latin letter capital E) would appear instead as #2E00. It is said then that the data are *byte swapped*, which can easily happen when files are transferred between computer systems having different architectures.

The ⌐surrogate blocks¬ are explained in the ⌐Unicode¬ book; if you are implementing software to process Unicode data, consult your computer's system libraries to see what Unicode or ISO/IEC 10646 support is offered.

> **The mechanism for ⌐encoding¬ ⌐character code points¬ into bit patterns may vary from ⌐entity¬ to entity. . . .**

You might have, for example, a Japanese paragraph in an Italian document. In this case, it might be simplest to use ⌐ISO 8859-1¬ (Latin 1) or ⌐UTF-8¬ for the Italian text, and to put the Japanese text in a separate file (an external entity). The Japanese text might be encoded using ⌐UTF-16¬ or (less portably outside of Japan) ⌐ISO 2022-JP¬.

> **. . . All ⌐XML processors¬ must accept the ⌐UTF-8¬ and ⌐UTF-16¬ encodings of [ISO/IEC] 10646; the mechanisms for signaling which of the two is in use, or for bringing other encodings into play, are discussed later, in Section 4.3.3, *Character Encoding in Entities*.**

If you have a character encoding that is more useful locally, you should nonetheless transform your documents to use ⌐UTF-8¬ or ⌐UTF-16¬ before distributing them to people or software in other environments. UTF-8 is more compact for Western languages, and UTF-16 is more useful for Eastern scripts such as Hangul and Kanji.

Support for both UTF-8 and UTF-16 is required in all XML software: This is not an optional feature.

2.3 Common Syntactic Constructs

This section defines some symbols used widely in the grammar.

[The production] S[3] (white space) consists of one or more space (#20) characters, carriage returns, line feeds, or tabs.

If you are used to working with parser generating programs such as yacc, bison, or jacc, it may be a surprise to see that white space is an explicit terminal in the grammar productions, rather than being handled in the rules for *lexing* or *tokenizing* the input. There have been experiments with reworking the XML grammar to do this, and these are described in more detail on the Web site for this book, but the reader should note that they are not normative, and must therefore be used with considerable caution.

White Space

```
[3]  White Space ::= (#x20 | #x9 | #xD | #xA)+
```

It is important to note that S[3] must always match at least one character, because of the + sign. This is a difference from SGML, as the prose of that standard permits S[3] to match zero characters if no ambiguity would result.

Characters are classified for convenience as ⌜letters⌝, ⌜digits⌝, or other characters. Letters consist of an ⌜alphabetic⌝ or ⌜syllabic⌝ ⌜base character⌝ possibly followed by one or more combining characters, or of an ⌜ideographic character⌝. Full definitions of the specific characters in each class are given in Appendix B, *Character Classes*.

The definition of a ⌜letter⌝ might seem complex, but it is necessary because XML is intended for worldwide use. More details of the terminology used here can be found in Appendix B in Part 2 of this book and in the Glossary in Part 3 of this book; the reader should also consult the Unicode standard, and the www.unicode.org Web site.

The definition of a letter is such that a ⌜composite character⌝ such as an o with an acute accent (ó), which may be represented as an o followed by a combining acute accent (´), can be considered as a single letter and hence may be used in a `name`[5] or in other contexts that demand the use of a letter.

> **A Name is a ⌐token⌐ beginning with a letter or one of a few punctuation characters, and continuing with letters, digits, hyphens, underscores, colons, or full stops, together known as ⌐name characters⌐. . . .**

Some legal names are:

```
Priscilla, priscilla, r™le, RiLE, Z39.50,
Ankle_Diameter, City.Population, X_1_2.3.4_jk, passers-by, _exit
```

These names are illegal:

```
301 (cannot start with a digit)
Ankle Diameter (cannot contain a space)
-3 (can't start with a hyphen)
.bp (can't start with a full stop)
```

> **. . . Names beginning with the string "xml", or any string which would match (('X'|'x') ('M'|'m') ('L'|'l')), are reserved for standardization in this or future versions of this specification.**

In other words, you can't use names like `XML1.0` or `XmlEphant`, because everything starting with XML, case-insensitively, is reserved. Watch out for names such as `XmListBox`, by the way (a name in the Motif toolkit for programming the X Window System), which are also illegal but harder to spot. If you are translating into XML, perhaps to create on-line documentation or to represent program objects and their methods, you need to use a scheme that avoids this problem

> **Note: The colon character within XML names is reserved for experimentation with ⌐name spaces⌐. Its meaning is expected to be standardized at some future point, at which point those documents using the colon for experimental purposes may need to be updated. (There is no guarantee that any name-space mechanism adopted for XML will in fact use the colon as a name-space delimiter.) In practice, this means that authors should not use the colon in XML names except as part of name-space experiments, but that XML processors should accept the colon as a name character.**

This paragraph is saying that you can't use the colon (:) in XML documents unless you are experimenting and agree to change your documents when the XML name space specification is approved, or unless you wait until that specification has been approved. At the time of writing this book (late in 1998), a preliminary namespace specification had been written, and this is described in Part 3, Appendix E of this book.

All XML software must accept the colon as if it were a letter, so that `:x` and `a:b:c` and `::::::` are all acceptable XML names.

See Appendix E in Part 3 of this book, and also see the namespace draft at the World Wide Web Consortium's site, www.w3.org/XML/.

An Nmtoken[7] (name token) is any mixture of name characters.

Hence, an `Nmtoken`[7] could start with a digit, for example, but still could not contain a space. This may sometimes be useful for attribute values, which may be declared to be of type `NMTOKEN`, but it is hard to argue that this is an important part of XML.

Names and Tokens

```
[4]  NameChar ::=
        Letter[84] | Digit[88] | '.' | '_' | ':' |
        CombiningChar[87] | Extender[89]
[5]  Name ::= (Letter[84] | '_' | ':' ) (NameChar[4])*
[6]  Names  ::= Name[5] (S[3] Name[5])*

[7]  Nmtoken ::= (NameChar[4])+

[8]  Nmtokens ::= Nmtoken[7] (S[3] Nmtoken[7])*
```

Some examples of names are given in our annotations to Chapter 1 of the XML specification in Part 2 of this book.

Literal data is any quoted string not containing the quotation mark used as a delimiter for that string. . . .

A string surrounded by double quotes (`"..."`) can't contain a double quote, and a string surrounded by single quotes (`'...'`) can't contain a single quote. There is no other significance to the type of quotation mark used. If you need to include both a single and a double quote in the same literal string, use the predeclared entity `&quot;` for a single quote, or use a ⌐character reference⌐ as described in Chapter 4 below.

> . . . Literals are used for specifying the content of ⌐internal entities⌐ (EntityValue[9]), the values of ⌐attributes⌐ (AttValue[10]), and ⌐external identifiers⌐ (SystemLiteral[11]). . .

The production rules that follow to define these various uses of literals all differ in subtle ways, unfortunately. This is why "literal" is not the name of a production, but rather the name of a whole group of related productions.

> . . . Note that a SystemLiteral[11] can be parsed without scanning for markup.

A `SystemLiteral`[11] contains a ⌐URI⌐—that is, a URL. Markup is not special inside a `SystemLiteral`[11], and the characters & and < can occur in them literally.

This rule does *not* apply to XML ⌐attribute⌐ values that happen to contain a URL, such as `<IMG SRC="http://....">`, which is an `AttValue`[10] literal and not a `SystemLiteral`[11].

Literals

```
:[9]  EntityValue ::=
         '"' ([^%&"] | PEReference[69] | Reference[67])* '"'
       | "'" ([^%&'] | PEReference[69] | Reference[67])* "'"

[10] AttValue ::=
         '"' ([^<&"] | Reference[67])* '"'
       | "'" ([^<&'] | Reference[67])* "'"

[11] SystemLiteral ::= ('"' [^"]* '"') | ("'" [^']* "'")

[12] PubidLiteral ::=
         '"' PubidChar* '"'
       | "'" (PubidChar - "'")* "'"

[13] PubidChar ::=
         #x20 | #xD | #xA | [a-zA-Z0-9] | [-'()+,./:=?;!*#@$_%]
```

2.4 Character Data and Markup

Text consists of intermingled ⌐character data⌐ and ⌐markup⌐. Markup takes the form of ⌐start-tags⌐, ⌐end-tags⌐, ⌐empty-element tags⌐, ⌐entity references⌐, ⌐character references⌐, ⌐comments⌐, ⌐CDATA section delimiters⌐, ⌐document type declarations,⌐ and ⌐processing instructions⌐.

The items listed here are explained in the sections that follow.

The alert reader may notice that entity references are not mentioned. This may be an oversight, or it may be because the markup is what is left after replacing each ⌜entity reference⌝ with its ⌜replacement text⌝.

All text that is not markup constitutes the character data of the document.

The ⌜character data⌝, then, is the stuff outside the pointy brackets! See the example in the notes to Chapter 1 of the specification, and also see Part 1 of this book for examples. The term "text" is sometimes used to mean character data and sometimes used to mean `content`[43], which is whatever can go inside a document.

> **The ampersand character (&) and the left angle bracket (<) may appear in their literal form only when used as markup characters, or within a comment, a processing instruction, or a CDATA section. They are also legal within the ⌜literal entity value⌝ of an ⌜internal entity declaration⌝; see Section 4.3.2, *Well-Formed Parsed Entities*. . . .**

The technical reason for this restriction is entirely one of convenience for the *desperate perl hacker*, the person who has to use a scripting or programming language that is not XML-aware to change a large number of XML documents in a short time. A sample task might be to change all occurrences of part number 1907, as found inside `partNumber` tags, into 3710 instead. Knowing that the less-than sign and the ampersand can't occur as data makes this task simpler, especially in regular-expression pattern-matching languages such as perl.

In fact, a few short months after the XML specification was published, Larry Wall produced a version of the perl programming language environment that included James Clark's XML parser and had native support for XML. But the restriction still stands, and still helps!

Note that strictly speaking, the < character is a less-than sign and not a left angle bracket, as these two characters are quite distinct in Unicode. Informally, however, the term "angle bracket" remains as a holdover from the good old days of 7-bit ASCII and the Model 33 Teletype.

> **. . . If they are needed elsewhere, they must be escaped using either ⌜numeric character references⌝ or the strings "&" and "<" respectively. . . .**

There are two good reasons to prefer the strings `"&amp;"` and `"&lt;"` (which are ⌜general entity references⌝) over using numerical character references. Firstly, the result is much more readable, since most people seem to find it easier to remember that & stands for an ampersand than to remember that & is the same thing. Secondly, the numeric character reference is not sufficient to escape the ampersand and less-than sign in all contexts: Within the literal value of an internal general entity, you must use either the cryptic and subtle string &#38; or &.

> **. . . The right angle bracket (>) may be represented using the string ">", and must, for compatibility, be escaped using ">" or a character reference when it appears in the string "]]>" in content, when that string is not marking the end of a CDATA section.**

This is because older SGML software recognizes]]> in all contexts, and produces a fatal error if the string occurs outside any marked section.

> **In the content of elements, character data is any string of characters which does not contain the start-delimiter of any markup. In a CDATA section, character data is any string of characters not including the CDATA-section-close delimiter, "]]>".**

In other words, ⌜character data⌝ is what you have left after taking away all the markup. Note that markup is not recognized within a CDATA section, so all that's left to take away is the delimiter that marks the end of the CDATA section.

> **To allow attribute values to contain both single and double quotes, the apostrophe or single-quote character (') may be represented as "'", and the double-quote character (") as """.**

As mentioned above, there is no difference as far as XML is concerned between using single and double quotes around an attribute value, as long as the quotes are the same at both ends of the value! Note that the ASCII straight double quote (") must be used, and not typographic or "smart" quotes! Macintosh users should also note carefully that the apostrophe mentioned here is actually the spacing grave accent from ASCII (') that is also called a typewriter quote, and not the proper apostrophe or single left quote character.

Character Data

```
[14] CharData ::= [^<&]* - ([^<&]* ']]>' [^<&]*)
```

2.5 Comments

Comments may appear anywhere in a document outside other markup; in
addition, they may appear within the ⌜document type declaration⌝ at places
allowed by the grammar. They are not part of the document's ⌜character data⌝;
an ⌜XML processor⌝ ⌜may⌝, but need not, make it possible for an application to
retrieve the text of comments. . . .

Anyone used to writing parsers or compilers may be a little surprised to
discover that comments are not stripped out at the lexical level in XML,
and even more surprised to discover that comments are not permitted
within declarations. The following example shows an illegal placement of
a comment:

```
<!ATTLIST Doggie              (illegal example)
    tailLength CDATA "8"  <!-- 8 inches long by default -->
    wagSpeed (medium|fast|frenetic) "fast"
>
```

. . . For compatibility, the string "--" (double-hyphen) must not occur within
comments.

Comments in SGML have different rules; the XML rules ensure that all
XML comments are legal SGML comments, as long as they do not contain
two minus signs in a row. Note, by the way, that the character in question
is an ASCII minus sign and *not* a hyphen. The 7-bit ASCII standard did not
include a hyphen, so people became accustomed to making the minus sign
do double duty.

Comments

```
[15] Comment ::=
        '<!--' ((Char[2] - '-') | ('-' (Char[2] - '-')))* '-->'
```

The regular expression in the production for Comment[15] matches any
string not containing two minus signs next to each other.

An example of a comment:

```
<!--declarations for <head> & <body> -->
```

2.6 Processing Instructions

Processing instructions (PIs) allow documents to contain instructions for applications.

The idea behind processing instructions is that they are used to give directives to a particular XML application or processor. A typical example would be to instruct a particular page formatter to put a page break in a specific place, knowing that the same document formatted by a different application would need that page break elsewhere.

The document should survive unscathed if all processing instructions are removed. In this regard they are very like the #pragma directive in the ANSI C programming language.

Note that informally in the SGML community, the abbreviation PI is used (confusingly) both for ⌜processing instruction⌝ and for ⌜public identifier⌝.

Processing Instructions

```
[16] PI ::=
        '<?' PITarget[17]
            (S[3] (Char[2]* - (Char[2]* '?>' Char[2]*)))?
        '?>'

[17] PITarget ::= Name[5] - (('X'|'x') ('M'|"m") ('L'|'l'))
```

The regular expression for PI[16] simply matches a string not containing ?> anywhere.

Note that no space is allowed between the <? at the start and the PITarget[17].

Note also that a ⌜text declaration⌝ and an ⌜XML declaration⌝ use exactly the same syntax as processing instructions, except that they use "xml" as the target, which is explicitly disallowed for a PITarget[17]. See Section 2.8, "Prolog and Document Type Declaration," below.

PIs are not part of the document's ⌜character data⌝, but ⌜must⌝ be passed through to the application. . . .

Compare this with comments (see Section 2.5 above), which the XML processor ⌜may⌝ pass through to the application.

> **... The PI begins with a target (PITarget[17]) used to identify the application to which the instruction is directed. The target names "XML", "xml" and so on are reserved for standardization in this or future versions of this specification. ...**

Applications should each have a list of targets that they obey, and respond only to processing instructions that begin with one of those targets, ignoring all others. The target "xml" is already used for the ⌜XML declaration⌝ and the ⌜text declaration⌝ described in Chapter 4 of the specification.

> **... The XML Notation mechanism ⌜may⌝ be used for formal declaration of PI targets.**

This is entirely optional. You can declare the targets you use with an XML notation, and an XML processor could decide to generate warnings for undeclared targets, as an error-checking feature. There is no significance to the notation in this context. Here is an example:

```
<!NOTATION troff
    SYSTEM "this string is required but not used"
>
. . .
<!--* tell troff to begin a new page here: *-->
<?troff .bp ?>
```

2.7 CDATA Sections

> **CDATA sections may occur anywhere ⌜character data⌝ may occur; they are used to escape blocks of text containing characters which would otherwise be recognized as ⌜markup⌝. CDATA sections begin with the string "<![CDATA[" and end with the string "]]>":**

See Part 1 of this book for examples of CDATA sections used to escape HTML markup embedded within an XML document. Another common use is writing documentation for XML markup, where you need a way to represent the examples and want to be able to use copy and paste from working code. CDATA sections might also be used to embed fragments of scripting languages inside a document, where a fragment like the following would be painful to type using & and < everywhere:

```
if (shoeSize < 9 && age > 32) {
    my.textStyle = BOLD;
}
```

The absurd syntax of CDATA marked sections is inherited from SGML; XML uses a subset of SGML's more powerful marked section feature, and the syntax has been retained for compatibility.

CDATA Sections

```
[18] CDSect ::= CDStart[19] CData[20] CDEnd[21]

[19] CDStart ::= '<![CDATA['

[20] CData ::= (Char[2]* - (Char[2]* ']]>' Char[2]*))

[21] CDEnd ::= ']]>'
```

Within a CDATA section, only the CDEnd[21] string is recognized as markup, so that left angle brackets and ampersands may occur in their literal form; they need not (and cannot) be escaped using "<" and "&". CDATA sections cannot nest.

The ampersand (&) and less-than character (<) are not special inside a CDATA section. This means that any non-XML programs or scripts that scan documents for specific elements (for example) by recognizing tags will get confused by them. It is generally better to forget about CDATA sections and to escape markup in the normal way whenever possible.

If necessary, ask the vendor of your favorite SGML or XML editor for an option to quote markup automatically whenever text is pasted from another application.

An example of a ⌈CDATA section⌉, in which "<greeting>" and "</greeting>" are recognized as ⌈character data⌉, not ⌈markup⌉:

```
<![CDATA[<greeting>Hello, world!</greeting>]]>
```

Here is the same example given as regular content:

```
&lt;greeting&gt;Hello, world!&lt;/greeting&gt;
```

2.8 Prolog and Document Type Declaration

XML documents ⌐may¬, and should, begin with an XML declaration which specifies the version of XML being used. . . .

The moral imperative here, *should*, is because the XML declaration allows files to be self-identifying as XML, and because it will help you avoid problems when some future version of XML is published, perhaps with some small but incompatible changes.

...For example, the following is a complete XML document, ⌐well-formed¬ but not ⌐valid¬:

```
<?xml version="1.0"?>
<greeting>Hello, world!</greeting>
```

and so is this:

```
<greeting>Hello, world!</greeting>
```

The XML declaration looks just like a processing instruction; see Section 2.6, "Processing Instructions," above.

The version number "1.0" should be used to indicate conformance to this specification: it is an ⌐error¬ for a document to use the value "1.0" if it does not conform to this version of this specification. It is the intent of the XML working group to give later versions of this specification numbers other than "1.0", but this intent does not indicate a commitment to produce any future versions of XML, nor if any are produced, to use any particular numbering scheme. Since future versions are not ruled out, this construct is provided as a means to allow the possibility of automatic version recognition, should it become necessary. Processors ⌐may¬ signal an ⌐error¬ if they receive documents labeled with versions they do not support.

The only sensible interpretation is that an XML processor should signal an error if it sees an XML declaration with a version other than 1.0, despite what seems to be somewhat evasive wording here.

> The function of the ⌜markup⌝ in an XML document is to describe its storage and ⌜logical structure⌝ and to associate attribute-value pairs with its logical structures. . . .

"It" here must be the document without the markup. This is a very abstract view of the function of markup; see Part 1 of this book for more concrete interpretations.

> . . . XML provides a mechanism, the ⌜document type declaration⌝, to define constraints on the ⌜logical structure⌝ and to support the use of predefined storage units. An ⌜XML document⌝ is **valid** if it has an associated ⌜document type declaration⌝ and if the document complies with the constraints expressed in it.

The constraints that can be imposed on the ⌜logical structure⌝ are described later in Part 2, in Chapter 3, "Logical Structure," along with document validity; the storage mechanism is described in Chapter 4, "Physical Structure."

> The ⌜document type declaration⌝ must appear before the first element in the document.

Prolog

```
[22] prolog ::=
       XMLDecl[23]? Misc[27]* (doctypedecl[28] Misc[27]*)?

[23] XMLDecl ::=
       '<?xml' VersionInfo[24] EncodingDecl[80]? SDDecl[32]? S[3]? '?>'

[24] VersionInfo ::=
       S 'version' Eq[25] (' VersionNum[26] ' | " VersionNum[26] ")

[25] Eq ::= S[3]? '=' S[3]?

[26] VersionNum ::= ([a-zA-Z0-9_.:] | '-')+

[27] Misc ::= Comment[15] | PI[15] | S[3]
```

> The XML document type declaration contains or points to ⌜markup declarations⌝ that provide a grammar for a class of documents. This grammar is known as a ⌜document type definition⌝, or **DTD**. The ⌜document type declaration⌝

can point to an ⌐external subset⌐ (a special kind of ⌐external entity⌐) containing
markup declarations, or can contain the markup declarations directly in an
⌐internal subset⌐, or can do both. The DTD for a document consists of both
subsets taken together.

The following examples illustrate each of these combinations.

First, an XML document with neither ⌐internal subset⌐ nor ⌐external sub-
set⌐, and hence no ⌐DTD⌐:

```
<?xml version="1.0">
<list>3</list>
```

This document is ⌐well-formed⌐, but, since it has no DTD, it is not also
⌐valid⌐.

Next we add a DTD using only an ⌐internal subset⌐:

```
<?xml version="1.0">
\!DOCTYPE list [
    <!ELEMENT list
        (#PCDATA)*
    >
]>
<list>3</list>
```

This document is both well-formed and valid.

If we find ourselves using this definition of list often, we may well wish
to store it in a separate ⌐external entity⌐ and refer to it. The next example has
an ⌐external subset⌐ and no ⌐internal subset⌐:

```
<?xml version="1.0">
<!DOCTYPE list
    SYSTEM "list.dtd"
>
<list>3</list>
```

The external document type entity list.dtd looks like this:

```
<!--* Simple DTD to record the angle of the mast
    * of a ship from the vertical, in degrees clockwise when
    * looking forward.  This is known as the list of a ship.
    * -->
<!ELEMENT list
    (#PCDATA)*
>
```

Using the same external entity, we will next present a document with both an internal and an external subset:

```
<?xml version="1.0">
<!DOCTYPE list
    SYSTEM "list.dtd" [
    <!ENTITY degrees
        "¡"
    >
    ]
>
<list>3&degrees;</list>
```

When a document has both an internal and an external subset, the internal subset is read first, and definitions there override those in the external subset. This means that you can declare an entity in the internal subset and set its value, so that an entity declaration for the same entity in the external subset will have no effect, and you have thereby in a sense changed the external DTD subset.

In other words, except for introducing a ⌜parameter entity⌝ named `list.dtd`, this last example is exactly equivalent to the previous one:

```
<?xml version="1.0">
<!DOCTYPE list [
    <!ENTITY degrees
        "¡"
    >
    <!ENTITY % list.dtd
        SYSTEM "list.dtd"
    >
    %list.dtd;
    ]
>
<list>3&degrees;</list>
```

A markup declaration is an ⌜element type declaration⌝, an ⌜attribute-list declaration⌝, an ⌜entity declaration⌝, or a ⌜notation declaration⌝. These declarations may be contained in whole or in part within ⌜parameter entities⌝, as described in the ⌜well-formedness⌝ and ⌜validity⌝ ⌜constraints⌝ below. For fuller information, see Chapter 4, *Physical Structures*.

In addition to the examples of each of these types of ⌜markup declaration⌝ given in the notes to Part 2, Chapter 3, "Logical Structures," there are introductory notes and examples in Part 1 of this book; ⌜entities⌝ are discussed in Part 2, Chapter 4, "Physical Structures."

Document Type Definition

```
[28] doctypedecl ::=
        '<!DOCTYPE' S[3] Name[5] (S[3] ExternalID[75])? S[3]?
        ('[' (markupdecl[29] | PEReference[69] | S[3] )* ']' S[3]?)?
        '>'                                    [VC: Root Element Type]


[29] markupdecl ::=
        elementdecl[45] | AttlistDecl[52]      [VC: Proper Declaration/PE Nesting]
      | EntityDecl[70] | NotationDecl[82]      [WFC: PEs in Internal Subset]
      | PI[16] | Comment[15]
```

Note: The heading for these productions was probably meant to be *Document Type Declaration* rather than *Document Type Definition*.

The markup declarations may be made up in whole or in part of the ⌐replacement text⌐ of ⌐parameter entities⌐. The productions later in this specification for individual ⌐nonterminals⌐ (elementdecl[45], AttlistDecl[52], and so on) describe the declarations *after* all the parameter entities have been included.

There are a number of restrictions on how a ⌐parameter entity⌐ interacts with markup declarations. The clearest of these is that any ⌐internal parameter entity⌐ referenced in the ⌐internal subset⌐ can only contain entire markup declarations, and cannot appear within a markup declaration. Other restrictions are scattered around the specification, mostly in Chapters 3 and 4.

Validity Constraint: Root Element Type

The Name[5] in the ⌐document type declaration⌐ must match the ⌐element type⌐ of the ⌐root element⌐.

As usual in XML, this is a case-sensitive ⌐match⌐. See the ⌐list⌐ examples given above, and notice how the element list is named in the ⌐document type declaration⌐ after the keyword DOCTYPE and is also the ⌐element type⌐ of the first (and only) element in the document in each case.

You can use any element that you have declared for a root element: there is nothing special about it apart from being named in the document type declaration as the root element.

Validity Constraint: Proper Declaration/PE Nesting

Parameter-entity ⌜replacement text⌝ must be properly nested with markup declarations. That is to say, if either the first character or the last character of a markup declaration (markupdecl[29] above) is contained in the replacement text for a parameter-entity reference, both must be contained in the same replacement text.

In other words, if either the first or last character is inside a parameter entity replacement value, the entire declaration must be! Here is an example:

```
<!ENTITY % content
    "(#PCDATA)*"
>
<!ENTITY % makeElements
    "
        <!ELEMENT one
            %content;
        >
        <!ELEMENT two
            %content;
        >
    "
>
%makeElements;
```

In this example, the declarations for the element types one and two are entirely contained within the replacement text of the makeElements internal parameter entity. Part of those markup declarations is contained in the content entity, but the start and end of each element declaration is directly within makeElements. Note also that the example shows that you can have more than one markup declaration within a single parameter entity.

Well-Formedness Constraint: PEs in Internal Subset

In the ⌜internal DTD subset⌝, ⌜parameter-entity references⌝ can occur only where ⌜markup declarations⌝ can occur, not within markup declarations. (This does not apply to references that occur in ⌜external parameter entities⌝ or to the ⌜external subset⌝.)

A non-validating XML processor is not required to read external parameter entities, and may therefore not have seen the definition for a parameter entity; this rule allows such a non-validating XML processor to skip reliably over parameter entity references even if it has not seen their declarations.

> **Like the ⌈internal DTD subset⌉, the ⌈external subset⌉ and any ⌈external parameter entities⌉ referred to in the DTD must consist of a series of complete markup declarations of the types allowed by the ⌈non-terminal⌉ symbol markupdecl[29], interspersed with ⌈white space⌉ or parameter-entity references. However, portions of the contents of the ⌈external subset⌉ or of external parameter entities may conditionally be ignored by using the ⌈conditional section⌉ construct; this is not allowed in the ⌈internal subset⌉.**

In other words, conditional sections (described in Section 3.4, "Conditional Sections") can appear in the external DTD subset and in external parameter entities, but *not* in the internal DTD subset. A non-validating XML processor that has not read external parameter entities does not know, in general, the values of parameter entities, so that in the (illegal) example that follows, it does not know whether the conditional section should be included:

```
<!--Example illegal inside internal DTD subset -->

<!ENTITY % externalDefs
    SYSTEM "mydefs.dtd"
>
%externalDefs;
<!--* a non-validating processor could not handle this
    * conditional section if it did not know the value
    * of %ifWednesday;, whether it is INCLUDE or IGNORE.
    *
    * It also violates the rule that parameter entities can
    * only contain complete markup declarations.
    *-->
<![%ifWednesday;[
]]>
```

External Subset

```
[30] extSubset ::= TextDecl[77]? extSubsetDecl[31]

[31] extSubsetDecl ::=
        (markupdecl[29] | conditionalsect[61] | PEReference[69] | S[3])*
```

Note: Processing instructions and comments are included in `markupdecl`[29], and thus are allowed in both the internal and external subsets.

The ⌜external subset⌝ and ⌜external parameter entities⌝ also differ from the ⌜internal subset⌝ in that in them, ⌜parameter-entity references⌝ are permitted *within* ⌜markup declarations⌝, not only *between* markup declarations.

This has been mentioned above, and is repeated in Chapter 4 in a slightly different wording. One of the most useful aspects of external parameter entities is the way that conditional sections and parameter entities can be used in them.

An example of an ⌜XML document⌝ with a ⌜document type declaration⌝:

```
<?xml version = "1.0"?>
<!DOCTYPE greeting SYSTEM "hello.dtd">
<greeting>Hello, world!</greeting>
```

The system identifier "hello.dtd" gives the URI of a DTD for the document.

In this case, the URI is actually a ⌜relative URL⌝, so that if the document had been fetched as *http://www.groveware.com/xmlbook/chapter3.xml*, the DTD would be *http://www.groveware.com/xmlbook/hello.dtd*, but if the document had been loaded from a local file called "`marvin.xml`", the DTD would be in the same directory as the document, with the name "`hello.dtd`".

The declarations can also be given locally, as in this example:

```
<?xml version= "1.0" encoding= "UTF8" ?>
<!DOCTYPE greeting [
  <!ELEMENT greeting
    (#PCDATA)
  >
]>
<greeting>Hello, world!</greeting>
```

It may be helpful to compare this to the examples given earlier in this section.

If both the external and internal subsets are used, the internal subset is considered to occur before the external subset. This has the effect that entity

and attribute-list declarations in the internal subset take precedence over those in the external subset.

This is a very important statement. The idea is that an external DTD can be written in such a way as to be modular, with various options that can be configured by setting parameter entities to INCLUDE or IGNORE in the internal subset. Since the DTD may be different depending on the value of those entities, it follows that the external subset must be read *after* the internal subset. This in turn means that earlier definitions of entities must override later ones.

2.9 Standalone Document Declaration

Markup declarations can affect the content of the document, as passed from an XML processor to an application; examples are ⌐attribute defaults⌐ and ⌐entity⌐ declarations. The ⌐standalone document declaration⌐, which ⌐may⌐ appear as a component of the XML declaration, signals whether or not there are such declarations which appear external to the document entity.

This is something that is generally created and maintained by humans, although it would be possible in principle to automate it. The idea is that a non-validating XML processor can determine whether it is changing the content of the document in not examining external parameter entities.

Standalone Document Declaration

```
[32] SDDecl ::= S 'standalone' Eq (
              ("'" ('yes' | 'no') "'")
            | ('"' ('yes' | 'no') '"'))
                    [VC: Standalone Document Declaration]
```

The ⌐standalone document declaration⌐ appears within the XML declaration (XMLDecl[23]) at the start of the main ⌐document entity⌐.

In a ⌐standalone document declaration⌐, the value "yes" indicates that there are no ⌐markup declarations⌐ external to the ⌐document entity⌐ (either in the DTD external subset, or in an external parameter entity referenced from the internal

subset) which affect the information passed from the XML processor to the application. . . .

Recall that the ⌜external DTD subset⌝ includes all ⌜external parameter entities⌝ that are referenced from external entities.

. . . The value "no" indicates that there are or may be such external ⌜markup declarations⌝. . . .

A value of "yes" means that an XML processor that does not read the external DTD subset will still produce the same document content as if it had read that subset. A value of "no", on the other hand, means that we can't tell whether this is so: It does *not* mean that there will definitely be a difference, but only that there may be. For example; suppose an element type was declared in an ⌜external parameter entity⌝ to have an attribute with a default value, but that no elements of that type occurred in the document. In this case, there would be no difference in the document content depending on whether the XML processor knew about the default attribute value, because the attribute was never used.

. . . Note that the standalone document declaration only denotes the presence of external *declarations*; the presence, in a document, of references to external *entities*, when those entities are internally declared, does not change its standalone status.

A document is *not* standalone if the external subset, directly or indirectly, declares default attributes for elements that are used, or declares general entities (whether internal or external) that are referenced. But if the same declarations occur only in an ⌜external parameter entity⌝ that is declared and referenced in the internal DTD subset, it would appear from this rule that the document *is* standalone.

It is probable that what is meant here instead is that ⌜external general entity references⌝ do not affect the standalone declaration, since they can contain no markup declarations.

If there are no external markup declarations, the standalone document declaration has no meaning. If there are external markup declarations but there is no standalone document declaration, the value "no" is assumed.

It would be better to say (especially in the light of the next paragraph in the specification) that if there are no external markup declarations, the document is standalone.

> **Any XML document for which standalone= "no" holds can be converted algorithmically to a standalone document, which may be desirable for some network delivery applications.**

One such algorithm would be to take all of the external markup declarations that might affect document content and put them in the internal document subset.

> **Validity Constraint: Standalone Document Declaration**
>
> **The standalone document declaration must have the value "no" if any external markup declarations contain declarations of:**
>
> ■ **attributes with default values, if elements to which these attributes apply appear in the document without specifications of values for these attributes, or . . .**

This is straightforward for a validating XML processor to determine, but does mean that the entire document may have to be scanned, at least up to the first element that omits a value for an attribute with a declared default value.

> ■ **entities (other than amp, lt, gt, apos, quot), if references to those entities appear in the document, or . . .**

You are not allowed to declare the five predeclared entities to have any other value than that given at the end of Part 2, Chapter 4, "Physical Structures," so it is not necessary to read external entities to determine their values.

> ■ **attributes with values subject to normalization, where the attribute appears in the document with a value which will change as a result of normalization, or . . .**

This means that any attribute values containing character references would automatically cause the document not to be standalone, which seems a little excessive.

- **element types with element content, if white space occurs directly within any instance of those types.**

⌜White space⌝ in ⌜element content⌝ can be ignored, whereas white space in ⌜mixed content⌝ must be passed back to the application (it might be the space between two words, for example). See the next section for a discussion of white space.

An example XML declaration with a standalone document declaration:

```
<?xml version="1.0" standalone="yes"?>
```

2.10 White Space Handling

In editing XML documents, it is often convenient to use "white space" (spaces, tabs, and blank lines, denoted by the nonterminal S[3] in this specification) to set apart the markup for greater readability. . . .

By *editing XML documents* is meant, editing XML documents using an editor that shows the markup and does not lay out the source automatically. The following two examples indicate the sort of use of white space that is being described:

```
<table><column type="heading" width="auto"><cell>Student
Name</cell><cell>Student Shoe Size</cell></columnn> . . .

<table>
  <column type="heading" width="auto">
    <cell>Student Name</cell>
    <cell>Student Shoe Size</cell>
  </columnn>
 . . .
</table>
```

. . . Such white space is typically not intended for inclusion in the delivered version of the document. On the other hand, "significant" white space that

should be preserved in the delivered version is common, for example in poetry and source code.

Somepeoplelikespacesbetweenwords,too. Consider also the space between the elements in the following example—it is clearly significant!

```
<p><det>The</det> <noun>boy</noun> <verb>smiled</verb/p>.
```

An XML processor must always pass all characters in a document that are not markup through to the application. A ⌜validating XML processor⌝ must also inform the application which of these characters constitute white space appearing in element content.

A non-validating XML processor may not have access to this information, for example if the element containing white space was declared in an ⌜external parameter entity⌝ that the processor did not read.

All of the white space is passed back to the application; this is important for implementors to note, as white space handling is particularly important in text processing applications.

A special attribute named xml:space may be attached to an element to signal an intention that in that element, white space should be preserved by applications. In valid documents, this attribute, like any other, must be declared if it is used. When declared, it must be given an enumerated type whose only possible values are "default" and "preserve". For example:

```
<!ATTLIST poem
    xml:space (default|preserve) 'preserve'
>
```

One might be tempted to infer that the default value here will make a difference; it will, but in general only for a validating XML processor and only if poem contains only other elements and not #PCDATA (i.e. has ⌜element content⌝ and not ⌜mixed content⌝).

A non-validating XML processor must respect default attribute values only if they are declared in the internal DTD subset before the first reference to an external parameter entity (if any). A declaration of xml:space in that circumstance would make a difference for all XML processors. Since only a validating XML processor has to inform the application about white space that can be ignored, telling a non-validating processor not to do so has no effect. But the validating processor will have read the element declaration to know if it has mixed content. Therefore, `xml:space="pre-serve"` should only be used for elements with element content, and `xml:space="default"` should only be used on element instances to override a declared default value of `"preserve"`.

Note: It is possible to declare `xml:space` as a `#FIXED` attribute having the value `"preserve"`, in which case no instance of the element type concerned would ever have an XML processor declare to the application that the white space within it could be discarded.

> **The value "default" signals that applications' default white-space processing modes are acceptable for this element; the value "preserve" indicates the intent that applications preserve all the white space. This declared intent is considered to apply to all elements within the content of the element where it is specified, unless overridden with another instance of the xml:space attribute.**

The attribute does no more than signal an intent: An application is free to discard white space if its designers felt that to be appropriate.

> **The root element of any document is considered to have signaled no intentions as regards application [white] space handling, unless it provides a value for this attribute or the attribute is declared with a default value.**

If you declare that your root element has an attribute of `xml:space` with a default value of "preserve", you will effectively ensure that white space is not ignored anywhere in your document, assuming that the application chooses to honor the message.

2.11 End-of-Line Handling

> **XML ⌐parsed entities⌐ are often stored in computer files which, for editing convenience, are organized into lines. These lines are typically separated by some combination of the characters carriage-return (#xD) and line-feed (#xA).**

Carriage return (CR, #xD) is Control-M on an ASCII keyboard; line feed (LF, #xA) is Control-J. MS-DOS, Microsoft Windows NT, and a number of other much older operating systems use CR-LF at the end of each line. The Macintosh operating system uses CR, and UNIX uses LF. The HTTP protocol specifies that lines are terminated by CR-LF, although not all implementations do this.

To simplify the tasks of applications, wherever an ⌐external parsed entity⌐ or the ⌐literal entity value⌐ of an ⌐internal parsed entity⌐ contains either the literal two-character sequence "#xD#xA" or a standalone literal #xD, an XML processor must pass to the application the single character #xA. (This behavior can conveniently be produced by normalizing all line breaks to #xA on input, before parsing.)

Normalizing a document in this way would involve processing every character in the input twice, which does not bode well for performance. It would probably be just as simple to treat #xD and #xA as white space matching S[3] in a markup declaration context, and within content to turn #xD (LF) into #xA and ignore a #xA that immediately follows a #xD.

2.12 Language Identification

In document processing, it is often useful to identify the natural or formal language in which the content is written. . . .

A natural language is one such as Cymric (Welsh) spoken by people in normal conversation; a formal language might be a programming language such as C or ADA. Some reasons to identify the language are: spell checking, where having different spell checkers for various elements of a document that are in different languages is very helpful; hyphenation, where rules vary by language; choice of typeface or other presentational variations; voice selection for speech synthesis software.

. . . A special attribute named xml:lang may be inserted in documents to specify the language used in the contents and attribute values of any element in an XML document. In valid documents, this attribute, like any other, must be declared if it is used. The values of the attribute are language identifiers as defined by IETF RFCC 1766, *Tags for the Identification of Languages*.

See Part 3 of this book for more information about RFC 1766. A sample declaration for xml:lang is given later in this section.

Language Identification

```
[33] LanguageID ::= Langcode[34] ('-' Subcode[38])*

[34] Langcode ::= ISO639Code[35] | IanaCode[36] | UserCode[37]
```

```
[35] ISO639Code ::= ([a-z] | [A-Z]) ([a-z] | [A-Z])

[36] IanaCode ::= ('i' | 'I') '-' ([a-z] | [A-Z]))+

[37] UserCode ::= ('x' | 'X') '-' ([a-z] | [A-Z]))+

[38] Subcode ::= ([a-z] | [A-Z])+
```

Note that the three types of language code are mutually distinguishable: An ISO 639 code (ISO[35]639Code) has a letter as its second character, whereas the other two have a minus sign, with either an I or an X as the first character (in either upper- or lowercase).

The Langcode[34] may be any of the following:

- **a two-letter language code as defined by ISO 639, Codes for the representation of names of languages . . .**

This is a ⌈normative reference⌉ to a document available from national standards bodies in ISO member countries, or from the ISO headquarters in Switzerland for people in other countries.

- **a language identifier registered with the ⌈Internet Assigned Numbers Authority⌉ (IANA); these begin with the prefix "i-" (or "I-") . . .**

This category is the most likely to be supported by other (non-XML) Internet-related software, and should be used where possible. See Part 3 of this book for more details.

- **a language identifier assigned by the user, or agreed on between parties in private use; these must begin with the prefix "x-" or "X-" in order to ensure that they do not conflict with names later standardized or registered with ⌈IANA⌉.**

If you have agreed with a friend to use x-Intercal or x-OldEnglish-Wessex, you are at least able to indicate this in a standard way using xml:lang, so that other users (and software) can detect that your documents use a language alien and unfamiliar to them.

If you expect your documents to be distributed widely, though, you should not use private language identifiers, as recipients of your documents might not be able to handle them. Of course, if there is no standard value for the language you are using, you have no choice, but in this case you need to provide clear enough documentation that other people can at least understand what action you expect their XML applications to take on seeing your language identifier.

> **There may be any number of Subcode[38] segments: . . .**

The intent is that the subcodes add precision. For example, EN-UK-cockney might be a value, with subcodes UK and cockney indicating a gradually more specific dialect of the English language.

> **. . . if the first subcode segment exists and the Subcode consists of two letters, then it must be a country code from ISO 3166, *Codes for the representation of names of countries*. . . .**

Appendix A of the XML specification, Section 1 "Normative References" gives a publication date of 1997 for ISO 3166; country codes change fairly frequently as new countries obtain independence and old ones are subsumed or merge. If a country code you need to use is not listed in the 1997 version of ISO 3166, the correct thing to do is to check to see if it is registered with IANA (see below), and, if not, to use a private use code. Do not use values from newer versions of ISO 3166.

> **. . . If the first subcode consists of more than two letters, it must be a subcode for the language in question registered with ⌈IANA⌉, unless the Langcode[34] begins with the prefix "x-" or "X-".**

If the Langcode[34] began with an x or X, the interpretation of subcodes is clearly undefined.

> **It is customary to give the language code in lower case, and the country code (if any) in upper case. Note that these values, unlike [most] other names in XML documents, are case insensitive.**

Encoding names (EncName[81]) in an encoding declaration (EncodingDecl[80]) are also case-insensitive, for similar reasons: They are defined outside the scope of XML, and are defined to be case-insensitive.

For example:

```
<p xml:lang="en">The quick brown fox jumps over the lazy dog.</p>
<p xml:lang="en-GB">What colour is it?</p>
<p xml:lang="en-US">What color is it?</p>
<sp who="Faust" desc='leise' xml:lang="de">
  <l>Habe nun, ach! Philosophie,</l>
  <l>Juristerei, und Medizin</l>
  <l>und leider auch Theologie</l>
  <l>durchaus studiert mit hei§em BemŸh'n.</l>
</sp>
```

The intent declared with xml:lang is considered to apply to all attributes and content of the element where it is specified, unless overridden with an instance of xml:lang on another element within that content.

There is no way to have a single element with multiple attributes whose values are in different languages. If you need to do this, you will have to change the attributes into sub-elements. Thus

```
<duomo xml:lang="it" city="Florence" city.it="Firenze">
```

can be turned into:

```
<duomo xml:lang="it">
  <city xml:lang="en">Florence</city>
  </city>Firenze</city>
</duomo>
```

A simple declaration for xml:lang might take the form

```
xml:lang NMTOKEN #IMPLIED
```

but specific default values may also be given, if appropriate. In a collection of French poems for English students, with glosses and notes in English, the xml:lang attribute might be declared this way:

```
<!ATTLIST poem
    xml:lang NMTOKEN 'fr'
>
<!ATTLIST gloss
```

```
    xml:lang NMTOKEN 'en'
>
<!ATTLIST note
    xml:lang NMTOKEN 'en'
>
```

The attribute xml:space can be declared to be of type NMTOKEN because the minus sign (-) is allowed inside an XML Name[5]. The XML specification does not mandate that NMTOKEN be used: You could declare it as CDATA if you preferred.

CHAPTER 3

Logical Structures

Each XML ⌐document⌐ contains one or more ⌐elements⌐, the boundaries of which are either delimited by ⌐start-tags⌐ and ⌐end-tags⌐, or, for ⌐empty elements⌐, by an ⌐empty-element tag⌐.

There are two kinds of XML document: ones containing nothing but a single ⌐empty-element tag⌐, and others. A document containing only a single element with no content might look like this:

```
<?xml version="1.0">
<!DOCTYPE Artifact SYSTEM "artifact.dtd">
<Artifact name="Crown" owner="Jack"/>
```

A document with ⌐content⌐ might look like this:

```
<?xml version="1.0">
<!DOCTYPE Artifact SYSTEM "artifact.dtd">
<Artifact status="broken">
  <Owner>Jack</Owner>
  <Name>Crown</Name>
  <Description>A <emph>very</emph\>> shiny golden
crown</Description>
</Artifact>
```

> **Each element has a type, identified by name, sometimes called its ⸢generic identifier⸣ (⸢GI⸣), . . .**

In the two examples above, the first element has a ⸢generic identifier⸣ of *Artifact*. This generic identifier shows that the element in the example has an ⸢element type⸣ of Artifact.

> **. . . and may have a set of attribute specifications. Each attribute specification has a name and a value.**

The name="Crown" in the second example is an ⸢attribute specification⸣. The name is tricky: It's called an attribute specification because it's where you specify (i.e., supply, give, state) the actual value of the attribute. The ⸢attribute declaration⸣ (AttDef[53]) in the ⸢attribute-list declaration⸣ (AttListDecl[52]) determines which values are actually acceptable here; the attribute declaration is found in the ⸢document type declaration⸣.

```
[39] element ::= EmptyElemTag[44]                    [WFC: Element Type Match]
               | STag[40] content[43] Etag[42]        [VC: Element Valid]
```

> **This specification does not constrain the semantics, use, or (beyond syntax) names of the element types and attributes, except that names beginning with a match to (('X'|'x') ('M'|'m') ('L'|'l')) are reserved for standardization in this or future versions of this specification.**

The XML specification does not say what any particular element means. You might have a "list" element that contains a program listing, and someone else might have a "list" element that contains a sequence of numbered paragraphs, and yet another person might use a "list" element to describe how much a ship was leaning (listing) to one side when it was sighted in a storm.

The regular expression matches XML in any combination of upper and lower case (xml, XML, xMl, XmL, and so forth), so that you can't use elements with names starting with xml, such as XMLEPHANT or XML1.0 or XmListAddItem. The phrase "reserved for standardization" should be taken to mean that if you use such a name in your document, you do so at your own risk, since the name might in the future be given a special meaning. It also means that you should not expect to be able to use such names in applications you write. However, if your application should see such a name, it is not an error: It might be written to a more recent version of the specification that says XMLwobble elements (say) have a specific meaning.

Older software should read such newer elements without rejecting them and also without doing anything special to them.

> **Well-Formedness Constraint: Element Type Match**
> **The Name in an element's end–tag must match the element type in the start–tag.**

In other words, the following are all illegal:

```
<Boy> . . . </boy> (not an exact match)
<Boy> .... </Girl> (different name)
<B> <I>.... </B> ... </I>  (the </B> doesn't match the <I>)
```

> **Validity Constraint: Element Valid**
> **An element is ⌜valid⌝ if there is a declaration matching elementdecl[45] where the Name[5] matches the ⌜element type⌝, and one of the following holds: . . .**

An element can only be ⌜valid⌝ if it is of an ⌜element type⌝ that has been declared. This means that if you want your document to be valid in addition to being well-formed, you must declare every element that you use. The Name[5] must ⌜match⌝ the ⌜element type⌝ in the declaration exactly: As usual in XML, it is a ⌜case-sensitive⌝ match. Section 3.2, "Element Type Declarations," shows how to declare an element type.

> **1. The declaration matches EMPTY and the element has no content.**

The word "EMPTY" here is a keyword that can appear as an element ⌜content model⌝, contentspec[46], in which case the corresponding element has no content, and uses an empty-element tag (see EmptyElemTag[44] below).

> **2. The declaration matches children[47] and the sequence of ⌜child⌝ elements belongs to the language generated by the ⌜regular expression⌝ in the ⌜content model⌝, with optional ⌜white space⌝ (characters matching the ⌜nonterminal⌝ s[3]) between each pair of ⌜child⌝ elements.**

This item is really two rolled into one. The first item says that the declaration matches children[47]. This simply means that the ⌜content model⌝ given in the declaration must use the right syntax, and must only allow child elements and not text. An example might be a <Chapter> element, whose content might be a title followed by one or more paragraphs, with all the text being in the title and the paragraphs and not directly contained in the chapter itself:

```
<!ELEMENT Chapter
    (Title, P+)
>
```

The second half of the constraint talks about a sequence of child elements belonging to a language generated by the regular expression in the content model.

The language generated by a regular expression, in formal computer science, is the set of all strings that match that expression. For our `Chapter` example, the generated language would include a `Title` followed by a single `P`, a `Title` followed by two `P` elements, a `Title` followed by three `P` elements, and so on.

Our rather fearsome-looking constraint is therefore saying no more than that the elements directly contained in the element we're considering must match the content model given in the declaration for elements of that name.

The note about ⌜white space⌝ is to make clear that you can also put white space between elements even though other text isn't allowed there. Such white space may be thrown away by some ⌜XML processors⌝, since it is (by definition) not important. One should therefore not rely on white space between elements as having any meaning unless text (#PCDATA) is allowed there too, as in item 3:

3. The declaration matches Mixed[51] and the content consists of ⌜character data⌝ and ⌜child⌝ elements whose types match names in the ⌜content model⌝.

A `Mixed`[51] content model, also called ⌜mixed content⌝, contains an ⌜or group⌝ in which the first item is #PCDATA, and which uses the * operator:

```
<!ELEMENT P
    (#PCDATA|Emphasis|Footnote|Quote|PartNumber)*
>
```

Within a mixed content model, ⌜white space⌝ is significant; thus the following three examples are all different:

```
But <emph>dahling</emph>,
you <emph> know</emph>  <person>Bleachie</person> is coming for
tea!
```

```
But <emph>dahling</emph>,
you <emph>know</emph><person>Bleachie</person> is coming for
tea!
(note the missing space between the tags in this example)

But <emph>dahling</emph>,
   you <emph>know</emph>
<person>Bleachie</person> is coming for tea!
(extra spaces and a newline instead of a space)
```

4. The declaration matches ANY, and the types of any ⌜child⌝ elements have been declared.

It's sometimes tempting to use ANY for every element in a DTD, as it seems so much easier than working out precise content models. Programmers may consider this to be like going from a language like C, which has some strong typing support, to one in which the compiler makes no distinction between a pointer, an integer, and some random piece of memory you referenced by mistake.

One common use for ANY, though, is for versioning: Consider an element called Revision that you can put around anything you have changed to mark the start and end of changes; the element might have attributes such as Purpose, Author, Date, and so on. Since the Revision element can be used anywhere, it cannot have a fixed content model, but only one of ANY.

If your DTDs all use ANY a lot, you might want to ask yourself whether you would be better off using a ⌜schema⌝ instead, such as ⌜XML-Data⌝ or a ⌜DCD⌝. See the discussion at www.w3.org/XML for more information on this topic.

3.1 Start-Tags, End-Tags, and Empty-Element Tags

A ⌜tag⌝ is the markup that marks the start or end of each ⌜element⌝ in an XML document.

The beginning of every non-empty XML element is marked by a *start-tag*.

Empty elements don't use start-tags, but all other elements do. Every start-tag must be matched by an end-tag, as specified below.

Start-tag

```
[40] Stag        ::= '<' Name[5] (S Attribute[41])* S? '>'
                                          [WFC: Unique Att Spec]
[41]Attribute  ::= Name[5] Eq[25] AttValue[10]        [VC: Attribute Value Type]
                               [WFC: No External Entity References]
                                  [WFC: No < in Attribute Values]
```

Note the places where white space ($S^{[3]}$) is allowed; see the comments under ETag[42] below about this, and especially about the optional space before the final > character at the end of the tag.

The Name[5] in the start- and end-tags gives the element's type . . .

The start- and end-tags surround ⌜content⌝; together with the content, they represent an ⌜instance⌝ of an ⌜element⌝ of the given Name[5].

Note that the name of an element is sometimes known as its ⌜generic identifier⌝, or GI.

The Name[5]-AttValue[10] pairs are referred to as the attribute specifications of the element . . .

The actual Name[5]-AttValue[10] pairs in the element instance are called the ⌜attribute specification⌝, not to be confused with the ⌜attribute-list declaration⌝. The attribute-list declaration goes in the DTD, and says what ⌜attributes⌝ are allowed on elements of a given ⌜element type⌝, and may also constrain the values of those attributes. The attribute specification is the place where an actual element of a given element type specifies real actual values for the attributes.

The following is an example of an attribute-list declaration taken from a DTD:

```
<!ATTLIST Artifact
    Worth (Trinket|Moderate|Valuable|Priceless) #REQUIRED
>
```

Within an XML document, one might then see the following:

```
<Artifact Worth="Priceless">The Amulet of Yendor</Artifact>
```

In this example, Worth="Priceless" is an ⌜attribute specification⌝, contained within the start-tag <Artifact Worth="Priceless">.

... with the Name[5] in each pair referred to as the **attribute name** and the content of the AttValue[5] (the text between ' or " delimiters) as the **attribute value.**

In the example, `Worth` is an attribute name and `Priceless` is the corresponding attribute value.

Although this looks simple, there are some subtleties described under "Well-Formedness Constraint: No External Entity References" below.

Well-Formedness Constraint: Unique Att Spec
No attribute name may appear more than once in the same start-tag or empty-element tag.

You can't use an attribute twice in the same tag:

```
<eg wf="yes" wf="no">illegal, wf used twice</eg>
```

There are no restrictions against using the same attribute multiple times in different tags:

```
<eg wf="definitely">first, wf used only once here</eg>
<eg wf="yes">second, wf used only once per tag</eg>
```

Validity Constraint: Attribute Value Type
The attribute must have been declared; the value must be of the type declared for it. (For attribute types, see *3.3 Attribute-List Declarations.*)

In order for the document to be ⌜valid⌝, all attributes must have been declared in the DTD, using attribute list declarations (`AttlistDecl`[52]) for each ⌜element type⌝ that can have attributes. The declaration gives the name and the type of each attribute, and whether the attribute must be given or has a default value. On the actual element where the value is given, all attribute values that are supplied must match the type given in the declaration, and all attributes that are declared as being required must be present.

This isn't really saying anything complicated. In the `Artifact` example just described, the type of the attribute `Worth` was an `Enumerated-Type`[57], and the value, `Priceless`, matched one of the possible values in that enumeration, so that element was valid.

Well-Formedness Constraint: No External Entity References

Attribute values cannot contain direct or indirect entity references to external entities.

An attribute value can contain ⌈entity references⌉, but those entities can only be to general text entities, like this:

```
<!ENTITY LETTER_AE "Æ">
. . .
<death year="1005" person="&LETTER_AE;lfric"/>
(Archbishop Ælfric died in the year of Our Lord 1005)
```

It would be an error to refer to an image file or other ⌈external entity⌉ inside an attribute value in this way.

An indirect reference occurs when one entity has ⌈replacement text⌉ that refers to another entity; the following example results in exactly the same attribute value for person, and it would be an error if LETTER_AT were an ⌈external entity⌉.

```
<!ENTITY LETTER_AE "Æ">
<!ENTITY bish "&LETTER_AE;lfric">
. . .
<death year="1005" person="&bish;"/>
(Archbishop Ælfric died in the year of Our Lord 1005)
```

Well-Formedness Constraint: No < in Attribute Values
The replacement text of any entity referred to directly or indirectly in an attribute value (other than "<") must not contain a <.

The less-than sign (<) is prohibited in attribute values, even indirectly as a result of expanding entity references; given the entity declaration:

```
<!ENTITY Bad
    "your <smile> here"
>
```

the following attribute specification is not well-formed:

```
<Anything text="here is &Bad; for you!">
```

as it expands as follows:

```
<Anything text="here is your <smile> here for you!">
```

Since attributes can't contain <, every < that appears within an actual document (after the document type declaration at the start) represents the start of an ⌈element⌉, a ⌈processing instruction⌉, or a ⌈comment⌉.

This means, for example, that a perl programmer can write code such as:

```
$input =~ s@<kw( [^>]*)?>(.*?)</kw>@<I CLASS="kw">$2</I>@gi
```

to change every kw element to an I element without having to worry about the possibility of kw having an attribute containing a < sign, such as this:

```
<oops expr="jw<kw">
```

which the preceding perl expression would match incorrectly as a `<kw>` element!

The restriction on < not appearing even in the replacement text of entities used in attribute values means that if you expand all the entities in attribute values (as a validating XML processor will do) you don't have to worry about < characters, simplifying life for script writers and programmers.[1]

An example of a start-tag:

```
<termdef id="dt-dog" term="dog">
```

The end of every element that begins with a start-tag must by marked by an end-tag containing a name that echoes the element's type as given in the start-tag:

The only elements that don't begin with a start-tag are empty elements, defined in production `EmptyElemTag`[44] below and explained in the text following that production.

End-tag

```
[42] Etag ::= '</' Name[5] S[3] '/>'
```

The space (S[3]) here may be a surprise; it's common to see software (such as Jade) that inserts newlines there so as to prevent the lines in the XML file from becoming too long without affecting the content.

1. But see also the discussion of CDATA sections in Section 2.7 of the specification for a circumstance in which < and & can occur without being interpreted.

One way to deal with any difficulty that spaces and newlines inside tags cause to programs handling XML is to write a pre-processor that removes spaces there, and perhaps also removes spaces in start-tags (see STag[40]) for the same reason.

An example of an end-tag:

```
</termdef>
```

Note that the Name[5] inside the tag is ⌈case-sensitive⌉: You can't use <Simon> with </simon>, for example.

The text between the start-tag and the end-tag is called the element's content:

An end-tag cannot contain ⌈attributes⌉, and every end-tag must correspond to a start-tag with the same name: Elements with start- and end-tags are containers, and the tags mark the boundaries of the container. If you want to use a start-tag without an end-tag, you need an ⌈empty element⌉ instead (see below).

Content of Elements

```
[43] content ::= (element[39] | CharData[14] | Reference[67]
                 | CDSect[18] | PI[17] | Comment[15])*
```

The expansion for element[39] allows content[43], so that the content[43] production is (indirectly) recursive. It is because of this that the XML format is inherently recursive, and it is this recursion, the fact that you can have elements within elements, that gives XML much of its expressive power.

If an element is empty, it must be represented either by a start-tag immediately followed by an end-tag or by an empty-element tag.

It is very useful to distinguish between an element that *might* have content but happens not to, and an element that can never have any content. An example of the latter might be an element marking a possible hyphenation point between two syllables, perhaps with attributes giving the desirability of breaking the word there and the hyphenation character to use.

Note that *a start-tag immediately followed by an end-tag* means you can't put white space between the tags: if you did, the element would contain the space, and wouldn't be empty:

```
<nothing-here></nothing-here>  -- empty
<nothing-here>
</nothing-here> -- not empty, because of the newline
<nothing-here/> -- empty, see next production
```

If the element is declared as containing only other elements, the white space may be ignored if you are using a ⌜validating parser⌝, but it is not prudent to rely on this. An application using an XML parser is of course free to ignore such white space, or any other content it likes, so for some applications it may be perfectly acceptable to use a start-tag followed by a newline and some spaces, then an end-tag, but this is not generally true.

An *empty-element tag* takes a special form:

Tags for Empty Elements

```
[44] EmptyElemTag ::= '<' Name[5] (S[3] Attribute[41])* S[3]? '/>'
                                        [WFC: Unique Att Spec]
```

See the comments under ETag[42] about the white space (S[3]) here and how it affects programs and scripts.

Empty-element tags may be used for any element which has no content, whether or not it is declared using the keyword EMPTY. . . .

Even in a ⌜valid⌝ document, you can use an empty-element tag for any element that has no content:

```
<!ELEMENT GoodIdea
    (#PCDATA)*
>
. . .
<GoodIdea></GoodIdea>   (nothing here)
<GoodIdea/>             (nothing here either)
```

An element declared as EMPTY cannot use start- and end-tags:

```
<!ELEMENT Bobble
    EMPTY
>
. . .
<Bobble></Bobble>  illegal example
```

```
<Bobble/>          OK
```

An XML processor may or may not report back to the application the distinction between these two representations.

It is probably not a good idea to use empty-element tags just to save space in your files, as this makes the files slightly harder to process for very little benefit. It is probably safest to use the empty-element tags only for elements declared EMPTY.

> **. . . For ⌜interoperability⌝, the empty-element tag must be used, and can only be used, for elements which are declared EMPTY.**

The phrase ⌜for interoperability⌝ refers to the ability to use XML files with older SGML tools that have not been modified for use with XML. Although XML permits the use of the ⌜empty-element tag⌝ with any element that happens not to have content, SGML allows this only for elements that have been declared EMPTY. (Being declared EMPTY is the same as being declared using the keyword EMPTY in the ⌜element type declaration⌝; the XML specification uses both wordings interchangeably.)

Examples of empty elements:

```
<IMG align="left"
 src="http://www.w3.org/Icons/WWW/w3c_home" />

<br></br>

<br/>
```

3.2 Element Type Declarations

Every element that occurs in a valid document has an ⌜element type⌝; the type of an element is defined by an element type declaration, and the element is matched by a validating ⌜XML processor⌝ to the right type declaration by the element's name. An element thus has both a name, which appears in the tags, and a type, which is declared in the DTD.

In order for a document to be valid, every element type used in that document must have a corresponding declaration.

This section of the book is important for you if you are writing an XML parser, or if you need to know how to skip any declarations that occur at the start of a document. Otherwise, since a DTD is optional in XML, and all element type declarations must be contained in the DTD (including the DOC-TYPE prolog at the start of the document), this section is optional reading.

The ⌜element structure⌝ of an ⌜XML document⌝ may, for ⌜validation⌝ purposes, be constrained using element type and ⌜attribute-list⌝ declarations. . . .

There are a number of reasons why one might wish to do this. Software for people writing documents (XML ⌜authoring software⌝) may read these constraints and enforce them. For example, an editor might not let a user insert a chapter inside a figure caption, or might insist that every attribute of type IDREF have a corresponding attribute of type ID somewhere in the document.

Another reason to constrain a document might be for error checking, so that you can reject an unfinished or incorrect document without doing any further processing.

A third reason might be to simplify software that handles the XML documents: If there are fewer possible cases to handle, the software may well be easier to write. For example, you might not need to check to see whether an <integer> element contains any other elements, because your DTD could use a declaration for the integer element to forbid it.

Unfortunately, you cannot constrain *text* using a DTD, so there is no way to say that the integer element in our example can only contain digits and cannot contain letters or Kanji characters. Worse, anywhere text is allowed (as indicated by the XML keyword PCDATA, as we shall see), zero or more text characters are allowed, so you can't require that an element that is allowed to contain ⌜character data⌝ be non-empty.

If you need to go beyond the ⌜validation⌝ provided by the XML declarations defined by the XML specification, you should look at a ⌜schema⌝ format such as ⌜DCD⌝. The important thing to remember about XML's declarations is that they are part of the main specification, and are also SGML conformant, so that you will find a lot of software available that understands and handles them. And of course, if you are writing a validating XML parser, you need to understand them.

. . . An ⌜element type declaration⌝ constrains the element's ⌜content⌝.

Element type declarations do not have any effect on whether a document is ⌜well-formed⌝. They only make a difference if you are checking a document for validity, in which case every element used in that document must have a corresponding element type declaration.

Element type declarations often constrain which types can appear as children of the element. . . .

The word "often" is used here because an element type declaration that uses the keyword ANY can avoid constraining which types of element may appear as children of elements of that type.

. . . ⌐At user option⌐, an ⌐XML processor⌐ ⌐may⌐ issue a warning when a declaration mentions an element type for which no declaration is provided, but this is not an ⌐error⌐.

This is a little misleading, since XML is nowhere explicit about what in programming language design is called the scope and extent of declarations. This warning about an undeclared element being referenced should not be issued until all declarations have been read, in order to determine whether a declaration is provided somewhere. For example, no error should be produced for the following fragment, since all the elements are in fact declared:

```
<!ELEMENT CHAPTER
      (Title,P+)
>
<!ELEMENT Title
      (#PCDATA)
>
<!ELEMENT P
      (#PCDATA)
>
```

An element type declaration takes the form:

Element Type Declaration

```
[45]   elementdecl   ::=
               <!ELEMENT' S[3] Name[5]S[3] contentspec[46] S[3]? '>'
                                    [VC: Unique Element Type Declaration]

[46]   contentspec   ::= 'EMPTY' | 'ANY' | Mixed[51] | children[47]
```

where the Name[5] gives the element being declared.

Like most other XML keywords, ELEMENT must be in uppercase (the main exception is the string XML in the XMLDecl[23] at the start of an XML document or entity; this must be in lowercase).

```
<!ELEMENT P
    (#PCDATA)
>
```

One of the options within the definition of `contentspec`[46] is `Mixed`[51], which matches (`#PCDATA`).

Validity Constraint: Unique Element Type Declaration

No element type may be declared more than once.

Since element names are ⌜case-sensitive⌝, it is legal to define two or more element types whose names differ only by case, such as `happy`, `Happy`, and `HAPPY`.

It is also legal to have multiple ⌜attribute-list declarations⌝ for the same element type.

If you are combining several different DTDs into a single larger one and you find that some element type or other occurs in more than one DTD, you may be able to use ⌜namespaces⌝ to help, although at the time of writing this book, namespaces did not work well with DTDs.

Examples of element type declarations:

```
<!ELEMENT br EMPTY>
<!ELEMENT p (#PCDATA|emph)* >
<!ELEMENT %name.para; %content.para; >
<!ELEMENT container ANY>
```

The notation `%name.para;` is a parameter entity reference, and is explained in Chapter 4 of the XML Specification, "Physical Structures".

3.2.1 Element Content

An ⌜element type⌝ has element content when . . .

Note that this sentence is talking about an element type: that is, what it says applies to all XML elements of a given type, and not just to a particular instance of an element type that happens to occur in a document.

. . . when elements of that type must contain only child elements (no character data) . . .

The element declaration is what determines whether an element is permitted to contain character data. Like many of the constraints in this chapter, this distinction is only meaningful when you use a validating parser, since a non-validating parser is not required to read the declarations.

> **. . . optionally separated by white space characters (characters matching the nonterminal S[3]).**

There is in fact no way to specify in a DTD that white space is not allowed between the child elements. Instead, every element type that can contain child elements but not character data also permits white space between the child elements.

> **In this case [i.e., element content], the constraint includes a ⌐content model⌐, a simple grammar governing the allowed types of the child elements and the order in which they are allowed to appear.**

The ⌐content model⌐ of an ⌐element type⌐ defines a grammar for a "little language".

> **The grammar is built on content particles (cp[48]s), which consist of names, choice lists of content particles, or sequence lists of content particles: . . .**

In more conventional computer science terminology, a ⌐grammar⌐ defines a set of rules over a set of symbols known as an ⌐alphabet⌐. The less technical way of looking at this is that a content model says what can appear inside elements of a given ⌐element type⌐, and the way it does this is to provide a pattern or grammar which the ⌐content⌐ of elements of that type must ⌐match⌐.

The ⌐content particles⌐ are the names of the child elements to be allowed in content, and also various pieces of punctuation. The punctuation specifies whether those child elements must occur in some particular order (using the , operator) and how many of them must appear in an instance of that element type (using ?, *, or +) before the content model is considered to have been matched so that that element may be pronounced valid.

Element Content Models

```
[47] children ::= (choice[49] | seq[50]) ('?' | '*' | '+')?
```

```
[48] cp       ::=
              (Name[5] | choice[49] | seq[50]) ('?' | '*' | '+')?

[49] choice   ::=
              '(' S[3]? cp[48] ( S[3]? '|' S[3]? cp[48] )* S[3]? ')'
                                              [VC: Proper Group/PE Nesting]

[50] seq      ::=
              '(' S[3]? cp[48] ( S[3]? ',' S[3]? cp[48] )* S[3]? ')'
                                              [VC: Proper Group/PE Nesting]
```

where each Name[5] is the type of an element which may appear as a child. . . .

Production children[47] is one of four possibilities allowed by contentspec[46] for the ⌐content model⌐ of an ⌐element type⌐ in an ⌐element type declaration⌐. The contentspec[46] production could be expanded as follows:

```
contentspec-expanded ::= 'EMPTY' |
                         'ANY' |
                         Mixed[51] |
                         (choice[49] | seq[50]) ('?' | '*' | '+') ?
```

An element whose content model matches the children[47] rule is said to have ⌐element content⌐; an element whose content model matches ANY or Mixed[51] is said to have ⌐mixed content⌐.

Note that white space is not allowed before the ?, *, or +, so that the following would all be illegal:

```
Daniel *      (the space before the "*" not allowed)
(Daniel | Martha) ?  (the space before the "?" not allowed)
```

. . . Any content particle in a choice list may appear in the element content at the location where the choice list appears in the grammar; content particles occurring in a sequence list must each appear in the element content in the order given in the list. . . .

For example, consider the following declaration:

```
<!ELEMENT Insect
    (head, body, (leg|tentacle|wing)+, tail)
>
```

An instance of an element of type Insect must contain a head followed by a body, one or more elements whose types are given in the or group, and finally a tail.

> **... The optional character following a name or list governs whether the element or the content particles in the list may occur one or more (+), zero or more (*), or zero or one times (?). The absence of such an operator means that the element or content particle must appear exactly once.**

The following examples may clarify this.

If a content model for an element type `Insect` contains `tail`, an `Insect` element in a document must contain exactly one `tail` element at that point:

```
<!ELEMENT Insect
    (tail)
>
. . .
<Insect><tail/><Insect>
```

If the content model had said `leg+` instead, elements of type `Insect` would be permitted to contain any number of `leg` elements at that point, one after the other, as long as there was at least one. White space would automatically be permitted between those elements:

```
<!ELEMENT Insect
    (leg+)
>
. . .
<Insect><leg/> <leg/>    <leg/>
    <leg/><Insect>
```

A content model of `foot*` would allow zero or more `foot` elements, so that they could be omitted altogether; a content model of `ankle?` would allow either zero or exactly one element of type `ankle`.

In the same way, a content model of `(foot, ankle, leg)*` would mean that a valid instance could contain any number of those elements, but only if all three occurred in that order, one immediately following another:

```
<!ELEMENT Insect
    (foot, ankle, leg)*
>
. . .
<foot/><ankle/><leg/><foot/><ankle/><leg/>
```

If the elements were not empty, the tags would appear like this:

Chapter 3: Logical Structures   179

```
<foot></foot><ankle></ankle><leg></leg>
```

**. . . This syntax and meaning are identical to those used in the productions in
this specification.**

The XML specification itself uses this syntax for the production rules, with
+, *, and ? having the same meaning as in XML content model declarations.

**The content of an element ⌈matches⌉ a content model if and only if it is possible
to trace out a path through the content model, obeying the sequence, choice,
and repetition operators and matching each element in the content against an
element type in the content model.**

As an example, consider the following element type declaration:

```
<!ELEMENT Insect
    (tentacle*, head, body, (leg|tentacle|wing)+, tail)
>
```

Now let us match the following instance against this content model:

```
<Insect>
  <head/head>
  <body>There could be all sorts of things in here!</body>
  <leg><foot/></leg>
  <leg><foot/></leg>
  <leg><foot/></leg>
  <wing></wing>
  <leg><foot/></leg>
  <leg><foot/></leg>
  <wing></wing>
  <leg><foot/></leg>
  <tail></tail>
  <head/head>
</Insect>
```

We start by noting that the first element inside our Insect is a head; there
are no tentacles, so we skip over the tentacle* and move inexorably
onwards to match the head element against the head in the content
model. The content model requires exactly one element of type head at
this point, and, looking ahead, we see that this is what we have.

We move on to match body in the same way. Note that the content of the
body element itself is not relevant to us here. Presumably it has its own

declaration somewhere, with its own content model, and will be validated against that content model in turn.

After `body` in the content model we have `(leg|tentacle|wing)+`, which means we must have at least one element whose type is taken from that list of three alternatives, and that we can have more than one. In fact, this insect has six `legs` and two `wings`. Each `leg` contains a `foot`, but, as with `body`, that does not concern us. The `wings` and `legs` are muddled up together, but as long as we have a sequence of elements each of which is a `leg`, a `tentacle`, or a `wing`, we are still matching the same particle in the content model.

The next element we have in our instance is a `tail`, and since `tail` is not allowed inside the content particle we're using, we move ahead. Sure enough, the content model allows (and requires!) exactly one element of type `tail`.

But what is this? The content model has ended, and yet there is a `head` element still unaccounted for! We have an element left over. Although an element of type `head` is allowed elsewhere in this content model, it is not allowed at the end, and we sadly declare that we have a malformed and invalid `Insect`. The instance is perfectly well-formed, but not valid.

For compatibility, it is an error if an element in the document can match more than one occurrence of an element type in the content model. For more information, see Appendix E, Deterministic Content Models.

The simplest way to build a parser to recognize and validate XML content models is almost certainly to build a Non-deterministic Finite State Automaton (an NDFA) and then to reduce this to a Deterministic Finite State Automaton (a DFA); a standard reference on compiler theory such as Aho and Ullman's *Principles of Compiler Design* gives techniques for doing this. If you use these techniques, this restriction will not concern you, except that you need to write extra code to test for it.

It is entirely possible that a future version of XML will remove this so-called ambiguous content model restriction.

Validity Constraint: Proper Group/PE Nesting:

⌜Parameter-entity⌝ ⌜replacement text⌝ **must be properly nested with parenthesized groups. That is to say, if either of the opening or closing parentheses in a choice[49], seq[50], or Mixed[51] construct is contained in the replacement text for a parameter entity, both must be contained in the same replacement text.**

This is so that XML software that doesn't expand ⌐parameter entities⌐ (for example because it has not gone off and fetched an external ⌐document type declaration⌐ that contains the definition for a given ⌐parameter entity⌐, and thus does not have access to the replacement text) can still match the parentheses correctly.

A content model such as (em | %part.em;+) is also invalid, since the expansion of the parameter entity introduces a space, and the + cannot be preceded by a space.

> **. . . For interoperability, if a parameter-entity reference appears in a choice[49], seq[50], or Mixed[51] construct, its replacement text should not be empty, and neither the first nor last non-blank character of the replacement text should be a connector (| or ,).**

The term *should* is used here but not defined by the standard; a reasonable interpretation would be ⌐may⌐, which is to say that this restriction is not formally binding. It is probably best thought of as a guideline for those people who need to use older SGML software, since SGML has complex restrictions on the ways that parameter entities can start or end.

Examples of element-content models:

```
<!ELEMENT spec
    (front, body, back?)
>

<!ELEMENT div1
    (head, (p | list | note)*, div2*)
>

<!ELEMENT dictionary-body
    (%div.mix; | %dict.mix;)*
>
```

See Appendix G in Part 3 of this book for some ideas about how to lay out element type declarations so that they are readable and easy to change.

3.2.2 Mixed Content

> An ⌐element type⌐ has **mixed content** when elements of that type may contain ⌐character data⌐, optionally interspersed with ⌐child elements⌐. In this case, the

⌜types⌝ of the child elements may be constrained, but not their order or their number of occurrences: . . .

Mixed content, in other words, is anywhere you can put ⌜character data⌝, whether or not other elements are allowed there.

Mixed-content Declaration

```
[51] Mixed  ::= '(' S[3]? '#PCDATA' (S[3]? '|' S[3]? Name[5]))*
                S[3]? ')*'
              | '(' S[3]? '#PCDATA' S[3]?  ')''
```

                                        [VC: Proper Group/P Nesting]
                                        [VC: No Duplicate Types]

where the Name[5]s give the types of elements that may appear as children.

A space is not allowed in the sequence ')*', and the keyword #PCDATA must be in ⌜uppercase⌝, exactly as shown.

Validity Constraint: No Duplicate Types:

The same name must not appear more than once in a single mixed-content declaration.

This constraint means that a content model such as (#PCDATA|X|Y|X)* is not legal, since X appears more than once.

Examples of mixed content declarations:

```
<!ELEMENT P (#PCDATA|a|ul|b|i|em)*>
<!ELEMENT p
    (#PCDATA | %font; | %phrase; | %special; | %form;)*
>
<!ELEMENT b (#PCDATA)>
```

Note: A content model that contains character data (#PCDATA) anywhere in it cannot use sequencing, so that the following is not allowed:

```
<!ELEMENT illegal
    (title, (#PCDATA|P)*)                    (illegal!)
>
```

3.3 Attribute-List Declarations

⌐Attributes⌐ are used to associate name-value pairs with elements. ⌐Attribute specifications⌐ may appear only within ⌐start-tags⌐ and ⌐empty-element tags⌐; thus, the productions used to recognize them appear in Section 3.1, *Start-Tags, End-Tags, and Empty-Element Tags.* . . .

Consider the following XML element:

```
<Student name="Simon" age="14"/>
```

Here, two attributes are specified, name and age, with their respective values of Simon and 14.

. . . Attribute-list declarations may be used:

■   **To define the set of attributes pertaining to a given element type.**

In a valid XML document, an element's tag can only contain attribute specifications for attributes that have been declared for elements of that type.

■   **To establish type constraints for these attributes.**

An ⌐attribute-list declaration⌐ can say (for example) that a particular attribute must contain one of a short list of keywords; the phrase *type constraints* here means that the declaration places constraints on the possible values of the attribute.

■   **To provide default values for attributes.**

A validating XML parser can supply a default value for an attribute that's not specified in an instance. For example, if for elements of type Insect the color attribute is given a default value of shiny black in the ⌐attribute declaration⌐, an Insect tag that does not mention color will be treated by a validating parser just as if it had been <Insect color="shiny black"> instead of just <Insect>.

Attribute-list declarations specify the name, data type, and default value (if any) of each attribute associated with a given element type.

Default values only work reliably with a ⌐validating parser⌐; this makes them much less useful than it might at first appear.

Attribute-list Declaration

```
[52] AttlistDecl    ::= '<!ATTLIST' S[3] Name[5] AttDef[53]* S[3]? '>'

[53] AttDef         ::=S[3] Name[5] S[3] AttType[54] S[3] DefaultDecl[60]
```

The keyword `ATTLIST` must be in uppercase, as shown.

```
The Name[5] in the AttlistDecl[52] rule is the type of an element....
```

All XML names are ⌐case-sensitive⌐: the `Name`[5] in each `AttlistDecl`[52] must exactly match the name in the corresponding ⌐element type declaration⌐, and must also be the same as the name of the element using that attribute in the document instance.

... At user option, an XML processor may issue a warning if attributes are declared for an element type not itself declared, but this is not an error. The Name[5] in the AttDef[53] rule is the name of the attribute.

The intent of the specification is not to forbid the following example, although it is not made clear whether the example is in error:

```
<!ATTLIST Student
    name #CDATA #REQUIRED
    age #CDATA #REQUIRED
>
<!ELEMENT Student EMPTY>
```

Since no ⌐element type⌐ called `Student` has been declared when the attribute-list declaration is encountered, a validating parser could conceivably issue a warning. The XML specification says that this warning is ⌐at user option⌐, meaning that if the software generates such warnings, users must be able to say, don't give me these warnings any more, and continue to read the input. In fact, the example is not at all unusual, and perfectly legal. A validating XML processor should read all of the declarations and only produce warnings about missing declarations at the end of the DTD.

One would also hope that a ⌐validating parser⌐ would at least remember the ⌐attribute-list declaration⌐ so that when the ⌐element type declaration⌐ for `Student` is later encountered, the ⌐XML processor⌐ can relate the two declarations.

It would also be possible for a validating XML parser to wait until it had read all the declarations before issuing any warnings, in which case it would not be necessary to issue a warning for the above example.

> **When more than one AttlistDecl[52] is provided for a given element type, the contents of all those provided are merged. When more than one definition is provided for the same attribute of a given element type, the first declaration is binding and later declarations are ignored. . . .**

Given the following attribute list declarations:

```
<!ATTLIST Student
    name #CDATA #REQUIRED
    age #CDATA #IMPLIED
>
<!ATTLIST Student
>
<!ATTLIST Student
    telephone #CDATA #REQUIRED
    age #CDATA #REQUIRED
>
```

the following merged definition is equivalent:

```
<!ATTLIST Student
    name #CDATA #REQUIRED
    age #CDATA #IMPLIED
    telephone #CDATA #REQUIRED
>
```

The earlier definition for age was used, and the second, empty, declaration list has no effect. If no element type Student were declared, this document would be invalid.

> **. . . For interoperability, writers of DTDs ⌈may⌉ choose to provide at most one attribute-list declaration for a given element type, at most one attribute definition for a given attribute name, and at least one attribute definition in each attribute-list declaration. . . .**

Although, strictly speaking, SGML allows both multiple and empty ⌈attribute-list declarations⌉ as per XML, this is a recent change to SGML and older SGML tools may not support these features.

Empty attribute-list declarations are particularly useful when combined with ⌈parameter entity references⌉ and ⌈conditional sections⌉. If Student.attributes is empty in the following example, it is not an error:

```
<!ENTITY % Student.attributes
    " "
>
<!Element Student
    EMPTY
>
<!ATTLIST Student
    %Student.attributes;
>
```

Earlier entity declarations override later ones, and the ⌈external document type declaration subset⌉ is read *after* the internal subset. This means that if the above example is contained in a file called `Student.dtd`, the following document will result in the `Student` element having two attributes:

```
<!DOCTYPE Student SYSTEM "Student.dtd" [
  <!ENTITY % Student.attributes

        Name CDATA #REQUIRED
        Volume CDATA #IMPLIED

  >
]><Student Name="Andrew" Volume="40 litres"/>
```

A ⌈validating XML processor⌉ reads this document as follows.

First, it notes that the ⌈document type⌉ is `Student`, and that after reading the ⌈internal subset⌉ there is an ⌈external subset⌉ found in `Student.dtd`.

Second, the XML processor reads the internal subset and finds the declaration for the ⌈parameter entity⌉ `Student.attributes`; it then reaches the end of the internal subset.

Third, after reading the internal subset but before reading the rest of the input document, the XML processor reads the ⌈external subset⌉, in this case the file shown in the previous example. It sees the declaration for the ⌈parameter entity⌉ `Student.attributes` but, since that entity is already defined, it ignores the new declaration.

The XML processor then sees the ⌈element type declaration⌉ for the `Student` ⌈element type⌉, stores it, and proceeds.

It then encounters the ⌈attribute-list declaration⌉ for elements of type Student. This attribute-list declaration contains a ⌈parameter entity reference⌉; when this is expanded (using the earliest definition for `Student.attributes`) it looks like this:

```
<!ATTLIST Student
```

```
Name CDATA #REQUIRED
Volume CDATA #IMPLIED
```

>

The attribute-list declaration is processed in that form, and the XML processor then reaches the end of the external DTD subset and continues reading the input document, which consists of a single empty element of type Student, which specifies acceptable string values for both of the required attributes, so the resulting document is in fact valid.

Note: The extra blank lines come from the parameter entity definition; the expansion also adds an extra space at the start and end of the expanded text, but that can't be seen in this example.

The reader may find it helpful to review this example after reading Section 3.4 below, "Conditional Sections," and consider the case where one or another attribute-list definition is included inside a conditional section.

> **. . . For interoperability, an XML processor may at user option issue a warning when more than one attribute-list declaration is provided for a given element type, or more than one attribute definition is provided for a given attribute, but this is not an error.**

Programmers familiar with the Unix *lint* command will understand the motivation for this suggestion! The idea is to help people find mistakes in large document type definitions, even where the mistakes are not actually errors. Giving more than one attribute-list declaration for the same element may very easily be done by mistake, and since the resulting document is quite likely to be valid but erroneous, this warning could be very helpful. Users must of course be able to disable any such warnings (⌈at user option⌉), whether they are being issued by a batch tool or by an interactive application.

3.3.1 Attribute Types

> **XML attribute types are of three kinds: a string type, a set of tokenized types, and enumerated types. The string type may take any literal string as a value; the tokenized types have varying lexical and semantic constraints, as noted: . . .**

In fact, there are a number of restrictions on the possible value of a string-typed attribute, as described in our comments on Section 3.3.3, "Attribute-Value Normalization."

Attribute Types

```
[54] AttType ::= StringType[55] | TokenizedType[56]
                 | EnumeratedType[57]


[55] StringType ::= 'CDATA'


[56] TokenizedType ::= 'ID':                          [VC: ID]
                                       [VC: One ID per Element Type]
                                         [VC: ID Attribute Default]
                    | 'IDREF'                          [VC: IDREF]
                    | 'IDREFS                          [VC: IDREF]
                    | 'ENTITY'                    [VC: Entity Name]
                    | 'ENTITIES'                  [VC: Entity Name]
                    | 'NMTOKEN'                    [VC: Name Token]
                    | 'NMTOKENS'                   [VC: Name Token]
```

Originally, SGML allowed all these different attribute types because it seemed like little extra effort to implement them. For most purposes, the only useful tokenized types are ID, IDREF, and ENTITY. If you find yourself using the others in documents, you will probably quickly find yourself needing others too, but the list is not extensible. See Part 3, Appendix F of this book, "Schema or DTD?" for another approach.

Validity Constraint: ID

Values of type ID must match the Name[5] production. A name must not appear more than once in an XML document as a value of this type; i.e., ID values must uniquely identify the elements which bear them.

Like any other Name[5], an ID is case-sensitive. Attributes of type ID are often used as destinations for cross-references or hypertext links, or, when combined with IDREF attributes (q.v.), to link a footnote with a marker, a database field with its schema definition, or any other form of link within a document.

If you are constructing an XML document by pasting together fragments, perhaps in a python script or a Java program, you must be careful to avoid duplicating ID-valued attributes. One way to do this might be to use different ⌐namespaces¬ for the ID values in the individual fragments.

Validity Constraint: One ID Per Element Type

No element type may have more than one ID attribute specified.

This means that you can't have a declaration like this:

```
<!ATTLIST Student
    ID ID #IMPLIED
    StudentID ID #REQUIRED
    Username ID #REQUIRED
>
```

Instead, you must make all but one of the attributes be of type CDATA or NAME.

Validity Constraint: ID Attribute Default

An ID attribute must have a declared default of #IMPLIED or #REQUIRED.

This means you can't give a constant string as a default, as in:

```
<!ATTLIST Student
    Username ID "Guest"     (illegal example)
>
```

If you could use such a declaration, and you had two elements of type Student in your document, and neither overrode the default value for Username, you would have an invalid document, because the ID value of Guest would have been duplicated:

```
<Student/>  <!-- ID defaulted to "Guest (illegal) *-->
<Student/>  <!-- ID defaulted again (illegal) *-->
```

For most applications, such as our example student whose login code will be Guest unless another is assigned, the best approach is to use NAME or CDATA rather than ID:

```
<!ATTLIST Student
    Username NAME "Guest"
>
```

Validity Constraint: IDREF

Values of type IDREF must match the Name[5] production, and values of type IDREFS must match Names[6]; each Name[5] must match the value of an ID

attribute on some element in the XML document; i.e., IDREF values must match
the value of some ID attribute.

The idea is that if you have a type of element declared as having an
attribute of type ID, you can use attributes of type IDREF or IDREFS to
refer to instances of that element type from elsewhere in the document:

```
<!ATTLIST StudentResidence
    ID ID #REQUIRED
>
<!ATTLIST Student
    CampusAddress IDREF #IMPLIED
>
. . .
<StudentResidence ID="SR401">Whitefields 7</StudentResidence>
<Student CampusAddress="SR401">Liam Quin</Student>
<Student CampusAddresss="SR401">James Bloggs</Student>
<Student>Erin Watts</Student>  <!--* lives off-campus *-->
```

In the example, two students (Liam and James) share an address at
Whitefields 7, as indicated by the value of the CampusAddress attribute
matching the value of the ID attribute of the StudentResidence element.

Validity Constraint: Entity Name

**Values of type ENTITY must match the Name[5] production, values of type
ENTITIES must match Names[6]; each Name[5] must match the name of an
unparsed entity declared in the DTD.**

The most common use for an attribute of type ENTITY is to refer to an
external file such as an image, sound, or video:

```
<!ENTITY syPic SYSTEM "simon.gif" NDATA GIF>
. . .
<Student picture="syPic">Simon</Student>
```

The SGML model that XML has inherited is that each external ⌐unparsed
entity⌐ has an associated NOTATION (called GIF in this example), so that
the document processor knows what to expect. This is quite different from
the World Wide Web model , where an agent uses HTTP (the ⌐HyperText
Transfer Protocol⌐) to request a resource, optionally including with the
request a list of preferred formats such as GIF, JPEG, or PNG. The remote
server then replies with the name of the format as well as the data. In the

Web model, the software has to accept whatever it receives, whether it's an HTML text or a JPEG image.

These two models seem very much at odds with each other: one in which the document specifies the format of a (possibly remote) external resource, and one in which the format is determined by asking the remote server responsible for managing that resource.

Practical compromises for XML include using the XML notation as a hint, or having a notation with a name such as WWW or HTTP that tells your software to use the HTTP rules for this resource. See also NOTATION-valued attributes described in production NotationType[58].

There is little practical advantage in ENTITY-valued attributes over CDATA. One advantage is that you can save typing:

```
<!ENTITY % serv "www.groveware.com">
<!ENTITY logoURL "http://%serv;/images/logo.gif">
<!ENTITY logo SYSTEM "http://%serv;/images/logo.gif NDATA GIF>
. . .
<Picture src="&logoURL;">Using CDATA</Picture>
<Image src="logo">Using an ENTITY saves typing</Image>
```

In either case, the definition of serv means that if all your images move to a different server, you only need to update a single line in your XML DTD. If you are using a validating parser, you could place the definition of serv in a single XML file that was included by every document, using a parameter entity as shown in the example at the end of Section 4.1, "Character and Entity References."

Validity Constraint: Name Token

Values of type NMTOKEN must match the Nmtoken[7] production; values of type NMTOKENS must match Nmtokens[8].

Attributes of type NMTOKEN or NMTOKENS may be useful if you happen to need strings that match those naming rules; they are also useful if you want to have multiple ID-valued attributes on the same element and can't, as you can instead use NMTOKEN. Unlike ID, IDREF, and IDREFS, attributes of types NMTOKEN and NMTOKENS do not have any predefined meaning in XML, and are not often used.

Several types of attribute that one might expect, such as INTEGER, are not available; see Part 3, Appendix F of this book, "Schema or DTD?" for possible approaches to handle numbers, regular expressions, and other types.

Enumerated attributes can take one of a list of values provided in the declaration. There are two kinds of enumerated types:

Enumerated Attribute Types

```
[57]  EnumeratedType   ::= NotationType[58] | Enumeration[59]

[58]   NotationType    ::= 'NOTATION' S[3] '(' S[3]? Name[5]
                              (S[3]? '|' S[3]? Name[5])* S[3]? ')'
                                              [VC: Notation Attributes]

[59]    Enumeration    ::=   '(' S[3]? Nmtoken[7]
                              (S[3]? '|' S[3]? Nmtoken[7])* S[3]? ')'
                                              [VC: Enumeration]
```

A NOTATION attribute identifies a notation, declared in the DTD with associated system and/or public identifiers, to be used in interpreting the element to which the attribute is attached.

Notation declarations are covered in production `NotationDecl`[82] in Section 4.7, "Notation Declarations."

See also the notes on `ENTITY`-valued attributes above.

The idea of a `NOTATION` attribute is to identify the format either of the ⌐content⌐ of an element to which it is attached or of an external ⌐unparsed entity⌐ specified as the value of an `ENTITY`-valued attribute on that element.

An example might be a ⌐MIME⌐ ⌐Base64⌐ encoding of a binary object:

```
<!ELEMENT blob
    (#PCDATA)
>
<!NOTATION base64 SYSTEM "mimedecode">
<!NOTATION uuencode SYSTEM "uudecode">
<!NOTATION raw SYSTEM "/bin/cat">
<!ATTLIST blob
    content-encoding NOTATION (base64|uuencode|raw) #REQUIRED
>


. . .
<blob content-encoding="base64">
. . . MIME Base64-encoded data goes here,
. . . with & and < escaped using &amp; and &lt;
</blob>
```

Neither `blob` nor `content-encoding` are words that are built into

XML, of course. This means that you would have to decide how your application would use these values yourself. See Section 4.7 in the following chapter, "Notation Declarations," for more information about NOTATION, and see Chapter 1 in Part 1 of this book for an introduction to unparsed entities and notations. For linking to external objects, see the ⌜XLink⌝ specification available from the XML Web page at www.w3.org/XML and also on the Web page for this book.

Validity Constraint: Notation Attributes

Values of this type must match one of the notation names included in the declaration; all notation names in the declaration must be declared.

An example of a notation attribute might be:

```
<!ATTLIST Insect
    pictureType NOTATION (GIF|JPEG|PNG|EPSI|TIFF) #REQUIRED
>
```

There must be a separate ⌜notation declaration⌝ in the DTD for each of the notation names GIF, JPEG, and so on:

```
<!NOTATION GIF SYSTEM "">
<!NOTATION JPEG SYSTEM "convert JPEG:- GIF:-">
<!NOTATION EPSI SYSTEM "gs -dump -device GIF -">
```

The significance of the SYSTEM identifiers in these declarations is discussed in Section 4.7 of the following chapter.

Validity Constraint: Enumeration

Values of this type must match one of the Nmtoken[7] tokens in the declaration.

This is probably the most commonly used attribute type after CDATA (a string). An example from North American higher education:

```
<!ATTLIST Student
    Year (Freshman|Sophomore|Junior|Senior|PostGraduate)
#REQUIRED
>
```

As with all XML names, the values are case-sensitive: An element instance in the document must use one of these values exactly as given in the DTD.

For interoperability, the same Nmtoken[7] should not occur more than once in the enumerated attribute types of a single element type.

This is a restriction for the benefit of old SGML software predating the 1997 WebSGML update to that standard. It forbids constructs like this:

```
<!ATTLIST Student
    PaidInAdvance (Yes|No) #REQUIRED
    MeetsLanguageRequirements (Yes|No) "No"
    WearsShoes (Usually|Sometimes) "Sometimes"
    Behaves (Always|Usually|Never) "Never"
>
```

Here, Yes and No occur twice, as does Usually. This is not an error in XML, but may cause problems in some older SGML software, because until the WebSGML update to SGML in 1997 it was illegal to allow duplicate attribute values like this in SGML documents.

3.3.2 Attribute Defaults

An ⌜attribute declaration⌝ provides information on whether the attribute's presence is required, and if not, how an XML processor should react if a declared attribute is absent in a document.

The attribute declaration affects all ⌜validating XML processors⌝; it may or may not affect a ⌜non-validating XML processor⌝, and for this reason attribute defaults should be used with care. The defaults would be ignored by a non-validating XML processor if they occurred in an ⌜external parsed entity⌝, or if an ⌜external parameter entity⌝ was referenced in the ⌜internal document type definition subset⌝ before the attribute-list declaration.

Attribute Defaults

```
[60] DefaultDecl    ::= '#REQUIRED' | '#IMPLIED'
                      | (('#FIXED' S[3])? AttValue[10])
                                                    [VC: Required Attribute]
                                                    [VC: Attribute Default Legal]
                                                    [WFC: No < in Attribute Values]
                                                    [VC: Fixed Attribute Default]
```

In an attribute declaration, #REQUIRED means that the attribute must always be provided, ...

That is, if an element type is declared as having a #REQUIRED attribute, that attribute must be given an explicit value in every instance of that element type.

Since only a validating parser can enforce this, #REQUIRED attributes are the same as #IMPLIED attributes (see below) for a non-validating XML processor. The presence of #REQUIRED in a DTD may be useful for documentation purposes, however, as it clearly expresses the DTD writer's intention that the attribute always be supplied.

... #IMPLIED [means] that no default value is provided. ...

The idea is that the attribute's value is implicit, so that the XML processor will infer it automatically: If the attribute is not given a value in some particular instance of the element, the software will usually treat it as if the attribute were not present.

The following example illustrates the difference between an implied attribute value and a default attribute value:

```
<!ATTLIST Chapter
    ChapterNumber CDATA #IMPLIED
    IncludeInOnlineEdition (yes|no) "yes"
>
```

In this example, the chapter number will presumably be supplied automatically by the formatting software, so that the chapters are numbered sequentially starting at Chapter One in the body of a book, and perhaps marked as Appendix I and so forth in the back of the book. Before the book is finished, though, it might be convenient to print a draft without the as-yet unwritten Chapter Three. In this case, one would set the Chapter Number attribute on Chapter Four to 4, so that the formatter might be able to deduce that Chapter Three was not present. If the ChapterNumber attribute is not present, the value, in other words, is supplied by the XML processor and may be an application-specific value or may vary from instance to instance, as with chapter numbers that are normally different for each chapter.

If on the other hand the IncludeInOnlineEdition attribute is not specified on a particular instance of a Chapter element, a validating XML processor will deduce that its value is the declared default of yes.

... If the declaration is neither #REQUIRED nor #IMPLIED, then the AttValue[10] value contains the declared default value; ...

A validating XML parser will supply the default value of the attribute to the application whenever an instance of that element type does not specify a value for it:

```
<!ATTLIST Insect
    Style (creepy|crawly|buzzy|zoomy) #REQUIRED
    Color CDATA "Shiny black"
    WhenSquashed CDATA #IMPLIED
>
. . .
<Insect Style="creepy">
  This one is shiny black (default) and unsquashed
</Insect>
<Insect Style="buzzy" Color="black and yellow"
WhenSquashed="today">
  This one gives all values explicitly
</Insect>
<Insect Style="crawly" WhenSquashed="last Tuesday">
  A shiny black insect that got squashed last Tuesday.
</Insect>
```

. . . The #FIXED keyword states that the attribute must always have the default value. . . .

One use for this is to check that the right version of a DTD is being used:

```
<!ATTLIST Document
    DTDversion #FIXED "1.2"
>
. . .
<Document DTDversion="1.2">
  It would be an error if the DTDversion attribute was
  given the value 1.3 here...
</Document>
```

Another use of `#FIXED` attributes is to associate extra information with all elements of a given type; This technique is known as using an Architectural Form, and can be seen on the Web site accompanying this book (www.wiley.com/compbooks/graham-quin).

. . . If a default value is declared, when an XML processor encounters an omitted attribute, it is to behave as though the attribute were present with the declared default value.

This sounds pretty obvious, but note that it means that a parser API (for example at the C++ or Java level) is not required to distinguish between the case that the attribute was omitted and the case that it was present but with the default attribute. If you are writing software that reads an XML document, processes it in some way, and then writes it out again, you may find that all default attributes (including #FIXED ones) become explicitly supplied when you write out the document. Default and #FIXED values are most useful when XML documents are used only in conjunction with validating XML processors.

Validity Constraint: Required Attribute

If the default declaration is the keyword #REQUIRED, then the attribute must be specified for all elements of the type in the attribute-list declaration.

That is, every occurrence of an element with a #REQUIRED attribute must give a value for that attribute. In the following example, every Student element must supply a value for the BarefootHeightInInches attribute:

```
<!ATTLIST Student
    BarefootHeightInInches CDATA #REQUIRED
>
. . .
<Student/>  <!-- illegal, BarefootHeightInInches not given -->
<Student BarefootHeightInInches="71.5" />
```

Validity Constraint: Attribute Default Legal

The declared default value must meet the lexical constraints of the declared attribute type.

In other words, the default value for an attribute must be a legal value for that attribute!

Validity Constraint: Fixed Attribute Default

If an attribute has a default value declared with the #FIXED keyword, instances of that attribute must match the default value.

If an element has a #FIXED attribute, and that attribute is given a value in an instance, then the value specified in the instance must be exactly the same as the default value given in the attribute declaration.

Examples of attribute-list declarations:

```
<!ATTLIST termdef
    id ID #REQUIRED
    name CDATA #IMPLIED
>
<!ATTLIST list
    type (bullets|ordered|glossary) "ordered"
>

<!ATTLIST form
    method CDATA #FIXED "POST"
>
```

3.3.3 Attribute-Value Normalization

Before the value of an attribute is passed to the application or checked for ⌐validity⌐, the ⌐XML processor⌐ must ⌐normalize⌐ it as follows: . . .

The underlying assumption of the entire XML specification is that a program (the application) is using an ⌐XML processor⌐, or ⌐parser⌐, to read an ⌐XML document⌐. The XML processor usually hands back the data to the application as it reads it, one piece at a time, often using an event-based processing model such as ⌐SAX⌐. Other XML processors (for example using the ⌐Document Object Model⌐, DOM), may attempt to read the entire document into memory before passing any of it back to the application. In either case, the XML processor will change the attribute value according to the rules that follow, and the original attribute value is not accessible to the application. Some XML parsers, such as that written by James Clark (see www.jclark.com/) and used in recent versions of the perl programming language (www.perl.org/), have extensions that allow the application to retrieve both the original value from the instance and the normalized value at the same time.

■ **a character reference is processed by appending the referenced character to the attribute value**

This is actually incorrect. As written, an attribute of the form x="Example" would turn into x="Examplea", since character 97 in ISO/IEC 10646 (Unicode) is a Latin small letter a.

In fact, what is intended is that the character reference is *replaced* by its value, turning x="Example" into x="Example" instead.

At the time of writing, this was not mentioned in the official errata at www.w3.org/XML/xml-19980210-errata.

- ■ **an entity reference is processed by recursively processing the replacement text of the entity**

By "recursively processing" is meant applying these normalization rules not just for the attribute value that occurred in the instance, but also for the replacement text of each ⌈internal general entity⌉ referenced therein.

Recall also that references to external and unparsed entities are not allowed inside attribute values, so that only internal general text entities may occur. Consider the following example:

```
<!ENTITY server "www.groveware.com">
. . .
<Link href="http://&server;/index.html">
```

Here, the value of the href attribute is normalized.

Since the processing is done recursively, if the replacement text of &server; had contained an ⌈entity reference⌉, it too would have been expanded, so that the following example yields exactly the same attribute value:

```
<!ENTITY protocol "http">
<!ENTITY server "&protocol;://www.groveware.com">
. . .
<Link href="&server;/index.html">
```

- ■ **a whitespace character (#x20, #xD, #xA, #x9) is processed by appending #x20 to the normalized value, except that only a single #x20 is appended for a "#xD#xA" sequence that is part of an external parsed entity or the literal entity value of an internal parsed entity**

A single space, line feed, carriage return (CR), or line feed (LF) is replaced by a space, but the sequence CR-LF is replaced by a single space. Multiple line feeds or spaces in a row are replaced by corresponding multiple spaces in the normalized attribute value: White space is not collapsed.

Note that despite what is said here, an external parsed entity cannot be referenced from within an attribute value (see Section 4.4 in the next chapter). This appears to be a minor error in the specification.

- other characters are processed by appending them to the normalized value.

Other characters are thus passed back to the application unchanged. See Chapter 1 of Part 1 of this book.

If the declared value is not CDATA, then the XML processor must further process the normalized attribute value by discarding any leading and trailing space (#x20) characters, and by replacing sequences of space (#x20) characters by a single space (#x20) character.

If the declared value *is* of type CDATA, all the spaces inside it are significant.

If the declared value is not of type CDATA, it is an enumerated type, a tokenized type such as an IDREF, or a notation type. Spaces inside the value (other than at the start or end) can only occur with tokenized types ENTITIES, IDREFS, or NMTOKENS, and are compressed into a single space.

All attributes for which no declaration has been read should be treated by a non-validating parser as if declared CDATA.

This means that if your document may be read by both validating and non-validating parsers, you should not put extra spaces into attribute values. Consider the following example:

```
<!ATTLIST XRef
    TO IDREF #REQUIRED
>
<!ATTLIST Artifact
    ID ID #REQUIRED
>
. . .
<Artifact ID="Crown" value="Priceless">The Golden
Crown</Artifact>
. . .
Jack fell down and broke his <XRef TO="Crown">Golden
Crown</XRef>
```

This will fail with a non-validating XML processor, as the application will see the string with the space before and after Crown, rather than without it as with a validating XML processor.

3.4 Conditional Sections

Conditional sections are portions of the document type declaration ⌐external subset⌐ which are included in, or excluded from, the ⌐logical structure⌐ of the ⌐DTD⌐ based on the keyword which governs them.

C and C++ programmers will recognize conditional sections as being a little like `#ifdef` albeit without any equivalents to `#else` or `#if (boolean-expression)`.

You can use ⌐conditional sections⌐ to declare elements, attributes, or entities differently depending on the value of a ⌐parameter entity⌐, as will be seen in the example at the end of this section.

The arcane syntax of conditional sections is unfortunate, but was chosen to make them compatible with the slightly more powerful SGML Marked Section feature.

Conditional Section

```
[61]    conditionalSect     ::= includeSect[62] | ignoreSect[63]
[62]    includeSect         ::=
        '<![' S[3]? 'INCLUDE' S[3]? '[' extSubsetDecl[31] ']]>'
[63]    ignoreSect          ::=
        '<![' S[3]? 'IGNORE' S[3]? '[' ignoreSectContents[64]* ']]>'
[64]    ignoreSectContents  ::=
        Ignore[65] (<![' ignoreSectContents[64] ']]>' Ignore)*
[65]    Ignore              ::= Char* - (Char* (<![' | ']]>') Char*)
```

This is really a *tour de force* in regular expression writing!

What it is saying (or trying to say) is that there are two kinds of conditional section: included and ignored. In either case, the format is <![followed by either IGNORE or INCLUDE as appropriate, followed by a [, then the contents, and then a closing]]>.

Productions `ignoreSectContents`[64] and `Ignore`[65] between them are saying that the contents of an ignored marked section can include other marked sections (which are all ignored in turn), and that any marked section delimiters inside an ignored marked section have to be properly paired.

Like the internal and external DTD subsets, a ⌐conditional section⌐ ⌐may⌐ contain one or more complete declarations, comments, ⌐processing instructions⌐, or nested conditional sections, intermingled with ⌐white space⌐.

Conditional sections can only occur in the ⌐external DTD subset⌐, including external parsed entities referenced from the internal or external subsets. The things that the conditional sections may contain are exactly those things that are legal at the point where the conditional section occurs. The important point here is that the enclosed declarations must be *complete*; in the following example, the conditional section does not surround a complete declaration, and is thus illegal:

```
<!ELEMENT Paragraph
    (#PCDATA|Emphasis
    <![IGNORE[
        |Author|Playwright                illegal example
    ]]>
    )*
>
```

If the keyword of the conditional section is INCLUDE, then the contents of the conditional section are part of the DTD. . . .

This means that markup included as a result of an included conditional section must result in a valid DTD. The following example, although legal according to the productions, is disallowed by this rule:

```
<!ELEMENT Paragraph
    <![INCLUDE[
        <!ELEMENT P (#PCDATA)>            (illegal example)
    ]]>
    (#PCDATA)
>
```

This is illegal because once the contents of the conditional section become part of the DTD, the example reads like this:

```
<!ELEMENT Paragraph
        <!ELEMENT P (#PCDATA)>            (illegal example)
    (#PCDATA)
>
```

This is not valid, as the syntax for element type declarations doesn't allow them to nest!

. . . If the keyword of the conditional section is IGNORE, then the contents of the conditional section are not logically part of the DTD. . . .

This means that you can use ignored conditional sections to disable part of a DTD. The examples below may help to clarify this.

... Note that for reliable parsing, the contents of even ignored conditional sections must be read in order to detect nested conditional sections and ensure that the end of the outermost (ignored) conditional section is properly detected. ...

It is only necessary for the XML processor to scan the contents of an ignored conditional section for the start and end delimiters <![and]]>; there is no need to ensure that the contents of the conditional section would be valid, or even syntactically correct, if the conditional section markers were removed.

Note that it is considered poor practice to use conditional sections as a kind of comment markup! It is better to use the XML comment form, as human readers will be more easily able to recognize this:

```
<!--* Make your comments like this, with a clear
    * row of asterisks lining up down the left hand side,
    * and they will stand out very clearly indeed.
    *-->
```

... If a conditional section with a keyword of INCLUDE occurs within a larger conditional section with a keyword of IGNORE, both the outer and the inner conditional sections are ignored.

This is so you can disable a large section of a DTD by enclosing it in an ignored conditional section, with no need to worry about whether there were conditional sections inside it.

If the keyword of the conditional section is a parameter-entity reference, the parameter entity must be replaced by its content before the processor decides whether to include or ignore the conditional section.

This is really what makes conditional sections useful in practice. An earlier definition of a ⌐parameter entity⌐ overrides any later definition, as specified in Section 4.2, "Entity Declarations," so that in the following example, Poetry is included in the definition of the TextBlocks element type:

```
<!ENTITY % UsePoetry 'INCLUDE'>
<![[%UsePoetry[[
```

```
    <!ENTITY % TextBlocks
        "(Paragraph|Note|Table|Poem)*"
    >
]]>
<!ENTITY % TextBlocks
        "(Paragraph|Note|Table)* "
>
```

An example:

```
<!ENTITY % draft 'INCLUDE' >
<!ENTITY % final 'IGNORE' >

<![%draft;[
    <!ELEMENT book
        (comments*, title, body, supplements?)
    >
]]>
<![%final;[
    <!ELEMENT book
        (title, body, supplements?)
    >
]]>
```

Physical Structures

An XML document may consist of one or many storage units. These are called entities; . . .

XML, like its parent standard ⌐SGML⌐, goes a long way to avoid talking about files directly. This is because an XML ⌐entity⌐ might be a file, but might also be a stream of data fetched over a network, or it might be data held entirely in memory.

The use of the term "entity" for a file is very confusing, because "entity" is also used for several other things, as we shall see. When reading this chapter, you should try to keep this in mind, and whenever the term "entity" appears, remember that the term can have several meanings. In this book, and especially in this chapter, we have tried to use qualified terms such as ⌐external entity⌐ or ⌐unparsed entity⌐ or ⌐document entity⌐, to try and make the meaning clearer.

Refer to Part 1 of this book for a discussion of the different kinds of entities in XML and how they are used.

. . . they all have content and are all (except for the ⌐document entity⌐, see below, and the ⌐external DTD subset⌐) identified by name. . . .

The ⌐content⌐ of an entity is simply whatever it contains.

> **... Each ⌜XML document⌝ has one ⌜entity⌝ called the ⌜document entity⌝, which serves as the starting point for the XML processor and may contain the whole document.**

If an XML document is contained in a single file, that is, in a single entity, then that entity is the document entity, and it obviously must contain the whole file, as there is only one file. If the document includes one or more other entities, then the document entity is the main part of the document but not all of it, as there are other parts too.

> **Entities may be either parsed or unparsed. A parsed entity's contents are referred to as its ⌜replacement text⌝; this text is considered an integral part of the document.**

A ⌜parsed entity⌝ is an ⌜external entity⌝ that can be included in an XML document.

The term ⌜replacement text⌝ is also used to describe the content of internal parsed entities; internal parsed entities are actually more properly called ⌜general entities⌝ and are described later in this section.

> **An unparsed entity is a resource whose contents may or may not be text, and if text, may not be XML. ...**

The most important distinction between a ⌜parsed entity⌝ and an ⌜unparsed entity⌝ is nothing to do with the format of the file, but rather, whether the entity is *included* in the document or whether it is simply *referred to* from the document.

The same external resource could be used both as a parsed entity and as an unparsed entity in the same document. The only constraint is that a parsed entity is read by the validating XML processor as part of its input, and thus must be well-formed and valid, whereas an unparsed entity is passed directly back to the application. The XML processor does not look inside an unparsed entity to try and read or interpret its contents, so although the contents might happen to be valid XML, they don't need to be anything of the sort, and could as easily be a binary image file or a letter to your grandmother.

A parsed entity is included as part of a larger XML document, and therefore it is not valid in itself, but merely well-formed. What must be valid is the overall document, with the replacement text of all parsed entities inserted in place of the references to them.

Note: Since the replacement text of the parsed entity is included wherever a reference to that entity occurs, ID attributes must be unique across the entire resulting document. You can't have two ID-valued attributes using the same ID value even if the elements bearing those attributes are in different entities. Entity references are discussed in more detail below.

> ... Each ⌈unparsed entity⌉ has an associated ⌈notation⌉, identified by name. Beyond a requirement that an XML processor make the identifiers for the entity and notation available to the ⌈application⌉, XML places no constraints on the contents of unparsed entities.

See Section 4.7, "Notation Declarations," for more information about how to use ⌈notations⌉.

The phrase "XML places no constraints on the contents of unparsed entities" means that an unparsed entity can contain any data, whether text or binary. The application is expected to take the identifiers for the notation and the entity (in each case both a name and an external reference such as a SYSTEM identifier) and use them to fetch or process the data in whatever way it deems appropriate.

An example of an unparsed entity might be a graphic image that could be displayed as if it were part of an XML document. The image data (a JPEG or TIFF image file, perhaps) would actually be stored in an unparsed entity.

> Parsed entities are invoked by name using ⌈entity references⌉; unparsed entities by name, given in the value of ENTITY or ENTITIES attributes.

There are two differences in syntax between parsed and unparsed entities. The first difference is that an ⌈unparsed entity⌉ is given an associated NOTATION in its declaration, using the NDATA keyword:

```
<!ENTITY leftFoot
    SYSTEM "leftfoot.jpg"
    NDATA JPEG
>
<!ENTITY description
    SYSTEM "leftfoot.xml"
>
```

This example assumes that the JPEG notation is declared elsewhere, and then declares leftFoot as an unparsed entity and description as a parsed entity. See Section 4.7, "Notation Declarations," for more information about NOTATION.

The second difference is in how the two kinds of entity are used.

Unparsed entities are never included in the document, but can only be used by mentioning them in an attribute value. Parsed entities, on the other hand, can never be referred to in that way, but instead are included inline using an ⌜entity reference⌝ of the form &name; or %name;.

```
<!ELEMENT Picture
    (#PCDATA)
>
<!ATTLIST Picture
    Image ENTITY #REQUIRED
>
.  .  .
<Picture Image="leftFoot">&description;</Picture>
```

General entities are entities for use within the document content. . . .

A ⌜general entity⌝ can only be referenced from within content[43], and not from the DTD (except in attribute default values and in the replacement text of internal entities).

A general entity may be internal or external. Where the declaration of an external parsed entity gives an ⌜external identifier⌝ (SYSTEM or PUBLIC) that can be used to retrieve the content, an internal general entity simply gives the content:

```
<!ENTITY longdesc
    SYSTEM "description.xml"
>
<!ENTITY shortdesc
    "tall, fair-haired, with a shy grin"
>
```

. . . In this specification, ⌜general entities⌝ are sometimes referred to with the unqualified term *entity* when this leads to no ambiguity. . . .

This usage may not lead to formal ambiguities, but there can be no doubt that it causes considerable confusion. It is to be hoped that a future version of the XML specification will be more careful in its use of the term ⌜entity⌝. In the meantime, we have tried to make the distinction clear whenever we felt there was any possibility of confusion on the part of the reader.

There are in fact only two kinds of entity in XML: ⌜parameter entities⌝ and ⌜general entities⌝; see the notes to the next item.

... ⌐Parameter entities⌐ are ⌐parsed entities⌐ for use within the DTD. These two
types of entities [⌐general entities⌐ and ⌐parameter entities⌐] use different forms
of reference and are recognized in different contexts. ...

A ⌐parameter entity⌐ is declared and used with a % sign, and can only be
used within the ⌐document type declaration⌐ (the DTD). The following
markup would include the file mydecls.dtd within a ⌐DTD⌐:

```
<!--* Declare and include the file "mydecls.dtd",
    * which contains element or other declarations:
    *-->
<!ENTITY % myDeclarations
    SYSTEM "mydecls.dtd"
>
%myDeclarations;
```

A ⌐general entity⌐ can be referenced from within the content of an element (including the value of an attribute) or can be named in an attribute
value of type ENTITY or ENTITIES. A ⌐parameter entity⌐ can be referenced
only from within either the document prolog or the external document
type declaration (the DTD).

... Furthermore, they occupy different namespaces; a parameter entity and a
general entity with the same name are two distinct entities.

Parameter entities are often used in conjunction with conditional sections (described in Section 3.4, "Conditional Sections") to customize a document type definition. General entities might be used by the author of a
document for convenience in editing. Since the author may not be familiar
with the design of the DTD, this rule allows authors to declare general entities for their own use without worrying that a parameter entity of the same
name might exist somewhere in the DTD.

Note: The term *namespace* here is not in any way related to the experi-
mental ⌐namespace⌐ feature in XML. The meaning of the sentence is
unchanged if the words "Furthermore, they occupy different namespaces"
are deleted.

4.1 Character and Entity References

This section describes how entities are actually used. Refer to Part 1 of this
book for introductory text and more examples.

A ⌈character reference⌉ refers to a specific character in the ISO/IEC 10646 character set, for example one not directly accessible from available input devices.

If you want to use a ⌈Unicode⌉ character that you can't reach from your keyboard, you can use a ⌈character reference⌉ to enter it.

Character Reference

```
[66] CharRef ::= '&#' [0-9]+ ';' | '&#' [0-9a-fA-F]+ ';'
```
[WFC: Legal Character]

Some examples of character references are given below, after the discussion of the well-formedness constraint.

Despite the fact that a ⌈character reference⌉ begins with an ampersand (&), it is not an entity reference—it just looks like one.

Well-Formedness Constraint: Legal Character

Characters referred to using ⌈character references⌉ must match the production for Char[2].

You cannot use a character reference to include a character that is not part of the ⌈document character set⌉, such as 0000 (NUL). Character references therefore cannot be used as an escape mechanism for arbitrary binary data; you instead must use something like the ⌈MIME⌉ ⌈base64⌉ encoding described in Section 3.3.1, "Attribute Types," under the heading ⌈NOTATION-valued attribute types⌉.

If the ⌈character reference⌉ begins with "&#x", the ⌈digits⌉ and ⌈letters⌉ up to the terminating ; provide a ⌈hexadecimal⌉ representation of the character's ⌈code point⌉ in ⌈ISO/IEC 10646⌉. If it begins just with "&#", the digits up to the terminating ; provide a decimal representation of the character's ⌈code point⌉.

See Appendix B in Part 3 of this book for a description of characters and their use and function in XML, and the related terminology.

Unicode uses hexadecimal codes where SGML traditionally used decimal; XML permits both. The next example shows some character references together with their corresponding characters. Note that the x in

"&#x" must be lowercase, even though the hexadecimal digits A to F may be in any combination of upper- and lowercase.

```
0, NUL,                              this character is not allowed
A, The Latin letter upper case   A, &#65;, &#x41;
```

You can use ⌜character references⌝ to escape ⌜markup⌝, but this is not recommended. Consider the following example ("<" is character 60 decimal, 3C hexadecimal):

```
This is &#60;emph>legal&#x3C;/emph>
```

This is bad practice, because people not using XML parsers (such as the ⌜Desperate Perl Hacker⌝ writing a script to modify a file but working under a tight deadline) may not expect it, and also because the markup will probably not survive being read into an XML editor and then saved—the character references would possibly (incorrectly) be turned back into markup:

```
This is <emph>legal</emph>
```

You should use < and & to escape the < and & characters.

See Appendix D of the XML specification, "Expansion of Entity and Character References," for more details of this.

> **An entity reference refers to the content of a named ⌜entity⌝. References to parsed ⌜general entities⌝ use ampersand (&) and semicolon (;) as delimiters. Parameter-entity references use percent sign (%) and semicolon (;) as delimiters.**

The ⌜delimiters⌝ are at the start and end of an entity reference:

```
<!--* an internal general entity: *-->
<!ENTITY myPeak
    "Everest"
>
<!--* a parameter entity: *-->
<!ENTITY % peaks
    SYSTEM "himalayas.dtd"
>
%peaks; <!--* include within DTD using % and ; delimiters *-->
. . .
<Mountain>Yesterday my grandmother and I climbed
&myPeak;.</Mountain>
```

Note: You cannot reference an ⌜unparsed general entity⌝ using the &
delimiter; instead, unparsed entities can only be used inside entity-valued
attributes.

Entity Reference

```
[67] Reference ::= EntityRef[68] | CharRef[66]

[68] EntityRef ::= '&' Name[5] ';'                    [WFC: Entity Declared]
                                                      [VC: Entity Declared]
                                                      [WFC: Parsed Entity]
                                                      [WFC: No Recursion]

[69] PEReference ::= '&' Name[5] ';'                  [VC: Entity Declared]
                                                      [WFC: No Recursion]
                                                      [WFC: In DTD]
```

Well-Formedness Constraint: Entity Declared

**In a document without any DTD, a document with only an ⌜internal DTD subset⌝
which contains no ⌜parameter entity references⌝, or a document with
"standalone='yes'", the Name[5] given in the ⌜entity reference⌝ must match that
in an ⌜entity declaration⌝, except that ⌜well-formed⌝ documents need not declare
any of the following entities: amp, lt, gt, apos, quot. . . .**

A document with no DTD obviously has no entity declarations, and so can
only use the five predefined general entities listed here. The meaning of the
predefined entities is given in Section 4.6 below.

. . . The declaration of a ⌜parameter entity⌝ must precede any reference to it. . . .

This includes references in entity values, so that the following is illegal:

```
<!ENTITY title "My Friend %friend;">  (illegal example)
<!ENTITY % friend "Daniella">
<!--* friend was used before it was
    * declared, so this is not a legal example.
    *-->
```

**. . . Similarly, the declaration of a general entity must precede any reference to
it which appears in a default value in an attribute-list declaration. . . .**

A default value in an attribute-list declaration is the only context in which a general entity can appear and be expanded in the DTD. Apart from this, general entity references are only expanded in the actual document instance, after the end of the document type declaration. The following example shows this:

```
<!ELEMENT Image
    (Caption, IfImageNotShown, Credits)
>
<!ATTLIST Image
    Icon ENTITY "default-icon"
>
<!ENTITY default-icon
    SYSTEM "default.bmp"
    NDATA BMP
>
<!--* Error: default-icon was referenced before it was defined
*-->
```

. . . Note that if entities are declared in the ⌜external subset⌝ or in external ⌜parameter entities⌝, a ⌜non-validating [XML] processor⌝ is not obligated to read and process their declarations; for such documents, the rule that an entity must be declared is a well-formedness constraint only if standalone='yes'.

This means that a well-formed document with standalone="yes" can use entities that are not defined in the ⌜internal DTD subset⌝, as long as they do not affect the way the document parses. (See Section 2.9, "Standalone Document Declaration," for a description of standalone=yes.)

Validity Constraint: Entity Declared

In a document with an external subset or external parameter entities with "standalone='no'", the Name[5] given in the entity reference must match that in an entity declaration.

In other words, the entity must have been declared. The ⌜match⌝ here (as always) is case-sensitive, so that SockColor and sockcolor would be two entirely unrelated entity names.

. . . For interoperability, valid documents should declare the entities amp, lt, gt, apos, quot, in the form specified in Section 4.6 *Predefined Entities*.

This is for compatibility with SGML, which does not pre-declare these entities; a valid SGML document needs them to be declared.

> **... The declaration of a ⌐parameter entity⌐ must precede any reference to it. Similarly, the declaration of a general entity must precede any reference to it which appears in a default value in an attribute-list declaration.**

See the comments on the preceding well-formedness constraint, *Entity Declared*.

Well-Formedness Constraint: Parsed Entity

An ⌐entity reference⌐ must not contain the name of an ⌐unparsed entity⌐. Unparsed entities may be referred to only in attribute values declared to be of type ENTITY or ENTITIES.

This constraint duplicates earlier prose, but states the point more precisely. It means that the following is not permitted:

```
<!ENTITY rose
    SYSTEM "rose.odf"
    NDATA OdorDefinitionFormat
>
. . .
Scratch and sniff &rose;   (illegal entity reference)
```

This is illegal because the rose entity has an associated notation, and hence is an unparsed entity. The rationale is that its contents would presumably not be legal if they occurred inline in the document at this point.

Well-Formedness Constraint: No Recursion

A parsed entity must not contain a recursive reference to itself, either directly or indirectly.

This is because an XML processor would never finish expanding the reference. Consider this example:

```
<!ENTITY A "A then &B;">
<!ENTITY B "B then &A;">
```

An XML processor would never finish expanding this entity, getting lost instead in an infinite recursion.

Well-Formedness Constraint: In DTD

Parameter-entity references may only appear in the ⌈DTD⌉.

Note: A ⌈parameter entity reference⌉ in the replacement text of an internal general entity is expanded when the declaration of the general entity is parsed, and thus only appears in the DTD. The following example shows a parameter entity in the replacement text of a general entity:

```
<!ENTITY % Tree "Oak">
<!ENTITY MyTree "A tall %Tree;">
<!--* MyTree is now defined as "A tall Oak". *-->
. . .
In the document, %MyTree; expands into A tall  Oak .
```

Note: The extra spaces around the expansion of Oak are explained in Section 4.4.8 of the specification, "Included as PE."

Examples of character and entity references:

```
Type <key> less-than </key> (&#x3C;) to save options.
This document was prepared on &docdate; and
is classified &security-level;.
```

Example of a parameter entity reference:

```
<!-- declare the parameter entity "ISOLat2"... -->
<!ENTITY % ISOLat2
    SYSTEM "http://www.xml.com/iso/isolat2-xml.entities"
>
<!-- ... now reference it. -->
%ISOLat2;
```

4.2 Entity Declarations

Entities are declared thus:

Entity Declaration

```
[70] EntityDecl ::= GEDecl[71] | PEDecl[72]

[71] GEDecl ::= '<!ENTITY' S[3] Name[5] S[3] EntityDef[73] S[3]? '>'
```

```
[72] PEDecl ::=
        '<!ENTITY' S[3] '%' S[3] Name[5] S[3] PEDef[74] S[3]? '>'

[73] EntityDef ::= EntityValue[9] | (ExternalID[75] NDataDecl[76]?)

[74] PEDef ::= EntityValue[9] | ExternalID[75]
```

Note that the space (S[3])after the % is required for a PEDecl[72]; if it is omitted, the % followed by a Name[5] signals the start of a ⌈parameter entity reference⌉.

Some examples of ⌈entity declarations⌉ here might help. The first example declares a general entity called `artist`, with replacement text `George Platt Lynes`; the productions matched are `EntityDecl`[70], `GEDecl`[71], `EntityDef`[73], and `EntityValue`[9]:

```
<!ENTITY artist
    "George Platt Lynes"
>
```

The second example declares an external parameter entity, matching `EntityDecl`[70], `PEDecl`[72], `PEDef`[73], and `ExternalID`[75]; the external entity is then included with a ⌈parameter entity reference⌉:

```
<!ENTITY % artistList
    SYSTEM "artists.dtd"
>
%artistList;
```

The Name[5] identifies the ⌈entity⌉ in an ⌈entity reference⌉ or, in the case of an ⌈unparsed entity⌉, in the value of an ENTITY or ENTITIES ⌈attribute⌉. . . .

A slightly less convoluted way of saying this is that the Name[5] in an ⌈entity reference⌉ must exactly ⌈match⌉ the Name[3] in an ⌈entity declaration⌉. The declaration must be of the right type, either for a general entity or a parameter entity, depending on whether the delimiter used to reference the entity was % or &, respectively. An entity named in the value of an attribute of type ENTITY or ENTITIES must always be an unparsed (and hence external) ⌈general entity⌉.

. . . If the same entity is declared more than once, the first declaration encountered is binding; ⌈at user option⌉, an ⌈XML processor⌉ ⌈may⌉ issue a ⌈warning⌉ if entities are declared multiple times.

This may at first seem surprising. Recall, however, that the ⌐internal DTD subset⌐ is read before the ⌐external DTD subset⌐. Any entities defined in the internal DTD subset will thus override definitions of the same entities in the external subset. Consider the following example:

```
<!DOCTYPE Story SYSTEM "story.dtd" [
  <!ENTITY % Story.contents
     'Poem'
  >
  <!ELEMENT Poem
     (Line+)
  >
  <!ELEMENT Line
     (#PCDATA)
  >
]>
<Story>
  <Poem>
    <Line>Jack and Jill went up the hill</Line>
    <Line>To fetch a pail of water.</Line>
    <Line>Jack fell down and broke his Crown</Line>
    <Line>And Jill came tumbling after.</Line>
  </Poem>
</Story>
```

When the document shown in this example is read by a validating XML parser, the parameter entity `Story.contents` is first defined to have the replacement text of `(Poem)`. Two element types, `Poem` and `Line`, are then defined, giving a somewhat simplistic representation of poetry.

After reading the ⌐internal DTD subset⌐, the validating XML processor goes on to locate and read the ⌐external DTD subset⌐, which is shown next:

```
<!--* DTD "story.dtd"
    * Author: Liam Quin
    * Date: September 1998; Version: 1.3
    *-->
<!ENTITY % Story.contents
    '(Paragraph)+'
>
<!ELEMENT Story
    (%Story.contents;)
>
<!ELEMENT Paragraph
    (#PCDATA)*
>
```

After skipping the initial ⌜comment⌝, the validating XML processor reads the ⌜parameter entity declaration⌝ for `Story.contents`, discovers that a parameter entity of that name has already been defined, and discards the newer definition, leaving the replacement text for the entity unchanged.

When the processor reaches the element type definition for Story, it is therefore expanded as follows:

```
<!ELEMENT Story
    ( Poem )
>
<!ELEMENT Paragraph
    (#PCDATA)*
>
```

Because the DTD was designed to be customized in this way, the content model of `Story` was changed without changing the original DTD at all.

This technique is also often used with parameter entities that are set to `INCLUDE` or `IGNORE` to control the inclusion of a conditional section.

Since this technique is so useful, an XML processor that issued a warning when entities were defined more than once would probably be very unpopular unless the warning could easily be disabled.

Note: The extra spaces around `Poem` in the expanded content model for `Story` are always supplied at the start and end of the replacement text of a parameter entity when it is referenced.

Note: Within the internal DTD subset, parameter entities are restricted; see the next section, "Internal Entities," for more information.

4.2.1 Internal Entities

If the entity definition is an EntityValue[9], the defined entity is called an ⌜internal entity⌝. There is no separate physical storage object, and the content of the entity is given in the declaration. . . .

An `EntityValue`[9] is a string inside double or single quotes, and which may contain any combination of text (⌜character data⌝), ⌜parameter entity references⌝, and ⌜general entity references⌝.

What is meant here is that the entity definition does not refer to an external object, so that instead of the `SYSTEM` or `PUBLIC` keyword in its declaration, it has the literal value of the entity.

. . . Note that some processing of entity and character references in the literal entity value may be required to produce the correct ⌜replacement text⌝: see Section 4.5, *Construction of Internal Entity Replacement Text.*

When an internal entity is defined, whether it is a ⌜parameter entity⌝ or a ⌜general entity⌝, any parameter entity references and ⌜character references⌝ in its value are expanded in place.

An internal entity is a parsed entity.

An ⌜unparsed entity⌝ is always an ⌜external entity⌝. The easiest way to remember this is probably to remember that a reference to an ⌜internal entity⌝ is expanded in place and parsed, so that the result must be proper XML. An external entity, on the other hand, can be referred to without being expanded, and so is not always parsed.

Example of an internal entity declaration:

```
<!ENTITY Pub-Status
    "This is a pre-release of the specification."
>
```

4.2.2 External Entities

If an entity is not internal, it is an external entity, declared as follows:

External Entity Declaration

```
[75] ExternalID ::=
        'SYSTEM' S[3] SystemLiteral[11]
        | 'PUBLIC' S[3] PubidLiteral[12] S[3] SystemLiteral[11]

[76] NdataDecl ::= S[3] 'NDATA' S[3] Name[5]          [VC: Notation Declared]
```

The meanings of PUBLIC and SYSTEM identifiers are discussed in the following paragraphs.

If the NDataDecl[76] is present, this is a ⌜general unparsed entity⌝; otherwise it is a ⌜parsed entity⌝.

This statement is central to understanding the difference between a ⌜parsed external entity⌝ and an ⌜unparsed external entity⌝; see Part 1 of this book for a more detailed discussion of entities, together with examples.

Validity Constraint: Notation Declared

The Name[5] must ˹match˺ the declared name of a ˹notation˺.

The idea is that the notation associated with an unparsed external entity determines the format of that entity in some way. One might, for example, use a notation to indicate that an external resource is encoded using the PostScript page description language.

This is a reasonable approach when all of the files and software involved are on a single local machine, or on a local area network but entirely under control of a single group of people. Specifying the format of external resources is not robust in a distributed environment such as the World Wide Web, where one might not have control over, or be informed when, a remote resource is changed.

On the Internet, ˹HTTP˺ and ˹MIME˺ supply a far more powerful and generally more useful model, in which ˹content negotiation˺ occurs between a client (such as a Web browser) and a server (such as the UNIX HTTP server process, *httpd*). The format of the remote resource is only discovered when the server supplies an HTTP Content-type header along with the actual data. Furthermore, the same data might be delivered in any of a number of formats, depending on the Accept HTTP header sent by the client along with the request for the resource.

It is unclear what is the best approach to using notations in general. It is most likely that it depends on your operating environment and existing software.

If you are working with the Internet, you should read the ˹IETF˺ ˹RFCs˺ for ˹HTTP˺, ˹MIME˺, and ˹content negotiation˺, and at least work with that existing infrastructure.

An example approach might be to define and use a notation as follows:

```
<!NOTATION notation.Image
    SYSTEM "image/png;image/jpeg;text/postscript;image/*"
>
<!ENTITY picture.Liam
    SYSTEM "http://www.groveware.com/~lee/images/liam/"
    NDATA notation.Image
>
```

Here, the idea is that the SYSTEM value given for notation.Image will be used in an HTTP Accept: header, so that if a PNG-format image is available, it should be sent back by the server in preference to a JPEG one, and so on. This, however, is an application-specific convention that is nowhere specified by XML.

The XML specification does not say explicitly that notation names are in their own namespace, but it is implied by the above constraint that you can have an element type (for example) with the same name as a notation name.

Since the specification is not explicit, it is better to make notation names different from all other names you use. This will also help to make your documents easier to read and understand! One way to do this is with a prefix, as shown in the example above; recall that a dot (full stop, period) is permitted within a name, so that `notation.Image` and `picture.Liam` match `Name`[5], and thus are acceptable names.

> **The SystemLiteral[11] is called the entity's ⌜system identifier⌝. It is a ⌜URI⌝, which may be used to retrieve the entity. . . .**

There is nothing subtle or unexpected here: The ⌜system identifier⌝ is the location of the contents of the external entity. In practice, a ⌜URI⌝ here means a ⌜URL⌝, but a ⌜URN⌝ can also be used.

Note: Some XML software supports the notation of an external catalogue file in which both system and public identifiers can be looked up and remapped, but this is not part of the XML specification, and at the time of writing there are at least two competing and incompatible catalogue formats.

> **. . . Note that the hash mark (#) and ⌜fragment identifier⌝ frequently used with URIs are not, formally, part of the URI itself; an XML processor may signal an error if a fragment identifier is given as part of a system identifier. . . .**

An example of a URI (actually a URL) with a fragment identifier might be:

```
http://www.somewhere.else.new/sf/authors.html#Zamyatin
```

An HTML browser would generally download the entire resource given here and then scroll to an `ID` or `NAME` attribute matching *Zamyatin*. The fragment identifier is not formally part of the URL, but is an HTML extension to the URL syntax. Since it does not make sense to start reading an XML entity partway through, the XML specification is saying here that an XML processor is not required to accept this extension, and may in fact refuse to process a document containing a fragment identifier in a system identifier.

As a result, fragment identifiers should not be used in XML documents that are to be interchanged between multiple and unknown XML processors.

> . . . Unless otherwise provided by information outside the scope of this
> specification (e.g., a special XML element type defined by a particular DTD, or a
> processing instruction defined by a particular application specification), relative
> URIs are relative to the location of the resource within which the entity
> declaration occurs. A URI might thus be relative to the document entity, to the
> entity containing the external DTD subset, or to some other external parameter
> entity.

A URL usually consists of a protocol, a server name, and a path starting at
a root directory (/), in the form *protocol://server/path/to/resource*. A ⌈relative
URL⌉, or ⌈partial URL⌉, is one that does not give all of the protocol, the
server name, and the root directory. The missing components are assumed
to be the same as those of the document containing that relative URL.

Note: A full URL actually has a more complex syntax; see the ⌈IETF⌉
⌈RFCs⌉ that specify ⌈URLs⌉, listed in the bibliography

It does not in general make sense for a ⌈URN⌉ to be relative; as of the time
of writing this book, only a ⌈URL⌉ can be relative.

> An XML processor should handle a non-ASCII character in a URI by representing
> the character in UTF-8 as one or more bytes, and then escaping these bytes
> with the URI escaping mechanism (i.e., by converting each byte to %HH, where
> HH is the hexadecimal notation of the byte value).

The XML specification does not make clear what "handle" means here. A
reasonable interpretation might be that the XML processor is required to
convert the characters to 8-bit bytes and then quote all the characters that
the HTTP and URL specifications require, in the manner and circumstances
which those specifications require, but it hardly seems necessary for XML
to specify that. See RFC 2396, *Uniform Resource Identifiers (URI) Common
Syntax*, and also www.w3.org/TR/WD-charreq for more information.

> In addition to a ⌈system identifier⌉, an ⌈external identifier⌉ may include a ⌈public
> identifier⌉. An ⌈XML processor⌉ attempting to retrieve the ⌈entity⌉'s content may
> use the public identifier to try to generate an alternative ⌈URI⌉. If the processor
> is unable to do so, it must use the URI specified in the ⌈system literal⌉. Before a
> ⌈match⌉ is attempted, all strings of ⌈white space⌉ in the public identifier must be
> normalized to single space characters (#x20), and leading and trailing white
> space must be removed.

The original idea was that a ⌐public identifier⌐ would function rather like a ⌐URN⌐: that is, it would be a name that was independent of the actual computer on which the resource was stored.

Unfortunately, XML does not specify how an XML processor is to take a public identifier and resolve it—that is, how to fetch the data that it names. The most common method is simply to ignore the public identifier and use the system identifier (which must always be given). The second most common method is to look up the identifier in a system-specific file, called a catalogue. Unfortunately, if one system looks up the public identifier and the other uses the system identifier, the two systems are likely to fetch entirely different resources for the same entity. This makes testing very difficult, and can impede interoperability.

Since those systems that support public identifier mapping via a catalogue generally also support mapping of system identifiers using the same catalogue file, there is in fact no practical benefit to using a public identifier.

We suggest that if you are creating documents, or writing software to generate XML documents, you use only system identifiers.

Note: The idea of a ⌐public identifier⌐ is taken from SGML, which supports a very structured syntax for formal public identifiers, but which also does not specify a resolution mechanism for them. Some SGML and XML software supports the notion of a catalogue file, as described above, to map public identifiers into system identifiers, but one cannot rely on the existence of such a mechanism unless the XML processor is known in advance.

Examples of external entity declarations:

```
<!ENTITY open-hatch
    SYSTEM "http://www.textuality.com/boilerplate/OpenHatch.xml"
>
<!ENTITY open-hatch
    PUBLIC "-//Textuality//TEXT Standard open-hatch boilerplate//EN"
    "http://www.textuality.com/boilerplate/OpenHatch.xml"
>

<!ENTITY hatch-pic
    SYSTEM "../grafix/OpenHatch.gif"
    NDATA gif
>
```

Notice that if the keyword PUBLIC is given, the keyword SYSTEM must be omitted, even though a system identifier is supplied. It is a common error to include the SYSTEM keyword by mistake in that situation.

4.3 Parsed Entities

This section describes both internal and external parsed entities. See Chapter 1 in Part 1 of this book for a general discussion and examples of entities.

4.3.1 The Text Declaration

⌈External parsed entities⌉ ⌈may⌉ each begin with a ⌈**text declaration**⌉.

Recall that the word ⌈may⌉ has a specific meaning in this specification. An ⌈external parsed entity⌉ therefore starts with an optional ⌈text declaration⌉.

Text Declaration

```
[77]  TextDecl ::=
            '<?xml' VersionInfo[24]? EncodingDecl[80] S[3]? '?>'
```

There are several things to note here; most of these also apply to the XML declaration that may appear at the start of an XML document (compare TextDecl[77] with XMLDecl[23] described in Section 2.8, "Prolog and Document Type Declaration").

First, the string xml at the start must be in lowercase, even though all other XML keywords are in uppercase.

Second, unlike the optional ⌈XML declaration⌉ at the start of the ⌈document entity⌉, a ⌈text declaration⌉ cannot contain a ⌈standalone declaration⌉; this is not surprising, since the standalone declaration applies to the document as a whole.

Third, the EncodingDecl[80] is allowed because an external parsed entity might use a different character ⌈encoding⌉ than the entity (either the ⌈document entity⌉ or an ⌈external entity⌉) that includes it. See the notes for EncodingDecl[80] and also Appendix B in Part 3 of this book, which discusses character sets and encodings.

Finally, be careful to note that the closing delimiter is "?>" and not just ">". A common mistake is to omit the question mark (?), causing massive chunks of document to be swallowed mysteriously, with the XML processor producing strange and faintly disturbing error messages. You have been warned.

The text declaration must be provided literally, not by reference to a parsed entity. . . .

This is also presumably intended to exclude starting an external parsed entity with a parameter entity reference as follows:

```
%textDecl;
```

where textDecl is declared in another entity, as follows:

```
<!ENTITY % textDecl
    '<&#38;xml version="1.0" ?>'        (illegal example)
>
```

> **... No ⌜text declaration⌝ may appear at any position other than the beginning of an ⌜external parsed entity⌝.**

This means that you cannot simply join together two external entities to make a single larger one: You must inspect the second one and if it has a text declaration at the beginning, remove it.

The best way to think of the text declaration is that it roughly corresponds to the ⌜MIME⌝ headers MIME-Version and Content-Transfer-Encoding, except with a different syntax.

4.3.2 Well-Formed Parsed Entities

> **The ⌜document entity⌝ is ⌜well-formed⌝ if it ⌜matches⌝ the production labeled document[1]. . . .**

The ⌜document entity⌝ is the file or resource containing the start and end of the document; the hub or core, if you will, that may in turn reference or include other entities.

It is entirely possible for the document entity to be ⌜well-formed⌝ but for one or more ⌜external parsed entities⌝ that it includes not to be well-formed. In this case the document as a whole is neither well-formed nor ⌜valid⌝, but since a ⌜non-validating XML processor⌝ is not required to fetch external parsed entities, the non-validness may never be detected. A ⌜validating XML processor⌝ would of course find the error.

> **... An ⌜external general parsed entity⌝ is ⌜well-formed⌝ if it ⌜matches⌝ the production labeled extParsedEnt[78]. . . .**

Production extParsedEnt[78] is described in more detail below. Note that every ⌜external parsed entity⌝ must be ⌜well-formed⌝.

> **... An ⌜external parameter entity⌝ is well-formed if it matches the production labeled extPE[79].**

An ⌜external parameter entity⌝ can only be included in the DTD (including the ⌜internal DTD subset⌝). As a result, whatever it `contains` must be legal in a DTD, and since textual content and element instances aren't allowed in the DTD, an external parameter entity can only contain declarations.

Well-Formed External Parsed Entity

```
[78] extParsedEnt ::= TextDecl[77]? content[43]

[79] extPE ::= TextDecl[77]? extSubsetDecl[31]
```

Both an ⌜external parameter entity⌝ and an ⌜external general entity⌝ can start with (and cannot otherwise contain) a ⌜text declaration⌝

An ⌜external parsed general entity⌝ contains `content`[43], defined as a mixture of ⌜elements⌝, text (⌜character data⌝), ⌜comments⌝, ⌜conditional sections⌝, and ⌜processing instructions⌝, just as for the main body of an XML document.

An ⌜external parameter entity⌝ (parameter entities are always ⌜parsed⌝) contains declarations rather than `content`[43]. As explained in Section 2.8, "Prolog and Document Type Declaration," one good reason for using an external parameter entity is that there are fewer restrictions on declarations there than in the ⌜internal DTD subset⌝. Another is that you can reuse the same set of declarations in many documents.

There are two main reasons why an external entity may have a different ⌜encoding⌝ from the document including it. One is that the entity may have been written by someone else or even published publicly for reuse, and you may not have control over its encoding. The other reason is that it is much more convenient to use some encodings for certain languages than others; the reader is referred to Appendix B in Part 3 of this book, and also to the *Japanese Information Processing* book published by O'Reilly and Associates for example.

> An ⌜internal general parsed entity⌝ is ⌜well-formed⌝ if its ⌜replacement text⌝ ⌜matches⌝ the production labeled content[43]. . . .

If this statement is clear at first glance, you've been spending too much time reading this book!

The subject has shifted to *internal* entities, and is saying that their ⌜replacement text⌝ must itself be well-formed. These examples may help:

```
<!--* first, a legal entity: *-->
<!ENTITY Shortpara
```

```
      '<p>This is a paragraph</p>'
   >
   <!--* now, an illegal example:
      * the problem is that the Chapter element is not closed
      *-->
   <!ENTITY StartChapter
      '<Chapter><Title>&theTitle;</Title>'        (illegal example)
   >
```

. . . All internal parameter entities are well-formed by definition.

It's not clear what, if anything, is meant by this. In fact, the well-formed-ness constraint applies not to the replacement text of an internal parameter entity but to the *context* in which the reference to that parameter entity occurs, be it the ⌐internal document type definition subset⌐ or an ⌐external parameter entity⌐.

> **A consequence of ⌐well-formedness⌐ in entities is that the logical and physical structures in an ⌐XML document⌐ are properly nested; no ⌐start-tag⌐, ⌐end-tag⌐, ⌐empty-element tag⌐, ⌐element⌐, ⌐comment⌐, ⌐processing instruction⌐, ⌐character reference⌐, or ⌐entity reference⌐ can begin in one ⌐entity⌐ and end in another.**

⌐Markup⌐ must begin and end in the same ⌐entity⌐ as it started, whether that's an ⌐internal entity⌐ or an ⌐external entity⌐.

Although the markup must start and end in the same entity, it is entirely at liberty to wander off elsewhere in the middle, as the examples show.

```
   <book>
      &Chapter1; <!--* wander off into chapter one... *-->
      &Chapter2;
      &Chapter3;
   </book>
   <!--* This fragment is from an external parameter entity;
      * it would not be legal inside the internal DTD subset,
   where
      * parameter entities can only contain complete declarations.
      *-->
   <!ENTITY % middleBit
      '(boy|girl)+'
   >
   <!--* The declaration of the Children element type starts and
      * ends in this entity, but part of the declaration is to be
      * found by the discerning parser in the replacement text
      * of the middleBit internal parameter entity:
      *-->
```

```
<!ELEMENT Children
    %middleBit;
>
```

4.3.3 ⌐Character Encoding⌐ in ⌐Entities⌐

Appendix B in Part 3 of this book discusses ⌐character encoding⌐ in some detail, and a quick trip to those pages may prove helpful before attempting this section.

In this section, "entity" is used to mean ⌐parsed external entity⌐, unambiguously, since only a parsed external entity can contain a ⌐text declaration⌐, and that is the only way to specify the ⌐character encoding⌐ of an ⌐entity⌐.

> **Each ⌐external parsed entity⌐ in an ⌐XML document⌐ ⌐may⌐ use a different ⌐encoding⌐ for its ⌐characters⌐. All ⌐XML processors⌐ ⌐must⌐ be able to read ⌐entities⌐ in either ⌐UTF-8⌐ or ⌐UTF-16⌐.**

There are four encodings that you can reasonably expect to work in most XML systems: the 7-bit U.S. American Standard Code for Information Interchange (⌐ASCII⌐), ⌐ISO 8859-1⌐ (Latin 1), ⌐UTF-8⌐, and ⌐UTF-16⌐. Neither the Macintosh character set nor the default MS-DOS and Windows code pages are supported, so that if you try to enter "smart double quotes," for example, you may get a nasty surprise when you view your file on another computer. If you are creating XML documents to send to other people or make available on the Internet, or for use with multiple pieces of software, you should get into the habit of using a ⌐validating XML processor⌐ to check your input, and, if possible, test on multiple platforms to ensure that you have not relied on any platform-specific characters.

Note: The phrase "either UTF 8 or UTF 16" should read "both UTF 8 and UTF 16".

> **Entities encoded in ⌐UTF-16⌐ must begin with the ⌐Byte Order Mark⌐ described by ⌐ISO/IEC 10646⌐ Annex E and ⌐Unicode⌐ Appendix B (the ZERO-WIDTH NO-BREAK SPACE character, #xFEFF).**

These appear to be ⌐normative references⌐, which means that, strictly speaking, every conforming XML processor must comply with all of the stipulations of both references. Happily, this is not too onerous a task. The ⌐Unicode⌐ specification suggests that the zero-width no-break space be used to detect ⌐byte ordering⌐, since a file (or, in the case of XML, any ⌐external entity⌐) with reversed ⌐byte ordering⌐ would start with #xFFFE instead of #xFEFF, but Unicode does not mandate this. Although the XML specification does not say what happens to the byte order mark, the only sensible interpretation is that the byte order mark is swallowed by the ⌐XML processor⌐ and not passed back to the ⌐application⌐. This is the only place in the specification where an input character cannot be passed back by the XML processor to the application, so an application that copies or generates XML must be prepared to issue the byte order mark automatically.

> **Although an ⌐XML processor⌐ is required to read only [parsed external] ⌐entities⌐ in the ⌐UTF-8⌐ and ⌐UTF-16⌐ ⌐encodings⌐, it is recognized that other encodings are used around the world, and it may be desired for XML processors to read entities that use them. Parsed [external] entities which are stored in an encoding other than UTF-8 or UTF-16 must begin with a ⌐text declaration⌐ containing an ⌐encoding declaration⌐: . . .**

There is a great danger that interoperability will suffer from this statement: It permits the use of platform- and locale-specific character encodings that may not be recognized by other XML processors. As a result, whenever possible, produce and store text entities using the standard character encodings; if this is not possible, write or obtain software to convert the entities from your local character encoding into a standard one, and use that if you deliver your entities over the Internet.

We also note in passing that the literal sense of the statement is incorrect: An XML processor is not required to read *only* UTF-8 and UTF-16; rather it is only *required* to read UTF-8 and UTF-16. The wording as written implies that an XML processor is forbidden to read any encoding other than the two that are listed, but what is meant is that an XML processor ⌐must⌐ read UTF-8 and UTF-16, and ⌐may⌐ read others.

Encoding Declaration

```
[80] EncodingDecl ::=
        S[3] 'encoding' Eq[25]
            ('"' EncName[81] '"' | "'" EncName[81] "'" )

[81] EncName ::= [A-Za-z] ([A-Za-z0-9._] | '-')*
     /* Encoding name contains only Latin characters */
```

It is not made clear why an encoding name (EncName[81]) is restricted to Latin characters, but this does help compatibility with ⌐HTTP⌐ and ⌐MIME⌐, where the Content-Type header is constrained to 7-bit ASCII by ⌐RFC 822⌐, the ⌜IETF⌝ electronic mail standard. The example shows a Content-Type header giving a charset parameter.

```
Content-Type: text/xml; charset="ISO-8859-1"
```

Note: The production for EncName[81] has '-' separated off because the minus sign (-) represents a character range inside a character class, and so can't be included in the [A-Za-z0-9._] item.

> In the ⌜document entity⌝, the ⌜encoding declaration⌝ is part of the ⌜XML declaration⌝. The EncName[81] is the name of the encoding used.

The EncodingDecl[80] is used in a ⌜text declaration⌝ (TextDecl[77]) as described in Section 4.3.1, "The Text Declaration."

> In an ⌜encoding declaration⌝, the values "UTF-8", "UTF-16", "ISO-10646-UCS-2", and "ISO-10646-UCS-4" should be used for the various encodings and transformations of Unicode / ISO/IEC 10646, the values "ISO-8859-1", "ISO-8859-2", . . . "ISO-8859-9" should be used for the parts of ⌜ISO 8859⌝, and the values "ISO-2022-JP", "Shift_JIS", and "EUC-JP" ⌜should⌝ be used for the various encoded forms of JIS X-0208-1997. . . .

The word "should" here is unfortunate: ⌜must⌝ would be appropriate, since, if there is to be interoperability, it is essential that all users of a character set share the same name for it!

See Appendix B in Part 3 of this book for some starting points in navigating this bewildering minefield of acronyms and numbers.

> . . . XML processors ⌜may⌝ recognize other encodings; it is recommended that ⌜character encodings⌝ registered (as ⌜charsets⌝) with the ⌜Internet Assigned Numbers Authority⌝ [IANA], other than those just listed, should be referred to using their registered names. Note that these registered names are defined to be case-insensitive, so processors wishing to match against them should do so in a case-insensitive way.

The list of encodings is maintained by the ⌜IANA⌝ and is available via anonymous ftp.

Since the encoding name is made up only of the 26 letters A-Z and the ten digits 0-9, with the addition of the full stop (.), minus sign (-), and underscore (_), case-insensitive matching is well defined. This is not true in general for multilingual text, which is why XML names are in all other situations case-sensitive.

> **In the absence of information provided by an external transport protocol (e.g. HTTP or MIME), it is an ⌐error⌐ for an entity including an encoding declaration to be presented to the XML processor in an encoding other than that named in the declaration, . . .**

This is not an error that can easily be detected: If the encoding is ⌐EBCDIC⌐, for example, the result will most likely be that an XML processor will generate syntax errors because it will think it sees a character that's illegal. Alternatively, if the ⌐external parsed entity⌐ in question happened not to contain any EBCDIC character whose byte values were equal to the byte values of markup characters in UTF-8, the XML processor would see nothing wrong but produce garbage text.

The best way to deal with this is to use only the basic required encodings in XML documents, and to use external character set or encoding translation software instead.

It is tempting to configure one's local systems to have a default character encoding other than the standard one. This is very convenient for internal use, but as soon as you try to interchange documents, it becomes a disaster. It is important not to rely on locally defined default character encodings, but instead always to specify them explicitly.

> **. . . for an encoding declaration to occur other than at the beginning of an external entity, . . .**

This is always an error, since encoding declarations are only allowed at the start of external entities.

> **. . . or for an [external] entity which begins with neither a Byte Order Mark nor an encoding declaration to use an encoding other than UTF-8. . . .**

If the external entity starts with a byte order mark, it's encoded in UTF-16. If it does not, it must either be in UTF-8 or start with an encoding declaration. Of course, if the file is encoded in a sufficiently strange manner, any attempt to read the encoding declaration will fail, since that will be in the same encoding as the rest of the file! For this reason, any attempt to share EBCDIC files between computer systems must use MIME headers instead of, or as well as, encoding declarations.

> **. . . Note that since ASCII is a subset of UTF-8, ordinary ASCII entities do not strictly need an encoding declaration.**

This is because an entity encoded using the 7-bit ANSI US ASCII standard will be byte-for-byte the same as if it had been encoded using UTF-8.

It is a ⌜fatal error⌝ when an XML processor encounters an [external parsed] entity with an encoding that it is unable to process.

This is another good reason for giving a ⌜text declaration⌝ at the start of every ⌜external parsed entity⌝ if you are not using ⌜UTF-8⌝. The error can only be detected if an entity is delivered to the XML processor with a ⌜MIME⌝ header (as is the case over ⌜HTTP⌝, for example) or with some other external indication of its encoding, or if the encoding is sufficiently compatible with ⌜ASCII⌝ that the ⌜encoding declaration⌝ contained in the ⌜text declaration⌝ at the start of it can be read and understood.

Examples of encoding declarations:

```
<?xml encoding='UTF-8'>
<?xml encoding='EUC-JP'>
```

Reminder: There must be no space in <?xml, and the xml must be in lowercase.

4.4 XML Processor Treatment of Entities and References

This section specifies where entity references are permitted and how they are treated.

The table below summarizes the contexts in which ⌜character references⌝, ⌜entity references⌝, and invocations of ⌜unparsed entities⌝ might appear and the required behavior of an ⌜XML processor⌝ in each case. The labels in the leftmost column describe the recognition context: . . .

Note: The terms "invocation" and "recognition context" are not used anywhere else in the XML specification, and are not formally defined.

The "table below" is actually several paragraphs further down, by the way, after the specification defines the various terms used in it.

Reference in Content

as a reference anywhere after the ⌜start-tag⌝ and before the ⌜end-tag⌝ of an ⌜element⌝; corresponds to the ⌜nonterminal⌝ content[43].

This is a reference to a general entity, whether external or internal, within the content of an element. The example shows one of each kind:

```
Entity Reference in Content
<!ENTITY country
    "Thailand"
>
<!ENTITY phoneCall
    SYSTEM "phone.xml"
>
. . .
<Paragraph>He had gone to &country; for the week;
he telephoned me, and said, &phoneCall;,
which was very interesting.</Paragraph>
```

Reference in Attribute Value

as a reference within either the value of an ⌜attribute⌝ in a ⌜start-tag⌝, or a ⌜default value⌝ in an ⌜attribute declaration⌝; corresponds to the ⌜nonterminal⌝ AttValue[10].

This is a reference to an ⌜internal general entity⌝, since that is the only kind of ⌜entity reference⌝ permitted in this context. The following example shows an ⌜internal general entity⌝ called AE being used to represent a character (the ⌜ligature⌝ Æ) that may be difficult to type directly on some systems, and also a reference to an internal entity called sources.harmsworth being used in the ⌜default value⌝ of an ⌜attribute⌝. The definition for sources.harmsworth is shown in the example accompanying "Reference in Entity Value" below.

```
Entity Reference in Attribute Value
<!ENTITY AE
    "Æ"
>
<!ELEMENT Earl
    (#PCDATA)
>
<!ATTLIST Earl
    authority CDATA "&sources.harmsworth;"
    name CDATA #REQUIRED
```

```
>
. . .
<Earl name="&AE;lfgar">Son of Leofric</Earl>
```

Occurs as Attribute Value

as a Name[5], not a reference, appearing either as the value of an attribute which has been declared as type ENTITY, or as one of the space-separated ⌐tokens⌐ in the value of an attribute which has been declared as type ENTITIES.

An entity whose name occurs as an attribute value must be an ⌐external unparsed entity⌐, because that is the only kind of entity that may be named in that context. See Section 3.3.1, "Attribute Types," and the validity constraint "Entity Name" in that section.

```
Entity Reference as Attribute Value
<!NOTATION oxf
    SYSTEM "http://www.ocf.org/OdourExchangeFormat.xml"
>
<!ENTITY oldSock
    SYSTEM "oldSock.oxf"
    NDATA oxf
>
<!ELEMENT Wine
    (#PCDATA)
>
<!ATTLIST Wine
    year CDATA #IMPLIED
    bouquet ENTITY #IMPLIED
>
. . .
<Wine year="1982" bouquet="oldSock">
  An execrable wine from Alaska with a pungent bouquet
</Wine>
```

Reference in Entity Value

as a reference within a parameter or ⌐internal entity⌐'s literal entity value in the entity's declaration; corresponds to the ⌐nonterminal⌐ EntityValue[9].

This is a reference within the declared value of an ⌐internal parameter entity⌐ or an ⌐internal general entity⌐. Both are shown in the following example.

```
Entity Reference in Entity Value
<!ENTITY ae
    "Æ "
>
<!ENTITY sources.Harmsworth
    "Harmsworth Encyclop&ae;dia, 1907"
>
<!ENTITY % defaultSourceAttribute
    'source CDATA "&sources.Harmsworth;"'
>
 .  .  .

<!ATTLIST Article
    %defaultSourceAttribute;
>
```

The defaultSourceAttribute ⌈internal parameter entity⌉ shown in the example can be used in the ⌈external DTD subset⌉ (included in the ⌈XML document⌉ using an ⌈external parameter entity⌉, or from the ⌈external entity⌉ mentioned with the DOCTYPE keyword) but *not* in the ⌈internal DTD subset⌉, because it is not a complete declaration. See the well-formedness constraint to markupdecl[29], "PEs in Internal Subset," in Section 2.8, "Prolog and Document Type Declaration," for an explanation of how parameter entity references are constrained in the ⌈document type declaration internal subset⌉.

Reference in DTD

as a reference within either the internal or external subsets of the DTD, but outside of an EntityValue[9] or AttValue[10].

Within the ⌈internal document type declaration subset⌉ or the ⌈external DTD subset⌉, or, more informally, within the DTD, this must be a ⌈parameter entity⌉, and may be either an ⌈internal parameter entity⌉ or an ⌈external parameter entity reference⌉.

Entity Reference Type Context Availability Matrix

We first reproduce the entire table (see Table 4.1) as given in the XML specification, then the definitions from the specification of the terms used within the table, and then comment on individual rows of the Table 4.1 one at a time.

This section is complex, but it should be stressed that it is also the key to understanding entities in XML.

4.4.1 Not Recognized

Outside the ⌈DTD⌉, the % character has no special significance; thus, what would be ⌈parameter entity references⌉ in the DTD are not recognized as ⌈markup⌉ in content[43]. Similarly, the names of ⌈unparsed entities⌉ are not recognized except when they appear in the value of an appropriately declared attribute.

Since *Not Recognized* does not appear in the column for unparsed entities in the table, the second sentence is simply an error. A reference to an ⌈external general entity⌉ is always recognized, whether it is allowed or produces an error.

Table 4.1 Entity Reference Type Context Availability Matrix

	Entity Type				
	Parameter	Internal General	External Parsed General	Unparsed	Character
Reference in Content	Not recognized	Included	Included if validating	Forbidden	Included
Reference in Attribute Value	Not recognized	Included in literal	Forbidden	Forbidden	Included
Occurs as Attribute Value	Not recognized	Forbidden	Forbidden	Notify	Not recognized
Reference in Entity Value	Included in literal	Bypassed	Bypassed	Forbidden	Included
Reference in DTD	Included as PE	Forbidden	Forbidden	Forbidden	Forbidden

4.1.2 Included

An ⌜entity⌝ is **included** when its ⌜replacement text⌝ is retrieved and processed, in place of the reference itself, as though it were part of the document at the location the reference was recognized. . . .

This form of inclusion is known in computer science as text macro processing. It has the advantage of being easy to implement, but the disadvantage that there is no concept of *scope*: An element in the replacement text of an ⌜external parsed entity⌝, for example, bearing an attribute whose type is declared as ID, must give that attribute a value that does not occur anywhere else in the entire document.

. . . The ⌜replacement text⌝ ⌜may⌝ contain both ⌜character data⌝ and (except for ⌜parameter entities⌝) ⌜markup⌝, which ⌜must⌝ be recognized in the usual way, . . .

The implication here that a ⌜parameter entity⌝ cannot contain markup is erroneous. What might be meant instead is that parameter entity references are not allowed in the replacement text of an external parsed entity, but the sentence is not clear.

. . . except that the replacement text of entities used to escape markup delimiters (the entities amp, lt, gt, apos, quot) is always treated as data. (The string "AT&T" expands to "AT&T" and the remaining ampersand is not recognized as an ⌜entity-reference delimiter⌝.) . . .

This irregularity means that the internal general entity `&Percival;` in the example shown here has the ⌜replacement text⌝ The energy & angst of youth display'd:

```
<!ENTITY % what
    "energy &amp; angst"
>
<!ENTITY % whom
    "youth"
>
<!ENTITY subject
    "%what; of %whom;"
>
<!ENTITY phrase
    "The &subject; display'd"
>
```

> ... A ⌜character reference⌝ is **included** when the indicated character is processed in place of the reference itself.

See Appendix E of the specification for examples of how character references are processed in various circumstances; see also Part 1 of this book for more examples and discussion.

Note that you cannot use a character reference to escape markup characters inside an internal entity declaration, because the resulting character is processed again in place of the reference, and the text re-scanned, when the entity is referenced.

4.4.3 Included If Validating

> When an ⌜XML processor⌝ recognizes a reference to a ⌜parsed entity⌝, in order to ⌜validate⌝ the document, the processor ⌜must⌝ include its ⌜replacement text⌝. . . .

This is true for all entities of all types.

> ... If the entity is external, and the processor is not attempting to ⌜validate⌝ the XML document, the processor ⌜may⌝, but need not, include the entity's ⌜replacement text⌝. . . .

Note that this applies both to a ⌜non-validating processor⌝ that cannot validate, and to a non-validating processor that can operate as a ⌜validating processor⌝ but that happens not to be doing so on this particular XML document. The phrase "but need not" is formally redundant, because of the definition of ⌜may⌝.

> ... If a non-validating parser [sic] does not include the replacement text, it ⌜must⌝ inform the ⌜application⌝ that it recognized, but did not read, the entity.

For "parser," read "processor."

A non-validating XML processor may well not have seen the declarations for all of the external parsed entities that a document is using, since that processor is not required to read the ⌜external document type declaration subset⌝. Including the replacement text of an ⌜external parsed entity⌝ is therefore optional for a non-validating processor (see the next paragraph), but the XML specification does not place any restrictions on exactly *which* entities should be included. A processor might start loading all ⌜external parsed entities⌐ as soon as it sees the declarations for them, but read only those that it manages to load within a certain time, or that are smaller than a given size. A more conventional approach might be to include either all external parsed entities or none, perhaps at ⌐user option⌐, but the XML specification does not mandate any particular strategy.

> **This rule is based on the recognition that the automatic inclusion provided by the ⌐SGML⌐ and XML ⌐entity⌐ mechanism, primarily designed to support modularity in authoring, is not necessarily appropriate for other applications, in particular document browsing. Browsers, for example, when encountering an ⌐external parsed entity reference⌐, might choose to provide a visual indication of the entity's presence and retrieve it for display only on demand.**

If the accompanying ⌐XLink⌐ specification had been ready when XML was published, it is likely that this scenario would have been handled with a different linking construct for optionally embedded document components. Anyone developing a new browser, document viewer, or editor should consider using XLink (or some other hypertext linking mechanism) that indicates whether any given reference should be included in the user's view, replaced by an icon until selected, included or not included depending on an option, displayed in a pop-up window, read out loud on the streets, or printed out, screwed up into a small ball, and thrown out of the window. See www.w3.com/XML/ for the current status of XLink, which is a draft at the time of this writing (late 1998).

4.4.4 Forbidden

The following are forbidden, and constitute ⌐fatal errors⌐:

- **the appearance of a reference to an ⌐unparsed [external] entity⌐**

This is because the assumption is that an ⌐unparsed external entity⌐ is not in XML, and would probably cause errors if it were included. The following is always an error:

```
<!ENTITY LiamPic
    SYSTEM "http://www.groveware.com/~lee/LiamPic.jpg"
    NDATA JPEG
>
. . .
and here is my picture: &LiamPic;    (illegal example)
```

- the appearance of any character or general-entity reference in the DTD
  except within an EntityValue[9] or AttValue[10].

Since `content`[43] is not allowed in a DTD except in these two places, this
restriction is not surprising.

- a reference to an external entity in an attribute value

References to external unparsed entities and external parameter entities
within attribute values have already been forbidden in the section describing attribute values in Chapter 3 above, so it should not be surprising.
There is no particular reason or rationale for this restriction in XML. If it
causes you problems in designing XML document structures, recall that an
attribute can always be replaced by an element, as indicated in the following two examples, which convey the same information in slightly different
forms; you can include references to external entities inside element content in the second example:

```
<Student name="Simon" age="24"/>
<Student>
    <name>Simon</name>
    <age>24</age>
    <!--* You could include an external parsed general entity
        * here if you wanted.
        *-->
</Student>
```

4.4.5 Included in Literal

When [a general internal] entity reference appears in an attribute value, or [an
internal] ⌈parameter entity reference⌉ appears in a literal entity value, its
⌈replacement text⌉ is processed in place of the reference itself as though it were
part of the document at the location the reference was recognized, except that
a single or double quote character in the replacement text is always treated as
a normal ⌈data character⌉ and will not terminate the literal. . . .

Attribute values (both in the document instance and in default values in
the DTD) and the ⌈replacement texts⌉ of ⌈internal entities⌉ are surrounded
with quotes. This rule says that an entity that is expanded within these

quote-delimited strings can itself contain quotes without making things go wrong.

. . . For example, this is well-formed:

```
<!ENTITY % YN
    '"Yes"'
>
<!ENTITY WhatHeSaid
    "He said &YN;"
>
```

while this is not:

```
<!ENTITY EndAttr
    "27'"
>
[. . .]
<element attribute='a-&EndAttr;>
(illegal example, not well formed)
```

4.4.6 Notify

When the name of an ⌐unparsed [external] entity⌐ appears as a ⌐token⌐ in the value of an attribute of declared type ENTITY or ENTITIES, a ⌐validating processor⌐ must inform the ⌐application⌐ of the system and public (if any) identifiers for both the entity and its associated ⌐notation⌐.

The ⌐system identifier⌐ and optional ⌐public identifier⌐ associated with an ⌐external entity⌐ are what tell the ⌐XML processor⌐ or ⌐application⌐ how to fetch the actual data contained in the entity. An XML processor never actually needs to inspect the contents of an ⌐external unparsed entity⌐, so it simply passes the information on how to fetch the resource back to the ⌐application⌐.

Note: A ⌐non-validating parser⌐ may well not have read the declarations for external entities, and so may not know the ⌐system identifier⌐ (nor the ⌐public identifier⌐, if one was given).

4.4.7 Bypassed

When a ⌜general entity reference⌝ appears in the EntityValue[9] in an ⌜entity declaration⌝, it is bypassed and left as is.

A ⌜general entity reference⌝ within the declared value of an entity is expanded not when the declaration is seen but when the entity is referenced. See Appendix D to the XML specification, "Expansion of Entity and Character References," and also Part 1 of this book, for more discussion of this together with examples.

4.4.8 Included as PE

Just as with ⌜external parsed entities⌝, ⌜parameter entities⌝ need only be included if validating. . . .

This is why, in the internal DTD subset that must be read by all XML processors, even if only to skip over it, parameter entities cannot occur within declarations, and why ⌜conditional sections⌝ cannot occur within the ⌜internal document type definition subset⌝. These restrictions mean that the first occurrence of] outside of a literal or comment terminates the doc-typedecl[28].

The XML specification does not require that a non-validating processor read external parameter entities. But this in turn means that internal general entities should not be defined using parameter entities if non-validating processors might be used. In the following example, a non-validating XML processor may not be able to expand the ⌜internal general entity⌝ ShortDescription correctly. If GirlBoy had instead been declared as a ⌜general external entity⌝, even a non-validating XML processor could expand ShortDescription correctly, provided of course that the two entity declarations were moved into the ⌜internal document type declaration subset⌝.

Note: The example must have been contained in an external entity— either the anonymous ⌜document type entity⌝ or an ⌜external parameter entity⌝—and not in the ⌜internal DTD subset⌝ at the start of the ⌜document entity⌝. This is because the ⌜internal parameter entity⌝ GirlBoy does not contain a complete declaration, and also because of the ⌜internal parameter entity reference⌝ to %GirlBoy; inside an entity declaration. Neither of these two things are legal inside the ⌐internal DTD subset⌐. Because of this, a non-validating XML processor is required to skip all entity definitions after the first reference to an external parameter entity that it does not include.

```
<!--* This example is legal but poor style; see the
    * accompanying text.  Use general entities and not
    * parameter entities for text substitution in
    * entity values.
    *-->
<!ENTITY % GirlBoy
    "Max"
>
<!ENTITY ShortDescription
    "%GirlBoy; was a boy born with a baby girl's body"
>
```

. . . When a ⌐parameter-entity reference⌐ is recognized in the DTD and included, its ⌐replacement text⌐ is enlarged by the attachment of one leading and one following space (#x20) character; the intent is to constrain the replacement text of parameter entities to contain an integral number of ⌐grammatical tokens⌐ in the DTD.

This means that in fact the ShortDescription example ends up with the following ⌐replacement text⌐: "Max was a boy born with a baby girl's body", where there is a space at the start and two spaces after Max. Now, Max is a pretty spaced out sort of person, so perhaps this doesn't matter too much, but in general it is another reason not to use parameter entities in this way.

What is meant by "an integral number of grammatical tokens" is *whole words*, so that the following example is not allowed, because <!ELE MEN T (with spaces) is a syntax error:

```
<!ENTITY % boyz
    "MEN"
>
<!ELE%boyz;T mangled        (illegal example)
    (#PCDATA)
>
```

We now return to the table showing where entities are allowed, one column at a time. See the notes above on the phrases used within the table—what follows is not a complete summary.

Entity type: Parameter
Reference in Content: Not Recognized
Reference in Attribute Value: Not Recognized
Occurs as Attribute Value: Not Recognized

An XML ⌜parameter entity reference⌝ is only recognized within the DTD; elsewhere, the % sign is treated as a regular character and not as introducing a parameter entity reference.

Reference in Entity Value: Included in Literal

The parameter entity is replaced by its value when an entity declaration is seen.

Reference in DTD: Included as PE

Parameter entities in a DTD ⌜must⌝ be understood by a ⌜validating XML processor⌝, and ⌜may⌝ be understood by a ⌜non-validating processor⌝.

Entity type: Internal General
Reference in Content: Included

The use of ⌜internal general entities⌝ was considered one of the major advantages of XML over HTML in even the simplest of applications, so all ⌜XML processors⌝ must handle them correctly.

Reference in Attribute Value: Included in Literal

⌜General internal entity references⌝ are always expanded inside attribute values. The difference between *Included in literal* and *Included* is the handling of quotes; see the notes above.

Occurs as Attribute Value: Forbidden
Reference in Entity Value: Bypassed

The embedded entity reference is expanded when the containing entity is used, not when it is declared.

Reference in DTD: Forbidden

General entity references are not allowed in a DTD outside default attribute values and entity literals.

Entity type: External Parsed General

Reference in Content: Included if Validating

⌈Non-validating XML processors⌉ are not required to handle ⌈external entities⌉.

Reference in Attribute Value: Forbidden
Occurs as Attribute Value: Forbidden
Reference in Entity Value: Bypassed

The embedded entity reference is expanded when the containing entity is used, not when it is declared.

Reference in DTD: Forbidden
Entity type: Unparsed
Reference in Content: Forbidden
Reference in Attribute Value: Forbidden
Occurs as Attribute Value: Notify

The XML processor never reads an ⌈unparsed entity⌉ itself, but only passes information about the entity back to the application.

Reference in Entity Value: Forbidden

Reference in DTD: Forbidden
Entity type: Character

That is, a ⌈character reference⌉.

Reference in Content: Included
Reference in Attribute Value: Included
Occurs as Attribute Value: Not Recognized

When an entity is used as an entity value, there is no delimiter (no % or &), so that a character reference as an attribute value would look like `image="x405"`, and the XML processor will look for an external unparsed entity of that name and never know that the author meant to use the character whose hexadecimal Unicode value was 405.

Reference in Entity Value: Included

Character references are always expanded as soon as they are seen.

Reference in DTD: Forbidden

4.5 Construction of Internal Entity Replacement Text

In discussing the treatment of ⌐internal entities⌐, it is useful to distinguish two forms of the entity's value. The *literal entity value* is the quoted string actually present in the ⌐entity declaration⌐, corresponding to the ⌐non-terminal⌐ EntityValue[9]. The *replacement text* is the content of the entity, after replacement of ⌐character references⌐ and ⌐parameter-entity references⌐.

Informally, the term ⌐replacement text⌐ is often used to mean the quoted string in the entity declaration, but this is incorrect. See Part 1 of this book for a discussion of this, and also see Appendix D of the XML specification, "Expansion of Entity and Character References."

The ⌐literal entity value⌐ as given in an internal entity declaration (EntityValue[9]) may contain character, parameter-entity, and general-entity references. . . .

See the previous section for a more detailed discussion of entity references and how they are treated in various contexts.

. . . Such references must be contained entirely within the ⌐literal entity value⌐. . . .

In other words, the following example is illegal:

```
<!ENTITY appearance
    "beautiful"
>
<!ENTITY Priscilla
```

```
    "I am very &app"     (illegal example)
>
. . .
<person>&Priscilla;earance;</person>
```

... The actual ⌐replacement text⌐ that is included as described above [in the previous paragraph of the specification] must contain the *replacement text* of any ⌐parameter entities⌐ referred to, and must contain the character referred to, in place of any ⌐character references⌐ in the ⌐literal entity value⌐; however, ⌐general-entity references⌐ must be left as-is, unexpanded. . . .

⌐General entity references⌐ are expanded only when the replacement text is used, not when it is defined.

. . . For example, given the following declarations:

```
<!ENTITY % pub
    "&#xc9;ditions Gallimard"
>
<!ENTITY rights
    "All rights reserved"
>
<!ENTITY book
    "La Peste: Albert Camus, &#xA9; 1947 %pub;. &rights;"
>
```

then the replacement text for the entity "book" is:[

```
La Peste: Albert Camus,
© 1947  Éditions Gallimard . &rights;
```

Note the extra (and almost certainly unwanted) spaces around the expansion of %pub; here. These spaces are not actually shown in the printed and on-line XML specification, presumably in error.

The ⌐general-entity reference⌐ "&rights;" would be expanded should the reference "&book;" appear in the document's ⌐content⌐ or [in] an ⌐attribute value⌐.

One useful consequence of this is that the general entity (rights, for example) need not actually be declared at the point at which the containing entity (book in this case) is declared. In particular, the definition for rights might appear in the ⌜internal document type declaration subset⌝ and the definition for book in the ⌜external DTD subset⌝. In this way, a single XML document could redefine rights without having to change the external DTD.

> These simple rules may have complex interactions; for a detailed discussion of a difficult example, see Appendix D, *Expansion of Entity and Character References.*

Whether the rules are simple or not is a matter of judgment! See Part 1 of this book for some introductory material explaining how entities work, as well as our comments on Appendix D of the specification, given in Part 2, Appendix D of this book.

4.6 Predefined Entities

> ⌜Entity [references]⌝ and ⌜character references⌝ can both be used to **escape the left angle bracket, ampersand, and other delimiters. A set of [internal] general entities (amp, lt, gt, apos, quot) is specified for this purpose. Numeric character references may also be used; they are expanded immediately when recognized and must be treated as character data, so the numeric character references "<" and "&" may be used to escape < and & when they occur in character data.**

This is not entirely correct. The predefined entities lt and amp may be used to escape the left angle bracket and the ampersand with impunity, but ⌜numeric character references⌝ will only protect these characters from a single level of entity expansion. See the example in Appendix D to the XML specification.

> All ⌜XML processors⌝ ⌜must⌝ recognize these entities whether they are declared or not. ⌜For interoperability⌝, valid ⌜XML documents⌝ should declare these entities, like any others, before using them. If the entities in question are declared, they ⌜must⌝ be declared as internal [general] entities whose replacement text is the single character being escaped or a character reference to that character, as shown below.

Recall that ⌜for interoperability⌝ means for older SGML software. The term "should" appears to have been used in error here for ⌜may⌝; there is no need to declare the entities unless SGML software is being used that pre-dates the WebSGML changes that were made to SGML to support XML.

```
<!ENTITY lt   "&#38;#60;">
<!ENTITY gt   "&#62;">
<!ENTITY amp  "&#38;#38;">
<!ENTITY apos "&#39;">
<!ENTITY quot "&#34;">
```

Note that the < and & characters in the declarations of "lt" and "amp" are doubly escaped to meet the requirement that entity replacement be well-formed.

When the declaration of lt is read, the replacement text stored is <, because character references are replaced when entities are declared. When the entity lt is used, the replacement value is again parsed, and the resulting character reference is expanded to yield a literal < character.

4.7 Notation Declarations

See also Chapter 3, Section 3.3.1, "Attribute Types," for information about NOTATION-valued attributes.

Notations identify by name the format of ⌜unparsed entities⌝, the format of ⌜elements⌝ which bear a ⌜notation attribute⌝, or the application to which a ⌜processing instruction⌝ is addressed.

An element with a notation attribute cannot contain arbitrary non-XML data—all element content must be well-formed XML, even if a notation attribute indicates that the content of that element is something other than XML.

An example use for a notation on an element might be to say that the content of that element is a JPEG image encoded using the MIME base64 mechanism.

Notation declarations provide a name for the notation, for use in entity and attribute-list declarations and in ⌜attribute specifications⌝, and an ⌜external identifier⌝ for the notation which may allow an ⌜XML processor⌝ or its client ⌜application⌝ to locate a helper application capable of processing data in the given notation.

Notation Declarations

```
[82] NotationDecl ::=
        '<!NOTATION' S[3] Name[5] S[3]
                        (ExternalID[75] | PublicID[83]) S[3]?
     '>'

[83] PublicID ::= 'PUBLIC' S[3] PubidLiteral[12]
```

It could be argued that a notation declaration is the only place in XML where a public identifier is of any real use. Various applications could agree, for example, on a public identifier for the TIFF image format, and another for JPEG. In fact, no such agreement has been made, and a public identifier is no better here than a system one. Furthermore, as we have commented elsewhere, in a World Wide Web (HTTP) environment, an application has to accept resources in the format in which they are delivered, rather than making assumptions before asking a remote server.

We suggest using a notation system or public identifier that is simply a semicolon-separated list of acceptable ⌈MIME⌉ media types.

> ⌈XML processors⌉ must provide ⌈applications⌉ with the name and ⌈external identifier⌉(s) of any ⌈notation⌉ declared and referred to in an ⌈attribute value⌉, ⌈attribute definition⌉ or [external unparsed] ⌈entity declaration⌉. They [the processors] ⌈may⌉ additionally resolve the external identifier into the system identifier, file name, or other information needed to allow the application to call a processor for data in the notation described. (It is not an error, however, for XML documents to declare and refer to notations for which notation-specific applications are not available on the system where the XML processor or application is running.)

There seems to be an assumption that there is only one action ever associated with an object that has an associate notation. An action for a C program might be *compile*, but other actions include *edit, print, save, send as e-mail, run, convert to Java,* or even *remove.*

The idea that the system identifier might be used to name a program to run could be taken as a mild form of humor in an Internet world; the idea that someone can send me an XML document that might cause my XML-aware mail reader to fetch an unknown resource over the Web and then run some arbitrary local program is neither pleasant nor acceptable in a security-conscious environment.

We urge XML implementors not to treat the system identifier of a notation as referring to an application to run. Instead, as mentioned above, treat it as a list of media types that are plausible for the given object.

4.8 Document Entity

The document entity serves as the root of the entity tree and a starting-point for an XML processor. This specification does not specify how the document entity is to be located by an XML processor; unlike other entities, the document entity has no name and might well appear on a processor input stream without any identification at all.

The document entity is the file or resource that contains the document. The document entity may refer to and/or include other entities in turn.

Note: The external entity referred to in the DOCTYPE declaration has no entity name, although it does have a system identifier.

CHAPTER

5

Conformance

This part of the specification deals with the relationship between the XML document, the XML processor and the concepts of well-formedness and validity.

5.1 Validating and Non-Validating Processors

> Conforming ⌜XML processors⌝ fall into two classes: ⌜validating⌝ and ⌜non-validating⌝.

Some ⌜XML processors⌝ can operate in either mode, but at any one time for a given document they fall into one or the other category.

> Validating and non-validating processors alike must report violations of this specification's ⌜well-formedness constraints⌝ in the ⌜content⌝ of the ⌜document entity⌝ and any other [external] ⌜parsed entities⌝ that they read.

If the input to an ⌜XML processor⌝ is not ⌜well-formed⌝, it is, by definition, not XML. Although the XML specification clearly cannot be binding on non-XML objects, it *is* binding on software that claims to be an XML processor. Automatic silent correction of errors (as is done by the HTML parsers inside most World Wide Web browsers, for example) is explicitly disallowed.

> **Validating processors must report violations of the constraints expressed by the declarations in the DTD, and failures to fulfill the validity constraints given in this specification. . . .**

There is no point in having declarations and constraints if errors are not reported. One of the hardest things for programmers in dealing with the World Wide Web is that so many web pages are full of errors. To see why this is so, consider the fact that the major browsers do not report errors in HTML documents. As a result, people edit their HTML until it looks right, and if it contains errors, they never know about them. But for a programmer writing a script, life is very complex, for the script will certainly see all the errors and will have to deal with them.

XML documents are always ⌈well-formed⌉, and can also be ⌈valid⌉, and one way to ensure that is to require that all XML processors that conform to the specification are required to report errors.

> **. . . To accomplish this, validating XML processors must read and process the entire DTD and all external parsed entities references in the document.**

See Chapter 4 of this specification for more details about the DTD and entities, and also see the examples in Part 1 of this book. The important point here is that reading an external entity may require fetching data over a network, so there is likely to be a significant performance overhead to using a validating XML processor in some applications.

> **⌈Non-validating processors⌉ are required to check only the ⌈document entity⌉, including the entire ⌈internal DTD subset⌉, for ⌈well-formedness⌉. . . .**

A ⌈non-validating XML processor⌉ checks only for ⌈well-formedness⌉ and not that the ⌈XML document⌉ is ⌈valid⌉, of course

Even a non-validating XML processor must be able to parse the declarations that might appear in the ⌈internal document type declaration subset⌉ at least well enough to find the end of the subset and the start of the document, but there are some additional capabilities that are required, described in the next sentence in the specification. The processor does not need to read declarations found in external parameter entities, nor the external DTD subset. A lot of care went into the design of XML to ensure that this would be the case, as it is *not* true in general for SGML systems.

> ... While they are not required to check the document for ⌜validity⌝, they are required to **process** all the declarations they read in the ⌜internal DTD subset⌝ and in any ⌜parameter entity⌝ that they read, up to the first reference to a parameter entity that they do *not* read; ...

As described in Section 4.4.3, "Included if Validating," a non-validating XML processor is not required to fetch and process ⌜external parameter entities⌝.

> ... that is to say, they must use the information in those declarations to normalize ⌜attribute values⌝, include the ⌜replacement text⌝ of ⌜internal entities⌝, and supply default attribute values. ...

For normalization of attributes, see Section 3.3.3 of the XML specification, "Attribute Value Normalization." For including ⌜replacement text⌝ of ⌜internal entities⌝, see Section 4.4, "XML Processor Treatment of Entities and References." For default ⌜attribute⌝ values, see Section 3.3.2, "Attribute Defaults."

> ... They ⌜must⌝ not process ⌜entity declarations⌝ or ⌜attribute-list declarations⌝ encountered after a reference to a ⌜parameter entity⌝ that is not read, since the entity may have contained overriding declarations.

Figure 5.1 shows a small document entity that refers to an ⌜external parameter entity⌝; that external parameter entity is shown in Figure 5.2, and contains an entity declaration that overrides one in the document entity. A non-validating processor that does not fetch the external parameter entity will not detect this and will not be able to construct the correct replacement text for the internal general entity `theBoy`, the string `"Matthew Harris"`.

The consequence for document design is that you should put any ⌜entity declarations⌝ local to the document near the *start* of the ⌜internal DTD subset⌝, before any ⌜parameter entity references⌝.

```
<?xml version="1.0">
<!DOCTYPE Student [
  <!ENTITY % definitions
      SYSTEM "student.dtd"
  >
  %definitions;
  <!ENTITY theBoy
      "Simon A. Pilgrim"
  >
]>
<Student>
  <Name>&boy;</Name>
  <Number>591</Number>
</Student>
```

Figure 5.1 Sample document entity.

5.2 Using XML Processors

The behavior of a ⌐validating XML processor⌐ is highly predictable; it must read every piece of a document and report all ⌐well-formedness⌐ and ⌐validity⌐ violations. Less is required of a ⌐non-validating processor⌐; it need not read any part of a document other than the ⌐document entity⌐. This has two effects that may be important to users of ⌐XML processors⌐:

- Certain well-formedness ⌐errors⌐, specifically those that require reading external entities, may not be detected by a ⌐non-validating processor⌐.

```
<!--* The following entity declaration overrides the
    * declaration in the instance shown in Example 5.1,
    * because this file is included before the
    * declaration in that file.
    *-->
<!ENTITY theBoy
    "Matthew Harris"
>
```

Figure 5.2 Student.dtd (excerpt).

Examples include the constraints entitled *Entity Declared*, *Parsed Entity*, and *No Recursion*, as well as some of the cases described as forbidden in Section 4.4, *XML Processor Treatment of Entities and References*.

The three well-formedness constraints mentioned are described in Section 4.1, "Character and Entity References." Violations of *Entity Declared* might not be detected because an ⌐entity⌐ might be declared in an ⌐external parameter entity⌐ that was not read, so that the ⌐non-validating XML processor⌐ did not see it. Violations of *Parsed Entity* might not be reported because the processor would not be able to tell if an entity was parsed or unparsed without having seen its declaration. Violations of *No Recursion* similarly cannot be enforced without expanding all entities.

For the creator of XML documents, this means that it is essential to use a ⌐validating XML processor⌐ to check for errors.

For the application developer, software architect, or programmer, it means considering carefully the choice of whether to use a validating or a non-validating XML processor, or to allow the user the choice of either (as for example does Peter Murray-Rust in Jumbo, the ⌐Chemical Markup Language⌐ browser).

■ **The information passed from the processor to the application may vary, depending on whether the processor reads parameter and external entities. For example, a ⌐non-validating processor⌐ ⌐may⌐ not normalize attribute values, where doing so depends on having read declarations in external or parameter entities.**

This does not mean to imply that reading the same document twice with the same XML processor might produce different results (although it might), but rather that if the same application can use two different XML processors, one validating and the other non-validating, or both non-validating, the two XML processors will not in general return exactly the same information back to the application, even though they are each given exactly the same input document.

Two validating XML processors must return all of the information back to the document that is demanded by the XML specification, but they may provide additional information, and the way in which the information is provided is not defined here. There are a number of widely used programming interfaces to XML processors, of which SAX is the simplest and most widespread but provides the least information.

CHAPTER 6

Notation

This chapter describes the notation used for the XML specification itself, rather than the ⌐notation⌐ concept in the XML language with its associated `NOTATION` keyword.

Refer to Part 1 of this book for an introduction to reading the specification, and also to Appendix A in Part 3 of this book, which lists the XML productions with brief annotations.

> **The formal grammar of XML is given in this specification using a simple Extended Backus-Naur Form (EBNF) notation. Each rule in the grammar defines one symbol, in the form**

```
symbol ::= expression
```

This is commonly read, "*Symbol* is defined as *expression*". The whole construct is known as a ⌐rule⌐ or ⌐production⌐ or ⌐production rule⌐.

> **Symbols are written with an initial capital letter if they are defined by a regular expression, or with an initial lowercase letter otherwise. Literal strings are quoted.**

The use of initial capital letters in the XML specification does not appear to follow this rule reliably in practice. For example, document and prolog do not start with a capital letter, but CDSect does.

Literal strings are surrounded with either single or double quotes; either double or single quotes can be used as long as they are the same at both ends.

> **Within the expression on the right-hand side of a ⌜rule⌝, the following expressions are used to ⌜match⌝ strings of one or more characters**

See Chapter 1 of the XML specification for the formal definition of ⌜match⌝.

> **#xN: where N is a hexadecimal integer, the expression matches the ⌜character⌝ in ISO/IEC 10646 whose canonical (⌜UCS-4⌝) code value, when interpreted as an unsigned binary number, has the value indicated. The number of leading zeros in the #xN form is insignificant; the number of leading zeros in the corresponding code value is governed by the character encoding in use and is not significant for XML.**

See Appendix B in Part 3 of this book on characters and encodings. The simple description is that #x4A on the right side of a production rule matches character 4A in Unicode, which (as a glance at a hexadecimal character chart will show) is an uppercase J. The part about leading zeros means that #x004A and #x4A are the same.

> **[a-zA-Z], [#xN-#xN]: ⌜matches⌝ any character with a value in the range(s) indicated (inclusive).**

For example, [a-d] matches any one of a, b, c, and d.

> **[^a-z], [^#xN-#xN]: matches any character with a value *outside* the range indicated.**

In other words, any character that matches [b-w] does not match [^b-w], and vice versa.

Note that the XML specification avoids using a minus sign in character ranges, as, for example, [—v] looks decidedly odd and, more importantly, might appear to be a mistake. Also, in a few places, most notably in the discussion of the xml:lang attribute in Chapter 2, the specification uses the form ([A-Z]|[a-z])+ instead of [A-Za-z]+, presumably to emphasize that the value is case-insensitive in that case.

[^abc], '^#xN#xN#xN]: matches any character with a value not among the characters given.

Thus, [^aeiou] would match a w but not an a.

"string": matches a literal string matching that given inside the double quotes.
'string': matches a literal string matching that given inside the single quotes.

The only difference between using single or double quotes for a string is whether you can put single or double quotes inside its value. As in XML literal values, the strings in the grammar productions in the specification do not expect the string value to be interpreted differently depending on the type of quotes that are used around it.

These symbols may be combined to match more complex patterns as follows, where A and B represent simple expressions: . . .

The phrase "simple expressions" is not defined; it appears to mean any of the above forms or any of the forms that follow, inside parentheses.

(expression): expression is treated as a unit and may be combined as described in this list.
A?: matches A or nothing; optional A.
A B: matches A followed by B.
A | B: matches A or B but not both.
A - B: matches any string that matches A but does not match B.

This form is unusual: It does not come from SGML, and is also not found in most computer science regular expression texts. Implementors will generally have to rework the expressions to avoid this construction, since underlying parsing and expression libraries do not usually support it directly.

A+: matches one or more occurrences of A.

This is the same as "A A*" (see next item).

A*: matches zero or more occurrences of A.

This could also be written as "(A+)?", as long as A+ is not already implemented in terms of A* itself.

An example of how to combine the expressions may be useful. Consider the rule for `SystemLiteral`[11]:

```
[11] SystemLiteral ::=  ('"' [^"]* '"') | ("'" [^']* "'")
```

The right-hand side of this rule is in the form A | B, where A is (`'"'` `[^"]*` `'"'`) and B is (`"'"` `[^']*` `"'"`), and can be thought of as being split by the | into two halves.

Each of these two halves (A and B) is of the form (`expression`).

The leftmost `expression` is `'"'` `[^"]*` `'"'`, which is a sequence of the form A B C. The rules above do not actually allow a three-term sequence, so we have to pretend that they do, and tread gently at this point.

The first and third expressions in the sequence are literal strings: `'"'`, a string matching exactly one double-quote character.

The middle term in our sequence of three expressions, `[^"]*`, is of the form A*, where A is the expression `[^"]`, matching any character other than a double quote. This middle term then matches a sequence of zero or more characters that are not double quotes.

The first half of production [11] could then be read as a double-quote character followed by any number of characters that are not double quotes, and ending in another double-quote character.

The right-hand half of the production is the same as the left side except with single quotes instead of double ones. Here are some examples:

```
"example"                            matches OK
"he stood 5'6" tall in his bare feet" not OK, contains a "-sign
" "                                  OK, zero characters
                                     between the double
                                     quotes
hello                                not OK, no double quotes
'single quotes'                      OK
"one of each'                        not OK, does not match
                                     either half
```

Other notations used in the productions are:

/* ... */ comment.

The specification twice includes comments on specific production rules using this notation; in each case, the comment is to explain an expression, and does not change the meaning of the text in any way.

[wfc: ...] ⌜well-formedness constraint⌝; this identifies by name a ⌜constraint⌝ on ⌜well-formed documents⌝ associated with a ⌜production⌝.

Since every XML document must be well-formed, the well-formedness constraints must be implemented by all XML processors. In general they are used for things that were difficult to describe using the grammar rules.

[vc: ...] ⌜validity constraint⌝; this identifies by name a ⌜constraint⌝ on ⌜valid documents⌝ associated with a ⌜production⌝.

XML documents that are ⌜well-formed⌝ but that are not also ⌜valid⌝ do not need to meet these constraints, and a ⌜non-validating XML processor⌝ therefore does not need to check for them.

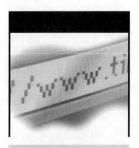

Appendixes

The XML Specification has seven appendixes, A through G*. In this part of the book (Part 2), we have annotated Appendix D, *Expansion of Entity and Character References* (Non-Normative) and Appendix E, *Deterministic Content Models* (Non-Normative). We reprint the other appendixes without change, for completeness. Appendix B, *Character Classes* and Appendix F, *Autodetection of Character Encodings,* are not ⌐Normative¬, and much of the material is discussed in *Part 3*, Appendix B.

*Note that these are not the same as the appendixes in Part 3 of this book; we have of necessity retained the numbering *(and lettering)* of the XML Specification.

References

A.1 Normative References

IANA (Internet Assigned Numbers Authority) *Official Names for Character Sets*, ed. Keld Simonsen et al. *See* ftp://ftp.isi.edu/in-notes/iana/assignments/character-sets.

IETF RFC 1766 IETF (Internet Engineering Task Force). RFC 1766: *Tags for the Identification of Languages*, ed. H. Alvestrand. 1995.

ISO 639 (International Organization for Standardization). ISO 639:1988 (E). *Code for the representation of names of languages.* [Geneva]: International Organization for Standardization, 1988.

ISO 3166 (International Organization for Standardization). ISO 3166-1:1997 (E). *Codes for the representation of names of countries and their subdivisions— Part 1: Country codes* [Geneva]: International Organization for Standardization, 1997.

ISO/IEC 10646 ISO (International Organization for Standardization). ISO/IEC 10646-1993 (E). *Information technology — Universal Multiple-Octet Coded Character Set (UCS) — Part 1: Architecture and Basic Multilingual Plane.* [Geneva]: International Organization for Standardization, 1993 (plus amendments AM 1 through AM 7).

Unicode The Unicode Consortium. *The Unicode Standard, Version 2.0.* Reading, Mass.: Addison-Wesley Developers Press, 1996.

A.2 Other References

Aho/Ullman Aho, Alfred V., Ravi Sethi, and Jeffrey D. Ullman. *Compilers: Principles, Techniques, and Tools.* Reading: Addison-Wesley, 1986, rpt. corr. 1988.

Berners-Lee et al. Berners-Lee, T., R. Fielding, and L. Masinter. *Uniform Resource Identifiers (URI): Generic Syntax and Semantics.* 1997. (Work in progress; see updates to RFC1738.)

Brüggemann-Klein Brüggemann-Klein, Anne. *Regular Expressions into Finite Automata.* Extended abstract in I. Simon, Hrsg., LATIN 1992, S. 97-98. Springer-Verlag, Berlin 1992. Full Version in Theoretical Computer Science 120: 197-213, 1993.

Brüggemann-Klein and Wood Brüggemann-Klein, Anne, and Derick Wood. *Deterministic Regular Languages.* Universität Freiburg, Institut für Informatik, Bericht 38, Oktober 1991.

Clark James Clark. Comparison of SGML and XML. *See* www.w3.org/TR/NOTE-sgml-xml-971215.

IETF RFC1738 IETF (Internet Engineering Task Force). RFC 1738: *Uniform Resource Locators (URL),* ed. T. Berners-Lee, L. Masinter, M. McCahill. 1994.

IETF RFC1808 IETF (Internet Engineering Task Force). RFC 1808: *Relative Uniform Resource Locators,* ed. R. Fielding. 1995.

IETF RFC2141 IETF (Internet Engineering Task Force). RFC 2141: *URN Syntax,* ed. R. Moats. 1997.

ISO 8879 ISO (International Organization for Standardization). ISO 8879:1986(E). *Information processing—Text and Office Systems—Standard Generalized Markup Language (SGML).* First edition—1986-10-15. [Geneva]: International Organization for Standardization, 1986.

ISO/IEC 10744 ISO (International Organization for Standardization). ISO/IEC 10744-1992 (E). *Information technology—Hypermedia/Time-based Structuring Language (HyTime).* [Geneva]: International Organization for Standardization, 1992. Extended Facilities Annexe. [Geneva]: International Organization for Standardization, 1996.

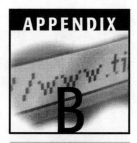

Character Classes

Following the characteristics defined in the Unicode standard, characters are classed as base characters (among others, these contain the alphabetic characters of the Latin alphabet, without diacritics), ideographic characters, and combining characters (among others, this class contains most diacritics); these classes combine to form the class of letters. Digits and extenders are also distinguished.

Characters

```
[84]Letter    ::=  BaseChar[85] | Ideographic[86]
[85]BaseChar  ::=  [#x0041-#x005A] | [#x0061-#x007A] | [#x00C0-#x00D6] |
                   [#x00D8-#x00F6] | [#x00F8-#x00FF] | [#x0100-#x0131] |
                   [#x0134-#x013E] | [#x0141-#x0148] | [#x014A-#x017E] |
                   [#x0180-#x01C3] | [#x01CD-#x01F0] | [#x01F4-#x01F5] |
                   [#x01FA-#x0217] | [#x0250-#x02A8] | [#x02BB-#x02C1] |
                   #x0386 | [#x0388-#x038A] | #x038C | [#x038E-#x03A1] |
                   [#x03A3-#x03CE] | [#x03D0-#x03D6] | #x03DA | #x03DC |
                   #x03DE | #x03E0 | [#x03E2-#x03F3] | [#x0401-#x040C] |
                   [#x040E-#x044F] | [#x0451-#x045C] | [#x045E-#x0481] |
                   [#x0490-#x04C4] | [#x04C7-#x04C8] | [#x04CB-#x04CC] |
                   [#x04D0-#x04EB] | [#x04EE-#x04F5] | [#x04F8-#x04F9] |
```

```
[#x0531-#x0556] | #x0559 | [#x0561-#x0586] | [#x05D0-
#x05EA] | [#x05F0-#x05F2] | [#x0621-#x063A] |
[#x0641-#x064A] | [#x0671-#x06B7] | [#x06BA-#x06BE] |
[#x06C0-#x06CE] | [#x06D0-#x06D3] | #x06D5 | [#x06E5-
#x06E6] | [#x0905-#x0939] | #x093D | [#x0958-#x0961]
| [#x0985-#x098C] | [#x098F-#x0990] | [#x0993-#x09A8]
| [#x09AA-#x09B0] | #x09B2 | [#x09B6-#x09B9] |
[#x09DC-#x09DD] | [#x09DF-#x09E1] | [#x09F0-#x09F1] |
[#x0A05-#x0A0A] | [#x0A0F-#x0A10] | [#x0A13-#x0A28] |
[#x0A2A-#x0A30] | [#x0A32-#x0A33] | [#x0A35-#x0A36] |
[#x0A38-#x0A39] | [#x0A59-#x0A5C] | #x0A5E | [#x0A72-
#x0A74] | [#x0A85-#x0A8B] | #x0A8D | [#x0A8F-#x0A91]
| [#x0A93-#x0AA8] | [#x0AAA-#x0AB0] | [#x0AB2-#x0AB3]
| [#x0AB5-#x0AB9] | #x0ABD | #x0AE0 | [#x0B05-#x0B0C]
| [#x0B0F-#x0B10] | [#x0B13-#x0B28] | [#x0B2A-#x0B30]
| [#x0B32-#x0B33] | [#x0B36-#x0B39] | #x0B3D |
[#x0B5C-#x0B5D] | [#x0B5F-#x0B61] | [#x0B85-#x0B8A] |
[#x0B8E-#x0B90] | [#x0B92-#x0B95] | [#x0B99-#x0B9A] |
#x0B9C | [#x0B9E-#x0B9F] | [#x0BA3-#x0BA4] | [#x0BA8-
#x0BAA] | [#x0BAE-#x0BB5] | [#x0BB7-#x0BB9] |
[#x0C05-#x0C0C] | [#x0C0E-#x0C10] | [#x0C12-#x0C28] |
[#x0C2A-#x0C33] | [#x0C35-#x0C39] | [#x0C60-#x0C61] |
[#x0C85-#x0C8C] | [#x0C8E-#x0C90] | [#x0C92-#x0CA8] |
[#x0CAA-#x0CB3] | [#x0CB5-#x0CB9] | #x0CDE | [#x0CE0-
#x0CE1] | [#x0D05-#x0D0C] | [#x0D0E-#x0D10] |
[#x0D12-#x0D28] | [#x0D2A-#x0D39] | [#x0D60-#x0D61] |
[#x0E01-#x0E2E] | #x0E30 | [#x0E32-#x0E33] | [#x0E40-
#x0E45] | [#x0E81-#x0E82] | #x0E84 | [#x0E87-#x0E88]
| #x0E8A | #x0E8D | [#x0E94-#x0E97] | [#x0E99-#x0E9F]
| [#x0EA1-#x0EA3] | #x0EA5 | #x0EA7 | [#x0EAA-#x0EAB]
| [#x0EAD-#x0EAE] | #x0EB0 | [#x0EB2-#x0EB3] | #x0EBD
| [#x0EC0-#x0EC4] | [#x0F40-#x0F47] | [#x0F49-#x0F69]
| [#x10A0-#x10C5] | [#x10D0-#x10F6] | #x1100 |
[#x1102-#x1103] | [#x1105-#x1107] | #x1109 | [#x110B-
#x110C] | [#x110E-#x1112] | #x113C | #x113E | #x1140
| #x114C | #x114E | #x1150 | [#x1154-#x1155] | #x1159
| [#x115F-#x1161] | #x1163 | #x1165 | #x1167 | #x1169
| [#x116D-#x116E] | [#x1172-#x1173] | #x1175 | #x119E
| #x11A8 | #x11AB | [#x11AE-#x11AF] | [#x11B7-#x11B8]
| #x11BA | [#x11BC-#x11C2] | #x11EB | #x11F0 | #x11F9
| [#x1E00-#x1E9B] | [#x1EA0-#x1EF9] | [#x1F00-#x1F15]
| [#x1F18-#x1F1D] | [#x1F20-#x1F45] | [#x1F48-#x1F4D]
| [#x1F50-#x1F57] | #x1F59 | #x1F5B | #x1F5D |
[#x1F5F-#x1F7D] | [#x1F80-#x1FB4] | [#x1FB6-#x1FBC] |
#x1FBE | [#x1FC2-#x1FC4] | [#x1FC6-#x1FCC] | [#x1FD0-
#x1FD3] | [#x1FD6-#x1FDB] | [#x1FE0-#x1FEC] |
```

```
                [#x1FF2-#x1FF4]  |  [#x1FF6-#x1FFC]  |  #x2126  |  [#x212A-
                #x212B]  |  #x212E  |  [#x2180-#x2182]  |  [#x3041-#x3094]
                |  [#x30A1-#x30FA]  |  [#x3105-#x312C]  |  [#xAC00-#xD7A3]
[86]Ideo-    ::=  [#x4E00-#x9FA5]  |  #x3007  |  [#x3021-#x3029]
   graphic
[87]Combining ::=  [#x0300-#x0345]  |  [#x0360-#x0361]  |  [#x0483-#x0486]  |
   Char              [#x0591-#x05A1]  |  [#x05A3-#x05B9]  |  [#x05BB-#x05BD]  |
                #x05BF  |  [#x05C1-#x05C2]  |  #x05C4  |  [#x064B-#x0652]  |
                #x0670  |  [#x06D6-#x06DC]  |  [#x06DD-#x06DF]  |  [#x06E0-
                #x06E4]  |  [#x06E7-#x06E8]  |  [#x06EA-#x06ED]  |
                [#x0901-#x0903]  |  #x093C  |  [#x093E-#x094C]  |  #x094D  |
                [#x0951-#x0954]  |  [#x0962-#x0963]  |  [#x0981-#x0983]  |
                #x09BC  |  #x09BE  |  #x09BF  |  [#x09C0-#x09C4]  |  [#x09C7-
                #x09C8]  |  [#x09CB-#x09CD]  |  #x09D7  |  [#x09E2-#x09E3]
                |  #x0A02  |  #x0A3C  |  #x0A3E  |  #x0A3F  |  [#x0A40-#x0A42]
                |  [#x0A47-#x0A48]  |  [#x0A4B-#x0A4D]  |  [#x0A70-#x0A71]
                |  [#x0A81-#x0A83]  |  #x0ABC  |  [#x0ABE-#x0AC5]  |
                [#x0AC7-#x0AC9]  |  [#x0ACB-#x0ACD]  |  [#x0B01-#x0B03]  |
                #x0B3C  |  [#x0B3E-#x0B43]  |  [#x0B47-#x0B48]  |  [#x0B4B-
                #x0B4D]  |  [#x0B56-#x0B57]  |  [#x0B82-#x0B83]  |
                [#x0BBE-#x0BC2]  |  [#x0BC6-#x0BC8]  |  [#x0BCA-#x0BCD]  |
                #x0BD7  |  [#x0C01-#x0C03]  |  [#x0C3E-#x0C44]  |  [#x0C46-
                #x0C48]  |  [#x0C4A-#x0C4D]  |  [#x0C55-#x0C56]  |
                [#x0C82-#x0C83]  |  [#x0CBE-#x0CC4]  |  [#x0CC6-#x0CC8]  |
                [#x0CCA-#x0CCD]  |  [#x0CD5-#x0CD6]  |  [#x0D02-#x0D03]  |
                [#x0D3E-#x0D43]  |  [#x0D46-#x0D48]  |  [#x0D4A-#x0D4D]  |
                #x0D57  |  #x0E31  |  [#x0E34-#x0E3A]  |  [#x0E47-#x0E4E]  |
                #x0EB1  |  [#x0EB4-#x0EB9]  |  [#x0EBB-#x0EBC]  |  [#x0EC8-
                #x0ECD]  |  [#x0F18-#x0F19]  |  #x0F35  |  #x0F37  |  #x0F39
                |  #x0F3E  |  #x0F3F  |  [#x0F71-#x0F84]  |  [#x0F86-#x0F8B]
                |  [#x0F90-#x0F95]  |  #x0F97  |  [#x0F99-#x0FAD]  |
                [#x0FB1-#x0FB7]  |  #x0FB9  |  [#x20D0-#x20DC]  |  #x20E1  |
                [#x302A-#x302F]  |  #x3099  |  #x309A
[88]Digit    ::=  [#x0030-#x0039]  |  [#x0660-#x0669]  |  [#x06F0-#x06F9]  |
                [#x0966-#x096F]  |  [#x09E6-#x09EF]  |  [#x0A66-#x0A6F]  |
                [#x0AE6-#x0AEF]  |  [#x0B66-#x0B6F]  |  [#x0BE7-#x0BEF]  |
                [#x0C66-#x0C6F]  |  [#x0CE6-#x0CEF]  |  [#x0D66-#x0D6F]  |
                [#x0E50-#x0E59]  |  [#x0ED0-#x0ED9]  |  [#x0F20-#x0F29]
[89]Extender ::=  #x00B7  |  #x02D0  |  #x02D1  |  #x0387  |  #x0640  |  #x0E46  |
                #x0EC6  |  #x3005  |  [#x3031-#x3035]  |  [#x309D-#x309E]  |
                [#x30FC-#x30FE]
```

The character classes defined here can be derived from the Unicode character database as follows:

- Name start characters must have one of the categories Ll, Lu, Lo, Lt, Nl.
- Name characters other than Name-start characters must have one of the categories Mc, Me, Mn, Lm, or Nd.
- Characters in the compatibility area (i.e. with character code greater than #xF900 and less than #xFFFE) are not allowed in XML names.
- Characters which have a font or compatibility decomposition (i.e. those with a "compatibility formatting tag" in field 5 of the database — marked by field 5 beginning with a "<") are not allowed.
- The following characters are treated as name-start characters rather than name characters, because the property file classifies them as Alphabetic: [#x02BB-#x02C1], #x0559, #x06E5, #x06E6.
- Characters #x20DD-#x20E0 are excluded (in accordance with Unicode, section 5.14).
- Character #x00B7 is classified as an extender, because the property list so identifies it.
- Character #x0387 is added as a name character, because #x00B7 is its canonical equivalent.
- Characters ':' and '_' are allowed as name-start characters.
- Characters '-' and '.' are allowed as name characters.

XML and SGML
(Non-Normative)

XML is designed to be a subset of SGML, in that every ⌈valid⌉ XML document should also be a conformant SGML document. For a detailed comparison of the additional restrictions that XML places on documents beyond those of SGML, see [Clark].

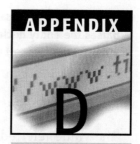

Expansion of Entity and Character References (Non-Normative)

This appendix contains some examples illustrating the sequence of entity- and character-reference recognition and expansion, as specified in Section 4.4 *XML Processor Treatment of Entities and References*.

This appendix is ⌜non-normative⌝, so if there are any differences between it and the specification (through error, for example), it is the specification which must be followed. You are urged to read Chapter 4 of the XML Specification in Part 2 of this book carefully rather than rely on this illustrative appendix.

These examples are *not* introductory: see Part 1 of this book for some simpler examples.

If the DTD contains the declaration

```
<!ENTITY example
    "<p>An ampersand (&#38;#38;) may be escaped
numerically (&#38;#38;#38;) or with a general entity (&amp;amp;).</p>"
>
```

then the 「XML processor」 will recognize the 「character references」 when it parses the entity declaration, and resolve them before storing the following string as the value of the entity "「example」":

```
<p>An ampersand (&#38;) may be escaped
numerically (&#38;#38;) or with a general entity (&amp;amp;).</p>
```

The value referred to is the 「replacement text」 of the 「internal general entity」 called example. Expanding character references has turned each occurrence of & into the corresponding character, &, so that &#38; becomes & and so on. Since general entity references have not been expanded, & has remained unchanged.

A reference in the document to "&example;" will cause the text to be reparsed, at which time the start- and end-tags of the "p" element will be recognized and the three [character and entity] references will be recognized and expanded, resulting in a "p" element with the following content (all data, no delimiters or markup):

```
An ampersand (&) may be escaped
numerically (&#38;) or with a general entity (&amp;).
```

The internal general entity & is expanded only at the last possible minute, not at the time when the entity &example; was declared.

A more complex example will illustrate the rules and their effects fully. In the following example, the line numbers are solely for reference.

```
1 <?xml version='1.0'?>
2 <!DOCTYPE test [
3 <!ELEMENT test (#PCDATA) >
4 <!ENTITY % xx '&#37;zz;'>
5 <!ENTITY % zz '&#60;!ENTITY tricky "error-prone" >' >
6 %xx;
7 ]>
8 <test>this example shows a &tricky; method.</test>
```

This produces the following:

■ in line 4, the reference to character 37 is expanded immediately, and the parameter entity "xx" is stored in the symbol table with the value "%zz;". Since the 「replacement text」 is not rescanned, the reference to parameter

> entity "zz" is not recognized. (And it would be an error if it were since "zz" is not yet declared.)

This is the only place in which *symbol table* is mentioned. It would be better to say that the replacement text of the parameter entity xx is stored as being %zz; after the character reference % has been converted into a %-sign.

■ **in line 5, the character reference "<" is expanded immediately and the [internal] parameter entity "zz" is stored with the replacement text "<!ENTITY tricky "error-prone" >", which is a well-formed entity declaration.**

Note the use of single quotes to contain the entity value on line 5, so that the embedded double quotes would not cause problems. An alternative would have been to use double quotes on the outside and character references " instead of double quotes on the inside:

```
<!ENTITY % zz
    "&#60;!ENTITY tricky &#34;error-prone&#34;>"
>
```

Note also that a multi-line layout makes complex examples such as these considerably easier to read and edit!

■ **in line 6, the reference to "xx" is recognized, and the replacement text of "xx" (namely "%zz;") is parsed. The reference to "zz" is recognized in its turn, and its replacement text ("<!ENTITY tricky "error-prone">") is parsed. The general entity "tricky" has now been declared, with the replacement text "error-prone".**

Let's take this slowly, one step at a time . . .
First, line 6 is changed from

```
%xx;
```
by expanding the internal parameter entity xx, yielding:
```
%zz;
```

Next, this is rescanned. A typical implementation model is to push entity replacement texts onto an input stack as they occur, so that the effect is as if the entity reference had not been there at all, and instead the replacement text had been seen. The scanning of the replacement text for zz changes the line into:

```
<!ENTITY tricky "error-prone">
```

This replacement text is now read in turn, and that causes the general internal entity called `tricky` to be declared.

■ in line 8, the reference to the general entity "tricky" is recognized, and it is expanded, so the full content of the "test" element is the self-describing (and ungrammatical) string, *This sample shows an error-prone method.*

Defining entities in this indirect manner is certainly legal in XML, but it is also not a good idea if you ever want to be able to go back to your entity definitions and understand them! If you find yourself doing things this complex, ask yourself whether you should perhaps be using a different representation and converting into simpler DTDs automatically. See Appendix F "Schema or DTD?" in Part 3 of this book for one approach.

APPENDIX

E

Deterministic Content Models (Non-Normative)

For compatibility, it is required that ⌜content models⌝ in ⌜element type declarations⌝ be deterministic.

This is required for compatibility in Part 3, Chapter 3, Section 3.2.1, "Element Content."

SGML requires deterministic content models (it calls them *unambiguous*); XML processors built using SGML systems may flag non-deterministic content models as errors.

In practice, almost all existing SGML processors can handle non-deterministic content models without any problems and will warn about them rather than producing fatal errors. The types of content model that are hardest to implement in SGML are not expressible in XML, since XML does not have *element inclusions*, *exclusions*, and *and groups* in its element declaration syntax.

For example, the content model ((b, c) | (b, d)) is ⌜non-deterministic⌝, because given an initial b the parser cannot know which b in the model is being matched without looking ahead to see which element follows the b. . . .

The SGML requirement, then, is that the SGML parser must be able to match each element in the input with a specific token in the corresponding content model. There is no significance whatsoever in which b is matched, except that the SGML parser has to choose one, and, since it does not know which one to choose, it takes the belligerent option and refuses to accept the content model in the first place.

> **...In this case, the two references to b can be collapsed into a single reference, making the model read (b, (c | d)). An initial b now clearly matches only a single name in the content model. The parser doesn't need to look ahead to see what follows; either c or d would be accepted....**

This sort of manual change of a content model is not technically necessary, since the XML processor must be able to do it internally, or at least must be able to handle the content model, which is in no way forbidden in XML. Most or all existing SGML parsers can also handle it, generally using the standard algorithm referred to below, or a variant of it.

> **...More formally: a finite state automaton may be constructed from the content model using the standard algorithms, e.g. algorithm 3.5 in section 3.9 of Aho, Sethi, and Ullman [Aho/Ullman]. In many such algorithms, a follow set is constructed for each position in the regular expression (i.e., each leaf node in the syntax tree for the regular expression); if any position has a follow set in which more than one following position is labeled with the same element type name, then the content model is in error and ⌜may⌝ be reported as an ⌜error⌝.**

If you are familiar enough with computer science concepts such as finite state automata theory, or have read the book cited (Aho/Ullman in Appendix A—it is a very widely recommended textbook on compiler design and parsing), you will also know that detecting this situation is in most or all cases the same problem as reducing the non-deterministic finite state automaton to a finite state one, and if you can do that you don't need to worry about the problem, because now you can parse the input! The cost of the transformation is that your XML processor may need more than one token of look-ahead, although this rarely causes difficulty in an age in which 64 megabytes of memory costs less than a day of a programmer's salary!

If you are unfamiliar with these concepts, you only need to worry about them when you are implementing a validating XML parser, in which case you should certainly consult Aho, Sethi, and Ullman, the book informally known as the "Dragon Book" because of its cover illustration.

> **Algorithms exist which allow many but not all non-deterministic content models to be reduced automatically to equivalent deterministic content models; see Brüggmann-Klein 1991.**

APPENDIX

F

Autodetection of Character Encodings (Non-Normative)

The XML encoding declaration functions as an internal label on each entity, indicating which character encoding is in use. Before an XML processor can read the internal label, however, it apparently has to know what character encoding is in use—which is what the internal label is trying to indicate. In the general case, this is a hopeless situation. It is not entirely hopeless in XML, however, because XML limits the general case in two ways: each implementation is assumed to support only a finite set of character encodings, and the XML encoding declaration is restricted in position and content in order to make it feasible to autodetect the character encoding in use in each entity in normal cases. Also, in many cases other sources of information are available in addition to the XML data stream itself. Two cases may be distinguished, depending on whether the XML entity is presented to the processor without, or with, any accompanying (external) information. We consider the first case first.

Because each XML entity not in UTF-8 or UTF-16 format must begin with an XML encoding declaration, in which the first characters must be '<?xml', any conforming processor can detect, after two to four octets of input, which of the following cases apply. In reading this list, it may help to know that in UCS-4, '<' is "#x0000003C" and '?' is "#x0000003F", and the Byte Order Mark required of UTF-16 data streams is "#xFEFF".

- 00 00 00 3C: UCS-4, big-endian machine (1234 order)
- 3C 00 00 00: UCS-4, little-endian machine (4321 order)
- 00 00 3C 00: UCS-4, unusual octet order (2143)
- 00 3C 00 00: UCS-4, unusual octet order (3412)
- FE FF: UTF-16, big-endian
- FF FE: UTF-16, little-endian
- 00 3C 00 3F: UTF-16, big-endian, no Byte Order Mark (and thus, strictly speaking, in error)
- 3C 00 3F 00: UTF-16, little-endian, no Byte Order Mark (and thus, strictly speaking, in error)
- 3C 3F 78 6D: UTF-8, ISO 646, ASCII, some part of ISO 8859, Shift-JIS, EUC, or any other 7-bit, 8-bit, or mixed-width encoding which ensures that the characters of ASCII have their normal positions, width, and values; the actual encoding declaration must be read to detect which of these applies, but since all of these encodings use the same bit patterns for the ASCII characters, the encoding declaration itself may be read reliably
- 4C 6F A7 94: EBCDIC (in some flavor; the full encoding declaration must be read to tell which code page is in use)
- other: UTF-8 without an encoding declaration, or else the data stream is corrupt, fragmentary, or enclosed in a wrapper of some kind

This level of autodetection is enough to read the XML encoding declaration and parse the character-encoding identifier, which is still necessary to distinguish the individual members of each family of encodings (e.g. to tell UTF-8 from 8859, and the parts of 8859 from each other, or to distinguish the specific EBCDIC code page in use, and so on).

Because the contents of the encoding declaration are restricted to ASCII characters, a processor can reliably read the entire encoding declaration as soon as it has detected which family of encodings is in use. Since in practice, all widely used character encodings fall into one of the categories above, the XML encoding declaration allows reasonably reliable in-band labeling of character encodings, even when external sources of information at the operating-system or transport-protocol level are unreliable.

Once the processor has detected the character encoding in use, it can act appropriately, whether by invoking a separate input routine for each case, or by calling the proper conversion function on each character of input.

Like any self-labeling system, the XML encoding declaration will not work if any software changes the entity's character set or encoding without updating the encoding declaration. Implementors of character-encoding routines should be careful to ensure the accuracy of the internal and external information used to label the entity.

The second possible case occurs when the XML entity is accompanied by encoding information, as in some file systems and some network protocols. When multiple sources of information are available, their relative priority and the preferred method of handling conflict should be specified as part of the higher-level protocol used to deliver XML. Rules for the relative priority of the internal label and the MIME-type label in an external header, for example, should be part of the RFC document defining the text/xml and application/xml MIME types. In the interests of interoperability, however, the following rules are recommended.

- If an XML entity is in a file, the Byte-Order Mark and encoding-declaration PI are used (if present) to determine the character encoding. All other heuristics and sources of information are solely for error recovery.
- If an XML entity is delivered with a MIME type of text/xml, then the charset parameter on the MIME type determines the character encoding method; all other heuristics and sources of information are solely for error recovery.
- If an XML entity is delivered with a MIME type of application/xml, then the Byte-Order Mark and encoding-declaration PI are used (if present) to determine the character encoding. All other heuristics and sources of information are solely for error recovery.

These rules apply only in the absence of protocol-level documentation; in particular, when the MIME types text/xml and application/xml are defined, the recommendations of the relevant RFC will supersede these rules.

W3C XML Working Group (Non-Normative)

This specification was prepared and approved for publication by the W3C XML Working Group (WG). WG approval of this specification does not necessarily imply that all WG members voted for its approval. The current and former members of the XML WG are:

- Jon Bosak, Sun (Chair); James Clark (Technical Lead); Tim Bray, Textuality and Netscape (XML Co-editor); Jean Paoli, Microsoft (XML Co-editor); C. M. Sperberg-McQueen, U. of Ill. (XML Co-editor); Dan Connolly, W3C (W3C Liaison); Paula Angerstein, Texcel; Steve DeRose, INSO; Dave Hollander, HP; Eliot Kimber, ISOGEN; Eve Maler, ArborText; Tom Magliery, NCSA; Murray Maloney, Muzmo and Grif; Makoto Murata, Fuji Xerox Information Systems; Joel Nava, Adobe; Conleth O'Connell, Vignette; Peter Sharpe, SoftQuad; John Tigue, DataChannel

PART
Three

Technical Appendixes

The third and last part of the book contains seven appendixes that cover some technical aspects related to the XML specification, and that are not discussed in detail in the specification. For example, Appendix A presents the EBNF (Extended Backus-Naur-Form) for XML in somewhat more detail than is done in the specification, and is given here to help familiarize you with the EBNF formalism. Indeed, once you know XML quite well, you may find this appendix a useful "quick reference" for the grammatical rules of XML.

Appendixes B and C cover character set and language issues—things that are central to building multilingual XML applications, but that are defined in specifications external to XML. Appendix B goes into the UCS character set in some detail, and will help you appreciate the intricacies of this character set—as well as some of the implementation problems you are likely to encounter. Appendix C covers RFC 1766—the Internet specification for identifying human languages and dialects. After all, if you are going to use the multilingual capabilities of UCS, you surely need to be able to identify the different languages in your documents!

Appendix D provides a brief summary of the main differences between XML and HTML. This is a useful reference for HTML experts, and helps to remind you about what is different—and what you have to watch out for.

Appendixes E and F cover some "advanced" XML issues that are not (yet!) defined by formal specifications—namely namespaces and schemas. XML namespaces will allow proper merging of elements from different (and possibly conflicting) DTDs, while schemas provide a way—without using DTDs—to constrain the grammar and structure of XML documents. Indeed, namespaces and schemas are probably the most important coming features of XML, and will allow for proper, distributed XML-based applications.

Appendix G provides some "good practice" guidelines for writing markup declarations. DTDs are hard enough to write correctly and understand, and the guidelines here will help you to produce DTDs that are easier to read, and easier to debug!

Finally, this part of the book includes an extensive glossary of terms, expressions, and abbreviations commonly found in technical documents related to XML and Internet protocols. Note that, for easy reference, Part 2 of this book used small half brackets around each term having a glossary entry. Parts 1 and 3, however, took the more traditional approach of italicizing the first reference to a term included in the glossary.

Annotated Extended Backus-Naur Form (EBNF) for XML

This appendix contains an annotated version of the complete *Extended Backus-Naur Form* (*EBNF*) for the XML language. In general, an EBNF expresses the grammar for a language, using a set of rules that defines the form for a single *symbol* important in the language. The grammar for the language is then given by the complete collection of rules. Indeed, the collection of statements of an EBNF is said to define a *context-free grammar*, since the EBNF mechanism can express grammar rules independent of the context in which the grammar is used. Thus we can happily use EBNF to define the rules for XML without having to worry about software implementation details.[1]

A single EBNF rule defines a symbol (some symbol relevant to the XML language) in terms of an expression (which may contain fixed strings called tokens, other symbols, and special tokens that define grammatical rules). The notation for definitions has the form:

```
symbol ::= expression
```

---

[1] This statement is a bit unfair to the authors of the XML specification, as much of the effort in creating XML was spent in making the grammar as easy to implement as possible, while keeping it consistent with the more complex grammar of SGML.

where expression defines the rule for constructing a valid symbol of the type named on the left-hand side. An example is:

```
EntityRef ::= '&' Name ';'
```

which defines a symbol called EntityRef (an entity reference—the names are chosen to be similar to the thing they represent) in terms of another symbol called Name (a name, as defined elsewhere in the EBNF) preceded by the token "&" and followed by the token ";", with no intervening space. A symbol such as EntityRef is also called a *nonterminal*, since it does not have a fixed (terminal) value, but can change depending on the values in the expression. Symbols that never vary, such as the ampersand character above, are sometimes called *terminals*.

EBNF statements are also called *production rules*, since they express the way in which valid symbols are constructed, or *produced*, using other symbols and/or specific fixed strings. An instance of this production rule is called a production. The rules themselves are also often referred to as productions, as you will see while reading both the following and the official XML specifications.

Throughout this book, numbers in square brackets ("[23]") indicate rule numbering in the official XML specification. However, in this appendix the rules have been regrouped to facilitate discussion of issues, and renumbered accordingly; this numbering is italicized ("*1*"). To help with cross-references to the official specification, at the left side of each rule both numbers are given ("*1* [23]"). Of course, the order is irrelevant as far as the grammar is concerned.

The grammar for XML is specified using the EBNF plus well-formedness and validity constraints, that restrict the ways in which well-formed and valid XML documents can be constructed (e.g., that no two attributes of type ID can have the same value). This appendix lists these constraints, numbered for easy reference within this appendix. There are 31 such constraints. In general, a constraint applies to a specific production rule or rules, and we indicate this in each EBNF statement, as described later.

The text of the EBNF, and some other useful EBNF goodies, such as an interactive cross-reference of the productions, and a hyperlinked index of symbols, are available at the book Web site, at

www.utoronto.ca/ian/books/xml/appa/

The Web site also provides an EBNF in a format more suitable for electronic processing (commentary and numbering is removed, and all references to validity constraints are placed inside comment strings).

A.1 Grammatical and Other Expressions of the BNF

The expressions on the right-hand side of each production rule are written using a simple EBNF grammar. This grammar makes use of the notations defined and described below. In these descriptions, "matches" means that a valid item contains a sequence of characters that matches the set of expressions allowed (or produced) by the statement.

(expression)	The group expression is treated as a unit and may be combined as described in this list (that is, it may be treated as a single token).
#xN	Where N is a hexadecimal integer, the expression matches the character at the indicated hexadecimal integer position in the UCS coded character set. The number of leading zeros in the #xN form is insignificant.
"string"	Matches a literal string matching that given inside the double quotes.
'string'	Matches a literal string matching that given inside the single quotes.
A?	Matches A or nothing; optional A.
A+	Matches one or more occurrences of A.
A*	Matches zero or more occurrences of A.
A B	Matches A followed by B.
A | B	Matches A or B, but not both.
A - B	Matches any string that matches A but does not match B.
[a-zA-Z], [#xN-#xN]	Matches any character with a value in the range(s) indicated (inclusive).
[^a-z], [^#xN-#xN]	Matches any character with a value outside the range indicated. This match is against the list of all allowed text characters—the list of all characters allowed in an XML document is given by first production below (1).

[^abc],	Matches any character with a value not among the
[^#xN#xN#xN]	characters given. This match is against the list of all
	allowed text characters (see: 1).

Note also the following notations used in the BNF:

/* text */	The text between and including the /* and */ is a comment. Cross-references to the well-formedness and validity constraints relevant to a production are given as comments.
[WFC: *nn*]	Indicates a *well-formed* document constraint relevant to the indicated rule. The actual constraint appears as part of the annotations.
[VC: *nn*]	Indicates a *valid-document* constraint relevant to the indicated rule. The actual constraint appears as part of the annotations.

A.1.1 Some Example Productions

The following are three example production rules, with explanations:

```
document ::= prolog element Misc*
```

A document symbol consists of a prolog production, followed by an element production, followed by zero or more Misc productions.

```
Misc ::= Comment | PI | S
```

A Misc symbol consists of a one of either a Comment, a PI (processing instruction), or an S (string of white space).

```
XMLDecl ::= '<?xml' VersionInfo EncodingDecl? SDDecl? S? '?>'
```

An XMLDecl symbol consists of a leading string token<?xml, followed by the symbol VersionInfo, followed by the optional symbol EncodingDecl, followed by the optional symbol SDDecl, followed by optional white space S, followed (and finished) by the string ?>.

A.1.2 Well-Formedness and Validity Constraints

It is important to note that the grammar defines the rules for constructing XML documents, but cannot define the meaning behind those documents, nor can it express validity constraints that go beyond grammatical correctness. Thus, the well-formedness and validity constraints must be stated explicitly and are an important part of the specification. In this appendix, we list the constraints just above or below the rules to which they apply, and have numbered the constraints, for easy reference within this appendix, by the order in which they are presented. For a document to be well-formed, all the well-formedness constraints must be obeyed. A valid document must obey all the validity constraints in addition to the well-formedness ones.

A.2 The Extended BNF for XML

In this appendix, the EBNF is presented in seven main sections: Basic Nonterminals, Global Document Structure, The Document Type Declaration, Elements and Element Content, Language Definition Attributes, Structure of a Declared External Subset, and Structure of External Parsed Entities.

A.2.1 Basic Nonterminals

The first eight rules define the basic rules for common nonterminal string tokens. The first statement defines the list of characters allowed in an XML document: any Unicode character, excluding the surrogate blocks, plus the characters $FFFE_{16}$ and $FFFF_{16}$. The second statement defines white space to be any number of space, tab, carriage return, or line feed characters, while production 3 defines the symbol that denotes equality.

The next five productions (*4–8*) define the basic string token types of XML: *name* (Name) and *name token* (Nmtoken) strings. Note how productions 6 and 8 state that multiple names or name tokens are simply separated one from another by white space. The only difference between a name and a name token is that the first character of a name must be a Letter (*9*), underscore, or colon, while a name token can begin with any NameChar character.

The actual characters corresponding to letters, digits, and so on are defined in statements *10* through *14* inclusive—these symbols are used only in production 4 (NameChar) and 5 (Name) to define the allowed characters in tokens. See Appendix B in Part 3 to find out why these lists are so complicated!

```
1   [2]  Char    ::= #x9 | #xA | #xD | [#x20-#xD7FF]
                    | [#xE000-#xFFFD]
                    | [#x10000-#x10FFFF]
2   [3]  S       ::= (#x20 | #x9 | #xD | #xA)+
3   [25] Eq      ::= S? '=' S?
```

```
 4  [4]   NameChar ::=  Letter | Digit | '.' | '-' | '_' | ':'
                        | CombiningChar | Extender
 5  [5]   Name     ::= (Letter | '_' | ':') (NameChar)*
 6  [6]   Names    ::= Name (S Name)*
 7  [7]   Nmtoken  ::= (NameChar)+
 8  [8]   Nmtokens ::= Nmtoken (S Nmtoken)*
 9  [84]  Letter   ::= BaseChar | Ideographic
10  [85]  BaseChar ::= [#x0041-#x005A] | [#x0061-#x007A]
                     | [#x00C0-#x00D6] | [#x00D8-#x00F6]
                     | [#x00F8-#x00FF] | [#x0100-#x0131]
                     | [#x0134-#x013E] | [#x0141-#x0148]
                     | [#x014A-#x017E] | [#x0180-#x01C3]
                     | [#x01CD-#x01F0] | [#x01F4-#x01F5]
                     | [#x01FA-#x0217] | [#x0250-#x02A8]
                     | [#x02BB-#x02C1] | #x0386 | [#x0388-#x038A]
                     | #x038C | [#x038E-#x03A1] | [#x03A3-#x03CE]
                     | [#x03D0-#x03D6] | #x03DA | #x03DC | #x03DE
                     | #x03E0 | [#x03E2-#x03F3] | [#x0401-#x040C]
                     | [#x040E-#x044F] | [#x0451-#x045C]
                     | [#x045E-#x0481] | [#x0490-#x04C4]
                     | [#x04C7-#x04C8] | [#x04CB-#x04CC]
                     | [#x04D0-#x04EB] | [#x04EE-#x04F5]
                     | [#x04F8-#x04F9] | [#x0531-#x0556] | #x0559
                     | [#x0561-#x0586] | [#x05D0-#x05EA]
                     | [#x05F0-#x05F2] | [#x0621-#x063A]
                     | [#x0641-#x064A] | [#x0671-#x06B7]
                     | [#x06BA-#x06BE] | [#x06C0-#x06CE]
                     | [#x06D0-#x06D3] | #x06D5 | [#x06E5-#x06E6]
                     | [#x0905-#x0939] | #x093D | [#x0958-#x0961]
                     | [#x0985-#x098C] | [#x098F-#x0990]
                     | [#x0993-#x09A8] | [#x09AA-#x09B0] | #x09B2
                     | [#x09B6-#x09B9] | [#x09DC-#x09DD]
                     | [#x09DF-#x09E1] | [#x09F0-#x09F1]
                     | [#x0A05-#x0A0A] | [#x0A0F-#x0A10]
                     | [#x0A13-#x0A28] | [#x0A2A-#x0A30]
                     | [#x0A32-#x0A33] | [#x0A35-#x0A36]
                     | [#x0A38-#x0A39] | [#x0A59-#x0A5C] | #x0A5E
                     | [#x0A72-#x0A74] | [#x0A85-#x0A8B] | #x0A8D
                     | [#x0A8F-#x0A91] | [#x0A93-#x0AA8]
                     | [#x0AAA-#x0AB0] | [#x0AB2-#x0AB3]
                     | [#x0AB5-#x0AB9] | #x0ABD | #x0AE0
                     | [#x0B05-#x0B0C] | [#x0B0F-#x0B10]
                     | [#x0B13-#x0B28] | [#x0B2A-#x0B30]
                     | [#x0B32-#x0B33] | [#x0B36-#x0B39] | #x0B3D
                     | [#x0B5C-#x0B5D] | [#x0B5F-#x0B61]
                     | [#x0B85-#x0B8A] | [#x0B8E-#x0B90]
                     | [#x0B92-#x0B95] | [#x0B99-#x0B9A] | #x0B9C
                     | [#x0B9E-#x0B9F] | [#x0BA3-#x0BA4]
```

```
                |  [#x0BA8-#x0BAA]  |  [#x0BAE-#x0BB5]
                |  [#x0BB7-#x0BB9]  |  [#x0C05-#x0C0C]
                |  [#x0C0E-#x0C10]  |  [#x0C12-#x0C28]
                |  [#x0C2A-#x0C33]  |  [#x0C35-#x0C39]
                |  [#x0C60-#x0C61]  |  [#x0C85-#x0C8C]
                |  [#x0C8E-#x0C90]  |  [#x0C92-#x0CA8]
                |  [#x0CAA-#x0CB3]  |  [#x0CB5-#x0CB9]  |  #x0CDE
                |  [#x0CE0-#x0CE1]  |  [#x0D05-#x0D0C]
                |  [#x0D0E-#x0D10]  |  [#x0D12-#x0D28]
                |  [#x0D2A-#x0D39]  |  [#x0D60-#x0D61]
                |  [#x0E01-#x0E2E]  |  #x0E30  |  [#x0E32-#x0E33]
                |  [#x0E40-#x0E45]  |  [#x0E81-#x0E82]  |  #x0E84
                |  [#x0E87-#x0E88]  |  #x0E8A  |  #x0E8D
                |  [#x0E94-#x0E97]  |  [#x0E99-#x0E9F]
                |  [#x0EA1-#x0EA3]  |  #x0EA5  |  #x0EA7
                |  [#x0EAA-#x0EAB]  |  [#x0EAD-#x0EAE]  |  #x0EB0
                |  [#x0EB2-#x0EB3]  |  #x0EBD  |  [#x0EC0-#x0EC4]
                |  [#x0F40-#x0F47]  |  [#x0F49-#x0F69]
                |  [#x10A0-#x10C5]  |  [#x10D0-#x10F6]  |  #x1100
                |  [#x1102-#x1103]  |  [#x1105-#x1107]  |  #x1109
                |  [#x110B-#x110C]  |  [#x110E-#x1112]  |  #x113C
                |  #x113E  |  #x1140  |  #x114C  |  #x114E  |  #x1150
                |  [#x1154-#x1155]  |  #x1159  |  [#x115F-#x1161]
                |  #x1163  |  #x1165  |  #x1167  |  #x1169
                |  [#x116D-#x116E]  |  [#x1172-#x1173]  |  #x1175
                |  #x119E  |  #x11A8  |  #x11AB  |  [#x11AE-#x11AF]
                |  [#x11B7-#x11B8]  |  #x11BA  |  [#x11BC-#x11C2]
                |  #x11EB  |  #x11F0  |  #x11F9  |  [#x1E00-#x1E9B]
                |  [#x1EA0-#x1EF9]  |  [#x1F00-#x1F15]
                |  [#x1F18-#x1F1D]  |  [#x1F20-#x1F45]
                |  [#x1F48-#x1F4D]  |  [#x1F50-#x1F57]  |  #x1F59
                |  #x1F5B  |  #x1F5D  |  [#x1F5F-#x1F7D]
                |  [#x1F80-#x1FB4]  |  [#x1FB6-#x1FBC]  |  #x1FBE
                |  [#x1FC2-#x1FC4]  |  [#x1FC6-#x1FCC]
                |  [#x1FD0-#x1FD3]  |  [#x1FD6-#x1FDB]
                |  [#x1FE0-#x1FEC]  |  [#x1FF2-#x1FF4]
                |  [#x1FF6-#x1FFC]  |  #x2126  |  [#x212A-#x212B]
                |  #x212E  |  [#x2180-#x2182]  |  [#x3041-#x3094]
                |  [#x30A1-#x30FA]  |  [#x3105-#x312C]
                |  [#xAC00-#xD7A3]
11 [86] Ideographic   ::= [#x4E00-#x9FA5]  |  #x3007  |  [#x3021-#x3029]
12 [87] CombiningChar ::= [#x0300-#x0345]  |  [#x0360-#x0361]
                |  [#x0483-#x0486]  |  [#x0591-#x05A1]
                |  [#x05A3-#x05B9]  |  [#x05BB-#x05BD]  |  #x05BF
                |  [#x05C1-#x05C2]  |  #x05C4  |  [#x064B-#x0652]
                |  #x0670  |  [#x06D6-#x06DC]  |  [#x06DD-#x06DF]
                |  [#x06E0-#x06E4]  |  [#x06E7-#x06E8]
                |  [#x06EA-#x06ED]  |  [#x0901-#x0903]  |  #x093C
```

```
                         | [#x093E-#x094C] | #x094D | [#x0951-#x0954]
                         | [#x0962-#x0963] | [#x0981-#x0983] | #x09BC
                         | #x09BE | #x09BF | [#x09C0-#x09C4]
                         | [#x09C7-#x09C8] | [#x09CB-#x09CD] | #x09D7
                         | [#x09E2-#x09E3] | #x0A02 | #x0A3C | #x0A3E
                         | #x0A3F | [#x0A40-#x0A42] | [#x0A47-#x0A48]
                         | [#x0A4B-#x0A4D] | [#x0A70-#x0A71]
                         | [#x0A81-#x0A83] | #x0ABC | [#x0ABE-#x0AC5]
                         | [#x0AC7-#x0AC9] | [#x0ACB-#x0ACD]
                         | [#x0B01-#x0B03] | #x0B3C | [#x0B3E-#x0B43]
                         | [#x0B47-#x0B48] | [#x0B4B-#x0B4D]
                         | [#x0B56-#x0B57] | [#x0B82-#x0B83]
                         | [#x0BBE-#x0BC2] | [#x0BC6-#x0BC8]
                         | [#x0BCA-#x0BCD] | #x0BD7 | [#x0C01-#x0C03]
                         | [#x0C3E-#x0C44] | [#x0C46-#x0C48]
                         | [#x0C4A-#x0C4D] | [#x0C55-#x0C56]
                         | [#x0C82-#x0C83] | [#x0CBE-#x0CC4]
                         | [#x0CC6-#x0CC8] | [#x0CCA-#x0CCD]
                         | [#x0CD5-#x0CD6] | [#x0D02-#x0D03]
                         | [#x0D3E-#x0D43] | [#x0D46-#x0D48]
                         | [#x0D4A-#x0D4D] | #x0D57 | #x0E31
                         | [#x0E34-#x0E3A] | [#x0E47-#x0E4E] | #x0EB1
                         | [#x0EB4-#x0EB9] | [#x0EBB-#x0EBC]
                         | [#x0EC8-#x0ECD] | [#x0F18-#x0F19] | #x0F35
                         | #x0F37 | #x0F39 | #x0F3E | #x0F3F
                         | [#x0F71-#x0F84] | [#x0F86-#x0F8B]
                         | [#x0F90-#x0F95] | #x0F97 | [#x0F99-#x0FAD]
                         | [#x0FB1-#x0FB7] | #x0FB9 | [#x20D0-#x20DC]
                         | #x20E1 | [#x302A-#x302F] | #x3099 | #x309A
13 [88] Digit      ::=[#x0030-#x0039] | [#x0660-#x0669]
                         | [#x06F0-#x06F9] | [#x0966-#x096F]
                         | [#x09E6-#x09EF] | [#x0A66-#x0A6F]
                         | [#x0AE6-#x0AEF] | [#x0B66-#x0B6F]
                         | [#x0BE7-#x0BEF] | [#x0C66-#x0C6F]
                         | [#x0CE6-#x0CEF] | [#x0D66-#x0D6F]
                         | [#x0E50-#x0E59] | [#x0ED0-#x0ED9]
                         | [#x0F20-#x0F29]
14 [89] Extender ::= #x00B7 | #x02D0 | #x02D1 | #x0387 | #x0640
                         | #x0E46 | #x0EC6 | #x3005 | [#x3031-#x3035]
                         | [#x309D-#x309E] | [#x30FC-#x30FE]
```

A.2.2 Global Document Structure

Statement *15* defines the global structure of a document: it consists of a prolog, followed by the *document element* (element), followed by any amount of white space, comments, or processing instructions (Misc), in any order.

Misc *(16)* is just what its name suggests—a miscellaneous collection of markup components that can appear in a variety of places, including the end of the document and at various places in the prolog (see *17*).

```
15 [1]  document      ::= prolog element Misc*
16 [27] Misc          ::= Comment I PI I  S
```

Statement *17* defines the content of the prolog—an optional XML declaration (XMLDecl), followed by zero or more Misc *(16)*, followed by an optional document type declaration (doctypedecl, *23*), which can also be followed by an optional, unordered collection of comments, processing instructions, and white space (our friend, Misc). The next five statements *(18–22)* define the structure of an XML declaration and of the three declarations that can appear as part (a bit like attribute specifications) of the XML declaration. The version information *(19)* and encoding declaration *(21)* are also used in text declarations describing external parsed entities *(87)*. However, the standalone declaration SDDecl is only valid in an XML declaration. Note the validity constraint on SDDecl, (numbered here as constraint 1—note that this numerical ordering is included only to aid referencing within this appendix) which limits those documents that can be declared standalone:

```
17 [22] prolog        ::= XMLDecl? Misc* (doctypedecl Misc*)?
18 [23] XMLDecl       ::= '<?xml' VersionInfo EncodingDecl?
                                          SDDecl? S? '?>'
19 [24] VersionInfo   ::= S 'version' Eq (' VersionNum ' I  "
                                          VersionNum ")
20 [26] VersionNum    ::= ([a-zA-Z0-9_.:] I '-')+
21 [80] EncodingDecl  ::= S 'encoding' Eq ('"' EncName '"' I
                                          "'" EncName "'" )
22 [81] EncName       ::= [A-Za-z] ([A-Za-z0-9._] I '-')*
23 [32] SDDecl        ::= S 'standalone' Eq (("'" ('yes' I
                                          'no') "'")
                     I ('"' ('yes' I 'no') '"'))
```
`/* [VC: 1] */`

1. **Validity Constraint: Standalone Document Declaration.** The standalone document declaration must have the value "no" if any external markup declarations contain declarations of:

   - attributes with default values, if elements to which these attributes apply appear in the document without specifications of values for these attributes, or

   - entities (other than amp, lt, gt, apos, quot), if references to those entities appear in the document, or

- attributes with values subject to normalization, where the attribute appears in the document with a value which will change as a result of normalization, or

- element types with element content, if white space occurs directly within any instance of those types.

A.2.3 The Document Type Declaration

Statement 24 defines the structure of a Document Type Declaration (doctypedecl). A declaration must have a Name (5), and can *contain*, enclosed between square brackets, an optional collection of markup declarations (markupdecl, 30) and parameter-entity references (PEReference, 29). A doctypedecl can also specify an optional External Identifier (ExternalID, 25), which references an *external DTD subset* for the document. Note that if such a subset is referenced and is retrieved by an XML processor, then the markup contained inside it is processed *after* any explicit content of the document type declaration. Note also the following validity constraint:

2. **Validity Constraint: Root Element Type.** The Name [5] in the document type declaration must match the element type of the root element.

```
24 [28] doctypedecl ::= '<!DOCTYPE' S Name (S ExternalID)? S?
                        ('[' (markupdecl | PEReference | S)*
                        ']' S?)? '>'
                                                /* [VC: 2] */
25 [75] ExternalID  ::= 'SYSTEM' S SystemLiteral
                      | 'PUBLIC' S PubidLiteral S SystemLiteral
```

The ExternalID (25) defines a reference to an external resource. This can be a URI-specified system identifier (SYSTEM) or a system and public identifier (PUBLIC). The allowed characters in these identifiers are described in statements 26 through 28. Note that, although current URI implementations (URLs) only support characters from ISO 8859-1, the specification here (26) allows any Char (1) character except for the quotation character surrounding the string. Character and entity references are not parsed here.

```
26 [11] SystemLiteral ::= ('"' [^"]* '"') | ("'" [^']* "'")
27 [12] PubidLiteral  ::= '"' PubidChar* '"' | "'" (PubidChar - "'")
                                                        * "'"
28 [13] PubidChar      ::= #x20 | #xD | #xA | [a-zA-Z0-9]
                         | [-'()+,./:=?;!*#@$_%]
```

A parameter entity reference (PEReference) references a parameter entity by its Name (5). Note that a parameter entity must be defined by a *parameter entity declaration* (53) prior to being referenced. There are important restrictions on the allowed use of parameter-entity references, described in Constraints 3 and 4.

```
29 [69] PEReference ::= '%' Name ';'
```

Statement *30* defines what is meant by a markup declaration—one of an element declaration (elementdecl, *31*), attribute list declaration (AttlistDecl, *38*), entity declaration (EntityDecl, *51*), notation declaration (NotationDecl, *58*), processing instruction (PI, *60*), or Comment (*62*). Note how constraints 3 and 4 govern the use of parameter-entity references in markup declarations. General entity references are discussed later (EntityRef, *49*).

Not explicitly stated is the fact that parameter entity references can *only* be used within the markupdecl, and have no meaning outside of this context.

```
30 [29] markupdecl ::= elementdecl | AttlistDecl
                     | EntityDecl | NotationDecl
                     | PI | Comment
                                        /* [WFC: 3;  VC: 4] /*
```

3. **Well-Formedness Constraint: PEs in Internal Subset.** In the internal DTD subset, parameter-entity references can occur only where markup declarations can occur, not within markup declarations. (This does not apply to references that occur in external parameter entities or to the external subset.)

4. **Validity Constraint: Proper Declaration/PE Nesting.** Parameter-entity replacement text must be properly nested with markup declarations. That is to say, if either the first character or the last character of a markup declaration (markupdecl above) is contained in the replacement text for a parameter-entity reference, both must be contained in the same replacement text.

Statements *31* through *37* define the structure of an element declaration. Line *31* defines the overall structure, where Name is the Name (5) to associate with the element type, and contentspec is the element content model. Statements *32* through *37* explain how content models are defined. Note the important validity constraint:

5. **Validity Constraint: Unique Element Type Declaration.** No element type may be declared more than once.

```
31 [45] elementdecl   ::= '<!ELEMENT' S Name S contentspec S? '>'
                                                    /* [VC: 5] */
```

There are lots of ways to specify an element content model (contentspec), and statements *32* through *37* define a small grammar specific to this task. In this grammar, the terminal symbols '+' (one or more), '?' (zero or one), '*' (zero or more), '|' (choice of options; 'or') and ',' (fixed sequence) are defined to have the same meanings as in the EBNF grammar. Note also the following important constraints on how valid content model grammars can be written:

6. **Validity Constraint: Proper Group/PE Nesting.** Parameter-entity replacement text must be properly nested with parenthetized groups. That is to say, if either of the opening or closing parentheses in a choice, seq, or Mixed construct is contained in the replacement text for a parameter entity, both must be contained in the same replacement text. For interoperability, if a parameter-entity reference appears in a choice, seq, or Mixed construct, its replacement text should not be empty, and neither the first nor last non-blank character of the replacement text should be a connector (| or ,).

7. **Validity Constraint: No Duplicate Types.** The same name must not appear more than once in a single mixed-content declaration.

```
32 [46] contentspec ::= 'EMPTY' | 'ANY' | Mixed | children
33 [47] children    ::= (choice | seq) ('?' | '*' | '+')?
34 [48] cp          ::= (Name | choice | seq) ('?' | '*' | '+')?
35 [49] choice      ::= '(' S? cp ( S? '|' S? cp )* S? ')'
                        /* [VC: 6] */
36 [50] seq         ::= '(' S? cp ( S? ',' S? cp )* S? ')'
                        /* [VC: 6] */
37 [51] Mixed       ::= '(' S? '#PCDATA' (S? '|' S? Name)* ? ')'*
                        | '(' S? '#PCDATA' S? ')'
                        /* [VC: 6; 7] */
```

Production *38* defines the structure of an attribute-list declaration—the Name defines the Name (*5*) of the element type to which the declaration applies, while AttDef is a list of definitions of attributes and their properties. Production *39* defines the structure of each attribute definition, which consists of an attribute Name, a data type for the attribute value (AttType, *40*), and a declaration of the default value and/or properties for the defined attribute (DefaultDecl, *46*).

```
38 [52] AttlistDecl ::= '<!ATTLIST' S Name AttDef* S? '>'
39 [53] AttDef      ::= S Name S AttType S DefaultDecl
```

There are lots of different attribute types, and statements *40* through *45* formalize the definition notation appropriate to each of them. Note the six validity constraints related to the use of tokenized attribute types (TokenizedType; *42*). The StringType attribute (*41*; declared by the keyword CDATA) simply takes a character string value, although there are restrictions on the types of characters that can appear in this string, as explained by production *47* and the surrounding discussion.

Statements *40* through *50* define the symbols required in an AttDef and that were not defined previously. Statements *40* through *46* are only relevant in the context of an attribute declaration, while statements *47* through *50* (definition of an attribute value, definition of entity and character references) are used in several other contexts, as noted.

```
40 [54] AttType       ::= StringType | TokenizedType |
                          EnumeratedType
41 [55] StringType    ::= 'CDATA'
42 [56] TokenizedType ::= 'ID'                    /* [VC: 8,9,10] */
                        | 'IDREF' | 'IDREFS'   /* [VC: 11]     */
                        | 'ENTITY' | 'ENTITIES'/* [VC: 12]     */
                        | 'NMTOKEN' | 'NMTOKENS'/* [VC: 13]    */
```

There are seven possible values for TokenizedType (*42*), and six validity constraints imposed on values of these types.

8. **Validity Constraint: ID.** Values of type ID must match the Name production. A name must not appear more than once in an XML document as a value of this type; i.e., ID values must uniquely identify the elements which bear them.

9. **Validity Constraint : One ID per Element Type.** No element type may have more than one ID attribute specified.

10. **Validity Constraint: ID Attribute Default.** An ID attribute must have a declared default of #IMPLIED or #REQUIRED.

11. **Validity Constraint: IDREF.** Values of type IDREF must match the Name production, and values of type IDREFS must match Names; each Name must match the value of an ID attribute on some element in the XML document; i.e. IDREF values must match the value of some ID attribute.

12. **Validity Constraint: Entity Name.** Values of type ENTITY must match the Name production, values of type ENTITIES must match Names; each Name must match the name of an unparsed entity declared in the DTD.

13. **Validity Constraint: Name Token.** Values of type NMTOKEN must match the Nmtoken production; values of type NMTOKENS must match Nmtokens.

     There are two enumerated attribute types: Enumeration and NotationType. Enumeration (44) simply specifies a list of one or more *name token* values. In a valid document, the actual attribute value must match one of the allowed values listed in the attribute-list declaration.

14. **Validity Constraint: Enumeration.** Values of this type must match one of the Nmtoken tokens in the declaration.

```
43 [57] EnumeratedType ::= NotationType | Enumeration
44 [59] Enumeration ::= '(' S? Nmtoken (S? '|' S? Nmtoken)* S?
')' /* [VC: 14] */
```

     NotationType (45) specifies a list of one or more Name values. In a valid document, any such name *must* be declared as a notation via a Notation declaration (NotationDecl, 58):

15. **Validity Constraint: Notation Attributes.** Values of this type must match one of the notation Names included in the declaration; all notation names in the declaration must be declared.

```
45 [58] NotationType ::= 'NOTATION' S
                          '(' S? Name (S? '|' S? Name)* S? ')'
                                              /* [VC: 15] */
```

     The DefaultDecl (46) declares requirements for attribute usage (e.g., it is or is not optional in elements of the given type) and can also define a default value (AttValue). The rules implied by these requirements are expressed by the following validity constraints. Note also the well-formedness constraint (19) that attribute values cannot contain left angle brackets (<), even after all entities within the attribute value string are replaced by their replacement text.

```
46 [60] DefaultDecl ::=  '#REQUIRED' | '#IMPLIED'
                       | (('#FIXED' S)? AttValue)  /* [VC: 16,17,18;
                                                    WFC:19] */
```

16. **Validity Constraint: Required Attribute.** If the default declaration is the keyword #REQUIRED, then the attribute must be specified for all elements of the type in the attribute-list declaration.

17. **Validity Constraint: Attribute Default Legal.** The declared default value must meet the lexical constraints of the declared attribute type.

18. **Validity Constraint: Fixed Attribute Default.** If an attribute has a default value declared with the #FIXED keyword, instances of that attribute must match the default value.

19. **Well-Formedness Constraint: No < in Attribute Values.** The replacement text of any entity referred to directly or indirectly in an attribute value (other than "<") must not contain a <.

    Statement 47 defines the allowed characters in an attribute value. Just about any characters are allowed, except for < (forbidden by Well-Formedness Constraint 19), the quotation symbol used to delimit the string, and the ampersand character, which can only be present as the start of an entity (EntityRef) or character (CharRef) reference (49–50).

    However, Validity Constraint 17 further restricts the allowed string content—for example, if the attribute is of type Enumeration (44), then the only allowed default value is a name token taken from the declared list of allowed values. Note that production 47 (AttValue) is also used in the rule for attribute-value specifications in start-tags and empty-element tags (see 65). Similarly, Reference is also used in the EntityValue (54) and content (68) productions.

```
47 [10] AttValue  ::= '"' ([^<&"] | Reference)* '"'
                    |  "'" ([^<&'] | Reference)* "'"
48 [67] Reference ::= EntityRef | CharRef
```

    Statement 49 defines the format for a general entity reference (referenced by the entity's Name). The many constraints on how and where such references can be used are listed following the production, and are generally self-explanatory.

```
49 [68] EntityRef ::= '&' Name ';'              /* [WFC: 20,21,22;
                                                     VC: 23] */
```

20. **Well-Formedness Constraint: Entity Declared.** In a document without any DTD, a document with only an internal DTD subset which contains no parameter entity references, or a document with stand-alone='yes', the Name given in the entity reference must match that in

an entity declaration, except that well-formed documents need not declare any of the following entities: amp, lt, gt, apos, quot. The declaration of a parameter entity must precede any reference to it. Similarly, the declaration of a general entity must precede any reference to it which appears in a default value in an attribute-list declaration. Note that if entities are declared in the external subset or in external parameter entities, a non-validating processor is not obligated to read and process their declarations; for such documents, the rule that an entity must be declared is a well-formedness constraint only if standalone='yes'.

21. **Well-Formedness Constraint: Parsed Entity.** An entity reference must not contain the name of an unparsed entity. Unparsed entities may be referred to only in attribute values declared to be of type ENTITY or ENTITIES.

22. **Well-Formedness Constraint: No Recursion.** A parsed entity must not contain a recursive reference to itself, either directly or indirectly.

23. **Validity Constraint: Entity Declared.** In a document with an external subset or external parameter entities with standalone='no', the Name given in the entity reference must match that in an entity declaration. For interoperability, valid documents should declare the entities amp, lt, gt, apos, quot, in the form specified in *4.6 Predefined Entities*. The declaration of a parameter entity must precede any reference to it. Similarly, the declaration of a general entity must precede any reference to it which appears in a default value in an attribute-list declaration.

Statement *50* defines character references—the constraint simply says that the reference must be to a valid XML character (see Char; *1*).

```
50 [66] CharRef ::= '&#' [0-9]+ ';' | '&#x' [0-9a-fA-F]+ ';'    /*
                                                       [WFC: 24] */
```

24. **Well-Formedness Constraint: Legal Character.** Characters referred to using character references must match the production for Char (*1*).

The preceding statements made use of entity references, while the next few, statements *51–57*, define how the two types of entities (parameter: PEDecl (*52*) and general: GEDecl (*55*)) are declared. Parameter entities (PEDecl, *52*) are declared by Name (statement *52*), and can be defined as either a text string entity value (Entity-

Value) or a reference to an external entity (ExternalID, 25). Note how an EntityValue can contain parameter or entity references, but cannot contain "bare" % or & characters (they can only be present as the start of such references) or the quotation symbol used to delimit the string.

```
51 [70] EntityDecl  ::= GEDecl | PEDecl
52 [72] PEDecl       ::= '<!ENTITY' S '%' S Name S PEDef S? '>'
53 [74] PEDef        ::= EntityValue | ExternalID
54 [9]  EntityValue ::= '"' ([^%&"] | PEReference | Reference)*
                                                                  '"'

                      |  "'" ([^%&'] | PEReference | Reference)*
                                                                  "'"
```

General entities (GEDecl, 55) are similarly declared, except that external entities can be either parsed or unparsed. If they are unparsed, then the NDataDecl symbol must be present, and defines the *notation* relevant to the entity. Note the validity constraint on this symbol—a notation must be defined before it is referenced by an NDataDecl.

25. Validity Constraint: Notation Declared. The Name must match the declared name of a notation.

```
55 [71] GEDecl     ::= '<!ENTITY' S Name S EntityDef S? '>'
56 [73] EntityDef ::= EntityValue | (ExternalID NDataDecl?)
57 [76] NDataDecl ::= S 'NDATA' S Name
                                              /* [VC: 25] */
```

Statement *58* defines the grammar for declaring a notation. Notation declarations are similar to entity declarations (*55*), although note how notation *always* references an external entity. Notation declarations also support external references via a PublicID, without a system identifier: this is purely for legacy compatibility with SGML processors, and should be avoided.

```
58 [82] NotationDecl ::= '<!NOTATION' S Name S (ExternalID |
                                                  PublicID) S? '>'
59 [83] PublicID     ::= 'PUBLIC' S PubidLiteral
```

Statements *60* through *62* define the syntax for processing instructions and XML comments. Although it is not stated as a constraint, the PITarget of a processing instruction should be the Name of a notation to which the instructions (the text content of the PI) should be sent (the specifications use the word "may" in this context).

```
60 [16] PI        ::= '<?' PITarget (S (Char* - (Char* '?>'
                                               Char*)))? '?>'
61 [17] PITarget ::= Name - (('X' | 'x') ('M' | 'm') ('L' |
                                               '1'))
62 [15] Comment  ::= '<!--' ((Char - '-') | ('-' (Char - '-')))*
                                               '-->'
```

A.2.4 Elements and Element Content

The preceding statements defined the overall grammar for the document, and for the content of the document type declaration. From statement 15, the only content of the document is element—this is the *document element*, which in turn has content that defines the content of the document. Statement 63 defines the production for element. Associated with this statement are two constraints, given after the production.

```
63 [39] element ::= EmptyElemTag| STag content ETag    /* [WFC: 26;
                                                          VC: 27] */
```

26. **Well-Formedness Constraint: Element Type Match.** The Name in an element's end-tag must match the element type in the start-tag.

27. **Validity Constraint: Element Valid.** An element is valid if there is a declaration matching elementdecl where the Name matches the element type, and one of the following holds:

   1. The declaration matches EMPTY and the element has no content.
   2. The declaration matches children and the sequence of child elements belongs to the language generated by the regular expression in the content model, with optional white space (characters matching the nonterminal S) between each pair of child elements.
   3. The declaration matches Mixed and the content consists of character data and child elements whose types match names in the content model.
   4. The declaration matches ANY, and the types of any child elements have been declared.

   Start tags (and empty element tags (67)) define the element type (via the Name) and attribute definitions. However, each attribute can only be defined once in a start or empty element tag:

28. Well-Formedness Constraint: Unique Att Spec. No attribute name may appear more than once in the same start-tag or empty-element tag.

```
64 [40] STag        ::= '<' Name (S Attribute)* S? '>'     /* [WFC:
                                                              28] */
65 [41] Attribute   ::= Name Eq AttValue             /* [WFC: 29,30;
                                                          VC: 31] */
66 [42] ETag        ::= '</' Name S? '>'
67 [44] EmptyElemTag ::= '<' Name (S Attribute)* S? '/>'   /* [WFC:
                                                              28] */
```

There are also several constraints on the allowed literal values for attributes (AttValue, *65*) appearing in an attribute assignment of a start- or empty-element tag:

29. Well-Formedness Constraint: No External Entity References. Attribute values cannot contain direct or indirect entity references to external entities.

30. Well-Formedness Constraint: No < in Attribute Values. The replacement text of any entity referred to directly or indirectly in an attribute value (other than "<") must not contain a <.

31. Validity Constraint: Attribute Value Type. The attribute must have been declared; and the value must be of the type declared for it. (For attribute types, see *3.3 Attribute-List Declarations*.)

Statements *68* through *73* define the possible content of an element—other elements, character data (CharData), general entity references (Reference), CDATA sections (CDSect), processing instructions, and comments. Note, of course, that the actual content may be restricted by the content model for a given element type. Note also how CharData disallows left angle brackets and ampersands (except as the start of a general entity reference), and further disallows the string]]> that marks the end of a CDATA section.

CDSect denotes a CDATA section, which contains character data to be "escaped" from any processing. The content can be any characters except those (]]>) denoting the end of the CDATA section.

```
68 [43] content ::= (element | CharData | Reference | CDSect |
PI | Comment)*
69 [14] CharData ::= [^<&]* - ([^<&]* ']]>' [^<&]*)
70 [18] CDSect   ::= CDStart CData CDEnd
```

```
71 [19] CDStart  ::= '<![CDATA['
72 [20] CData    ::= (Char* - (Char* ']]>' Char*))
73 [21] CDEnd    ::= ']]>'
```

A.2.5 Language Definition Attributes

XML defines the special attribute Name, **xml:lang,** for identifying the language used within the content of an element. The allowed values (defined by 75) are formalized by RFC 1766, as discussed in Appendix C, Part 3 of this book.

```
74 [33] LanguageID ::= Langcode ('-' Subcode)*
75 [34] Langcode   ::= ISO639Code | IanaCode | UserCode
76 [35] ISO639Code ::= ([a-z] | [A-Z]) ([a-z] | [A-Z])
77 [36] IanaCode   ::= ('i' | 'I') '-' ([a-z] | [A-Z])+
78 [37] UserCode   ::= ('x' | 'X') '-' ([a-z] | [A-Z])+
79 [38] Subcode    ::= ([a-z] | [A-Z])+
```

A.2.6 Structure of a Declared External Subset

The *external subset* consists of the external entity explicitly referenced by the ExternalID of a doctypedecl (24), and of any external parameter entities referenced from within the content of the doctypedecl (i.e., from within the internal subset). Entities in the external subset must follow the grammar described in 80–81.

```
80 [30] extSubset     ::= TextDecl? extSubsetDecl
81 [31] extSubsetDecl ::= ( markupdecl | conditionalSect |
PEReference | S )*
```

Productions 82 through 86 define the structure of conditional sections—that is, sections of the DTD that are INCLUDEd and/or IGNOREd. These sections can only be present in the external DTD subset—namely, an external parameter entity (extPE, 89) or the external subset explicitly declared in the document type declaration (referenced by an externalID; see doctypedecl 24, and 80, 81). Note how the grammar allows sections within sections—thus an INCLUDE section can contain excluded subsets as well as included ones.

```
82 [61] conditionalSect ::= includeSect | ignoreSect
83 [62] includeSect     ::= '<![' S? 'INCLUDE' S? '[' extSubsetDecl
                                                           ']]>'
```

```
84 [63] ignoreSect ::= '<![' S? 'IGNORE' S? '[' ignoreSectContents*
                                                              ']]>'
85 [64] ignoreSectContents ::= Ignore ('<![' ignoreSectContents
                                                  ']]>' Ignore)*
86 [65] Ignore          ::= Char* - (Char* ('<![' | ']]>') Char*)
```

A.2.7 Structure of External Parsed Entities

Production *87* defines the markup declaration that can optionally precede the content of an external parsed entity—that it, a file containing XML markup to be included within another document or entity. This is very similar to the XML declaration *17* except that the standalone property is not supported, since a text entity is not intended, in general, to be treated as a document on its own.

```
87 [77] TextDecl     ::= '<?xml' VersionInfo? EncodingDecl S? '?>'
88 [78] extParsedEnt ::= TextDecl? content
89 [79] extPE        ::= TextDecl? extSubsetDecl
```

A.3 References

The normative reference for the EBNF grammar is the official XML specification, and you should look there to resolve any inconsistencies or errors in the EBNF and well-formedness/validity constraints presented here.

For a good overview of parsing, lexical analysis, and context-free grammars, please see:

Compilers: Principles, Techniques and Tools, Alfred V. Aho, Ravi Sethi, and Jeffrey D. Ullman, Addison-Wesley, 1986.

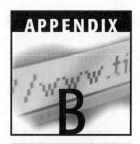

Character Sets, Character Encodings, and Document Character Sets

The universal communication of digital, text-based information is a far more complicated problem than most people—including many software developers—appreciate. The fundamental reason for this is that text is fundamentally complicated—humanity's many different writing systems use tens of thousands of characters, and employ many different sets of rules for written or spoken expression of those characters. Consequently, the task of creating a digital representation of characters and text is a complex problem that must satisfy complex technical, cultural, and linguistic constraints.

In the past, these issues were dealt with on a piecemeal basis, with many different (and mutually incompatible) encoding schemes being developed, each optimized for a different "set" of characters corresponding to specific language or writing systems. Indeed, many of these schemes were further optimized for "national" variants of a language or writing system. This gave rise to many compatibility problems when documents needed to be exchanged between systems supporting different, and often incompatible, standards.

The last fifteen years, however, have seen a vigorous re-investigation of character sets and character encoding issues, from both technical and cultural perspectives. The results were specifications for two "universal" computer character sets, formally known as ISO/IEC 10646:1993 (a specification developed by ISO, the International Organization for Standards) and Unicode 2.0 (a specification developed by the Unicode Consortium). Fortunately, the two organizations realized that it was neither sensible nor practical to have two *different* universal character sets, and the two schemes were soon merged such that Unicode and ISO 10646 define the same sets of characters, at the same locations in a common coded character set. They are thus identical, for all practical purposes, and will be treated as such here. Indeed, we will generally refer to a single character set, which we will call the *Universal Character Set*, or *UCS*, to indicate this single universal standard.

Formally, UCS is the "document" character set of *all* XML documents. This means that XML documents can only contain characters defined in UCS. It also means that numeric character references in an XML document must reference characters by their positions in UCS.

However, to explain what this means in practice requires a more detailed understanding of the differences between characters, glyphs (the graphic symbols that represent characters), character sets, and character encoding. Indeed, even these terms need to be more carefully defined. These issues are the topics of the next section.

B.1 Characters, Glyphs, and Encodings

Most people go about their days believing that they understand the meaning of the word "character." Indeed, we traditionally think of a character as a symbol with some associated meaning. For example, the letter "a" is a character with a special function, or identity (it has a certain sound, and is part of a phonetic alphabet), and a shape ("a"). The rendered illustration of the character is also called a *glyph*—that is, the symbol "a" is the glyph corresponding to this letter. Indeed, many text layout and rendering subsystems often have a component called a *glyph engine* or *glyph renderer* that actually takes a character and draws it to a display.

The above description does not clearly distinguish between a character and the glyph that represents it. However, a simple thought experiment illustrates that there is indeed a distinction—one that turns out to be quite important. For this experiment, simply imagine that you are listening to an individual speaking the entire English alphabet out loud. In doing so, the speaker is directly communicating to you the *abstract* concept of the characters, without ever producing glyphs that represent them.

Such a distinction may seem unimportant, as common experience (at least in the English speaking world) tells us that each character is associated with a single glyph, and vice versa. For example, the character "Latin small letter a" has a simple one-to-one relationship to the graphic symbol "a," while the concept of "one" has a one-to-one relationship with the graphic symbol "1."

However, this one-to-one relationship is not universal, particularly for languages other than English—it is only in Modern English where we can be fooled into thinking that the character-glyph relationship is so simple. We can even illustrate this example using traditional English letters, for example the letter "lowercase letter a." This letter can be represented by two distinctly different glyphs—"a" and "*a*"—two different glyphs corresponding to exactly the same character.

This simple example illustrates a critical point—that characters can often be represented, using glyphs, in more than one way. You may think that a useful simplification would be to forbid this situation, and require that each character correspond to only a single glyph (perhaps, in the preceding example, by adding a new character "lowercase letter italic a"). This, however, is not practical, as many languages have specific rules for how characters should be rendered as glyphs, for how adjacent glyphs may be combined, or for what glyph variations are not significant (i.e., that variations in font or style are irrelevant). Furthermore, using different characters for each such case would break important aspects of text processing, such as alphabetical ordering of words. For example, one would not want the words "alphabet" and "*alphabet*" to be treated as different sequences of characters! It is thus critical that any universal character set take into account the difference between characters and glyphs.

B.1.1 Characters

Because of the complex relationship between characters and glyphs, it is important to distinguish these concepts clearly, and to introduce explicit terminology. In particular, we need a careful definition for the concept of a character: after all, if we are going to be talking about computer character sets, we had better know what a set consists of! Formally, we think of a character as representing the abstract *function* associated with a character, independent of any glyphs associated with it. Then, a given character is distinguished from others by the fact that they serve different functions. Note that, in this sense, a "character" has no intrinsic appearance. For example, the character "e" can best be thought of as "Latin small letter e" (this is, in fact, a formal definition from the Unicode character set). Of course, you can see from this example how hard it can be to describe a character in the absence of an example glyph representing it!

B.1.2 Coded Character Sets

Given a definition for characters, we now require a definition for a set of characters. A *coded character set*[1] is simply an agreed-upon relationship between a set of *characters* and a sequence of integral positions in a defined code space.[2] As an example, consider the ISO 8859-1 character set, also know as ISO Latin-1. This coded character set has a code space allowing 256 possible characters, ranging from position 0 to 255 (the set was defined so as to fit comfortably within the space supported by a byte). The definition of ISO 8859-1 specifies a set of 191 characters (essentially the letters, digits, punctuation, and other characters common to most Western European languages) and the positions of these characters in the code space. Thus, the character "exclamation mark" (glyph "!") is the character at code position 33. Note that ISO 8859-1 does *not* define characters for all the positions in the available code space. In the case of applications that use ISO 8859-1, the code positions not used for defined characters are reserved for use by software, which use the binary codes corresponding to these positions to do such things as control data transmission or manipulate a display device. Indeed, another ISO standard (ISO 6429) defines meanings associated with these positions—for example, that tab, line feed, carriage return, and "delete character" functionality are encoded at positions 9, 10, 13, and 127, respectively.

> **NOTE** Code Positions and Numerical Notation. In this appendix, we often refer to the position of a character both by its decimal and hexadecimal position. In general, hexadecimal positions are given using the format $123F_{16}$ where the subscript indicates a base 16 number). Decimal positions are indicated by a number without a subscript.

Since most computers use *bytes* (8 bits) as the basic storage unit, there are many coded character sets designed to fit nicely in a 256 position code space. Indeed, the International Organization for Standards alone defines several such character sets, known as ISO/IEC 8859-1, ISO/IEC 8859-2, and so on. There are also many coded character sets with 128 code positions, such as US-ASCII and ISO/IEC 646. These are called 7-bit character

---

[1] The term *coded character set* is used instead of just *character set* as the second term is poorly—and often conflictingly—defined in a variety of standards. ISO 10646 and Unicode (and hence XML) chose to choose a different formalism for describing "character sets," and use the term *coded character set* to refer to this more precise definition. Please see *www.w3.org/MarkUp/html-spec/charset-harmful.html* for a more detailed discussion of this issue.

[2] More formally, one can think of a coded character set as being a function whose domain is a subset of non-negative integers, and whose range is a set of characters.

sets, as they can (and were designed to) fit within a 7-bit data item. The Unicode character set supports a base of 1,114,112 possible positions, and is designed (using a special encoding mechanism) such that each character can be encoded using one or two 16-bit words.

B.1.3 Representation of Characters Using a Coded Character Set

When a text document is to be represented using a coded character set, software (or the person controlling the transformation) must decide how to represent a given character in the document using the characters in the character set. For example, the character é can be represented by the character corresponding to the description "Latin small letter e with an acute accent," or it can be represented by two characters, a "Latin small letter e" joined together with a special "acute accent" *combining character* (combining characters are those, such as an acute accent or other diacritic, that join with a preceding character to change that character's meaning). After completing this transformation, an original source document becomes a sequence of code positions that define the ordered set of characters representing the document. For example, the string "égale" might be represented, using the ISO/IEC 8859-1 character set, by the sequence of characters at the five code positions 233, 103, 097, 108, and 101 (see Table B.1).

Note that this representation is actually more complicated than this example would suggest. We will revisit this issue later in the appendix.

B.1.4 Character Set Encoding

To store a document in digital format, one must next (and finally) encode the positions of the sequence of characters in a binary format suitable for communication or storage. With 7- or 8-bit character sets, the encoding of each character is generally accomplished by converting the integer position of each character into the corresponding 8-bit value.[3] For example, the character "Latin small letter g" at the code position 103 would be represented by the octet "01100111." All 7- and 8-bit character sets are encoded in this way, so that once such a character set is specified, the encoding mechanism is implied.

---

[3] You will sometimes see the word "octet" used in place of "byte." This is done because some computer architectures of the past employed basic storage units that used more than eight bits, and on these machines, the "byte" data type referred to a nine or even a ten-bit storage unit. You would be hard-pressed to find such machines today, but the legacy lives on in the word "octet."

Table B.1 ISO 8879-1 (Latin-1) characters and common control characters (ISO 6429), showing decimal positions and hexadecimal codes (equivalent to the 256 characters defined in UCS (Unicode/ISO 10646) at positions 0000_{16} through $00FF_{16}$).

CHARACTER	POSITION IN CHARACTER SET		CHARACTER	POSITION IN CHARACTER SET	
	DECIMAL	HEXADECIMAL		DECIMAL	HEXADECIMAL
NUL	0	00	SOH	1	01
STX	2	02	ETX	3	03
EOT	4	04	ENQ	5	05
ACK	6	06	BEL	7	07
BS	8	08	HT	9	09
LF	10	0a	VT	11	0b
NP	12	0c	CR	13	0d
SO	14	0e	SI	15	0f
DLE	16	10	DC1	17	11
DC2	18	12	DC3	19	13
DC4	20	14	NAK	21	15
SYN	22	16	ETB	23	17
CAN	24	18	EM	25	19
SUB	26	1a	ESC	27	1b
FS	28	1c	GS	29	1d
RS	30	1e	US	31	1f

Char	Dec	Hex	Char	Dec	Hex
SP	32	20	!	33	21
"	34	22	#	35	23
$	36	24	%	37	25
&	38	26	'	39	27
(	40	28	)	41	29
*	42	2a	+	43	2b
,	44	2c	-	45	2d
.	46	2e	/	47	2f
0	48	30	1	49	31
2	50	32	3	51	33
4	52	34	5	53	35
6	54	36	7	55	37
8	56	38	9	57	39
:	58	3a	;	59	3b
<	60	3c	=	61	3d
>	62	3e	?	63	3f
@	64	40	A	65	41
B	66	42	C	67	43
D	68	44	E	69	45
F	70	46	G	71	47

Table B.1 continues

Table B.1 *Continued*

CHARACTER	POSITION IN CHARACTER SET		CHARACTER	POSITION IN CHARACTER SET	
	DECIMAL	HEXADECIMAL		DECIMAL	HEXADECIMAL
H	72	48	I	73	49
J	74	4a	K	75	4b
L	76	4c	M	77	4d
N	78	4e	O	79	4f
P	80	50	Q	81	51
R	82	52	S	83	53
T	84	54	U	85	55
V	86	56	W	87	57
X	88	58	Y	89	59
Z	90	5a	[	91	5b
\	92	5c	]	93	5d
^	94	5e	_	95	5f
`	96	60	a	97	61
b	98	62	c	99	63
d	100	64	e	101	65
f	102	66	g	103	67
h	104	68	i	105	69

Dec	Char	Hex	Dec	Char	Hex
106	j	6a	107	k	6b
108	l	6c	109	m	6d
110	n	6e	111	o	6f
112	p	70	113	q	71
114	r	72	115	s	73
116	t	74	117	u	75
118	v	76	119	w	77
120	x	78	121	y	79
122	z	7a	123	{	7b
124	|	7c	125	}	7d
126	~	7e	127	DEL	7f
128	—	80	129	—	81
130	—	82	131	—	83
132	—	84	133	—	85
134	—	86	135	—	87
136	—	88	137	—	89
138	—	8a	139	—	8b
140	—	8c	141	—	8d
142	—	8e	143	—	8f
144	—	90	145	—	91

Table B.1 continues

Table B.1 Continued

CHARACTER	POSITION IN CHARACTER SET		CHARACTER	POSITION IN CHARACTER SET	
	DECIMAL	HEXADECIMAL		DECIMAL	HEXADECIMAL
—	146	92	—	147	93
—	148	94	—	149	95
—	150	96	—	151	97
—	152	98	—	153	99
—	154	9a	—	155	9b
—	156	9c	—	157	9d
—	158	9e	—	159	9f
NBSP	160	a0	¡	161	a1
¢	162	a2	£	163	a3
¤	164	a4	¥	165	a5
¦	166	a6	§	167	a7
¨	168	a8	©	169	a9
ª	170	aa	«	171	ab
¬	172	ac		173	ad
®	174	ae	¯	175	af
°	176	b0	±	177	b1
²	178	b2	³	179	b3

Char	Dec	Hex	Char	Dec	Hex
´	180	b4	µ	181	b5
¶	182	b6	·	183	b7
¸	184	b8	¹	185	b9
º	186	ba	»	187	bb
¼	188	bc	½	189	bd
¾	190	be	¿	191	bf
À	192	c0	Á	193	c1
Â	194	c2	Ã	195	c3
Ä	196	c4	Å	197	c5
Æ	198	c6	Ç	199	c7
È	200	c8	É	201	c9
Ê	202	ca	Ë	203	cb
Ì	204	cc	Í	205	cd
Î	206	ce	Ï	207	cf
Ð	208	d0	Ñ	209	d1
Ò	210	d2	Ó	211	d3
Ô	212	d4	Õ	213	d5
Ö	214	d6	×	215	d7
Ø	216	d8	Ù	217	d9
Ú	218	da	Û	219	db

Table B.1 continues

Table B.1 *Continued*

CHARACTER	POSITION IN CHARACTER SET		CHARACTER	POSITION IN CHARACTER SET	
	DECIMAL	HEXADECIMAL		DECIMAL	HEXADECIMAL
Ü	220	dc	Ý	221	dd
–	222	de	ß	223	df
à	224	e0	á	225	e1
â	226	e2	ã	227	e3
ä	228	e4	å	229	e5
æ	230	e6	ç	231	e7
è	232	e8	é	233	e9
ê	234	ea	ë	235	eb
ì	236	ec	í	237	ed
î	238	ee	ï	239	ef
–	240	f0	ñ	241	f1
ò	242	f2	ó	243	f3
ô	244	f4	õ	245	f5
ö	246	f6	÷	247	f7
ø	248	f8	ù	249	f9
ú	250	fa	û	251	fb
ü	252	fc	ý	253	fd
–	254	fe	ÿ	255	ff

Control character short names are shown slightly indented, and in italics. Control characters that are both printable and allowed in XML documents are shown in boldface. The control characters that are forbidden in XML documents (0000_{16}–0007_{16}, $000B_{16}$–$000C_{16}$, and $000E_{16}$–$001F_{16}$) are shown against a gray background. Note that the printable "space" (0020_{16}) and "non-breaking space" ($00A0_{16}$) characters are denoted by the strings SP and NBSP, as they would otherwise be invisible.

This is referred to as the *character encoding* of the document. For example, a document created using the Latin-1 character set is said to be *encoded* using ISO Latin-1. To put the distinction more formally, a character set is an abstract relationship between characters and a set of integers, whereas a character encoding is the specific instance of one such relationship as applied to a particular document, combined with an *encoding* of the integer positions of each character in a well-defined digital format.

The UCS character set is quite different, in that it uses an integer code space ranging from 0 to 1,114,111 ($10FFFF_{16}$), and the character set specification defines four possible encodings for these characters. The simplest encoding, known as UCS-2, can encode only the first 65,536 positions (the rest are not supported in UCS-2), and encodes each character in a single 16-bit word. A second encoding, known as UTF-16,[4] is essentially the same as UCS-2, except that it supports a type of "escape" mechanism to address all the UCS code space (each position greater than 65,535 is encoded using two 16-bit words, as described later in the appendix).[5] Note that UTF-16 is the standard representation for UCS characters when text data is resident in memory and being processed by an application (such as a word processor).

UCS also supports two encodings that use single bytes as the basic encoding unit. The first of these, known as UTF-8, represents Unicode characters as a stream of bytes and makes use of all the bits in the byte for encoding purposes. The second encoding, known as UTF-7, represents Unicode characters as a stream of bytes, but the encoding algorithm only uses seven of the least significant bits.

The Unicode specification refers to the seven- and eight-bit encodings as *transformation formats*, since they do not correspond to a useful in-memory representation of a document, but instead to a serialized format suitable for storage or transmission. In this context, UTF-8 has the advantage of compactness (the size of the file will be small compared with a corresponding UTF-7 or UTF-16-encoded file), while UTF-7 is best when a file is to be transported via older communications technologies (which may not properly transport information present in the most significant bit, an example being older mail gateways).

The existence of different character sets and encodings can create problems when files are stored on disk, or sent over the Internet, since informa-

---

[4.] UTF stands for *Universal Character Set Transformation Format*.
[5.] If a document does not use characters encoded at positions greater than 65,535, then the UTF-16 and UCS-2 encodings are equivalent—UCS conveniently does not define any characters at positions corresponding to the 16-bit words used as part of the "escape" mechanism.

tion about these character sets and encodings must now tag along with the data, and be available to subsequent software. If this information is not available, then the next program to see the text will not know how to decode the data and convert it back into the correct characters. Mechanisms for indicating the encoding, when data are passed from machine to machine, are discussed later.

B.2 Example: ISO/IEC 8859-1 Character Set

Probably the most common set in current use is the ISO/IEC 8859-1 character set. Commonly called ISO Latin-1, or simply Latin-1, this ISO-specified character set was designed for representing Latin-based Western European languages, and consists of characters common to English, French, Spanish, and Italian, amongst others. Latin-1 was also designed to support a simple, "flat" 8-bit encoding, so that the character set only defines 191 characters and their encoded locations within the 256 available positions. In a specific document encoding, each character is encoded in a single byte, which encodes the position of the character as an unsigned integer. [6]

The first 128 encoding positions in the ISO Latin-1 character set are equivalent to the 128 characters of the US-ASCII character set. [7] (US-ASCII is known as a 7-bit character set, since it defines only 128 characters, and can be represented using just seven bits—128=2^7.) Of these 128 positions, the first 32 (0–31) and the last (127) are *undefined* in both Latin-1 and US-ASCII. These positions are reserved for *control* characters, which are defined in a separate specification.

Control characters and their encodings are defined in another ISO specification, known as ISO 6429. Control characters are defined separately because they, and their common 8-bit encodings, are shared across several

[6] At present, Latin-1 is the most common character set—bar none—in current use. Indeed, most current Web documents are encoded using Latin-1, while many Internet protocols (such as HTTP) require Latin-1 encoding of the protocol control messages. For this reason, the UCS character set encodes all Latin-1 characters at exactly the same positions in UCS. Thus, the 61st character in Latin-1 (the equals sign, "=") is also the 61st character in UCS.

[7] ISO specifies, via ISO 646, a framework standard for 7-bit character sets. ISO 646 is similar to US-ASCII, but does not specify characters at 10 of the available code positions—these were left unspecified, to permit customization of the character set for particular national or linguistic environments (e.g., changing currency symbols, or adding important accented characters). US-ASCII is one of these variants, and is also known as the *International Reference Version* of ISO-646, in recognition of its pre-eminence amongst the ISO 646 variants.

different character set encodings. [8] In general, control characters encode information used to control printing devices and serial communications lines or devices (such as modems or terminals). Since most control characters are not printable (although some, such as "tab" or "carriage return," are), it is convenient to assign them two- or three-character short names, as shown in Table B.1: NUL for a null character, BEL for a bell character (rings a bell), CR for a carriage return, BS for a backspace character, and so on. In addition, Table B.1 represents the space character (decimal 32) with the symbol SP, since this would otherwise be invisible. Some important "printable" control characters, and their meanings, are:

CHARACTER MNEMONIC	FUNCTION	DECIMAL CODE POSITION
BS	Backspace	08
HT	Tab	09
LF	Line Feed or New Line (sometimes called NL)	10
VT	Vertical Tab	11
NP	New Page or Form Feed (sometimes called FF)	12
CR	Carriage Return	13
SP	Space character	32
DEL	Delete	127

Note that several of these, namely Backspace (BS), Vertical Tab (VT), and New Page (NP), are not allowed in XML documents.

ISO Latin 1 has an additional 128 code positions, corresponding to positions 128 to 255. The first 32 are undefined by ISO 8859-1, and are marked in Table B.1 by a long dash "—". The remaining positions encode printable characters, consisting of many of the accented and other special characters common in Western European languages.

There are several additional coded character sets defined by the ISO 8859 specifications, labeled ISO 8859-2, ISO 8859-3, and so on. These sets all encode identical characters (control and US-ASCII) in the first 128 code

---

[8] The ISO 2022 specification defines those aspects that are common to all 7-bit and 8-bit codes defined by the ISO, including the treatment of control characters (defined in ISO 6429). It also specifies how such encodings can be created using different coded character sets, including ways of indicating, within the encoding, which coded character set is being used.

positions, but thereafter encode characters relevant to several other phonetic languages, such as Cyrillic, Arabic, Hebrew, and Greek. Some details about these character sets are listed in Table B.2.

B.3 Fully Internationalized Character Sets

Eight-bit character sets are insufficient for encoding all types of text, since at best, the 256-character limit cannot represent characters from more than one *script*. [9] Although there are many 8-bit character sets, optimized for different languages, it is impossible, using a single 8-bit character set, to encode characters from different sets within the same document (for example, Japanese characters alongside Cyrillic text).

As mentioned at the beginning of the appendix, this limitation was rectified by the definition of new character sets that supported much wider repertoires of characters. One of these, ISO/IEC 10646, defines a 31-bit code space (a four-byte encoding of this character set is called UCS-4), sufficient for encoding approximately 2 billion characters—clearly enough for the most complex of documents. The other, known as Unicode, supports 1,114,112 code positions. Unicode also provides a special encoding mechanism allowing all positions to be encoded using 16-bit words (some characters are encoded as special two-word sequences, as described later). Unicode also specifies some constraints on the characters, to aid developers in developing common rules for processing character sequences, and for transparent transmission of character data. These extra semantic rules are not defined in the ISO/IEC 10646 standards.

To ensure compatibility, the two organizations agreed to make the two character sets equivalent over the entire 1,114,112 code positions supported by Unicode. We use the phrase *Universal Character Set*, or *UCS*, to denote this range (although the name Unicode may slip in, from time to time). The formalism of UCS is discussed in the next few sections.

Note that, up to now, all defined characters are encoded in the range 0 to 65,535. ISO 10646-1 calls this 16-bit portion the *Basic Multilingual Plane*, or *BMP*. You will often find reference to the BMP in other documents that describe coded character sets, ISO 10646, and Unicode.

[9.] Some examples of scripts are the Latin script, Cyrillic script, and so on. A writing system is then the use of one (or perhaps more) of these scripts to write a certain language, and may also include special orthographic conventions governing the way the characters should be written or combined.

B.3.1 Encoding the UCS Coded Character Set

As mentioned earlier, there are four ways in which UCS can be encoded. The UCS-2 encoding (Universal Character Set, coded in two bytes) is a two-byte encoding that can reference *only* the first 65,536 positions (i.e., the BMP) of the UCS character set (each position is encoded as a two-byte integer). However, there is a range of 2048 positions ($D800_{16}$ through $DFFF_{16}$) to which no characters are assigned. These positions are reserved for an extension reference mechanism, discussed below, and cannot be used in a UCS-2 encoding.

UCS also defines an encoding known as UTF-16 (Universal Character Set transformation format, encoded in 16 bits). UTF-16 is similar to UCS-2 in that any character from the BMP is encoded identically in UTF-16 and UCS-2. However, UTF-16 makes use of the 2048 reserved positions and a *surrogate code pair* mechanism to reference the code positions 65,536 through 1,114,111.

In this mechanism, the 2048 reserved positions are divided into two *zones*: The first 1024 positions ($D800_{16}$ through $DBFF_{16}$) are referred to as the *high surrogate*, and the second 1024 ($DC00_{16}$ through $DFFF_{16}$) as the *low surrogate*. The surrogate pair mechanism uses pairs of these characters—a high followed by a low—to reference specific positions in the range 65,536 to 1,114,111 (to be precise, 1,048,576 positions). The formula for calculating the character position for a given high/low pair is:

$$N = (H - D800_{16}) \times 400_{16} + (L - DC00_{16}) + 10000_{16}$$

where H is the (hexadecimal) value of the high-surrogate, L is the (hexadecimal) value of the low-surrogate, and N is the code position (in hexadecimal) of the character being referenced. This supports addressing of any position between 10000_{16} and $10FFFF_{16}$. Just to be confusing, the ISO/IEC 10646 standard refers to this range as the *S (Special) Zone* of the BMP, or S-BMP.

Note that the UCS-2 and UTF-16 encodings are identical provided the encoded text does not contain characters that are outside the BMP, and that need to be encoded using surrogate code pairs.

UCS also defines an 8-bit encoding known as UTF-8. UTF-8 encodes characters using a variable-length encoding scheme, in which a single character is encoded in from one to four bytes, depending on the code position of the character. UTF-8 can encode all the characters of UCS, but is less efficient (i.e., the files are bigger) than UTF-16 when encoding non-Latin script text.

The most important aspect of UTF-8 is *ASCII transparency*: All ASCII characters are encoded in a single byte, and in the same way as they are encoded in the standard ASCII or ISO 8859-1 encodings. Furthermore, these values never appear in the encoded data as part of another character's encoding—they only appear as a direct representation of an ASCII character.

The last encoding is known as UTF-7. Like UTF-8, this encoding represents Unicode characters using a variable-length byte-encoding scheme, but in this case, the encoding algorithm only uses the seven least significant bits of each byte. UTF-7 is appropriate when a file is to be transported via older communications technologies which do not properly transport information present in the most significant bit (e.g., older mail gateways). It is otherwise not widely used.

UCS/Unicode has been well received by software developers, and is being incorporated as the system character set by a number of modern operating systems (e.g., NetWare 4, Windows NT, AIX) and programming languages (e.g., Java).

B.3.2 Relationship to ISO 8859-1 (Latin-1)

UCS was designed so that characters from ISO 8859-1 were encoded into equivalent positions in ISO 10646. Thus, the 198th character in ISO 10646 is also the 198th character in ISO 8859-1 (AE letter/ligature " Æ ").

B.3.3 Control Characters

Further, UCS provides 65 code positions, at positions 0–31, 127, and 128–159, for representing control characters. Positions 0–31 and 127 are assigned the same control characters as defined in ISO/IEC 6429 and ISO/IEC 2022, although how an application actually treats or processes these characters must be defined by a higher-level protocol, and is outside the scope of the UCS standard. XML also places specific requirements on the allowed characters in an XML document, as discussed in Section B.4. Note that XML expressly forbids control characters at positions 0–8, 11, 12, and 14–31, but does allow 9 (Tab), 10 (Line Feed), 13 (Carriage Return), and 127 (Delete).

The defined control characters were indicated in Table B.1.

B.3.4 Character Allocation Areas of UCS

There are approximately 39,000 characters defined in the UCS standard, with more being added as new languages and characters are included. To simplify referencing (and understanding) of the different types of characters available in the character set, Unicode defines various ranges of the available code space, and places specific groups of characters in specific ranges. For example, the range 0000_{16} through $1FFF_{16}$ is called the *General Scripts* area, and encodes alphabetic and syllabic scripts that have rather small character sets, such as Latin, Cyrillic, and Greek. The range 2000_{16} through $2FFF_{16}$ is called the *Symbols* area, and encodes special symbols, such as punctuation, dingbats, and mathematical and other symbols used for technical purposes. There are various other areas, such as *CJK phonetics* (for Chinese-Japanese-Korean phonetic characters, amongst others), *CJK ideographs*, and more. Of course, not all positions within each range are assigned characters, and indeed whole ranges of the BMP plane are as yet unassigned. In general, space has been left in the various areas to allow for the addition of new characters of the indicated type.

Private Use and Compatibility Areas

Of particular relevance for XML, and portable documents in general, are the *private use* ($E00016$ through $F8FF_{16}$) and *compatibility* ($F900_{16}$ through $FEFF_{16}$) areas. Characters from these areas are *expressly forbidden* within XML markup (they cannot be used in *names*, *name tokens*, or *system identifier literals*). They should also be avoided within character data content, as these characters are likely not portable when the document is moved from one system to another.

The private use area is for use by developers or users who need a special, otherwise undefined, set of characters for a specific application. Different characters may be defined at these code positions by different applications, so that these positions cannot be used by documents designed to be portable between applications.

The compatibility area contains miscellaneous glyphs or characters that are in some way variants of characters coded at other positions (e.g., a character that can be composed using other characters, or a character that is simply a smaller or superscript version of another character [a font variation]). These characters are included in UCS only for compatibility with earlier character set standards. These characters should be avoided when document portability is important, and for that reason are forbidden in XML markup.

Not all compatibility characters lie in the compatibility area—many other compatibility characters lie throughout the UCS code space, often because they already existed in other character sets that were incorporated as a block into the UCS code space. For example, the circumflex character at position $005E_{16}$ (^), which is inherited from the ISO 8859-1 character set, is designated a compatibility character because it can also be written as a space character (0020_{16}) followed by a *combining* circumflex (0302_{16}). In looking at the XML BNF expression for basechar [85], you will note that the character $005E_{16}$ (^) is also not allowed in XML markup.

B.3.5 Base and Combining Characters

The preceding section introduced the idea of a combining character. UCS essentially divides characters into two groups, called *base* and *combining*. *Base characters* are those that essentially stand on their own, such as "Latin capital letter I." Such characters can be thought of as having standalone functionality—they can be processed individually. A *combining character* is one that is intended to be joined or combined with a preceding base character, and serves to modify the function or meaning of the base character in some way. An example combining character is the combining circumflex (0302_{16}) mentioned in the previous section. The function of this character is to join with a preceding base character, and add a circumflex accent to it. For example, to produce the character "Latin lowercase e with a circumflex accent," one would use the character "Latin small letter e" (0065_{16}) followed by the character "combining circumflex accent" (0302_{16}).

UCS defines approximately 400 combining characters, of which diacritics (accents) are the ones most familiar to those of us with Latin language roots. However, many of the combining characters originate from non-Latin languages.

A single base character can take on more than one combining character—for example, the letter "e" having both an acute and a circumflex accent. However, the rules for typographically combining these characters must also be given, so as to denote the order in which the characters should be combined—for example, should a circumflex appear above an acute accent, or vice versa? In general, Unicode says that the characters should be combined in the order in which they are listed, so that the sequence

"Latin small letter e" followed by "combining circumflex" followed by "combining acute accent" would place the circumflex above the letter e, and the acute accent above the circumflex.

Many characters are present in UCS in what is called a *precomposed form*—that is, there is a single code position that represents a character that could also be written as a base character plus one or more combining characters. For example, the character "Latin small letter e with circumflex" ($00EA_{16}$; ê) can also be written as "Latin small letter e" (0065_{16}) combined with "combining circumflex" (0065_{16}), that is: "e + ^."

The Unicode specification defines two types of relationships between a precomposed form and a base character plus combining characters. A *canonical decomposition* is one where the two forms (precomposed and decomposed) are formally identical—the example just given is of this type. A *compatibility decomposition* is one where there is a possible decomposition, but the decomposition may lead to loss of meaning. For example, the "degree Celsius" character (3103_{16}; °C) can also be written as the two-character sequence "degree sign" ($00B0_{16}$; °) plus "Latin capital letter c" (0043_{16}; C), but represented thus, the function of the character (denoting degrees Celsius) is lost. It is possible (albeit rare) that the sequence ° C could be used for something that is not a temperature measure—at least, in Unicode, one occurrence cannot guarantee that the sequence means the same thing as an explicit degrees centigrade. This may not be a good example, but there are other languages where decompositions lose meaning in a non-retrievable way.

B.3.6 Character Normalization

If a character is decomposable into more than two characters, then the order of these characters is important—in practice, two different sequences of base plus combining characters represent different composed characters. When the extra characters (e.g., an acute accent plus a circumflex) interact, the order is determined by how they interact—the combining character closest to the base character is listed first. However, combining characters often do not interact—for example, a circumflex (^) above a base character and a cedilla (ˌ) below—in which case some other ordering mechanism is needed.

To handle this case, Unicode groups combining characters into *combining classes* (an integer value), and mandates that combining characters be given in *increasing* order according to their class value. For example, the class for the circumflex is 230, and the class for a cedilla is 220, so that the canonical decomposition for the character "Latin small c with an acute accent and a cedilla" would be "c + ˛ + ˆ ".

The process of converting a string of characters into a sequence of fully precomposed or fully decomposed characters is called *string normalization*. Normalization is important because it is the only way to determine if two sequences of characters are equivalent—standard string comparison will consider two strings to be different if they consist of different sequences of characters, even if the two strings produce identical glyph renderings. Normalization can ensure that two strings yielding identical glyph renderings are matched as equivalent strings. Normalization is also important to allow controlled editing of characters (for example, to change accents on a character), as it permits predictable precomposed forms (the ones that are actually viewed) for a given decomposed (and hence editable) sequence.

The Unicode specification provides guidance for the normalization process, but does not specify a "universal" normalization mechanism to be imposed on all applications that process UCS text. Normalization inconsistencies can lead to interoperability problems, with some systems normalizing one way, others another. Some preliminary work aimed at establishing Internet norms for normalization and text string comparison are presented in a recent working draft published by the World Wide Web Consortium. This draft is available at: *www.w3.org/TR/WD-charreq*.

B.3.7 Character Properties

A combining class value is just one of the many properties that UCS can assign for a given character—indeed, much of the UCS specification, once a character is assigned a code position, involves determining the appropriate properties for that character, in addition to appropriate canonical or compatibility decomposition. These properties are specified, for each character in UCS, in the official Unicode database (a text file available from the Unicode Web site at *www.unicode.org*).

An example of such a property is *case*—that is, whether a character appears as an uppercase or lowercase variant of a single letter. Another is directionality—does the character display from left to right, or right to left? We will omit discussion of many of these properties, including case and directionality, as they are not relevant to the handling of text by an XML processor (of course they may very well be important to the XML application, such as an editor, that is using the processor to handle the XML data!). Instead we will focus on the properties that are important for defining the set of characters allowed within XML markup. Chapter 4 of the Unicode specification formally defines which characters belong to the various property groups, including the ones defined below, and you are referred there for details about character properties not discussed here.

We are particularly interested in five properties:

Letters. Essentially all the characters that are used to write words, including alphabetical characters, ideographs, and a variety of spacing-modifying characters. The set of letters can be subdivided into two subsets, *Alphabetic* and *Ideographic*.

Alphabetic. Corresponds to characters from alphabets and syllabic scripts, including combining and non-combining characters.

Ideographic. Corresponds to Unified Han (and other Han) characters.[4] Chapter 4 of the Unicode specification formally defines which characters have alphabetic and which have ideographic properties.

Numeric Values. Corresponds to those characters that represent numbers.

Decimal Digits. An important subset of numeric values that corresponds to digits that can be used in decimal numbers.

B.3.8 Character Types

The preceding discussions simply discussed the assignment of different regions of the UCS code space to different groups of characters, or the assignment of generic properties to sets of characters. However, for parsing or lexical analysis purposes, one needs to know additional semantic details, such as where *boundaries* exist between elements of the text, and how to identify *tokens* (called *identifiers* in the Unicode vocabulary) when a document is parsed. Both are important for text processing, and allow software to know where line breaks can occur, where one letter/symbol ends and the next begins, or where a word ends and another word begins. The latter is particularly important when processing XML *markup*, as the parser must know (and the XML grammar must specify) the rules by which valid markup strings, such as names, name tokens, and literal strings, can be constructed from UCS characters.

To facilitate the identification of letter boundaries, the Unicode character database designates each character as belonging to a specific character type, such as uppercase letter, decimal number, enclosing character, combining

---

[4.] Han characters are ideographic characters that originated in China. Unified Han refers to a unified set of characters that are common to several Asian writing systems, including Chinese, Japanese, and Korean.

character, and so on. Of course, there are many precisely defined types, given the many different characters encoded in Unicode and their very different functions. Table B.2 summarizes the Unicode character type designations and gives some examples of characters that fall in each class, but you are referred to the Unicode standard and the Unicode database for details.

Note that some of these types are *normative* (a rigorous part of the character set specification) while others are *informative*, and are intended more as a guide to implementation.

B.3.9 Identifier Classes

For parsing strings and identifying tokens (known in Unicode as *identifiers*), it is useful to identify several other character groups. One such group is known as the *initial alphabetic* characters, and consists of all alphabetic characters that are not combining characters. This is a useful distinction, as a string token generally cannot begin with a combining character. Another such group is called *extenders*. This group consists of characters that conceptually "extend" the preceding character in some way. Most characters in this group encode the concept of a repeated or iterated character, or a length.

Unicode just defines a basic outline for identifiers, and provides example BNF grammars that use identifier classes to define a grammar for identifying string tokens—these examples are found in Chapter 5 of the Unicode specification, and you are referred there for further details. In general, the identifier classes and grammatical rules need to be tailored to the language or application in question.

In general, the characters that appear in a given identifier class can be specified using the character types discussed in the preceding section. For example, we could define an "initial alphabetic" class to consist of the characters of type Lu, Ll, and Lo (uppercase, lowercase, and "other" letters). Indeed, XML does just this to define the allowed characters that can appear in name and name token strings in an XML document, as discussed in the next section.

B.4 XML and Character Sets

The XML specification defines ISO/IEC 10646-1/Unicode (what we are calling UCS) as the *document character set* for XML documents, and further restricts the list of characters allowed within a document, by forbidding most control characters. In particular, XML 1.0 allows the following char-

Table B.2   Unicode character type designations.

XML	NORMATIVE CATEGORY DESIGNATIONS		
N	Mn	Mark, non-spacing	[e.g., 0300_{16}—combining grave accent]
N	Mc	Mark, combining	[e.g., $0D02_{16}$—Malayalam sign visarga]
N	Me	Mark, enclosing	[e.g., $20DD_{16}$—combining, enclosing circle]
N	Nd	Number, decimal digit	[e.g., 0031_{16}—Digit one (1)]
N, NS	Nl	Number, letter	[e.g., 2162_{16} -Roman numeral three (iii)]
	No	Number, other	[e.g., $00B2_{16}$—Superscript 2 (^{2}); also ideographic numbers]
	Zs	Separator, space	[e.g., SP and non-breaking space]
	Zl	Separator, line	[2028_{16}—Line separator (only one character in this class)]
	Zp	Separator, paragraph	[2029_{16}—Paragraph separator (only one character in this class)]
	Cc	Other, control	[e.g., $000D_{16}$—Carriage return]
	Cf	Other, format	[e.g., $200C_{16}$—Zero-width non-joiner]
	Cs	Other, surrogate	[Surrogates for accessing "special" BMP]
	Co	Other, private use	[$E000_{16}$–$F8FF_{16}$]
	Cn	Other, not assigned	[No designated positions]
	INFORMATIVE CATEGORY DESIGNATIONS		
NS, N	Lu	Letter, uppercase	[e.g., Latin capital letter A]
NS, N	Ll	Letter, lowercase	[e.g., Latin lowercase letter a]
NS,N	Lt	Letter, titlecase	[e.g., $01CB_{16}$—Latin capital letter N with small letter j (Nj)]
N	Lm	Letter, modifier	[e.g., $02B0_{16}$—Modifier letter small h (^{h})]
NS, N	Lo	Letter, other	[e.g., $01AA_{16}$ Latin letter reversed esh loop, ideographic symbols]
	Pc	Punctuation, connector	[e.g., Low line _]
	Pd	Punctuation, dash	[e.g., Hyphen minus -]
	Ps	Punctuation, open	[e.g., Left parenthesis (]
	Pe	Punctuation, close	[e.g., Right parenthesis)]
	Po	Punctuation, other	[e.g., Exclamation mark !]

continues

Table B.2 *Continued.*

INFORMATIVE CATEGORY DESIGNATIONS		
Sm	Symbol, mathematics	[e.g., Plus sign +]
Sc	Symbol, currency	[e.g., Cent sign ¢]
Sk	Symbol, modifier	[e.g., Circumflex accent ^]
So	Symbol, other	[e.g., Section sign '§']

The Unicode character database specifies a character type for each character. "NS" in the first column indicates those types that are allowed (with some restrictions) as XML *name start* characters (see production [5]), while "N" indicates those allowed as XML *name* characters [4].

acter positions within a well-formed XML document:

$$0009_{16}, 000A_{16}, 000D_{16}, 0020_{16}-D7FF_{16}, E000_{16}-FFFD_{16}, 100000_{16}-10FFFF_{16}$$

Note that this expressly forbids control characters at positions $0000_{16}-0008_{16}$, $000B_{16}$, $000C_{16}$, and $000E_{16}-001F_{16}$, but does allow 0009_{16} (Tab), $000A_{16}$ (Line Feed), $000D_{16}$ (Carriage Return), $007F_{16}$ (Delete), and all the "undefined" control characters at positions 0080_{16} through $009F_{6}$. It also forbids characters at positions $D800_{16}$ through $DFFF_{16}$, which correspond to the surrogate pairs.

Furthermore, numeric character references within an XML document *always refer* to the position of a character within the document character set. Character references permit symbolic referencing of any Unicode character via its position in the Unicode character set. For example, a character reference for the character é is é (the semicolon is required, and terminates the reference). XML supports both decimal and hexadecimal character references. The general forms are:

&#*num*;   Decimal reference: *num* is the decimal position of the character

&#x*num*;   Hexadecimal reference: *num* is the hexadecimal position of the character

For example, the two possible references for the character are é and é. The hexadecimal numbers are case-insensitive, so that the references é and é are equivalent; however, the "x" in a hexadecimal character reference must be lowercase. Leading zeros are allowed and are irrelevant to the reference: thus, expressions like é and é are also allowed. A character reference must reference a valid UCS character that is allowed within an XML document. It is an error for a document to contain a character reference to a disallowed character (such as a control character or a surrogate).

B.4.1 Allowed String Tokens in XML

The XML grammar defines, via productions [4] through [8] and [84] through [89], the rules for constructing valid XML *names* and *name tokens*. The grammar bases these definitions on the Unicode character types and identifier classes discussed above, with additional restrictions that were imposed to improve portability of XML documents, and avoid problems associated with compatibility characters. Thus, the following conditions were set prior to defining the characters allowed in markup:

1. Characters from the private use area were forbidden ($E000_{16}$–$F8FF_{16}$).
2. Characters from the compatibility area were forbidden ($F900_{16}$ –$FFFE_{16}$).
3. Compatibility characters not in the special "compatibility" area are also forbidden. Compatibility characters are marked as such in the Unicode database (a text file, provided as part of the Unicode specification, that lists all the characters and the properties that apply to that character).
4. Name start characters must not be combining characters, and must be one of the types Ll, Lu, Lo, Lt, or Nl.
5. Name characters must not be combining characters, and must be either name start characters or characters of type Mc, Me, Mn, Lm, or Nd.
6. The characters ":" and "_" must be allowed as name start characters.
7. The characters "-" and "." must be allowed as name characters.

To define the grammar for token recognition, the authors of the XML specification decided to define five important nonterminal symbols: BaseChar, Ideographic, CombiningChar, Digit, and Extender (we are using fixed-width font to stress that these are the actual names of the symbols in the XML BNF). The basic meanings associated with these symbols are:

CombiningChar. Combining characters (character types Mn, Mc, and Me), excluding the characters $20DD_{16}$ –$20E0_{16}$ (combining/enclosing characters; type Me), as the Unicode standard recommends against allowing these in identifiers.

Digits. Characters that represent decimal digits (character type Nd).

Ideographic. Ideographic characters from Korean, Chinese, and Japanese, excluding any compatibility characters because of the third rule mentioned above (character type: Lo, plus some Nl).

Extender. Corresponds to extender characters, described in an earlier section. (These are mostly of class Lm, but $00B7_{16}$ and 0387_{16} [type Po] are included in this group because the Unicode property list identifies $00B7_{16}$ as an extender, and 0387_{16} as being canonically equivalent to $00B7_{16}$).

BaseChar. Script letters, excluding compatibility characters (character types Ll, Lu, Lo, Lt, and Nl, excluding ideographs), and including the characters $02BB_{16}02C1_{16}$, 0559_{16}, $06E5_{16}$, and $06E6_{16}$ (character type Lm), as Unicode classifies them as *alphabetic* (an informative property of characters).

Note that these assignments will change, as new characters are added to UCS, or as properties of existing characters are modified (to correct errors in the current specification).

XML next defines Letter to be equal to a BaseChar or Ideographic:

```
[84] Letter ::= BaseChar | Ideographic
```

This puts us in a position to define the rules for constructing names and name tokens. A general name character is defined by the rule:

```
[4] NameChar ::= Letter | Digit | '.' | '-' | '_' | ':' |
                 CombiningChar | Extender
```

so that a name character is any character of the classes defined above, plus the specific punctuation characters given here. Finally, a name (Name) and name token (Nmtoken) are given by:

```
[5] Name ::= (Letter | '_' | ':') (NameChar)*
[7] Nmtoken ::= (NameChar)*
```

which defines the two string token types allowed in XML.

B.4.2 Encoding of Document Instances

Although the characters that appear within an XML document must be defined in the UCS character set, the document itself need not be encoded using UCS (although it is obviously much easier to process if it is). Indeed, a document can be encoded using any of the commonly used encoding schemes (ISO 8859-1, EUC-KR, Shift-JIS, etc.), provided that the document contains only characters that are defined in the Unicode character set, and provided that all character references refer to characters by their position in the UCS character set, and not by their position in the character set used to encode the document.

An application reading such data must then know the encoding used to create the data, and must be able to decode the data so as to create a valid stream of Unicode characters. The steps required are:

1. Determine the character encoding used for the specified data.

2. Decode the data stream and write it to memory, mapping each character in the input data into the appropriate Unicode character, and storing this character in memory using the defined encoding.

Once the data are internally converted to UCS, an XML processor can begin processing the XML data.

Entities encoded in UTF-16 must begin with the *Byte Order Mark (BOM)* (the character "zero width no-break space," FEFF$_{16}$) described by ISO/IEC 10646-1: 1993, Annex E and Unicode 2.0, Section 2.4. This encoding signature is not part of the markup or character data of the XML document. XML processors can (and must be able to) use this character to differentiate between UTF-8 and UTF-16 encoded documents (the byte sequence will be absent if a document is encoded using UTF-8). If the document is encoded using UTF-16, then the BOM also indicates the byte ordering of the data (big-endian or little-endian). Such issues are discussed in Appendix F of the XML specification (in Part 2 of this book). This appendix also gives some suggestions for algorithms that can auto-detect the encoding used in a given document, should the encoding suggested by an external mechanism (such as MIME or HTTP headers) be in error.

B.4.3 Predefined XML Character References

The XML 1.0 specification explicitly defines five character-entity references that must be understood by all compliant XML applications. The entities and the corresponding characters are:

NAME	ENTITY REFERENCE	CHARACTER CODE POSITION DECIMAL	HEX	CHARACTER
quot	"	34	22	"
amp	&	38	26	&
apos	'	39	27	'
lt	<	60	3c	<
gt	>	62	3e	>

These entities are defined for convenience, as they make it easier to write down "escaped" markup (by escaping the <), entity references (by escaping the &), or attribute values (by escaping the " or ').

SGML software does not support predefined entities, so that for interoperability with such software, you should properly declare these entities within a document type declaration. An appropriate set of declarations is:

```
<!ENTITY quot   "&#34;" >
<!ENTITY amp    "&#38;#38;" >
<!ENTITY apos   "&#39;" >
<!ENTITY lt     "&#38;#60;" >
<!ENTITY gt     "&#62;" >
```

B.5 Character Encodings for URLs

The rules for URLs are quite different from the rules for XML documents. The URL specification (RFC 2396) states that a URL must be written using a subset of the printable ASCII characters, but that the URL itself can contain bytes from a UTF-8 encoding of the original URL text, wherein each byte not representable by an allowed, printable ASCII character must be included in the URL using a special URL encoded form:

```
%xx
```

where xx is the *hexadecimal* code corresponding to the value of the byte. The actual URL encoding rules vary according to the type of the URL and the mechanism by which the URL is constructed—you are referred to the URL specification for details.

Note that this is different from the original URL specification (RFC 1738), which stated that a URL must be written using a subset of the printable ASCII characters, but that the URL itself can contain any *ISO Latin-1* character, where each character not representable by an allowed printable ASCII character could be included in the URL using a special URL encoded form:

```
%xx
```

where xx is the *hexadecimal* code corresponding to the position of the character. Of course, this is different from the newer specification only for URLs that encode non-ASCII characters.

In practice, however, the newer definition conflicts with the current HTTP specification (RFC 2068; RFC 1945), which requires that HTTP headers be encoded using the ISO 8859-1 character set. Consequently, if an XML application extracts a URL from a document and wishes to use this URL to request data from an HTTP server, it must transform the string into one encoded in ISO 8859-1 and using the encoding mechanisms expressed in RFC 1738, for inclusion in the HTTP header.

B.6 Character Encoding and MIME Content-Types

The MIME specification supports a *charset* parameter to indicate the character encoding used within a text component of a MIME message. The mechanism uses a content-type header of the form

```
Content-type: text/subtype; charset=character_set
```

where *subtype* gives the subtype of the text document (html, plain, xml, etc.) and *character_set* indicates the character set (charset) used to encode the data. Such headers are included with each part of a MIME-encoded mail message, while every HTTP request or response header must include a content-type header to indicate the type of the data being sent.

Unfortunately, many current servers do not send charset information, while some older browsers and applications do not understand content-type headers containing charset specifications, and will not properly identify the MIME type if a charset parameter is present. It is thus both useful and important that a document include appropriate markup to indicate the encoding used to create it. With XML, this information can be placed in the XML declaration, while HTML supports **META** tags for this purpose. The forms in these two cases are

XML: <?xml encoding="*char-encoding*"?>

HTML: <META HTTP-EQUIV="Content-Type" CONTENT="text/ html; charset= *char-encoding* ">

Where *char-encoding* is a name that indicates the character encoding used to create the document instance. A list of common names is given in Table B.3. This approach is practical because most character encodings use the standard ASCII characters in positions 0 to 127, so that a browser can assume just about any character encoding, "guess" the size of the basic encoding unit (1 or 2 bytes—this can usually be guessed by looking for standard patterns in the first few bytes), and then read the initial (ASCII-character) markup up to where markup is encountered that gives the encoding being used.

Table B.3   Some common (and not always "official") names for character set encodings, with descriptions.

CHARSET LABEL	DESCRIPTION
US-ASCII	US ASCII
ISO-8859-1	ISO Latin-1
UTF-8	ISO 10646/Unicode, one-byte (8-bit) encoding—universal transformation format
UTF-16	ISO 10646/Unicode, two-byte encoding, including surrogate extension mechanism
Unicode-1-1	Unicode, Version 1.1, two-byte encoding
Unicode-2.0	Unicode, Version 2.0, two-byte encoding (equivalent to UTF-16)
UTF-7	Unicode, one-byte (8-bit) encoding—universal transformation format
ISO-10646-UCS-4, or UCS-4	ISO 10646, four-byte encoding
ISO-10646-UCS-4, or UCS-2	ISO 10646/Unicode, two-byte encoding (BMP only)
x-mac-roman	Like Latin-1; with extra characters in positions 0080_{16}–$009F_{16}$ (Macintosh only)
windows-1250; or win-1250; or CP-1250	Central European (Windows)
windows-1251; or win-1251; or CP-1251	Russian and Central/Eastern European (Windows)
ISO-8859-2	Central/East European (Slavic: Czech, Croat, German, Hungarian, Polish, Romanian, Slovak, and Slovenian)
x-mac-ce	Central/East European (Macintosh)
ISO-8859-3	Southern European (Esperanto, Galician, Maltese, and Turkish)
x-mac-cyrillic	Cyrillic (Macintosh)
KOI8-R	Cyrillic (RFC 1489)
ISO-8859-4	Cyrillic (Estonian, Latvian, Lithuanian)
ISO-8859-5	Cyrillic (Bulgarian, Byelorussian, Macedonian, Serbian, and Ukrainian)
ISO-8859-6	Arabic

CHARSET LABEL	DESCRIPTION
windows-1256; or win-1256; or CP-1256	Arabic (Windows)
iso-8859-7	Greek
windows-1253; or win-1253; or CP-1253	Greek (Windows)
ISO-8859-8	Hebrew
windows-1255; or win-1255; or CP-1255	Hebrew (Windows)
x-mac-turkish	Turkish (Macintosh)
ISO-8859-9	Turkish
windows-1254; or win-1254; or CP-1254	Turkish (Windows)
ISO-8859-10	Greenlandic/Icelandic/Lapp
ISO-2022-jp	Japanese (RFC 1468; not that this encoding can use more than one coded character set)
Shift_JIS, or x-sjis	Japanese Shift-JIS (Microsoft code set)
euc-jp, or x-euc-jp	Japanese; Extended UNIX Code
ISO-2022-kr	Korean (RFC 1557)
euc-kr, or x-euc-kr	Korean; Extended UNIX Code (RFC 1557)
gb_2312-80	Chinese, Simplified —People's Republic (RFC 1345)
x-euc-tw	Chinese-Taiwan; Extended UNIX Code
Big5	Chinese, Traditional—Taiwan—multi-byte set

Note that the charset names are *case-insensitive*. For interoperability, you should avoid distributing text using most of these encodings. The names of encodings that are widely supported (or that must be supported by an XML application) are indented, and in boldface.

In general, software receiving XML or HTML data by some communications medium should determine the character encoding used in the data from information in the message's control data (e.g., the MIME or HTTP header). If such information is absent, heuristics such as those described above can be used to "guess" at the employed encoding.

Note that XML processors must be able to read data encoded using UTF-8 or UTF-16, but are under no obligation to be able to read data encoded using any other character set encoding.

B.6.1 Common Names for Common Character Encodings

There are dozens of character sets and character encodings in common use. The ISO/IEC, for example, specifies several 8-bit character sets, in addition to ISO/IEC 10646, and specifies encoding appropriate to them. The ISO, however, is not the only organization to define character sets—many common sets were defined by national standards bodies, independent of ISO. Table B.3 lists some of the more common ones. Many of the text labels used here (left-hand column) are not standardized names (note the leading x-). Where available, the table lists the Internet RFCs that document the encoding and associated coded character set.

It is important to note that most of these character sets are not widely supported. For portable documents, you should only produce and send text encoded using UTF-8 or UTF-16, although us-ascii and iso-8859-1 are an option for compatibility with current Web software.

An "official" list of Internet-supported charset names is maintained by IANA (Internet Assigned Numbers Authority). The URL for the IANA lists is given at the end of this appendix. Note that having a name in this list does not guarantee that most Internet software understands the name, or knows how to process data so encoded!

B.7 References

UNOFFICIAL OVERVIEWS OF CHARACTER SETS AND ENCODINGS

www.ewos.bg/tg-cs/gtop.htm　(History of character sets, and overview of ISO character set specifications)

babel.alis.com:8080/codage/index.html　(Character encoding issues)

www2.echo.lu/oii/en/chars.html　(Character set standards)

www.isi.edu/in-notes/rfc1345.txt　(Mnemonics for character set names)

www.ifcss.org/ftp-pub/software/info/cjk-codes/　(Notes on Chinese/Japanese/Korean [CJK] character codes)

www.ifcss.org/ftp-pub/software/info/cjk-codes/Unicode.html　(ISO 10646 and Unicode)

MORE OFFICIAL ONLINE RESOURCES

www.w3.org/TR/WD-charreq	(Requirements for UCS string identity matching and string indexing)
www.w3.org/International/	(W3C area on internationalization issues)
www.w3.org/MarkUp/html-spec/charset-harmful.html	(Discussion of why the phrase "character set" is confusing, and should be avoided)

IANA REGISTERED NAMES FOR CHARSET VALUES

ftp://ftp.isi.edu/in-notes/iana/assignments/character-sets

SOFTWARE FOR PROCESSING ENCODED TEXT

ftp://ftp.unicode.org/Public/PROGRAMS/

RELEVANT INTERNET STANDARDS

www.isi.edu/in-notes/rfc1808.txt	(Relative URLs)
www.isi.edu/in-notes/rfc2277.txt	(IETF Policy on Character Sets and Languages)
www.isi.edu/in-notes/rfc1738.txt	(Uniform Resource Locators (URL))
www.isi.edu/in-notes/rfc2046.txt	(Multipurpose Internet Mail Extensions (MIME) Part Two: Media Types)
www.isi.edu/in-notes/rfc2279.txt	(UTF-8, a transformation format of ISO 10646)
www.isi.edu/in-notes/rfc2396.txt	Uniform Resource Identifiers (URI): Generic Syntax)

BOOKS AND STANDARDS

Understanding Japanese Information Processing, by Ken Lunde, O'Reilly & Associates, Inc. (1993). Provides a good overview of character encoding issues, with particular emphasis on the problems of Japanese text.

The Unicode Standard, Worldwide Character Encoding, Version 2.0 (1996). Complete description of the Unicode character set, with a CD-ROM illustrating all the defined characters. The book is not exactly fireside reading, but it is very useful for practical work. The standard can be purchased directly from the Unicode Consortium (*www.unicode.org*). Ordering information, and access to online updates to the standard (Technical Report #8 brings the standard up to Version 2.1) are provided at the Unicode standards page, at *www.unicode.org/unicode/uni2book/u2.html*. Note that the actual Unicode database (a text file) and associated character property tables are available from the Unicode FTP site (*ftp://ftp.unicode.org/Public/*), in directories with names beginning with the string *2.1-Update*.

ISO/IEC 10646-1:1993, *Information Technology—Universal Multiple-Octet Coded Character Set (UCS)—Part 1: Architecture and Basic Multilingual Plane*. There are several amendments to the original specification, which you will need to bring the standard up-to-date. Information about these amendments is found at *www.iso.ch/cate/d18741.html*. Information about the ISO, and instructions for purchasing ISO standards documents—including the amendment text—can be accessed via the Web at *www.iso.ch*.

Identifying Languages: RFC 1766

Text processing or presentation depends strongly on the language in which a document is written. For example, software displaying a document must know the language in order to: choose appropriate punctuation or currency symbols; format the display of large numbers (e.g., commas instead of periods as the decimal separator); appropriately capitalize lowercase letters; or alphabetically order selections of text. Software processing a document must be able to do these things and more—such as load in an appropriate language-specific spelling dictionary. Thus, when communicating a document or encoding text components within a document, it is important to be able to identify the language of a document, and of parts of a document.

For Internet applications, RFC 1766 specifies ASCII character strings for identifying languages. These strings are widely used in Internet applications. For example, the HTTP protocol uses headers containing RFC 1766 language identifiers to communicate requests for documents written in specific languages, while both HTTP and MIME use such strings to identify the language of a text document being transmitted. At the document level, HTML 4.0 defines a **LANG** attribute, supported by most elements, for identifying the language content of that element—the value of which must be an RFC 1766 language code.

C.1 The xml:lang Attribute

Much like HTML, XML 1.0 supports a reserved attribute name, **xml:lang**, for identifying the language used inside an element. If used, this attribute gives the language appropriate to the character data content of the element. The value assigned to this attribute must be a name token, and this name token must be of the form defined by RFC 1766. For example, the markup

```
<!ATTLIST p    xml:lang  NMTOKEN  "en">
. . .
<p xml:lang="en-US"> This is in the center. </p>
<p xml:lang="en-UK">This is in the centre. </p>
```

shows two paragraphs, the first containing text in U.S.-style English, and the second British-style English. This markup snippet also shows a possible attribute-list declaration, here assigning an initial default value. This attribute *must* be declared in a valid XML document—it is an error if it is not. However, an XML application handling *well-formed* documents should understand the special nature of **xml:lang**, should this be relevant to correct processing of the document (e.g., to change the rendering of the text, or properly configure a text editor).

Note that although name token attributes are case-sensitive in XML, the value assigned to **xml:lang** is actually *case-insensitive*. This requirement arises from RFC 1766, which specifies language strings as being case-insensitive.

C.2 The RFC 1766 Standard

RFC 1766 is based on the ISO standards for language (ISO 639) and country codes (ISO 3166), with extensions for situations not covered by these standards. In RFC 1766, language tags take the general form

```
lang-subtag
```

where *lang* is a string of case-insensitive ASCII letters (a–z and A–Z, plus dashes) specifying the language, and *subtag* is an optional, case-insensitive extension defining a subgroup of that language. Each string can have at most eight letters, with the special prefix x- (or X-) indicating a value defined for private use. Although uppercase letters are allowed in either portion, their use is by convention discouraged within the *lang* portion of the tag. The following is a more detailed description of the meanings and allowed values for these two fields.

Lang. This gives the base language. If this string contains only two ASCII letters (a–z, A–Z), then it indicates one of the language codes specified in ISO 639. For example, fr refers to the French language, and ja to Japanese. The only other allowed values are private codes, beginning with the prefix x- or X , or special IANA-registered language names, beginning with i- or I- (these IANA names are largely unused). This string is case-insensitive, but is usually given in lowercase. A list of ISO 639 language codes is provided later in this appendix, in Table C.1.

Subtag. This refers to a variant of a language. If this is a two-ASCII-letter code (a–z, A–Z), then it must be one of the *national identification* codes specified in ISO 3166 (e.g., fr-CA for Canadian French). Traditionally, two-letter national variant subtags are written in uppercase (as in fr-CA), although this is not required—the value is case-insensitive. A list of ISO 3166 country codes is provided later in this appendix, in Table C.2. Three- to eight-letter codes are also allowed: such codes may refer to dialects (e.g., en-cockney), or to specific physical script variations appropriate to a language. Private extension values are also allowed, and should begin with the string x- or X-.

Language codes can be used without country codes, to imply generic settings appropriate to the language.

The following list illustrates some language tags:

LANGUAGE TAG	DESCRIPTION
en-US	American English
en-cockney	Cockney dialect of English
x-romulan	Romulan language
ar-EG	Egyptian Arabic
fr	French (generic)

Most Web browsers allow the user to select language tags within the browser's configuration menus, and use this information to compose an *Accept-Language* HTTP header field, sent by the browser when requesting a resource.

C.2.1 ISO 639 Language Codes

The International Organization for Standards specifies, via ISO 639, two-letter ASCII codes for the world's various languages. Note that language codes are *not related* to the character set encoding used in a particular document—in practice, the same text content can be encoded using several different character sets, but in all these cases the language code would be the same.

References to the ISO department maintaining the ISO 639 standard are given at the end of this appendix. Table C.1 provides an unofficial list of the currently defined codes. This list is also available at the URLs listed at the end of this appendix.

C.2.2 ISO 3166 Country Codes

The International Organization for Standards, via the ISO 3166 standard, also specifies two-letter codes for the different countries of the world. As with language codes, these country codes are case-insensitive, although these codes are traditionally written in upper-case. Table C.2 provides an unofficial list of the currently defined country codes. This list is also available at the URLs given at the end of this appendix.

ISO 3166 codes are identical to the codes used in the Internet domain name scheme to identify the country domain of an Internet address. However, the Internet DNS system also uses some non-national names, such as ARPA (old-style Arpanet—obsolete), COM (commercial), EDU (educational), GOV (government), INT (international), MIL (U.S. military), NATO (for NATO, largely unused at present), NET (network), and ORG (non-profit organization). Additional domain names have also been proposed (WEB, etc.), but these are not yet in common use. Note that, when used as a part of a domain name, these strings are given in lowercase (e.g., server.net, machine.domain.org).

C.3 References

RFC 1766 AND INTERNET LANGUAGE IDENTIFICATION
ftp://ftp.isi.edu/in-notes/rfc1766.txt (Tags for the Identification of Languages)
see also:
ftp://ftp.isi.edu/in-notes/rfc2277.txt (IETF Policy on Character Sets and Languages)
For information on locating and obtaining RFCs, see:
http://www.rfc-editor.org/
http://www.rfc-editor.org/rfc.html

Table C.1   Two-letter language codes, from ISO 639.

CODE	LANGUAGE	CODE	LANGUAGE
aa	Afar	ab	Abkhazian
af	Afrikaans	am	Amharic
ar	Arabic	as	Assamese
ay	Aymara	az	Azerbaijani
ba	Bashkir	be	Byelorussian
bg	Bulgarian	bh	Bihari
bi	Bislama	bn	Bengali; Bangla
bo	Tibetan	br	Breton
ca	Catalan	co	Corsican
cs	Czech	cy	Welsh
da	Danish	de	German
dz	Bhutani	el	Greek
en	English	eo	Esperanto
es	Spanish	et	Estonian
eu	Basque	fa	Persian
fi	Finnish	fj	Fiji
fo	Faeroese	fr	French
fy	Frisian	ga	Irish
gd	Scots, Gaelic	gl	Galician
gn	Guarani	gu	Gujarati
he	Hebrew	ha	Hausa
hi	Hindi	hr	Croatian
hu	Hungarian	hy	Armenian
ia	Interlingua	id	Indonesian
ie	Interlingue	ik	Inupiak
in	Indonesian	is	Icelandic
it	Italian	iu	Inuktitut
iw*	Hebrew	ja	Japanese

*Obsolete codes.   *Continues*

Table C.1 *Continued.*

CODE	LANGUAGE	CODE	LANGUAGE
ji*	Yiddish	jw	Javanese
ka	Georgian	kk	Kazakh
kl	Greenlandic	km	Cambodian
kn	Kannada	ko	Korean
ks	Kashmiri	ku	Kurdish
ky	Kirghiz	la	Latin
ln	Lingala	lo	Laothian
lt	Lithuanian	lv	Latvian, Lettish
mg	Malagasy	mi	Maori
mk	Macedonian	ml	Malayalam
mn	Mongolian	mo	Moldavian
mr	Marathi	ms	Malay
mt	Maltese	my	Burmese
na	Nauru	ne	Nepali
nl	Dutch	no	Norwegian
oc	Occitan	om	(Afan), Oromo
or	Oriya	pa	Punjabi
pl	Polish	ps	Pashto, Pushto
pt	Portuguese	qu	Quechua
rm	Rhaeto-Romance	rn	Kirundi
ro	Romanian	ru	Russian
rw	Kinyarwanda	sa	Sanskrit
sd	Sindhi	sg	Sangro
sh	Serbo-Croatian	si	Singhalese
sk	Slovak	sl	Slovenian
sm	Samoan	sn	Shona
so	Somali	sq	Albanian
sr	Serbian	ss	Siswati
st	Sesotho	su	Sudanese

CODE	LANGUAGE	CODE	LANGUAGE
sv	Swedish	sw	Swahili
ta	Tamil	te	Tegulu
tg	Tajik	th	Thai
ti	Tigrinya	tk	Turkmen
tl	Tagalog	tn	Setswana
to	Tonga	tr	Turkish
ts	Tsonga	tt	Tatar
tw	Twi	ug	Uigur
uk	Ukrainian	ur	Urdu
uz	Uzbek	vi	Vietnamese
vo	Volapuk	wo	Wolof
xh	Xhosa	yi	Yiddish
yo	Yoruba	za	Zuang
zh	Chinese	zu	Zulu

*Obsolete codes.

ISO 639:1988—LANGUAGE CODES

Code for the representation of names of languages. The International Organization for Standardization, 1st edition, 1988. Prepared by ISO/TC 37—Terminology (principles and coordination).

The registry agency for additions or changes to the ISO language codes is:

International Information Centre for Terminology (Infoterm)
P.O. Box 130
A-1021 Wien
Austria
Phone: +43 1 26 75 35 Ext. 312
Fax: +43 1 216 32 72
An unofficial summary list is found at:
www.utoronto.ca/ian/books/xml/appc/iso639.html

ISO 3166:1988—COUNTRY CODES

Code for the representation of names of countries. The International Organization for Standardization, 1st edition, 1988.

Table C.2 Two-letter country codes, from ISO 3166

CODE	COUNTRY	CODE	COUNTRY
AD	Andorra	AE	United Arab Emirates
AF	Afghanistan	AG	Antigua and Barbuda
AI	Anguilla	AL	Albania
AM	Armenia	AN	Netherland Antilles
AO	Angola	AQ	Antarctica
AR	Argentina	AS	American Samoa
AT	Austria	AU	Australia
AW	Aruba	AZ	Azerbaijan
BA	Bosnia-Herzegovina	BB	Barbados
BD	Bangladesh	BE	Belgium
BF	Burkina Faso	BG	Bulgaria
BH	Bahrain	BI	Burundi
BJ	Benin	BM	Bermuda
BN	Brunei Darussalam	BO	Bolivia
BR	Brazil	BS	Bahamas
BT	Bhutan	BV	Bouvet Island
BW	Botswana	BY	Belarus
BZ	Belize	CA	Canada
CC	Cocos (Keeling) Islands	CF	Central African Republic
CG	Congo	CH	Switzerland
CI	Ivory Coast	CK	Cook Islands
CL	Chile	CM	Cameroon
CN	China	CO	Colombia
CR	Costa Rica	CS*	Czechoslovakia
CU	Cuba	CV	Cape Verde
CX	Christmas Island	CY	Cyprus
CZ	Czech Republic	DE	Germany

*Obsolete codes.

**Europe only.

CODE	COUNTRY	CODE	COUNTRY
DJ	Djibouti	DK	Denmark
DM	Dominica	DO	Dominican Republic
DZ	Algeria	EC	Ecuador
EE	Estonia	EG	Egypt
EH	Western Sahara	ER	Eritrea
ES	Spain	ET	Ethiopia
FI	Finland	FJ	Fiji
FK	Falkland Isl.(Malvinas)	FM	Micronesia
FO	Faroe Islands	FR	France
FX	France**	GA	Gabon
GB	Great Britain (UK)	GD	Grenada
GE	Georgia	GF	Guyana (Fr.)
GH	Ghana	GI	Gibraltar
GL	Greenland	GM	Gambia
GN	Guinea	GP	Guadeloupe (Fr.)
GQ	Equatorial Guinea	GR	Greece
GS	South Georgia & South Sandwich Islands	GT	Guatemala
GU	Guam (US)	GW	Guinea Bissau
GY	Guyana	HK	Hong Kong
HM	Heard & McDonald Islands	HN	Honduras
HR	Croatia	HT	Haiti
HU	Hungary	ID	Indonesia
IE	Ireland	IL	Israel
IN	India	IO	British Indian Ocean Terr.
IQ	Iraq	IR	Iran
IS	Iceland	IT	Italy
JM	Jamaica	JO	Jordan
JP	Japan	KE	Kenya

Continues

Table C.2   *Continued.*

CODE	COUNTRY	CODE	COUNTRY
KG	Kyrgyz Republic	KH	Cambodia
KI	Kiribati	KM	Comoros
KN	St. Kitts Nevis Anguilla	KP	Korea (North)
KR	Korea (South)	KW	Kuwait
KY	Cayman Islands	KZ	Kazachstan
LA	Laos	LB	Lebanon
LC	Saint Lucia	LI	Liechtenstein
LK	Sri Lanka	LR	Liberia
LS	Lesotho	LT	Lithuania
LU	Luxembourg	LV	Latvia
LY	Libya	MA	Morocco
MC	Monaco	MD	Moldova
MG	Madagascar	MH	Marshall Islands
MK	Macedonia (prev. Yug.)	ML	Mali
MM	Myanmar	MN	Mongolia
MO	Macau	MP	Northern Mariana Islands
MQ	Martinique (Fr.)	MR	Mauritania
MS	Montserrat	MT	Malta
MU	Mauritius	MV	Maldives
MW	Malawi	MX	Mexico
MY	Malaysia	MZ	Mozambique
NA	Namibia	NC	New Caledonia (Fr.)
NE	Niger	NF	Norfolk Island
NG	Nigeria	NI	Nicaragua
NL	Netherlands	NO	Norway
NP	Nepal	NR	Nauru
NU	Niue	NZ	New Zealand
OM	Oman	PA	Panama
PE	Peru	PF	Polynesia (Fr.)

CODE	COUNTRY	CODE	COUNTRY
PG	Papua New Guinea	PH	Philippines
PK	Pakistan	PL	Poland
PM	St. Pierre & Miquelon	PN	Pitcairn
PR	Puerto Rico (US)	PT	Portugal
PW	Palau	PY	Paraguay
QA	Qatar	RE	Reunion (Fr.)
RO	Romania	RU	Russian Federation
RW	Rwanda	SA	Saudi Arabia
SB	Solomon Islands	SC	Seychelles
SD	Sudan	SE	Sweden
SG	Singapore	SH	St. Helena
SI	Slovenia	SJ	Svalbard & Jan Mayen Islands
SK	Slovakia (Slovak Republic)	SL	Sierra Leone
SM	San Marino	SN	Senegal
SO	Somalia	SR	Suriname
ST	St. Tome and Principe	SU*	Soviet Union
SV	El Salvador	SY	Syria
SZ	Swaziland	TC	Turks & Caicos Islands
TD	Chad	TF	French Southern Territory
TG	Togo	TH	Thailand
TJ	Tadjikistan	TK	Tokelau
TM	Turkmenistan	TN	Tunisia
TO	Tonga	TP	East Timor
TR	Turkey	TT	Trinidad & Tobago
TV	Tuvalu	TW	Taiwan
TZ	Tanzania	UA	Ukraine
UG	Uganda	UK	United Kingdom
UM	US Minor (outlying islands)	US	United States

Continues

Table C.2 *Continued.*

CODE	COUNTRY	CODE	COUNTRY
UY	Uruguay	UZ	Uzbekistan
VA	Vatican City State	VC	St. Vincent & Grenadines
VE	Venezuela	VG	Virgin Islands (GB)
VI	Virgin Islands (US)	VN	Vietnam
VU	Vanuatu	WF	Wallis & Futuna Islands
WS	Samoa	YE	Yemen
YT	Mayotte	YU*	Yugoslavia
ZA	South Africa	ZM	Zambia
ZR	Zaire	ZW	Zimbabwe

The official registry agency for additions or changes to the ISO country codes is:

ISO 3166 Maintenance Agency Secretariat
c/o DIN Deutsches Institut für Normung
Burggrafenstrasse 6
Postfach 1107
D-10787 Berlin
Germany
Phone: +49 30 26 01 320
Fax: +49 30 26 01 231

An unofficial summary of the codes can be found at:
ftp://ftp.isi.edu/in-notes/iana/assignments/country-codes
www.utoronto.ca/ian/books/xml/appc/iso3166.html

XML for HTML Experts

XML is superficially similar to HTML, in that it uses a similar markup tag structure, and uses markup tags to define a logical structure for text data. However, HTML is a single language with a fixed set of markup tags and element nesting rules, whereas XML has no fixed set of tags, and no predefined nesting rules. In essence, XML lets you define an almost infinite number of "languages," and lets you use the document type declaration to define the allowed elements and their grammar.

The following items summarize the most important structural differences between HTML and XML markup. The main difference, of course, lies in the XML document type declaration, and the absence of a fixed element vocabulary. This book has, essentially, been about the ramifications of those features.

In XML, element names are *case-sensitive.* In XML, all element names are case-sensitive, while in HTML they are not. Thus in HTML, the markup paragraph </p> is correct, while in XML it is a fatal error, as the end tag </p> does not have a matching start tag.

In XML, attribute names are *case-sensitive.* In XML, attribute names are also case-sensitive, so that the tag <a href="ref1" Href="ref2"> is correct XML, as the two attributes ref1 and Ref1 are different. In HTML, attribute names are case-insensitive, so that the preceding tag would be an error—the two attributes would be seen as identical, and it is illegal (in both XML and HTML) to specify the same attribute value more than once on the same element.

In XML, attributes must have an *assigned value*. In XML, every attribute present in a given element must be assigned a value—you can never have an attribute that is simply given by name, but that is not assigned a value. This is not true in HTML, where values can be omitted in some cases, such as <OPTION VALUE="val1" SELECTED> ... </OPTION> to indicate a particular option (inside a **SELECT** list) that is pre-selected.

In XML, all attribute values must be *quoted*. In XML, all attribute values must be enclosed in quotes (matched single or double), whereas in HTML, some attributes do not require quotes. For example, in HTML, the tag <INPUT TYPE=text NAME="myVar"> is correct, whereas it would be invalid XML (you would need <INPUT TYPE="text" NAME="myVar">.

In XML, end-tags are *always* required. In XML, a start-tag must *always* have an end-tag, while in HTML, some end-tags are optional. For example, in HTML the markup

<p>here is a paragraph. <p> here is a second paragraph.

is correct (the </p> is optional), whereas this would produce a fatal error in an XML processor. The equivalent well-formed XML would need to be written (changes in boldface) as:

<p>here is a paragraph. **</p>** <p> here is a second paragraph. **</p>**.

XML uses a special notation for *empty elements*. In XML, empty elements must be written using a special empty element tag of the form *<ename attributes />* (it has a slash at the end of the tag, just before the closing angle bracket). In HTML, empty-elements tags are not distinguished from non-empty ones. For example, in HTML, the empty element **IMG** (here enclosed in an anchor element) can be written as:

```
<a href="whereto.html"><img src="imagefile.gif"
     alt=" text describing image"></a>
```

which is an XML error. In XML, this would need to be written:

```
<a href="whereto.html"><img src="imagefile.gif"
     alt=" text describing image"/></a>
```

XML has only five *predefined* **entities.** HTML defines many dozens of predefined entities (close to one hundred) that represent common Latin, mathematical, or symbol characters. These entities are not predefined in XML (which only defines five entities: **gt, lt, quot, amp,** and **apos**).

XML supports *CDATA sections*. XML supports CDATA sections inside markup elements. The content of a CDATA section is "escaped" from processing by an XML processor—markup and entity references are ignored inside it. HTML has no such escape mechanism, so that any escaping of marked-up text to be included within an HTML document must be done before the text is inserted into the document (e.g., by explicitly escaping characters using character or entity references).

XML allows *arbitrary element and attribute names.* In HTML the set of element and attribute names is fixed by the DTD that formalizes HTML. XML, on the other hand, can have arbitrary element and attribute names, provided the resulting markup is well-formed.

XML allows *processing instructions.* XML allows processing instructions inside any non-empty element (and also in the document type declaration). HTML does not support processing instructions.

XML supports *document type declarations.* The grammar of HTML is fixed, whereas XML lets you use a document type declaration to define new document grammars, and to define new entities which can be included, via entity references, inside the content of elements. Via the document type declaration, XML supports the following features not available in HTML:

- Use of **element and attribute-list declarations** to define grammatical rules for a type of document

- Use of **internal** or **external parsed general entities** (declarations and references) to define data for inclusion within the element content (or within attribute values) of a document

- Use of **external unparsed general entities** (declarations and ENTITY-type attributes) to define external non-XML data (such as binary files) and to reference such types via a special ENTITY attribute type

- Use of **notations** (notation declarations and notation attributes, and NDATA declarations in unparsed general entity declarations) for defining external utilities appropriate for processing types of non-XML data (indicated by the notation name of an unparsed general entity declaration), or for processing specially formatted content of XML elements (so denoted by a notation attribute)

- Use of **processing instructions** (plus a specified notation) to send directives to an external application

- Use of **internal** or **external parameter entities** (declarations and references) to define markup declaration rules for reuse within a document type declaration

- Use of **conditional sections** within external parameter entities to define a document type declaration that "includes" or "excludes" certain markup declarations, depending on keyword settings (rather like an *ifdef* directive to a C preprocessor)

- Support for **validation** of document markup, to ensure correctness as defined by the document type declaration

- Support for **well-formed** documents, which allows using the DTD to set default attribute values, or to declare external entities for use within a document

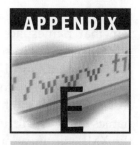

XML Namespaces

In making the language much more flexible than SGML, XML has introduced two important changes:

- It has made the use of a document type declaration optional.
- It allows for easy mixing of sets of element definitions from different sources.

This indeed sounds wonderful in theory: Start with the *Basic Prose* tag set and include the *Bibliography* tag set for citing your sources; add in the *e-commerce* tag set and let people purchase books by clicking on entries in your reading list, and last, include the *Postal Address* tag set for easy delivery.

But let's look at this in more detail.

Suppose the *Postal Address* tag set contains elements such as **FirstName**, **LastName**, **Title**, **Address**, and so forth. The *Bibliography* tag set adds in **Date, Author, Title, Publisher,** and so forth. The *Postal Address* tag set adds **Area, Name, NearestStreet, Title,** and so on.

But wait! All these elements named **Title** mean different things! In fact, they probably need very different attributes, and have widely differing content models.

This is a namespace problem—the different **Title** tags have different

meanings, because they are defined in different places. Thus, the first problem that namespaces have to solve is keeping all of the element (and
attribute) names in separate spaces, where they don't conflict.

The current World Wide Web Consortium proposal for namespaces does
that by allowing a document author to give each namespace a special prefix. Thus, you might distinguish the different Title elements by using
names such as **Bibliography:Title, PostalAddress:Title,** and so on. Since
the XML specification explicitly allows the colon (:) in names (see Production Name [5]) for just this purpose, an existing XML processor that does
not know about namespaces will happily read an XML document and
think that there just happen to be lots of names in it that contain colons.

But if I see an element called **Bibliography:Title** in an XML document,
how do I know whether it's the *Bibliography* tag set published by the British
Library or the tag set from the Association of Computing Machinery, or
some other one?

Thus, the second problem that namespaces need to solve is one of identifying which namespace a document is using.

The current draft does this by associating a URI (a URL or URN) with
each namespace prefix within the document. The namespace prefix then
becomes a shorthand within the document for that URI—somewhat similar to using a name to identify a notation, although here everything is done
directly in the XML markup, and not in the document type declaration.
Indeed, authors can then choose whatever short name they want for the
name space—and in the case of the preceding example, could use **bib**
instead of **Bibliography**, yielding smaller documents.

The current draft of the XML Namespaces specification reserves the special attribute name xmlns for specifying namespaces. The following is a
simple example illustrating how this name can be used:

```
<bibliography
    xmlns:bib='http://www.bibliography.org/XML/bib.ns'
    xmlns='urn:royal-mail.gov.uk/XML/ns/postal.ns,1999'
>
    <bib:book>
      <bib:title> . . .
    </bib>
</bibliography>
```

Here, the xmlns keyword in xmlns:bib declares bib to be a prefix that can
be used anywhere within the bibliography element to refer to the corresponding namespace URI. The unqualified xmlns attribute means that any
elements or attributes inside the content of this particular bibliography ele-

ment whose names *do not* contain colons are to be treated as if they came from the *Royal Mail* namespace.

The XML Namespaces specification is still under development, so we have presented here only a brief introduction to the ideas behind it. For up-to-date information, see *www.w3.org/TR/1998/WD-xml-names* on the World Wide Web Consortium's Web site.

Schema or DTD?

The XML specification describes a syntax for specifying a document type definition (that is, the syntax used to declare elements, attributes, notations, and entities) that is different from the syntax used for the main body of XML documents. A number of people have proposed using XML *element syntax* instead—that is, to define a special type of XML document that can be used to describe the allowed syntactic structure of other XML documents.

For example, consider the following document type declaration "snippet":

```
<!ELEMENT Shoe
    (Sock?, foot)?
>
```

This declaration might be represented, using regular XML markup, as:

```
<Define-element name="Shoe"
  <Content>(Sock?, foot)?</Content>
  <Description>A hard, uncomfortable torture
device</Description>
  <Example href="foot.xml">Example of use of Shoe</Example>
>
```

Note that the second example contains *more* information than can be expressed in an XML document type declaration. For example, there is no standard way in the DTD syntax to link a DTD to related documentation, or to provide a short description that might be used in an editor or style sheet dialog box. One can use comments, but comments in a DTD are discarded by most XML processors, and not passed back to the application.

Such XML "dialects" are generally called XML schemas, since they are used to define the schema by which other documents can be constructed. Several such schema languages have been proposed. At the time of writing, there was no single dominant schema, but the proposed languages named *XSchema, XData/DSD,* and *DCD/DCF/RDF* were the leading contenders for adoption as an XML standard. The web site accompanying this book has pointers to these proposals, and to any additional information on this topic that may have come into existence since this book went to press.

Since current XML software generally requires the DTD syntax, most people who work with (or who are developing) schema languages have written programs to translate automatically from one or another of these schema formats into the DTD syntax. Some software is available over the Web, should you wish to use these languages yourself.

The following list gives a summary of some of the benefits and drawbacks of the two approaches.

TRADITIONAL DTD SYNTAX	SCHEMA WITH INSTANCE SYNTAX
The DTD syntax is different from that of XML documents, so that authors need to learn a new syntax.	Same syntax as XML documents, so easy to learn
Must be written with an ASCII editor, or with a special-purpose DTD editor.	Can be written using an XML editor and normal XML tools
Not extensible: can't express additional properties of markup such as links to documentation or examples for each element	Extensible, can specify additional properties, such as documentation and examples, or links to external help
Cannot constrain element content at all, cannot constrain the content of CDATA attributes	Can specify additional constraints, such as that the content of an element must match a pattern, or that an attribute must contain a positive whole number
Standard, so every XML and SGML tool can use them	Not standard, so XML tools don't generally understand them yet

Layout of Document Type Declarations

This short summary gives some ideas for ways to lay out XML declarations so that they are most easily read and edited. We have used boldface for the name of the item being declared in each case; although obviously you can't do that in an actual DTD, where only plain unformatted text can be used, you can do so for printed documentation. We have also found useful pretty-printing software that takes a DTD or an external parameter entity and formats it with the names in bold, adds an index, and so forth. The one we use was written in-house for use with the Unix *troff* formatter and Post-Script language printers, but if you are interested, look at the Web site that accompanies this book for pointers to other useful pieces of software we have found for this task.

A paper by one of the authors on this subject, but targeted for SGML DTDs, can be found at *www.groveware.com/~lee/* under the heading *Writing a Readable DTD*.

G.1 Overview

There are four main tricks that can be used, with plain text files containing document type declarations, to organize the text for clearer reading and better error-detection.

Indentation. Use indentation to show nesting or containment. For example, attribute declarations are contained within an attribute definition list, so indent them to show this containment.

Proximity. Keep related things close together. Where items relate to one another in columns, align them vertically. Note, however, that this is rare in XML declarations. Usually, items relate to each other in horizontal rows, so keep such items within a row, and close together.

White space. Blank lines are perfectly legal within and between declarations, and can be used for grouping to good effect. For example, they can be used to separate one declaration from another, or a particularly complex attribute definition from preceding and subsequent definitions in the same attribute-list declaration.

Contrast. Make comments in particular look very different from declarations. One way to do this, borrowed from programming languages, is to use a vertical line of asterisks all the way down the left-hand side of a comment. We will illustrate this approach below.

G.2 Declaration Examples

The following sections contain examples of each of the main forms of declarations, and demonstrate the use of the layout rules discussed above.

G.2.1 Comments

Note the use of the asterisks on the left-hand side to mark out the lines covered by the comment. This helps the eye to find the beginning and end of the comment, and separate it from the markup.

```
<!--* It can be difficult to notice that a declaration is
    * commented out, or to see a single line of comment
    * amongst lots of declarations.
    *
    * This style makes comments stand out clearly.
    *-->
```

G.2.2 Element Declarations

XML does not allow comments within declarations, so it is useful to adopt a convention of placing a comment before an element declaration. You can use this space to give a short description and perhaps a pointer to documentation, rather as in the *JavaDoc* system.

Notice the placement of the trailing > on a line by itself—this helps to space declarations out, and also helps you catch errors, both when reading declarations, and while editing them.

```
<!ELEMENT C-Program
    (Inclusions?, Declarations?, Main, Functions?)
>
```

G.2.3 Attributes

Note how each attribute is declared on its own line. This makes it easy to look through the list of attributes, and separate one from another.

```
<!ATTLIST C-Program
    DTDVersion"1.1" #FIXED
    ProgramVersion CDATA #REQUIRED
    Level (V6Unix|KandR|ANSI) ANSI
>
```

G.2.4 Notations

With notations, one can generally place the external identifier (SYSTEM or PUBLIC) on a line following the declaration of the notation name. This again helps to mark out the name of the notation, and makes it easy to spot the identifiers, and the end of the declaration.

```
<!NOTATION Image
    SYSTEM "image/png,image/jpeg,image/gif,image/*"
>
```

G.2.5 External Entity Declarations

External entities, like notations, take an external identifier (SYSTEM or PUBLIC), so that once again it is useful to place this identifier on a separate line following the declaration of the entity name. This is shown in the following *external parameter entity:*

```
<!ENTITY % MyDefs
    SYSTEM "http://www.groveware.com/xmlbook/lib/bookdefs.dtd"
>
%MyDefs;
```

and the following external parsed general entity:

```
<!ENTITY ChapterFive
    SYSTEM "http://www.groveware.com/xmlbook/chap5.xml"
>
```

With *external unparsed general entities,* it is useful to place the notation reference (NDATA *notation-name*) on a separate line following the external identifier. This makes it easy to identify the entity as unparsed, and to locate the notation name for the entity:

```
<!ENTITY PictureOfLiam
    SYSTEM http://www.groveware.com/~lee/liam.jpg
    NDATA Image
>
```

G.2.6 Internal Entity Declarations

With internal entities, it is best to place the line defining the entity's literal value on a line separate from the start and end of the declaration. This is particularly important for entities containing > characters, as these are often misinterpreted (by the person editing the document) as the end of the entity, instead of as part of the literal entity value. This is shown here for an *internal parameter entity:*

```
<!ENTITY % RunningText
    "(#PCDATA|Emphasis|Phrase|Place|Person|Anchovy)*"
>
```

and an internal general entity:

```
<!ENTITY ProductName
    "Campus MainEvent &CME.Version;"
>
```

Glossary

This glossary defines, describes, and gives examples of terms and vocabulary used (and in some cases, formally defined) in the XML specification. In addition, this glossary defines terms and vocabulary in general use among those working with XML, or the UCS character set, but that not defined or mentioned in the XML specifications. Terms related to describing character sets and character encodings are indicated by the word [Char], in square brackets, following the term, while miscellaneous terms related to XML software development are indicated by the word [Misc], in square brackets, following the term.

Where possible, specific definitions were adapted from official specifications. However, the descriptions here are not *normative*, and you are referred to the official XML, SGML, and Unicode and ISO/IEC character set standards for official definitions arising from these standards.

The character used in XML to denote various keywords (see following entries). Also used in XML to indicate character references, as in the expression <. This character is also used in the EBNF for XML to reference characters by their code positions, as in #x3F (in the EBNF, the references use hexadecimal notation).

#FIXED A keyword used in an attribute default specification to indicate that the value for an attribute is fixed. See also: *attribute default*.

#IMPLIED A keyword used in an attribute default specification to indicate that the value for an attribute is optional. See also: *attribute default*.

#PCDATA A keyword that stands for parsed character data. Within an *element type declaration*, this keyword is used to indicate that *character data* is allowed as content within the given element type. For example, the element type declaration

```
<!ELEMENT Pname (#PCDATA ) >
```

indicates that elements of type **Pname** can only contain character data, and no markup, while the declaration

```
<!ELEMENT emph ( emph | #PCDATA ) >
```

indicates that the element **emph** can contain either an element of type **emph**, or character data, but not both.

#REQUIRED A keyword used in an attribute default specification to indicate that the value for an attribute is required, and must be given for all elements of the specified type. See also: *attribute default*.

% The character used in XML to denote the start of a *parameter-entity reference*. An example of such a reference is %pdata;. Note that such references are only recognized within the document type declaration—in other contexts (such as in element markup) % is simply the percent character.

& The character used in XML to denote the start of a *parameter-entity reference*. An example of such a reference is &mrBlobby;.

(. . .) Round brackets (parenthesis) are used in *content model* specifications, as well as in the *EBNF* for XML, to denote collections of expressions that should be treated as a group. For example, the sequence (a, b, c)+ corresponds to one or more occurrences of the sequence a b c, that is, "a b c", "a b c a b c", and so on.

* A "repeat" operator, used in *content model* specifications, as well as in the *EBNF* for XML, to indicate that the preceding expression can appear zero or more times. Thus the expression a* can correspond to nothing (zero occurrences), or else the patterns "a", "a a", "a a a", and so on. For other repeat patterns, see: +, ?.

+ A "repeat" operator, used in *content model* specifications, as well as in the *EBNF* for XML, to indicate that the preceding expression can appear one or more times. Thus the expression a+ can correspond to the expressions "a", "a a", "a a a", and so on. For other repeat patterns, see: *, ?.

, A "sequence" operator, used in *content model* specifications, as well as in the *EBNF* for XML, to indicate that the expressions on either side of the , must appear in the listed order. For example, the expression a , b means that both a and b must appear, and must appear in the order a followed by b. For other sequence operators (operators that define allowed sequences of symbols), see: |.

- A "range" operator, used in the *EBNF* for XML to indicate an allowed range of characters. For example, the expression [a-z] corresponds to all UCS characters with code positions between those of the lowercase letters a and z, inclusive. Instead of actual characters, one can also use explicit code positions, as in [#x61-#x7a]. For other range expressions, see: ^.

; The character used in XML to denote the end of an *entity reference*, as in %pdata; or &mrBlobby;. If it does not mark the end of an entity reference, then the semicolon is treated as a regular character.

<, > The delimiters used for an XML markup declaration, such as a *markup tag*, or an *element type declaration*.

? A "repeat" operator, used in *content model* specifications, as well as in the *EBNF* for XML, to indicate that the preceding expression can appear zero or one times. Thus the expression a? can correspond to nothing (zero occurrences) or the expression "a". For other repeat patterns, see: *, +.

^ An "exclude" operator, used in the *EBNF* for XML, to indicate an excluded character or range of characters. For example, the expression [^a-z] corresponds to all UCS characters except those with code positions between those of the lowercase letters a and z, inclusive. Instead of actual characters, one can also use explicit code positions, as in [^#x61-#x7a].

| An "or" operator, used in *content model* specifications, as well as in the *EBNF* for XML, to indicate that one of the expressions on either side of the | must appear, but both cannot. For example, the expression a | b means that an allowed expression is a, or b, but that a b is not allowed.

alphabet [XML, Char] An alphabet consists of a collection of symbols that generally represent the sounds of a language (as in the Latin alphabet used by Western European languages). However, there is not always a simple relationship between the symbols (letters) and sounds—as any spelling instructor can attest! The Unicode database explicitly states which characters are considered to be alphabetic, as discussed in Part 3, Appendix B.

amp An XML-predefined general entity corresponding to the ampersand (&) character. The corresponding entity reference is: &.

anchor [Misc] One end of a hypertext link in a document. An anchor can be either the start or end of a hypertext link.

ANY A keyword used in the definition of an element-type *content model* to indicate that elements of the specified type can contain any mixture of *elements* and/or *character data*. See also: EMPTY.

apos An XML-predefined general entity corresponding to the single-quote/apostrophe (') character. The corresponding entity reference is: '.

application A software module on behalf of which the *XML processor* is used to read and process XML data. For example, a database *application* would use an *XML processor* to process data coded in XML. Note that this differs from the SGML definition, wherein an SGML application is equivalent to a defined DTD.

application profile XML is said to be an *application profile* of SGML, in that XML is an application language defined using SGML. In SGML terminology, every language specified using SGML is referred to as an application profile of SGML.

ASCII [Char] American Standard Code for Information Interchange. a 7-bit *coded character set* representing 128 characters. Thirty-three of these characters are *control characters* used in communications and printing control. Only three of these control characters—the horizontal tab, line feed, and carriage return—are allowed within XML documents.

ATTLIST The markup declaration keyword that denotes an attribute-list declaration. An attribute list declaration always begins with the character string <!ATTLIST.

attribute A named property that can be assigned a value and that is associated with an *element*. Attributes can often be assigned values within an element *start-tag* (for non-empty elements) or *an empty-element tag* (for empty elements). For example, <IMG SRC="image.gif" /> means that the empty element **IMG** has an attribute **SRC**, assigned the value image.gif. Within a DTD, an attribute declaration within an *attribute-list declaration* can set a default *attribute value* for all instances of an *element type*, and can also specify if an attribute is fixed (cannot be changed), or required (must be specified in every start-tag or empty-element tag).

attribute declaration A declaration, within an *attribute-list declaration*, that defines the name, type, and *attribute default* properties of an attribute. The general form is:

```
attr-name  TYPE  attr-default
```

where *attr-name* is the name for the attribute, *TYPE* is one of CDATA, ENTITY, ENTITIES, NMTOKEN, NMTOKENS, ID, IDREF, and IDREFS, and *attr-default* (defined below) specifies the properties and possibly the default value of the attribute. An example is:

```
href  CDATA #REQUIRED
ALT   CDATA "an Image"
```

attribute default An attribute default, within an *attribute declaration*, provides information on whether the attribute's presence is required in an instance of the element type, and if not, how an XML processor should react if a declared attribute is absent from an element. There are four possible forms:

- **#REQUIRED** The attribute must be specified for all elements of the type in the associated *attribute-list declaration*.

- **#IMPLIED** No default value is provided, and assignment of a value within an element is optional.

- **#FIXED followed by a** *literal data* **token** The literal data token is the default attribute value, for all instances of that attribute, in all instances of elements of the type given in the associated attribute-list declaration. Note that #FIXED means that this value cannot be changed in an element's *attribute specification*.

- **A single** *literal data* **token** This defines the default value, which may be overridden by an attribute specification in a specific element. An example is "Default Value".

attribute-list declaration Specifies, using a set of *attribute declarations*, the name, data type, and default value (if any) of each attribute associated with a given *element type*. The following is an example attribute-list declaration, for the element-type EXAMP that contains four attribute declarations :

```
<!ATTLIST EXAMP
          LOCAT ID    #IMPLIED
          HREF  CDATA #REQUIRED
          LANG  CDATA #FIXED "fr-qc"
```

```
    TYPE  CDATA  "internal"
>
```

attribute name The *name* by which an attribute is identified.

attribute specification The attribute name/value assignments that appear in *start-tags* or *empty-element tags*. An example is the string ATTR="value" in the start-tag <PARA ATTR="value">.

attribute type The type of an attribute, defined in the *attribute declaration*. There are three possible types: a string type, identified by the type keyword *CDATA*, tokenized types, indicated by the keywords ID, IDREF, IDREFS, ENTITY, ENTITIES, NMTOKEN, and NMTOKENS, and enumerated types, which can take only one of a list of values provided in the declaration. There are two kinds of enumerated types: a bracketed list of allowed name token values, separated by vertical bars, such as ("value1" | "value2" | "value3"), and a notation type, which defines a list of allowed notation names, where each name must be defined in a *notation declaration*.

attribute value The value assigned to a given attribute.

at user option In the XML specification, certain functional features of an XML processor are said to be "at user option." In other words, users must be able to enable and disable the feature, at their option. Some things that are at user option are character data normalization or canonicalization (as described in Part 3, Appendix B of this book), and the reporting of warnings or errors.

authoring software Any application that can be used to create XML documents. This can vary from a simple text editor to a complex XML editor that enforces grammatical correctness and that can validate against a given DTD.

base64 [Misc] An encoding scheme (defined in RFC 2045) that encodes an arbitrary sequence of bytes (formally "octets") using 64 different ASCII characters. Each of these ASCII characters denotes a number in a base-64 numbering system. In the encoding, each group of three bytes (24 bits) is encoded as a sequence of four base-64 "digits."

base characters [XML, Char] Those characters that do not graphically combine with preceding characters. See also: *combining characters*.

BNF See: *EBNF.*

byte ordering, byte order mark When a single piece of information (such as a character) is encoded in two or more bytes, then it is important to indicate the order in which these bytes are stored (e.g., in memory) or transmitted (e.g., via HTTP). For example, UCS characters encoded in the UTF-16 encoding are stored in two bytes each (e.g., labeled 1 and 2), which could be sent or stored in the byte order 12 or 21. The particular choice used (both are equally valid) is referred to as the *byte ordering*. UCS (and XML) specifies the character at position $FEFF_{16}$ to be the *byte order mark*, or *BOM*, and suggests that this be the first character sent (or present) in UTF-16 data. Then, an application reading the data can use the order of the bytes in this first character (FE followed by FF, or vice versa) to determine the order of all subsequent bytes.

canonical, canonical form The adjective *canonical* refers to an idea or object reduced to its simplest or clearest schema. Thus, a *canonical form* is the simplest base form or structure of an object. An *XML processor*, at the option of the user or application developer, may *normalize* characters to some canonical form prior to comparing strings. This would be useful for comparing strings that contain characters for which multiple representations are possible in UCS (for example, characters that can appear as a single character, or as a combination of a *base character* plus a *combining character*, such as a *diacritic*).

canonicalize To convert an object into its *canonical form*.

cascading style sheets (CSS) A language designed for specifying the formatting presentation and layout of structurally marked-up documents, such as HTML or XML documents. CSS is *not* a dialect of XML. The CSS language is being developed under the auspices of the *World Wide Web Consortium*. See also: *XSL*.

case folding With characters that have both uppercase and lowercase forms, it is sometimes useful to compare strings while ignoring difference in case. In this situation, one often invokes *case folding* to convert all lowercase characters into the "equivalent" uppercase letter.

case-insensitive Indicates that the processing of the characters *does not* depend on differences in case. For example, the strings "stuff" and "StuFF" are equivalent to a case-insensitive application. Note that the concept of case does not apply to many characters in the ISO/IEC 10646 / Unicode. XML is, in general, a *case-sensitive* application.

case-sensitive Indicates that the processing of the characters depends on differences in case. For example, in a case-sensitive application, the strings "stuff" and "Stuff" are *not* equivalent. XML is, in general, a case-sensitive application.

CDATA A keyword used only within an *attribute declaration* to declare the type of an attribute value. The CDATA keyword indicates that the value is a string of characters that, prior to processing by an XML application, should be recursively parsed to expand any *entity references*, and to expand any *character references*. There are also some special rules related to white space handling, as described in Section 3.3.3 of the XML specification, and in Chapter 10 of Part 1 of this book. In practice, an XML application must expand an attribute value before using it in any context. For example, in the attribute-value assignment DBVAR="xyzzy<©>&quot" the value must be expanded to the string "xyzzy<©>" prior to processing in the application.

CDATA section These are specially "quoted" sections of text that are escaped from processing by the XML processor. CDATA sections may occur anywhere *character data* may occur, and are used to escape blocks of text containing characters which would otherwise be recognized as markup or character/entity references. CDATA sections begin with the string <![CDATA[and end with the string]]>.

character [Char] A generally ambiguous word, with many varied definitions. For computer software, it is best to think of a character as a quantity that represents the abstract function associated with a character, independent of any graphical representation of it. Alternatively, you can think of a character as a basic unit that represents "data" or codes used to organize and control "data." And, if this is still confusing (which it probably is), you can look to Part 3, Appendix B of this book for a more complete explanation. In XML, legal characters are tab, carriage return, line feed, and the graphic characters of Unicode and ISO/IEC 10646: See also: *character set*; *coded character set*.

character class [Char; XML] A term that distinguishes different classes of characters, following the characteristics defined in the Unicode standard. Unicode defines the following character classes: *base characters* (among others, this class contains the alphabetic characters of the Latin alphabet, without diacritics), *ideographic characters*, and *combining characters* (characters that combine with preceding characters—among others, this class contains most diacritics); these classes combine to form the class of letters. Other classes are *digits* (characters that refer to numbers) and *extenders* (a type of combining character that affects the meaning of a previous character, usually by changing the sense of size or length associated with the meaning of the character).

character data The actual text component of a document, excluding that portion that is considered to be *markup*—the non-markup data content of the document. For example, in <TAG>bleeble bla < foo</TAG>, the string "bleeble bla < foo" is the character data. In the content of elements, character data is any string of characters which does not contain the start-delimiter (i.e., the character "<") of any markup. Within a *CDATA section*, character data is any string of characters not including the CDATA-section close delimiter, "]]>", that marks the end of the CDATA section.

character encoding [Char] A mapping from a *coded character set* to a set of *bytes*. A given coded character set may allow more than one character encoding scheme. For example, the Unicode character set can be encoded such that each character is encoded in two octets (UTF-16, a 16-bit encoding), in from one to four octets (UTF-8, an 8-bit encoding), or in one to four octets, making use of only the seven least-significant bits in each octet (UTF-7, a 7-bit encoding).

character reference A reference to a specific Unicode character, using the decimal or hexadecimal number referencing the position of that character in the XML document character set (ISO/IEC 10646 / Unicode). For example, the character references é (decimal) and é (hexadecimal) both reference the character "e with an acute accent" (é). One can think of a character reference as the escape mechanism for Unicode characters.

character set [Char, XML] See: *coded character set*.

charset A property name used in a variety of Internet-based applications (such as MIME and HTTP) to indicate the *character encoding* used in a given piece of data. For example, in a MIME content type header, one could indicate the type and character encoding of a stream of XML data using a MIME content type header of the form: content-type: text/x-xml; charset=UTF-8.

Chemical Markup Language (CML) A markup language, defined using XML, for specifying the structure of molecular structures. CML was developed by Dr. Peter Murray-Rust.

child, child element Consider a non-*root element* **P** in a document. If there is an element **P** in the document such that **C** is in the content of **P**, but is not in the content of any other element that is in the content of **P**, then **P** is referred to as the *parent* of **C**, and **C** as a *child* of **P**. More simply, an element that lies directly within another element is called the *child element* of the containing element, while the containing element is called the *parent element* of the child element. For example, in the markup <P> This person is <EMPH> not <NAME> Stephen </NAME></EMPH>, I'm afraid.</P> , the element **EMPH** is a child of the element **P** and is also the *parent* of the element **NAME**, while **P**

is the parent element of **EMPH**. However, **NAME** is the child of **EMPH** but *not* a child of **P**.

children The set of all child elements of a given element.

CJK [Char] Chinese/Japanese/Korean. This acronym is often used in the discussion of character sets and of the issues important to these language/character set groups.

coded character set [Char] A set of unambiguous rules that establishes a set of characters, and a mapping from each character onto a position in a sequence of integers. One can also think of a coded character set as a mapping from a set of *characters* to a set of integers. ISO 10646/Unicode and ISO 8859-1 are examples of coded character sets. In most cases, the phrase *character set* means the same thing as coded character set.

code point, code position [Char, XML] The integer position of a specific *character* in a *coded character set*.

combining characters [Char, XML] The set of characters that join, or combine, with preceding character(s) to form a composite character. An example is a diacritic combining with a preceding letter (e.g., the letter "e" combined with a combining acute accent "´" to give é).

comment A type of *markup* that contains commentary text related to the document, but that is not treated as part of the document's character data. The general form is <!— comment text —> (the comment text itself cannot contain a double hyphen, i.e., the string "—"). Comments can appear within the *character data* of an XML document, and also within a document type declaration, where allowed by the DTD grammar. However, comments cannot appear inside other markup.

conditional section A portion of the *document type declaration external subset* which is included in, or excluded from, the logical structure of the DTD based on the keyword (either INCLUDE or IGNORE) used to declare a given conditional section. The two forms are:

```
<![ INCLUDE [  markup & character data to include ]]>
```

for included content, and

```
<![ IGNORE  [  markup & character data to ignore  ]]>
```

for markup that is to be ignored.

Most often, the keyword of the conditional section is given as a *parameter-entity reference*, which is defined previously in the document type declaration. Then, by changing the value of the parameter entity reference, an author can change the rules of the DTD. An example is given in Part 1, Chapter 9.

conforming document A document that conforms to the grammar and constraints given in the XML specification.

content Simply, the characters or markup that are contained within a given element. Thus, in the markup <para> stuff <break/> more stuff </para> The text and markup stuff <break/> more stuff is the *content* of the element **para**. Content can then consist of *character data* and *markup*.

content model A rule for the type of *elements* and/or *character data* allowed within a given element. Such rules are specified in *element type declarations* within a *DTD*.

content particles A fancy name for the different parts (element names, choice lists of names and/or other content particles, or sequence lists of names and/or other content particles) that appear as part of a *content model* specification. For example, in the content model (par1 | (par2, par3)*) the content particles are par1, par2, par3, (par2, par3) and (par1 | (par2, par3)*).

control character [Char] A character that controls the interpretation, presentation, or other processing of the characters that follow it; for example, a tab character. Control characters are indicated in Table B.1 in Part 3, Appendix B of this book.

CRLF [Misc] The combination of the two control characters carriage-return (CR) and linefeed (LF). This combination is used by several Internet protocols, including *HTTP,* to mark the end of a line.

CSS [Misc] See: *cascading style sheets.*

declaration In the XML specification, a declaration is any markup that defines grammatical properties of, or external entities and objects related to, a document or class of documents. The different types are: *XML declaration, document type declaration, markup declarations (element type declaration, attribute-list declaration, entity declaration, notation declaration),* and *text declaration.*

default value A value assigned to an attribute in an attribute-list declaration. This is the default value, for example, should no other value be given in an explicit *instance* of an element.

Desperate Perl Hacker One of the goals in designing XML was to allow a developer desperate to get a simple XML application up and running (the *Desperate Perl Hacker*) to produce a functional (if not beautiful) program in less than a day. Indeed, the specification is largely successful in this regard.

digits [Char, XML] Characters corresponding to decimal digits, as represented in a variety of language systems. As discussed in Part 3, Appendix B, *digits* is a subset of all characters that are associated with the concept of number.

DOCTYPE The markup declaration keyword that denotes a *document type declaration*. A document type declaration always begins with the string <!DOCTYPE.

document See: *XML document*.

document character set The set of characters allowed in an XML document, defined as a list of *code positions* of allowed characters from the UCS character set. This in turn defines the numeric positions for *character references* that are valid within the document. The document character set is essentially the list of characters defined in the production for Char [1], combined with the statement that the code positions referenced in Char [1] correspond to positions in Unicode/ISO/IEC 10646. Note that the term *document character set* is never formally used in the XML specification, but is often used in discussions of it.

document element Also called the *root element*, this is the single element that contains all the other elements and character data that comprise a given XML document. One can think of this element as the root node for the element tree that defines a document. Note that the name in the *document type declaration* (if such a declaration is present) must match the *element type* of the root element. By definition, a document has one and only one document element.

document entity The actual resource that serves as the starting point for processing a given document, and that in turn serves as the starting point for processing of the document by an *XML processor*. Formally, you can think of the document entity as the root of the *entity tree* corresponding to a given XML document. Unlike other entities, the document entity has no name, and might well appear on a processor input stream without any identification at all. The document entity may contain *external entity references* that reference additional data (files or data streams) to be included within the document entity when it is processed by an XML processor.

Document Object Model (DOM) An object-oriented software model for abstract HTML or XML documents, complete with a generic programming interface for accessing and modifying the element tree, element attribute values, and other rendering-specific properties of the elements.

document type declaration An optional declaration that can contain markup declarations to define constraints on the logical structure of a document or class of documents, and to provide support for the use of predefined storage units (*entity references*) within the document. If present, the document type declaration must precede the first element of an XML document. The document type declaration can point to an external subset (a special kind of external entity called a *document type declaration external subset*) containing markup declarations, or it can contain the markup declarations directly in an internal subset, or it can do both. The *grammar* defined by the document type declaration is referred to as the *document type definition*. The abbreviation DTD can mean either *document type definition* or *document type declaration*, depending on the context.

document type declaration external subset The part of the document type declaration contained (a) within *external parameter entities* referenced from inside the DOCTYPE element, and (b) within an external entity referenced by a *system* or *public identifier* explicitly named in the DOCTYPE element. For example, the following document type declaration:

```
<!DOCTYPE  dbapp
     SYSTEM "http://www.utoronto.ca/dtds/papp.dtd" [
... markup declarations [internal subset]
] >
```

references an external subset, located at the indicated URL. Note that a document type declaration can also directly contain markup declarations (at the location indicated in the above example). The collection of markup declarations directly within the declaration is called the *document type declaration internal subset*.

document type declaration internal subset The collection of markup declarations that are directly inside a document type declaration element. See also: *document type declaration external subset*.

document type definition The *grammar* allowed in a given class of documents, as defined by the *markup declarations* within *a document type declaration*, together with any processing conventions specified by *notations* or *processing instructions*. This is often abbreviated as the DTD, although DTD can also be an abbreviation for *document type declaration*.

DOM See: *document object model.*

DTD Can mean either *document type definition* or *document type declaration*, depending on the context (and the confusion of the author!).

DTD external subset See: *document type declaration external subset.*

DTD internal subset See: *document type declaration internal subset.*

EBCDIC A coded character set originating from the 1960s and old IBM mainframe computers.

EBNF Extended Backus-Naur Form. A notation, also called a context-free *grammar,* for expressing the syntax rules of a language. The XML specification uses an EBNF, along with validity and well-formedness constraints, to define the rules for constructing well-formed and *valid* XML documents.

ECMAscript [Misc] An internationally standardized scripting language, based on the *JavaScript* language developed by Netscape Inc., and the JScript language developed by Microsoft Inc. (ISO/IEC DIS 16262).

ELEMENT The keyword that denotes an element-type declaration. An element-type declaration always begins with the character string <!ELEMENT .

element The basic logical unit defining the structure of an XML document. Elements in a document are organized as a tree, with the *document element* being the root node of the tree. XML documents use *start-* and *end-tags* to define the structural elements in the document. Some elements are empty (cannot contain character data or markup) and do not have an end-tag: Such elements are defined by *empty-element tags.* Elements that are not empty are often called containers. The name or *generic identifier* for each element is given in the tag, and corresponds to the *element type* of that element. One can think of an *element type declaration* as defining a class of elements, with an element in a document being an instance of that class. For example, <P> *some text* </P> is an element of type **P**, with the name **P** being the generic identifier of this element type.

element content An *element type* is said to have *element content* when elements of that type can contain only *child elements,* and cannot contain *character data.* See also: *mixed content.*

element type The type of an element, as defined by the *element type declaration* in a DTD. The name or *generic identifier* of an element identifies the type of a given element. For example, the element <EMPH> some text </EMPH> is of element type **EMPH**.

element type declaration A declaration, inside a *document type declaration*, that defines the *content model* for a specific *element type*. One can think of an element type declaration as defining a class of elements, with an element in a document being an *instance* of this class. The name or *generic identifier* of a specific element gives the element type for the element. An example element type declaration is:

```
<!ELEMENT p (#PCDATA|emph)* >
```

which defines an element type labeled p, and declares that elements of type **p** can contain zero or more blocks of character data content and/or elements of type **emph**.

element valid A *validity constraint* for an instance of an element. An element is valid if there is an *element type declaration* for the given element, and if the content (if any) of the given element is valid according to the content rules expressed in the *element type declaration*.

EMPTY A keyword used in the definition of an element-type *content model* to indicate that elements of the specified type are empty, and cannot contain any content. Elements with this content model must be present, in a document, via an *empty-element tag*. See also: ANY.

empty element An element that cannot contain anything. Empty elements are denoted by *empty-element tags*. For example, the element <IMAGE SRC="foo.org"/> is an empty element.

empty-element tag A *markup* tag that denotes an empty element. In XML, empty-element tags must have the general form *<name ... />* , where *name* is the name or *generic identifier* for the element, and ... corresponds to (possible) attribute value assignments relevant to the element. An example is <IMAGE SRC="foo.org"/>. See also: *element*, *start-tag*.

encoding See: *character encoding.*

encoding declaration A declaration of the *character encoding* scheme used in a particular XML parsed *external entity*. An encoding declaration must appear in the *text declaration* that precedes any other markup or character data in a parsed external entity. An example is <?xml encoding='UTF-8'?>. The XML 1.0 specifications require that any entity not encoded in UTF-8 or UTF-16 must begin with an XML encoding declaration. See also: *XML declaration.*

end-tag A markup tag that denotes the end of a non-empty XML element. The general form of an end-tag is </*name*>, where *name* is the name *generic identifier* for the element. Every *start-tag* must have a corresponding end-tag. See also: *start-tag, empty-element tag*.

ENTITIES An attribute type declaration keyword that indicates that the associated attribute can only take, as its value, one or more white space–separated *names*, which must in turn correspond to the names of *unparsed entities*. In a *valid* XML document, these unparsed entities must be declared using an *entity declaration*.

ENTITY A keyword within an attribute type declaration that indicates that the associated attribute can only take, as its value, a single *name*, which must in turn be equivalent to the name of an *unparsed entity*. In a *valid* XML document, this unparsed entity must be declared using an *entity declaration*.

entity Physically, an XML document is composed of units called entities, with the document itself being the "root" or *document entity*. The document entity may then refer, using *entity references*, to other entities that should be included into the document. Entities that are used in this way must be defined by name using an *entity declaration*. Entities that are to be included into a document can come in several varieties: *external entities*, which exist as units outside the document entity, and *internal entities*, which act rather like a macro expansion facility and are defined inside the document type declaration of the document entity. External entities can in turn contain internal entities, and there are also *parameter entities, general entities,* and *unparsed entities*. See Part 1 of this book, Chapters 2 through 6, for an introduction to entities.

entity declaration A declaration, within a *document type declaration*, that defines a name for an entity and that associates this named entity with either explicitly defined *replacement text* (an *internal entity*), or an external resource (*external entity*). External entities come in two varieties: *parsed external entities* (containing valid XML character data and markup) and *unparsed external entities* (containing non-XML, possibly binary, data). See also *parsed entity, unparsed entity*.

entity reference The mechanism, within an XML document, for referencing the content of an *entity*. There are two types of entity references: *general entity references*, which can be used anywhere within an XML document except inside the *document type declaration*, and *parameter entity references*, which can be used only within a document type declaration. General entity references use ampersand (&) and semicolon (;) as delimiters (e.g., &entity;), while parameter-entity references use percent-sign (%) and semicolon (;) as delimiters (e.g., %entity;).

enumerated attribute types Those types of attributes whose allowed values are specified, in an attribute-list declaration, as an enumerated list. There are two such types, one in which the allowed values are given as a list of possible name token values (e.g., (value1 | value2 | value3)) and the other in which the allowed values are given as a list of allowed notation name (e.g., NOTATION (not1 | not2 | not3)).

error The XML specification defines an error to be any violation of the *normative* rules given in the specification. Software that conforms to the rules laid down in the XML specification may report errors, when they occur, and may—if an error is not *fatal*—also attempt to recover from the error, and continue processing.

external document type declaration subset See: *document type declaration external subset*.

external DTD subset See: *document type declaration external subset*.

external entity An entity that is physically separate from a given document entity. In practice, an external entity is usually a file on disk. See also: *entity declaration, internal entity*.

external identifier A string that, within an external *entity declaration*, identifies an external resource. An external identifier must specify, using a *URI* enclosed in quotation marks, the *system identifier* for the external resource. In addition, an external identifier may optionally specify a *public identifier* for the resource—this is a name that identifies the resource, but that does not specify a location for that resource. An example external identifier, within the context of an entity declaration, is:

```
<!ENTITY odi-schema
        PUBLIC "-//Groveware//Schema Definition for ODI
Application//EN"
        "http://www.groveware.com/public/odi-schema.xml"
>
```

This identifier contains both a public identifier (indicated by the keyword PUBLIC) and a system identifier (the URL).

external subset See *document type declaration external subset*.

extenders [Char, XML] A class of characters that conceptually extend the character that they follow. For details, see Part 3, Appendix B.

external parsed general entity A general entity that is both external and parsed. See: *external parsed entity, general entity*.

external parsed entity An external entity that is also a parsed entity (i.e., one that contains well-formed XML markup). Within an XML document, an external parsed entity must be declared and named in an entity declaration within the document type declaration. It can then be referenced, within the document, via an entity reference.

fatal error In XML, an error which a conforming XML processor must detect and report to the application. After encountering a fatal error, the processor may continue processing the data to search for further errors and may report such errors to the application. In order to support correction of errors, the processor may make the unprocessed data from the document (intermingled character data and explicit markup) available to the application. Once a fatal error is detected, the processor must not continue normal processing (i.e., it must not continue to pass character data and information about the document's logical structure to the application in the normal way).

font [Char] A collection of glyph images having the same basic design, e.g., Courier Bold Oblique. Alternatively, a set of printable or displayable glyphs sharing a specific style or size. See also *typeface.*

for compatibility The XML specification uses this phrase to refer to an XML feature included solely to ensure that XML remains compatible with SGML.

for interoperability The XML specification uses this phrase to refer to a recommended usage of XML that, if employed, will make the resulting XML data compatible with older SGML software that is not compliant with the WebSGML Adaptations Annex.

fragment identifier [Misc] A text string, appended to a URL, that references a named internal location within the URL-specified resource. An example would be the string "#priscilla" within the URL http://www.desert.org/queenofthe.xml#priscilla.

FTP File Transfer Protocol. A common Internet protocol for transferring data files between machines.

general entity A parsed entity for use within the document content. General entities are sometimes referred to with the unqualified term "entity." These should be contrasted with parameter entities, which are parsed entities that can only be used within a document type declaration. These two entity types use different forms of reference.

general entity declaration A declaration for a general entity. An example general entity declaration is:

```
<!ENTITY introduction
      SYSTEM "http://www.where.org/docs/intro.xml"
>
```

A general entity can be referenced from within a document via a *general entity reference*. Note, however, that an entity referenced from within a document must be a *parsed entity*, since it must itself be a *well-formed* XML document.

general entity reference An *entity reference* that references a *general entity*. The general form for a general entity reference is &*name*;, where *name* is the name of the general entity. This should be contrasted with a *parameter entity reference*, which has the general form &%*name*;, where *name* is the name of the system entity. See also: *parameter entity*.

generic identifier (GI) The *name* that identifies the *element type* of an element.

GI See: *generic identifier*.

glyph [Char] In general discussion, refers to the shape of a character. More precisely, one can think of a glyph as a graphical symbol that provides the appearance or form for a *character*. A glyph contains distinction in form, but has no intrinsic meaning separate from its relationship to a character. "A recognizable abstract graphic symbol which is independent of any specific design" (ISO/IEC 9541-1:1991). See also: *character*.

grammar [Misc] A set of rules that define the allowed syntax of a language. More precisely, a grammar defines the rules for constructing valid *tokens*, the allowed ways in which these tokens can be grouped to define symbols (called *nonterminals*), and finally the way in which tokens and/or statements can be hierarchically structured. The extended Backus-Naur Form (*EBNF*) is a formal mechanism for expressing the rules of a grammar, and is used in the XML specification to define the grammar for XML documents. Also, the content of a *document type declaration* defines, for a valid XML document, the allowed grammar for the XML markup content of the *document element*. Note that a grammar defines the syntax rules for a language, but does not define the meaning, or semantics, of documents written in that language, or even the meanings of the tokens defined in that language. See also: *parser, token, lexical analysis*.

grammatical production See: *production*.

grammatical token See: *token*.

gt An XML-predefined general entity corresponding to the ">" greater than character. The corresponding entity reference is: >.

hexadecimal Integer numbers written using a base-16 notation. Allowed digits in this notation are typically written as [0–9, A–F].

HTML [Misc] HyperText Markup Language, a markup language defined by an SGML *document type declaration*. HTML documents are not, in general, well-formed XML documents. The latest version, HTML 4.0, is formally defined by the World Wide Web Consortium, at: *www.w3.org/TR/REC-html40*.

HTTP [Misc] See: *HyperText Transfer Protocol*.

HTTP header [Misc] The leading part of an HTTP data message. HTTP messages are sent with an HTTP header preceding the actual communicated data. See also: *MIME header*.

hyperlink [Misc] See: *hypertext link*.

hypertext [Misc] Any document that contains hypertext links to other documents, or that can be reached by such links. HTML documents are examples of hypertext documents.

hypertext link [Misc] A hypertext relationship between two *anchors*, leading from the head anchor to the tail anchor. On the Web, this is usually a link from one hypertext document to another. Linking points are associated with anchors.

HyperText Transfer Protocol (HTTP)   An Internet communications protocol designed expressly for the distribution of hypertext documents and related data. This protocol includes various mechanisms for indicating the type of the data being sent to or from a server , and provides support for data caching and message proxying. The HTTP protocol (Version 1.1) is defined in RFC 2068.

HyTime An accompanying standard to SGML for representing hypermedia. It is an acronym for Hypermedia/Time-based structuring language. ISO/IEC 10744. Some of the ideas developed in HyTime are also employed in the proposed *XLink* XML linking specification.

I18N [Misc] See: *internationalization*.

IANA [Misc] Internet Assigned Naming Authority. The *IETF* agency which registers names for common use on the Internet. General information is found at: *www.iana.org/*.

ID A keyword within an *attribute type declaration* that indicates that the associated attribute can only take, as its value, a single *name* that uniquely identifies the element. As a result, no element can have more than one attribute of type ID, and no two elements can assign the same *name* to attributes of type ID.

ideographic characters [Char, XML] The class of abstract characters that correspond to ideographic characters, in particular ideographic Han characters, as unified under the CJK unification scheme. See the Unicode specification for more details (referenced at the end of Part 3, Appendix B).

IDREF A keyword within an *attribute type declaration* that indicates that the associated attribute can only take, as its value, a single *name* equivalent to a *name* assigned to an attribute of type ID elsewhere in the document. That is, an attribute of type IDREF must take, as its value, a single name that references an element elsewhere in the document that is labeled by an attribute of type ID with the same value. Note that any number of IDREF attribute values can share (that is, reference) the same ID value.

IDREFS A keyword within an *attribute type declaration* that indicates that the associated attribute can only take, as its value, one or more white space-separated *names* that are equivalent to *names* assigned to attributes of type ID elsewhere in the document. That is, all the individual *names* in an attribute of type IDREFS must match names assigned to attributes of type ID elsewhere in the document. Note that any number of IDREFS attribute values can share (that is, reference) the same ID value.

IEC International Electrotechnical Commission. An international body devoted to electrotechnical standardization, particularly in the areas of electrical and electronic engineering. The ISO collaborates with the IEC on all issues related to the mandate of the IEC—one of which is the standardization of computer character sets. A joint ISO/IEC technical committee, known as JTC1, carries out standardization work in the field of information technology.

IETF [Misc] Internet Engineering Task Force. A collection of task forces that develop and specify standards for Internet protocols and architectures. There are IETF groups working on such issues as URLs, HTTP, and MIME. See information at: *www.ietf.org/*.

ignorable white space *White space* that is not considered part of the *character data* of the document. For example, inside an element with element content (i.e., that can only take elements as content, and not character data), any white space between tags is ignorable.

IGNORE A keyword used within a condition section to indicate that a given section should be left out of the *document type declaration*. Examples are found in Part 1 of the book, Chapter 5, Section 5.4. See also: INCLUDE.

IMPLIED See: *#IMPLIED*.

INCLUDE A keyword used within a condition section to indicate that a given section should be included in the *document type declaration*. Examples are found in Part 1 of the book, Chapter 5, Section 5.4. See also: IGNORE.

included entity An entity is *included* when an associated entity reference is replaced by the *replacement text* of the entity.

instance The actual occurrence of an element inside a document is called an instance of that element. One can think of an *element type declaration* as defining a type of an element, and any elements of that type within a document as corresponding to *instances* of the defined type.

internal document type declaration subset The set of all markup declarations that explicitly appear inside the DOCTYPE element of a given document entity. The internal subset does not include the content of any external parameter entities referenced from and included within this context. See also: *external document type declaration subset*.

internal DTD subset See: *Internal document type declaration subset*.

internal entity A *parsed entity* that is declared and defined within a *document type declaration*. An internal entity is declared using an *entity declaration*. An example is:

```
<!ENTITY  copy  "Copyright (&#169;) Ian S. Graham and Liam Quin,
All rights reserved" >
```

where the string between the quotation marks is the *literal entity value*.

internal subset See: *internal document type declaration subset*.

internationalization [Misc] Refers to any software development issues related to providing software that can serve a multilingual, internationalized audience. Often abbreviated as I18N, since there are 18 letters between the "I" that begins the word and the "n" that ends it.

interoperability See: *for interoperability*.

ISO The formal name for the International Organization for Standards, an international organization responsible for setting international standards such as the ISO 8859-x character sets and ISO 8879:1986 (the

SGML specification). The name "ISO" is actually not an abbreviation. Rather, it is derived from the Greek isos, meaning "equal." Isos is the root for the prefix "iso-" used in many words or terms, such as "isobar" (regions of equal pressure), or "isometric" (of equal measure or dimensions). The ISO collaborates with the International Electrotechnical Commission (IEC) on issues related to standardization in the field of information technology.

ISO 639 An ISO standard for two-letter codes that represent the names of spoken languages.

ISO 646 An ISO standard for a 7-bit coded character set, based on (but not exactly the same as) ASCII. See Part 3, Appendix B of this book for more details.

ISO 3166 An ISO standard for two-letter codes that represent the names of countries.

ISO/IEC 8859-1 An 8-bit character set developed by the International Organization for Standards. An 8-bit code contains 256 different characters. The first 128 characters are equivalent to the 128 characters of the US-ASCII character set (also called ISO 646). The remaining 128 characters consist of control characters and a large collection of accented and other characters commonly used in Western European languages.

ISO/IEC 10646 A coded character set promoted by the ISO and IEC as a universal character set for all the world's languages. The most important subset of this coded character set (in fact, the only part used) is formally equivalent to the Unicode character set. See also: *Unicode, UCS.*

ISO Latin-1 [Misc] Equivalent to ISO/IEC 8859-1.

Java [Misc] A programming language, developed by Sun Microsystems, designed specifically for use in applet and agent applications. Java programs can only run under a Java interpreter, which is designed to eliminate the risk of a rogue Java applet damaging the local computer.

JavaScript [Misc] A scripting language developed by Netscape Inc. JavaScript program listings can be included within an HTML document, and are then executed by the Web browser when the document is loaded. An essentially equivalent language known as JScript has been developed by Microsoft. The international standard ECMAscript is designed to be a vendor-neutral base for document scripting, and to provide a base upon which JavaScript and JScript will evolve.

JScript A variant of the JavaScript language, developed by Microsoft, Inc. See also: *ECMAscript*.

letter [Char, XML] A class of characters that consists of alphabetic characters, syllabic characters, and ideographic characters. See Part 3, Appendix B of this book for more details.

lexical analysis, lexing [Misc] The process by which a string of input characters is analyzed and grouped into *tokens*, where these tokens are sequences of characters that have collective meaning. Lexical analysis is also called scanning. See also: *parsing, grammar, EBNF.*

ligature A glyph that represents a combination of two or more characters, such as an "A" and "E" combined to form an "Æ" ligature.

link [Misc] See: *hypertext link*.

literal See: *literal data*.

literal data Any string enclosed within single or double quotes but not containing the quotation mark used as a delimiter for that string. An example is "string" . Literals are used for specifying the content of *internal entities*, the values of *attributes*, and *external identifiers*.

literal entity value The quoted string actually present in the *entity declaration* for an *internal entity*. This should be contrasted with the *replacement text*, which is the content of the entity after replacement of character references and parameter entity references (but *not* general entity references). For example, in the declaration

```
<!ENTITY  examp  "Here is an &#xA9; &%frame; example entity." >
```

the literal entity value for the entity **examp** is the string:

```
Here is an &#xA9; &%frame; example entity.
```

logical structure The parsed structure of a document as defined by the *markup elements* and associated *attribute values*.

lowercase A property of a given character, as defined in a coded character set. Some characters (but not all) come in uppercase and lowercase forms—as in the letters "e" and "E". The term "lowercase" denotes the smaller of these two forms.

lt An XML-predefined general entity corresponding to the "<" character. The corresponding entity reference is: <.

markup Text that is added to the data of a document in order to convey information about the logical structure of the *character data*. In XML, markup takes the form of *start-tags, end-tags, empty elements, entity ref-*

erences, character references, comments, CDATA section delimiters, document type declarations, and *processing instructions.*

markup declaration One of a class of declarations that can appear only within the *document type declaration,* and that define the grammar for a class of XML documents. There are four types of markup declarations: *element type declaration, attribute-list declaration, entity declaration,* and *notation declaration.* These declarations may be contained in whole or in part within *parameter entities.*

match This word is used in many contexts in the XML specification. For simple strings, two strings "match" if they are the same sequence of UCS characters. When production rules of a grammar are involved (e.g., the rules of the *EBNF,* or the rules of a *content model*), a string *matches* the production if the sentence contained in the string is one that is permitted by the given production. For elements, an element matches its declaration if the content of the element is consistent with the *content model* specified in the *element-type declaration.*

MathML Mathematical Markup Language. A specific dialect of XML (defined by a MathML *document type declaration*) designed for encoding structural and semantic information corresponding to mathematical expressions and equations. The MathML language is being developed under the auspices of the *W3C.*

may Used in the XML specification to define behavior that a *conforming* XML processor is permitted—but not required—to follow. See also: *must.*

MIME Multipurpose Internet Mail Extensions. A scheme that lets Internet electronic mail messages contain mixed media (sound, video, image, and text). The World Wide Web uses MIME content types to specify the type of data being sent between an HTTP server and a client.

mixed content An *element type* has mixed content when elements of that type may contain *character data,* optionally interspersed with *child elements.* This should be contrasted with: *element content.*

must Used in the XML specification to define behavior that a *conforming XML processor* must follow. If a processor does not behave as described, then this is an error under the definitions of the XML specification. An example from the specification is: " Once a fatal error is detected, however, the processor *must* not continue normal processing."

name A *token* beginning with a *letter,* underscore (_), or colon (:) character (called a *name start character*), and continuing with zero or more *name characters* (*letters, digits,* hyphens (-), underscores (_), colons (:), full stops (.), *combining characters,* or *extenders*). *Names* beginning with the *case-insensitive* string "xml" are reserved for XML-standardization purposes. The colon character (:) is reserved within or at the beginning of a name for special use in declaring element *namespaces*. Note that names cannot contain *white space* characters. See also: *name token.*

name characters Any of the characters identified as: *letters, digits,* hyphens (-), underscores (_), colons (:), full stops (.), *combining characters,* or *extenders*. Note that name characters do not include *white space* characters.

namespace An abstract space in which a name has a defined meaning.

name start characters Those characters that are permitted as the first character of a *name*. In XML, a name start character must be a *letter,* underscore (_), or colon (:).

name token Any string consisting of a *name start character* followed by zero or more *name characters*. Note that name tokens are *case-sensitive,* and cannot contain *white space* characters. White space characters are used to separate multiple name tokens listed in a series.

NDATA A keyword used in an *entity declaration* to denote an *unparsed entity*. The name appearing after the NDATA keyword is the name of a *notation* appropriate to this entity.

NMTOKEN A keyword within an *attribute type declaration* that indicates that the associated attribute can only take, as its value, a single *name token*.

NMTOKENS A keyword within an *attribute type declaration* to indicate that the associated attribute can only take, as its value, one or more *white space*–separated *name tokens*. This is essentially the plural of NMTOKEN.

nonterminals The symbols, within a context-free grammar, that represent valid structures—a *production* defines the grammatical rule by which a nonterminal can be constructed. For example, the following statement (from the EBNF for XML) defines the production for the nonterminal XMLDecl:

```
XMLDecl ::= '<?xml' VersionInfo EncodingDecl? SDDecl? S? '?>'
```

The right-hand side defines the way in which this nonterminal can be constructed, and consists of *tokens* <?xml and ?> and nonterminals

(VersionInfo, EncodingDecl, SDDecl, and S) joined together by notational rules (here the ?) defined within the EBNF. See also: *parsing*, *lexing*, *EBNF*.

non-validating processor A processor that does not (or need not) validate a document against the grammar defined in the document type declaration. A non-validating processor must, however, process the document type declaration so as to, as far as possible, obtain information about external and internal entities, and obtain the types and default values for any declared attributes. There are specific limitations on what a non-validating processor is required to do (XML specification, Chapter 5, Section 5.1).

normalization The process by which an XML processor converts a string to a canonical form prior to passing the string to an application. XML defines specific normalization rules for attribute values (XML Specification, Chapter 3, Section 3.3.3), and for normalizing *public identifiers* (all strings of white space must be normalized to single space characters (#x20), and leading and trailing white space must be removed) before attempting to use the public identifier to generate an URI for the referenced resource.

normative A statement or collection of statements is *normative* if it explicitly forms a part of a specification. For example, the XML specification (www.w3.org/TR/REC-xml) contains text that is normative, and also text that is non-normative, and that serves to illustrate or explain the normative text. The text in Part 2 of this book is the normative specification for XML, except for those parts which are explicitly noted as being non-normative.

normative reference A reference to an externally published document, usually a standard of some sort, whose content applies to the standard containing the reference. For example, the XML standard refers to ISO/IEC 639 as the external normative standard for language codes used within an XML application.

NOTATION An XML keyword that is used in two contexts: (1) as the start of a *notation declaration*, as in <!NOTATION , and (2) as the type declaration, in an *attribute-list declaration*, that declares a specific attribute to be of the notation enumerated type (e.g., NOTATION (not1 | not2 | not3) "not1").

notation A *notation* identifies, by name, the format of an *unparsed entity*, or the application to which a *processing instruction* is addressed. For an illustrative example, see: *notation declaration*.

notation attribute An attribute type that corresponds to an enumerated list of allowed notation names. These names should be defined as notations somewhere in the document type declaration.

notation declaration Provides a name (a *name*) for the notation, along with an *external identifier* which identifies a resource, typically an external application, that can process data in the given notation. The name for the notation can then be used in *entity declarations* and *attribute-list declarations* and in attribute specifications, with the notation indicating how such declared resources can be processed. Notation names are also referenced by processing instructions: The XML application can forward the instructions in the processing instruction to the application referenced by the notation. For example, consider the following set of notation declarations, processing instructions, and attribute-list declarations:

```
<!NOTATION  gif  "http://www.somewhere.org/apps/gifplugin.exe" >
<!NOTATION  jpeg "http://www.somewhere.org/apps/jpegplugin.exe" >
<!NOTATION  pproc "http://www.somewhere.org/apps/fontgen.exe" >
<?pproc "outfilter -s100 -f=helvetica" ?>
<!ATTLIST img
    itype NOTATION (gif | jpeg | png | bmp ) "gif"
>
....
<IMG SRC="imagefile.gif" itype="jpeg"/>
```

Here the processing instruction indicates that the instruction outfilter -s100 -f=helvetica should be forwarded to the application referenced by the associated notation. Similarly, the attribute specification itype="jpeg" tells the application that there is software, at the URI indicated by the associated notation declaration, which can be used to process these data.

octet An 8-bit-long data storage unit. The ISO/IEC character set specifications use the term "octet" instead of "byte," as some computers define a byte as having a length different than eight bits.

parameter entity A *parsed entity* for use only within a DTD. A parameter entity must be a *parsed entity*, and can be either an *internal* or *external entity*. A parameter entity is declared via a *parameter entity declaration*. For an example, see: *parameter entity declaration*.

parameter entity declaration A declaration for a *parameter entity*. An example of a declaration for an internal parameter entity is:

```
<!ENTITY % draft.version "INCLUDE" >
```

where the percent (%) character preceding the name of the entity identifies it as a parameter entity. Parameter entities can be referenced only within a *document type declaration*, and are referenced using *parameter entity references*.

parameter entity reference A reference to a *parameter entity*. A parameter-entity reference has the form &%*name*;, where the percent character (%) indicates this is a parameter entity reference, and where *name* is the name declared in a *parameter entity declaration*. See also: *general entity, general entity reference.*

parent element See: *child element.*

parsed data Data that is parsed for markup, character references, and entity references. By definition, parsed data must be well-formed XML. See also: *unparsed data.*

parsed entity An entity that contains *text*, and that may represent *markup* and/or *character data*. A parsed entity's content is called its *replacement text*; this text is considered an integral part of the document. Note that the content of a parsed entity must itself be a *well-formed* XML document. Note also that a parsed entity *cannot* contain an entity reference that references itself, either directly or indirectly (i.e., recursive inclusion of an entity within itself is forbidden).

parser, parsing, parsable [Misc] A *parser* uses a set of syntax rules to convert an actual instance of input data into a hierarchical tree representing the structure of the data; or it can use these rules to verify whether or not an instance of the data properly satisfies the syntax rules; or it can do both: This process is known as *parsing*. A document is called *parsable* if it can be parsed without error. In the XML specification, the syntax rules—called the *grammar*—are specified using a notation called the extended Backus-Naur Form (*EBNF*). See also: *lexing, token.*

partial URL [Misc] A location scheme containing only partial information about the resource location. To access the resource, a user-agent must construct a full *URL*, based on the partial URL. It does so by assuming that all the information not found in the partial URL is the same as that used when the client accessed the document containing the partial URL reference. A partial URL is often called a relative URL, since the location of the linked resource can be determined relative to the location of the document containing the partial URL.

PCDATA See: *#PCDATA.*

PI See: *processing instruction.*

port number [Misc] Any Internet application communicates at a particular port number specific to the application. For example FTP, HTTP, Gopher, and telnet are all assigned unique port numbers so that the computer knows what to do when contacted at a particular port. There are accepted standard numbers for these ports so that computers know which port to connect to for a particular service. For example, Gopher servers generally "talk" at port 70, while HTTP servers generally "talk" at port 80. These default values can be overridden in a URL. For example, the URL http://www.groveware.com:31313/ references port number 31313 at the server *www.groveware.com.*

precomposed [Char] Coded character sets often support many ways of representing the same character. For example, the character "Latin small letter e with an acute accent" (é) can be represented by the single character of that name, or by two characters—the base character e, plus the combining accent character. The first of these is called the *precomposed* form (since all the parts of the character are precomposed into a single unit), while the latter is called the decomposed form.

protocol In computer networks, a protocol is simply a convention for inter-computer communication. Thus the TCP/IP protocol defines how messages are passed on the Internet, while the FTP protocol, which is built using the TCP/IP protocol, defines how FTP messages should be sent and received.

processing instruction A type of *markup* containing instructions specific to an application that processes an XML document. The general form is <?*target string* ?>, where *target* is a *name* identifying the *application* for which the instruction is intended, and *string* corresponds to a *white space*–separated sequence of character strings containing instructions for the application. A *notation declaration* can be used to identify the location of the application referenced by the target name. Note that the value *string* cannot contain the character sequence?>, and that the string *target* (a *name*) cannot be the *case-insensitive* string "XML."

production Each statement in a context-free grammar is called a production, and defines the rules by which, within a given grammar, a valid statement can be constructed. A valid statement that can result from a given production is said to *match* the production.

PUBLIC A keyword used in external identifiers to allow specification of a *public identifier.*

public identifier A type of *external identifier*. A public identifier may be used when declaring an *external entity* or a *notation*, and is indicated by the keyword PUBLIC preceding the public identifier string. Two examples are:

```
<!ENTITY boilerplate
        PUBLIC "-//GROVEWARE//DOC BOILERPLATE//EN"
        "http://www.groveware.com/docs/boiler.html">
<!DOCTYPE html
        PUBLIC "-//W3C//DTD HTML 4.0//EN"
        SYSTEM "http://www.w3.org/TR/REC-html40/strict.dtd">
```

XML does not assign any meaning whatsoever to public identifiers. Note that, in an XML document, a public identifier may not appear in the absence of a *system identifier*.

quot An XML-predefined general entity corresponding to the double quote character ("). The corresponding entity reference is: &guot;.

regular expression An expression, built using the basic grammatical units of a language, that defines the allowed form for a specific token or nonterminal.

replacement text The content of an *entity* after replacement of *character references* and *parameter entity references*, but not general entity references. For example, given the following entity definitions:

```
<!ENTITY % author  "Luc Pich&#233; and Ian Graham" >
<!ENTITY   journal "Journal of Condensed Matter Physics" >
<!ENTITY   refer   "by %author;, published in &journal;, &#xA9;
1994 " >
```

then the replacement text for the entity refer is:
    by Luc Piché and Ian Graham, published in &journal;, © 1994
See also Part 1, Chapter 3, Section 3.3.1 and Chapter 4, Section 4.4.

REQUIRED See: *#REQUIRED*.

RDF Resource Description Format. A specific dialect of XML (defined by an RDF *document type declaration*) designed for encoding metadata about a wide variety of resources. The RDF syntax is being developed under the auspices of the *W3C*.

relative URL See: *partial URL*.

RFC Request For Comments. An RFC is a document, written by groups or individuals involved in Internet development and published by the

IETF, that describes agreed-upon standards or proposes new standards for Internet protocols. For example, the rules for electronic mail message composition are specified in the document RFC 822.

RFC 822 The Internet RFC that specifies the format for Internet mail messages. The syntax for mail has been substantially updated since this RFC, and you should also read RFC 2045–RFC2049 for complete details on the mail message format and the *MIME* mechanisms.

root element Also called the *document element*. The element that contains all other elements. If there is a *document type declaration*, then the name in the document type declaration must match the *element type* of the root element.

SAX Simple API for XML. A specification for a simple, language-neutral programming interface for processing XML data.

schema A way of specifying formats and relationships of data objects. A schema is similar to a document type definition, but permits more rigorous specification of the types of data associated with an object.

SGML Standard Generalized Markup Language. A standard for describing markup languages. Both the HTML and XML languages are defined as instances of SGML. SGML is defined by ISO/IEC 8879-1:1993, plus various technical corrigenda.

SGML Editorial Review Board A group of approximately eleven people responsible for writing the XML specification. It was renamed the XML Working Group in 1997.

SGML Working Group A group that is part of ISO and is responsible for writing the SGML standard. It recently moved from being a Working Group to an official Subcommittee.

SMIL Synchronized Multimedia Integration Language. A specific dialect of XML (defined by an SMIL *document type declaration*) designed for encoding structural and semantic information corresponding to multimedia and hypermedia presentations. The SMIL language is being developed under the auspices of the *W3C*.

standalone A *standalone* document is one that can be safely processed by an XML processor and passed to an application unaffected by any markup declarations that may be found in a *document type definition external subset*, or in an external *parameter entity* referenced from the internal subset. In this context, "safely processed" means that the content of the document is unaffected by the absence of these entities. For example, if the external subset (or an external parameter entity referenced by the internal subset) contains attribute default declarations or entity declarations that affect the content of the document (e.g., by defining otherwise undefined entities, or otherwise unspecified attribute values), then the document is not standalone, as it cannot be processed independent of these entities.

standalone document declaration A declaration which may appear as a component of the XML declaration, and signals whether or not the document is *standalone*. The declaration takes the form standalone="yes" or standalone="no", with the value "yes" indicating the document is standalone. An example XML declaration corresponding to a standalone document is <?xml version="1.0" standalone="yes" ?>. By default, an XML processor will assume the declaration standalone="no" for a given document, if no standalone status is specified.

Standard Generalized Markup Language See: *SGML*.

start-tag A markup tag that denotes the start of an element. The general form of a start-tag is <*name ...*>, where *name* is the *generic identifier* (or name) for the element type, and where "…" corresponds to zero or more *attribute* value assignments.

storage layout The physical layout of a document, and how it is distributed amongst a set of external objects (i.e., entities). This is the same as the physical structure of a document.

SYSTEM A keyword used to indicate a URI-specified *system identifier* for an external resource.

system identifier May be used when declaring an *external entity*, and is indicated by the keyword SYSTEM preceding the entity's system identifier. The value is a URI, which may be used to retrieve the entity. Examples are:

```
<!ENTITY blobby SYSTEM
"http://www.groveware.com/ent/blobby.xml">
<!ENTITY blobby SYSTEM
        'http://www.groveware.com/images/blobby.gif'
        NDATA gif>.
```

An external entity may also be declared using a *public identifier*.

tag The basic markup unit that divides an XML document into markup *elements*. There are three types of tags: *start-tags*, (e.g., <tag>) *end-tags* (e.g., </tag>), and *empty-element tags* (e.g., <e-tag/>).

target Used in the context of a *processing instruction* (PI), a *target* corresponds to the *name* to which the PI is directed. For example, in the PI

```
<? Ppixl "xmac=23 plic=11 thibald='mortified'" ?>
```

the name Ppixl is the PI target. Often (although this is not formally required), the target of a PI is declared by a *notation declaration*. This then lets the XML application resolve the target to a specific external application declared by the notation.

TCP/IP [Misc] Transmission Control Protocol/Internet Protocol, one of the basic communication protocols of the Internet. Many other protocols, such as HTTP, FTP, and Gopher, are built on top of TCP/IP.

text XML defines text to be a sequence of *characters*, which may represent *markup* or *character data*.

text declaration A declaration of the version number and character encoding used in an *external parsed entity*. This declaration, if present, must appear as the very beginning of the entity. The form is <?xml version="*version-info*" encoding="*encoding-info*" ?> , where *version-info* gives the version of the XML specification corresponding to the content of the entity, and *encoding-info* is a well-known string indicating the character encoding used within the entity. Parsed entities which are not stored in either a UTF-8 or UTF-16 encoding must begin with a text declaration defining the correct encoding. Note that the version information is optional.

token [Misc] A sequence of characters that have a collective meaning according to a defined set of lexical rules. In general, a lexical analyzer uses a set of lexical rules to decompose a stream of input characters into a sequence of such tokens. Note the appearance of this word in the XML *name token* data type. See also: *lexical analysis, parsing.*

typeface [Char] A design for a set of printable or displayable *glyphs* sharing a common style. Each instance of a typeface, with a specific size or style, is called a font. The collection of fonts that share the same typeface design (e.g., with variations in size, slant, italic nature, etc.) are called members of the typeface family. For example, the font "Helvetica bold 10pt" is one member of the Helvetica typeface family. See also: *font.*

UCS Universal Character Set. In this book, we use the term UCS to refer to the unified Unicode / *ISO/IEC 10646* coded character set.

UCS-2 A particular encoding of the UCS character set, wherein each character is encoded in two bytes. See also: *UTF-8, UTF-16, UCS, Unicode.*

Unicode A 2-byte coded character set, developed as a universal character set for international use. The current version of Unicode (Version 2.1) is equivalent to the ISO/IEC 10646 coded character set. Both XML and HTML 4.0 use Unicode /ISO 10646 as the *document character set*.

Uniform Resource Locator See: *URL*.

unparsed entity A resource whose contents may or may not be text and, if text, may or may not be XML. Unparsed entities must always be *external entities*. Each unparsed entity defined within an XML document must also have an associated *notation* that relates the entity (via the entity *name*) to an external resource, which may be able to help the application process data in the unparsed entity. For example, if the external entity were a GIF image file, the notation might refer to an application capable of displaying GIF images. Within an XML document, unparsed entities may be referred to only in attribute values declared to be of type ENTITY or ENTITIES.

uppercase A property of a given character, as defined in a coded character set. Some characters (but not all) come in uppercase and lowercase forms—as in the letters "e" and "E". The term "uppercase" denotes the larger of these two forms.

URI Uniform Resource Identifier, the generic term for a coded string that identifies a (typically Internet) resource. There are currently three practical examples of URIs: Uniform Resource Locators (*URLs*), partial URLs, and Uniform Resource Names (*URNs*).

URL Uniform Resource Locator, the scheme used to address Internet resources on the World Wide Web. A URL specifies the protocol, domain name/IP address, port number, path, and resource details needed to access a resource from a particular machine. Partial URLs are an associated scheme that specify a location relative to the location of a document or resource containing the URL reference.

URN Uniform Resource Name. A scheme for addressing and referencing Internet-accessible resources independent of the actual servers on which the resources are found. A URN is one type of a URI.

user option See: *at user option*.

UTF-8, UTF-16 Eight bit-(UTF-8) and sixteen-bit (UTF-16) *encodings* of the *UCS coded character set*.

valid, validation An XML document is called *valid* if the document is associated with a *document type declaration*, if the document complies with the *grammar* constraints expressed in this document type declaration, and if the document complies with all *validity constraints* and *well-formedness* constraints. In essence, a document that is *valid* is guaranteed to be *parsable* by XML software, and the resulting parse tree is guaranteed to be consistent with the structure and rules defined by the document type declaration.

validating parser; validating XML processor An *XML processor* that reports all violations of the constraints expressed by the declarations in the DTD. It must also report all failures to fulfill the *validity constraints* given in the XML specifications.

validity constraint A rule that applies to all *valid* XML documents. Violations of validity constraints are errors; they must, *at user option*, be reported by validating XML processors. Validity constraints are explicitly defined in the XML specification. For example, the "Attribute Value Type" validity constraint states that: "the attribute must have been declared; and the value must be of the type declared for it."

W3C See: *World Wide Web Consortium.*

warning A notification from the XML processor that indicates a possible problem with the markup, but one that did not lead to an error. A warning may be issued if: an element type declaration mentions an undefined element type; if attribute types are declared for an element type that is not declared; if more than one attribute type declaration is present for a given element type; or if an entity is declared more than once.

WebSGML Adaptations Annex A collection of addenda to the SGML standard (ISO 8879) in support of Web applications.

well-formed A document is said to be *well-formed* if it is consistent with the *grammar* defined in the XML specification, it meets all the *well-formedness* constraints defined in the specification, and if each of the parsed entities referenced directly or indirectly from the document is itself *well-formed*. In essence, a document that is well-formed is guaranteed to be *parsable* by XML software.

well-formed constraint A rule that applies to all *well-formed* XML documents. For example, the "No External Entity References" well-formedness constraint states: "Attribute values cannot contain direct or indirect entity references to external entities." Violations of well-formedness constraints are *fatal errors*.

white space Any combination of one or more space, tab, carriage return, or line feed characters.

World Wide Web Consortium (W3C) A business and academic consortium devoted to developing international standards for use in Internet software applications. Many common standards, such as XML, *SMIL*, *MathML*, *HTML*, and *RDF*, have been (and are being) developed under the guidance of the W3C.

XLink A draft specification for an XML document-to-document linking language. This specification is being drafted under the auspices of the W3C. See www.w3.org/TR/ for the most recent public drafts, or for the official specification, once they release it.

XML-Data A schema syntax, written in XML, and designed to replace DTDs as a tool for constraining the grammar of XML documents. The XML-Data proposal has been subsumed by the DCF (Document Content Format) proposal. See the W3C Web site for the latest details.

XML declaration An optional markup declaration, at the beginning of a document, that declares the document to be XML. The declaration can also specify the character *encoding* used in the document, the Version of XML the document is consistent with, and whether or not the document is *standalone*. For example, the XML declaration:

```
<?xml version="1.0" standalone="yes" encoding="euc-jp"?>
```

indicates that the document is compliant with Version 1.0 of the XML specification, that it is encoded using the euc-jp character encoding, and that it is a *standalone* document.

XML document A data object is an XML document if it is well-formed as defined by the XML specification.

XML processor A software module that can read XML documents and provide access to their content and structure. See also: *validating XML processor*.

XML Special Interest Group Originally called the SGML Working Group, this was the group that set out to develop a simplified version of SGML for use with Web applications. The group was renamed the XML SIG in late 1997, once XML had been formalized as the name for the new language.

XML Working Group An invitation-only working group that reviews and critiques proposals for the specifications for XML.

XSL XML Stylesheet Language. A specific dialect of XML (defined by an XSL *document type declaration*) designed for specifying rules for restructuring the content of an XML document (transforming one instance of an XML document into another instance) and for specifying the presentational formatting for an XML document. The XSL syntax is being developed under the auspices of the *W3C*. See also: *CSS*.

Index

Production Rule Index